Hume's True Scepticism

David Hume is famous as a sceptical philosopher but the nature of his scepticism is difficult to pin down. *Hume's True Scepticism* provides the first sustained interpretation of Part 4 of Book 1 of Hume's *Treatise*, his deepest engagement with sceptical arguments. Hume notes there that, while reason shows that we ought not to believe the verdicts of reason or the senses, we do so nonetheless. Donald C. Ainslie argues that Hume uses our reactions to the sceptical arguments as evidence in favour of his model of the mind. If we were self-conscious subjects, superintending our rational and sensory beliefs, nothing should stop us from embracing the sceptical conclusions. But instead our minds are bundles of perceptions with our beliefs being generated, not by reflective assent, but by the imagination's association of ideas. We are not forced into the sceptical quagmire. Nonetheless, we can reflect and philosophy uses this capacity to question whether we should believe our instinctive rational and sensory verdicts. It turns out that we cannot answer this question because the reflective investigation of the mind interferes with the associative processes involved in reason and sensation. We thus must accept our rational and sensory capacities without being able to vindicate or undermine them philosophically.

Hume's True Scepticism addresses Hume's theory of representation; his criticisms of Locke, Descartes, and other predecessors; his account of the imagination; his understanding of perceptions and sensory belief; and his bundle theory of the mind and his later rejection of it.

Donald C. Ainslie is a Professor of Philosophy at the University of Toronto, where he also serves as Principal of University College.

Hume's True Scepticism

Donald C. Ainslie

OXFORD
UNIVERSITY PRESS

OXFORD
UNIVERSITY PRESS

Great Clarendon Street, Oxford, OX2 6DP,
United Kingdom

Oxford University Press is a department of the University of Oxford.
It furthers the University's objective of excellence in research, scholarship,
and education by publishing worldwide. Oxford is a registered trade mark of
Oxford University Press in the UK and in certain other countries

First published 2015
First published in paperback 2017

Published in the United States of America by Oxford University Press
198 Madison Avenue, New York, NY 10016, United States of America

British Library Cataloguing in Publication Data
Data available

Library of Congress Cataloging in Publication Data
Data available

ISBN 978-0-19-959386-6 (Hbk.)
ISBN 978-0-19-880141-2 (Pbk.)

Dedicated to the memory of Annette Baier,
who started me on this project,
and to Mike Twamley, who helped me finish it

Acknowledgements

It has taken me far longer than I would have liked to finish this book. I first started exploring the issues I discuss here as a doctoral student at the University of Pittsburgh. Annette Baier was my supervisor there, and we continued to correspond after I graduated and she moved back to her beloved New Zealand. While she read and responded to—and criticized!—earlier versions of many of the chapters here, including those where I disagree with her, I regret that she did not live to see the final product. This book is dedicated, in part, to her memory, because she taught me how to read texts, like Hume's *Treatise*, productively; and she taught me how the history of philosophy can serve as a vehicle for philosophical inquiry.

I am also grateful to my colleagues in the Department of Philosophy at the University of Toronto; it is hard to imagine a better environment for work in the history of philosophy. I have benefited enormously over the years from colleagues who share my research interests in the history of modern philosophy—the late André Gombay, Ian Hacking, Karolina Hübner, Elmar Kremer, Martin Lin, Jennifer Nagel, Calvin Normore, Martin Pickavé, Marleen Rozemond, Bill Seager, Sergio Tenenbaum, and Fred Wilson—as well as from those whose work focuses on other periods—Tom Hurka, Brad Inwood, Mohan Matthen, Cheryl Misak, and Jennifer Whiting, in particular. I owe special thanks to Arthur Ripstein, not just for his friendship and support, but also for his giving me the final nudge I needed to complete this project. I have also learned from my students at the University of Toronto, especially those who attended my graduate seminars, and also from John Bunner, Karen Detlefsen, Adam Harmer, Hugh Hunter, Owen Pikkert, Brandon Watson, and Shelley Weinberg. Jessy Giroux in particular deserves mention for his assistance in producing the index. In 2010–11, an interdisciplinary group of faculty and graduate students at the University of Toronto, under the auspices of the Jackman Humanities Institute, met regularly to discuss Hume and the eighteenth-century culture of letters, culminating in a celebration of Hume's 300th birthday. I would especially like to thank Deidre Lynch and Tom Keymer for helping to coordinate that effort.

Scholars working on David Hume benefit enormously from the community brought together by the International Hume Society. I have been attending Hume conferences since I was a graduate student, and I have learned so much from the friends I have made there. For their help with the ideas developed in this book, I want to acknowledge Lilli Alanen, Donald Baxter, Charlotte Brown, Annemarie Butler, Rachel Cohon, Johnny Cottrell, Graciela De Pierris, Lorne Falkenstein, Aaron Garrett, Don Garrett, James Harris, Peter Kail, David Landy, Wim Lemmens, Peter Loptson, Tito Magri, Peter Millican, Ted Morris, David Owen, Terence Penelhum, Dario Perinetti, Lewis Powell, Hsueh Qu, Elizabeth Radcliffe, Stefanie Rocknak,

Karl Schafer, Eric Schliesser, Amy Schmitter, Lisa Shapiro, Corliss Swain, Jackie Taylor, Saul Traiger, and Ken Winkler.

I presented preliminary versions of the arguments that follow at many conferences, workshops, and symposia, and I am grateful to the audiences on those occasions for their questions and criticisms.

Portions of the book were published previously in various guises. Chapter 1 borrows heavily from "Hume's Scepticism and Ancient Scepticisms," in Jon Miller and Brad Inwood (eds.), *Hellenistic and Early Modern Philosophy* (New York, NY: Cambridge University Press, 2003), 251–73 and is reprinted with permission, copyright © Cambridge University Press. §6.1, uses some paragraphs from my portions of the co-written essay (with Owen Ware) "Consciousness and Personal Identity," in Aaron Garrett (ed.), *Routledge Companion to Eighteenth Century Philosophy* (New York, NY: Routledge, 2014), 245–64. Most of §§6.2 and 6.3 first appeared in "Hume's Anti-*Cogito*," in Lorenzo Greco and Alessio Vaccari (eds.), *Hume Readings* (Rome: Edizioni di Storia e Letteratura, 2013), 91–120, and §6.5 and some of §8.2, borrow from portions of "Hume on Personal Identity," in E. Radcliffe (ed.), *A Companion to Hume* (Malden, MA: Blackwell, 2008), 140–57.

I first tried to start this project during a visit to the Center for Philosophy of Science at the University of Pittsburgh in the autumn of 2002, and I owe thanks to Jim Lennox for inviting me there. I properly began the manuscript in 2008–9 during a sabbatical when I was visiting Stanford University, and I am grateful to Ken Taylor for facilitating my time in the Bay Area. Jackie Taylor, Alice Sowaal, and I met regularly throughout my year there, and I appreciate their critical comments on early drafts of various chapters. I owe special thanks to David Owen, Eric Schliesser, Alison Simmons, and referees for the press who read the whole manuscript and offered very helpful feedback.

In addition, I would like to recognize the friends and family who patiently encouraged me with this project, especially Janet Ainslie, Jim Ainslie, Bob Greenbaum, Michael MacLennan, Lisa Shapiro, and Elinor Whitmore. The members of the Downtown Swim Club in Toronto and the San Francisco Tsunami Swim Team deserve special mention; their camaraderie in and out of the pool helped to dispel the "philosophical melancholy and delirium" to which I sometimes succumbed.

Finally, this book is also dedicated to my partner, Mike Twamley. I am lucky to have him in my life.

Contents

Abbreviations

Full details of the editions used are provided in the Bibliography.

Works by David Hume

T   *A Treatise of Human Nature*
References to this work indicate Book, Part, Section, and paragraph numbers as given in the Norton and Norton editions, followed by the page numbers as given in the Selby-Bigge and Nidditch edition (prefaced by 'SBN'). I use the following abbreviations for Sections within the *Treatise:*

IEEE   "Of the idea of existence, and of external existence" (T 1.2.6)

SwR   "Of scepticism with regard to reason" (T 1.4.1)

SwS   "Of scepticism with regard to the senses" (T 1.4.2)

AP   "Of the antient philosophy" (T 1.4.3)

MP   "Of the modern philosophy" (T 1.4.4)

IS   "Of the immateriality of the soul" (T 1.4.5)

PI   "Of personal identity" (T 1.4.6)

CtB   "Conclusion of this book" (T 1.4.7)

LG   "Letter from a Gentleman to his Friend in *Edinburgh*"
References to this work indicate the paragraph numbers as given in the Norton and Norton *Critical Edition.*

Es   *Essays: Moral, Political, and Literary*
References to this work indicate the page numbers as given in the Miller edition, accompanied by an indication of the essay in which the passage occurs.

EU   *An Enquiry concerning Human Understanding*
References to this work indicate Section, Part, and paragraph numbers as given in the Beauchamp edition, followed by the page numbers as given in the Selby-Bigge and Nidditch edition (prefaced by 'SBN').

EM   *An Enquiry concerning the Principles of Morals*
References to this work indicate Section, Part, and paragraph numbers as given in the Beauchamp edition, followed by a page reference to the Selby-Bigge and Nidditch edition (prefaced by 'SBN').

L   *Letters of David Hume*
References to this work indicate the volume and page numbers of the Grieg edition of the *Letters.*

MOL   "My Own Life"
       References to this work indicate the page numbers as given in the Miller
       edition of the *Essays*.

Works by other key philosophers

HCD   Bayle, Pierre. *Historical and Critical Dictionary*
       References to this work indicate the name of the Entry and the page
       numbers as given in the Popkin edition.

P   Berkeley, George. *A Treatise concerning the Principles of Human Knowledge*
       References to this work indicate Part and Section numbers as given in the
       Luce and Jessop edition.

D   Berkeley, George. *Three Dialogues between Hylas and Philonous*
       References to this work indicate the Dialogue and page numbers as given in
       the Luce and Jessop edition.

TISU   Cudworth, Ralph. *The True Intellectual System of the Universe*
       Reference to this work indicate the Book, Chapter, and page numbers using
       capitalized Roman numerals, small Roman numerals, and Arabic numerals
       respectively, as given in the Friedrich Fromann reprint of the 1678 edition.

AT   Descartes, René. *Meditations on First Philosophy, Objections and Replies*,
       and *Principles of Philosophy*
       References to these works indicate the volume and page numbers in Charles
       Adam and Paul Tannery's *Oeuvres de Descartes*, as given in the margins of
       the Cottingham *et al. Philosophical Writings*.

DL   Diogenes Laertius. *Lives of Eminent Philosophers*
       References to this work indicate Chapter and Section numbers, using capita-
       lized and small Roman numerals respectively, as given in the Hicks edition.

E   Locke, John. *An Essay concerning Human Understanding*
       References to this work indicate Book, Chapter, and paragraph numbers,
       using capitalized Roman numerals, small Roman numerals, and Arabic
       numerals respectively, as given in the Nidditch edition.

ST   Malebranche, Nicolas. *The Search after Truth*
       References to this work indicate Book, Part (if applicable), Chapter, and
       page numbers, using capitalized Roman numerals, small Roman numerals,
       Arabic numerals, and Arabic numerals respectively, as given in the Lennon
       and Olscamp edition.

PH   Sextus Empiricus. *The Outlines of Pyrrhonism*
       Reference to this work indicate Part and Section numbers, using small Roman
       numerals and Arabic numerals respectively, as given in the Bury edition.

Introduction

Hume is an ambivalent philosopher. On the one hand, he wrote what is now recognized as one of the greatest works in the English-language philosophical canon, *A Treatise of Human Nature*, as well as the two *Enquiries* that recapitulate and develop themes from the *Treatise*. In these works, he argues that a philosophical understanding of human nature is the "foundation" (T Intro.6–7, SBN xvi) for the other sciences; it shows "the extent and force of human understanding" (T Intro.4, SBN xv) and thus determines what the sciences can legitimately aim for in their investigations. Further, he holds that, because the human mind is located within nature, it is to be examined using the same experimental methods as we use to understand the rest of nature. Thus Hume stands as one of the founders of a kind of naturalism that remains among the dominant philosophical positions of our time.

On the other hand, in both his life and works he worried about the dangers of philosophy—especially its tendency to inspire its practitioners to hubristically claim special insight into a deep structure in nature. This tendency is hubristic because the depth of these so-called insights means that they have become unmoored from the only evidence that could establish them: our experiences. This tendency is dangerous, both to the individual philosophers and sometimes also to society. Should these philosophers start to recognize the shortcomings of their claims, they might succumb to what Hume so vividly describes in the final Section of Book 1 of the *Treatise*: a debilitating "melancholy and delirium" (T 1.4.7.9, SBN 269) in which they lose their grip on reality entirely. But if they do manage to delude themselves into maintaining their claims, they might make the further mistake of attempting to reform their lives around what they take to be their deep understanding of things. They might end up, like the "Cynics," embracing "as great extravagancies of conduct as any *Monk* or *Dervise* that ever was in the world" (T 1.4.7.13, SBN 272). Even worse, their positions might be recruited by religion. And because religious "superstition," Hume thinks, "arises naturally and easily from the popular opinions of mankind, it seizes more strongly on the mind, and is often able to disturb us in the conduct of our lives and actions" (T 1.4.7.13, SBN 271–2). Religion fortified with philosophical systems is especially dangerous. It creates "keenness in dispute," thus making "parties of religion ... more furious and enraged than the most cruel factions that ever arose from interest and ambition" (Es, 63).[1]

---

[1] This quotation is from "Of parties in general."

In the *Treatise*, Hume argues that the correct response to the double dangers of philosophy is a "true" scepticism, where he is "diffident of his philosophical doubts, as well as of his philosophical conviction" (T 1.4.7.14, SBN 273). In what follows, I offer a new understanding of this claim by developing the first[2] detailed and sustained interpretation of Part 4 of Book 1 of the *Treatise*, "Of the sceptical and other systems of philosophy"—what has been called Hume's "natural history of philosophy."[3]

I argue that true scepticism involves a domestication of philosophy. It no longer has a privileged place as a special way of knowing, but rather uses the same faculties as those it investigates and the same methods as those used in our everyday "vulgar" encounters with the world. We will see that this domestication has two effects. First, it means that philosophy turns out to be unable to offer a justification or repudiation of our fundamental tendencies to believe. We must learn to live with a kind of "blind" (T 1.4.7.10, SBN 269) embrace of our natural epistemic propensities. Second, there is no special *obligation* to philosophize, as if the unexamined life were not worth living. Rather, because philosophy's lessons can be useful in helping us understand how best to investigate the world, those who have an inclination for it should pursue it, while keeping its limitations in mind. But those who are not interested in things philosophical should not be thought to exemplify some kind of failing. Rather, philosophers should learn from them how the mind operates in its normal, non-reflective posture.

0.1 Philosophy and the "Disease of the Learned"

Hume's personal experiences with philosophy seem to have played a role in his recognition of its strengths and limitations. In a remarkable letter of 1734, addressed to an unknown doctor in London, he describes how he discovered philosophy and how his first trials at it left him worse for wear. The rather desperate, anonymous letter, clearly written in Hume's hand, was discovered by John Hill Burton, in the course of producing one of the first biographies of Hume.[4] The letter describes both its author's experiences with various physical and mental ailments and the contexts in which these ailments arose. It is, Hume says there, a "kind of History of my Life" (L 1, 13). It is unknown what exactly Hume's plan was in sending the anonymous letter—presumably he meant to have it delivered to the doctor with the idea of

[2] Robert Fogelin, *Hume's Skeptical Crisis: A Textual Study* (New York, NY: Oxford University Press, 2009) also focuses on *Treatise* 1.4 but, as he admits, his book takes the form of study notes rather than a fully detailed analysis (see ix–x, 8).

[3] The phrase is Fogelin's title for Chapter 7 in *Hume's Skepticism in the "Treatise of Human Nature"* (London: Routledge and Kegan Paul, 1985). See also Donald Livingston, "Hume on the Natural History of Philosophical Consciousness," in P. Jones (ed.), *The 'Science of Man' in the Scottish Enlightenment: Hume, Reid and their Contemporaries* (Edinburgh: Edinburgh University Press, 1989), 68–84.

[4] John Hill Burton, *Life and Correspondence of David Hume* (New York, NY: Burt Franklin, n.d.).

coming by to pick up a response some time later. The addressee is a matter of debate, with Burton and more recently John Wright suggesting George Cheyne, while Ernest Mossner argues for the Scriblerian, John Arbuthnot.[5] We do not even know if Hume actually followed up on his plan by sending the letter, as the copy we have is a draft. But the letter is one of the few pieces of evidence about Hume's state of mind as he wrote the *Treatise*, published in 1739–40.[6]

The letter starts with Hume's explanation of why he has sent an anonymous letter to a physician with whom he has had no previous acquaintance. He feels that his ailments are peculiar to the kind of life he has adopted—a life of letters—and that only a physician who shares in that life would be able to understand his situation well enough to diagnose it successfully (L 1, 12). Hume goes on to describe how, after his schooling, he came to pursue philosophy. At the age of 18, while reading "Books of Reasoning & Philosophy, & . . . Poetry, & the polite Authors," he stumbled upon "a new Scene of [philosophical] Thought," which, he felt, would not suffer from the "endless Disputes" to which other approaches to philosophy were subject, "even in the most fundamental Articles" (L 1, 13). As becomes apparent later in the letter, this "new Scene" was brought about by the recognition that the experimental investigation of human nature—the "science of man" that Hume later was to outline in the "Introduction" to the *Treatise*—was the necessary foundation for any philosophical study. For only if scholars have a clear understanding of how human nature is structured will they be able to reach any conclusions that will be adequate to human life.

Hume next describes how he planned to elaborate on this "new Scene," only to be hindered by ongoing physical and mental distress. After an initial period of enthusiasm, he soon found that he could no longer sustain the "pitch" of mind requisite for intense philosophical study. Attributing this failure to "a Laziness of Temper," he "redoubled [his] application" (L 1, 13) to his philosophical research and, at the same time, embarked on a series of exercises designed to reform his character.[7] But, to Hume's chagrin, these exercises served only to exacerbate his condition, and his

---

[5] Burton, *Life and Correspondence*, 42, who is followed in this by J. Y. T. Greig, the editor of a more recent edition of Hume's letters (L 1, 12n2); Mossner, "Hume's Epistle to Dr. Arbuthnot, 1734: The Biographical Significance," *Huntington Library Quarterly* 7 (1944), 135–52; Wright, "Dr. George Cheyne, Chevalier Ramsay, and Hume's Letter to a Physician," *Hume Studies* 29 (2003), 125–41.

[6] See M. A. Stewart, "Hume's Intellectual Development, 1711–1752," in M. Frasca-Spada and P. J. E. Kail (eds.), *Impressions of Hume* (Oxford: Clarendon Press, 2005), 11–58; and David Fate Norton, "Historical Account of *A Treatise of Human Nature* from its Beginnings to the Time of Hume's Death," in David Fate Norton and Mary J. Norton (eds.), *David Hume, A Treatise of Human Nature: A Critical Edition*, Vol. 2, *Editorial Material* (Oxford: Clarendon Press, 2007), 433–588.

[7] "[H]aving read many Books of Morality, such as Cicero, Seneca & Plutarch, & being smit with their beautiful Representations of Virtue & Philosophy, I undertook the Improvement of my Temper & Will, along with my Reason & Understanding. I was continually fortifying myself with Reflections against Death & Poverty, & Shame, & Pain, & all the other Calamities of Life" (L 1, 14).

mental distress was compounded by the onset of physical maladies such as "a slight Scurvy" and "Ptyalism or Wattryness in the mouth." He reports his physician's response to these complaints: "[H]e laught at me & told me that me I was now a Brother, for I had fairly got the Disease of the Learned" (L 1, 14). The official diagnosis was the "Vapours," and Hume was prescribed "a course of Bitters, & Anti-hysteric Pills," to drink "an English Pint of Claret Wine every Day," and to regularly "ride 8 or 10 Scotch Miles" (L 1, 14).

Hume tells us that he followed his physician's advice, engaging in his philosophical pursuits only when his "Spirits" were at "their highest Pitch" and ceasing his academic work when he no longer felt energetic. He established a regimen of outdoor exercise that included frequent rides in the countryside and walks around town. And he was, he tells the letter's recipient, "able to make considerable Progress in [his] former Designs" (L 1, 15). But, by the next summer, in 1731, new symptoms had appeared. He developed a ravenous appetite and acquired the corpulence for which he was later to be famous in the Paris salons. And he was bothered by a "Palpitation of the heart" and a "good deal of Wind" in his stomach. Repeated application of "the Bitters" and another course of "Anti-hysteric Pills" were of only limited help (L 1, 15–16).

But Hume's real concern was how his malady affected his mental abilities. He worried that he could no longer concentrate in the manner he thought was required for philosophical research:

I found that I was not able to follow out any Train of Thought, by one continued Stretch of View, but by repeated Interruptions, & by refreshing my Eye from Time to Time upon other Objects.... [B]ut when one must bring the Idea he comprehended in gross, nearer to him so as to contemplate its minutest Parts & keep it steddily in his Eye, so as to copy these Parts in Order, this I found impracticable for me, nor were my Spirits equal to so severe an Employment. (L 1, 16)

And so he despairs to the physician that he will never be able to "deliver [his] Opinions with such Elegance & Neatness, as to draw [him] the Attention of the World" (L 1, 17).

Hume writes that the only way he could successfully complete his philosophical project would be if he could return to good health. And to do this, he says, he must make a clean break from the life of "Study & Idleness," both of which he takes to be contributing causes of his melancholia; instead he must enter into a life of "Business & Diversion" (L 1, 17). To this end, Hume says that he plans to work for a Bristol merchant until he has escaped from his "Distemper." The letter ends with a series of questions for the physician, all centring on the issue of whether his "Spirits [will] regain their former Spring & Vigor, so as to endure the Fatigue of deep & abstruse thinking" (L 1, 18).

We know that, as it turned out, Hume did not find the life of a Bristol merchant much to his liking, but it seems to have cured him of his disease. For within a few months he quit the post and went to France. After three years of study in the Jesuit monastery at La Flèche, Hume returned to Britain with a complete manuscript of Books 1 and 2 of the *Treatise* and a draft of Book 3. His short autobiographical essay, "My Own Life" (hereafter 'MOL'), written in 1776—the last year of his life—says only that in his youth his health had become "a little broken by [his] ardent application" (MOL, xxxiii). He gives no indication that he ever suffered from similar ailments again.

In the "Conclusion of this book," the final Section of Book 1 of the *Treatise* (T 1.4.7; hereafter 'CtB'), Hume reflects on what he has accomplished in it and describes his reactions in a way that must have been inspired by the personal experiences detailed in the 1734 letter. He narrates how his philosophy has caused him to feeling growing dismay at his cognitive situation, ultimately leading to the near paralysis of "philosophical melancholy and delirium" (T 1.4.7.9, SBN 269):

Where am I, or what? From what causes do I derive my existence, and to what condition shall I return? Whose favour shall I court, and whose anger must I dread? What beings surround me? and on whom have I any influence, or who have any influence on me? I am confounded with all these questions, and begin to fancy myself in the most deplorable condition imaginable, inviron'd with the deepest darkness, and utterly depriv'd of the use of every member and faculty. (T 1.4.7.8, SBN 269)

He escapes this despair only by leaving philosophy: "I dine, I play a game of back-gammon, I converse, and am merry with my friends" (T 1.4.7.9, SBN 269). And just as he went to Bristol to escape from philosophy as a young man, Hume in CtB describes wanting to reject philosophy: "I am ready to throw all my books and papers into the fire, and resolve never more to renounce the pleasures of life for the sake of reasoning and philosophy" (T 1.4.7.10, SBN 269). But just as Hume left Bristol for La Flèche, the narrator of CtB eventually finds his "curiosity and ambition" (T 1.4.7.13, SBN 271) return, and he rededicates himself to philosophy, though now as a "true sceptic" (T 1.4.7.14, SBN 273). In the two Books of the *Treatise* that follow, "Of the passions" and "Of morals," he shows almost no trace of the anxiety about philosophy that characterized CtB.

0.2 "Of the sceptical and other systems of philosophy" (*Treatise* 1.4)

I believe that understanding Hume's embrace of true scepticism in CtB requires that it be fully contextualized in what has preceded it, especially elsewhere in Part 4, where he openly takes philosophy as his topic. And it is must also be read as setting the stage for what follows—his much less dramatic account of the passions and morals.[8]

---

[8] Annette Baier has driven this lesson home in her important *A Progress of Sentiments* (Cambridge, MA: Harvard University Press, 1991).

Hume explains his overall agenda for the *Treatise* in its "Introduction," where he notes that philosophers have failed to make progress in their attempts to understand the fundamental nature of reality:

Principles taken upon trust, consequences lamely deduced from them, want of coherence in the parts, and of evidence in the whole, these are every where to be met with in the systems of the most eminent philosophers, and seem to have drawn disgrace upon philosophy itself.

(T Intro.1, SBN xiv)

The solution, he suggests, is the study of human nature, so that we can recognize what we can hope to accomplish given our cognitive capacities. And this study is to be undertaken using the same experimental method that, in the seventeenth century, had allowed natural philosophy to enter a new era of understanding. But just as the best scientists of the day (presumably he has the Newtonians in mind) accept the need for unexplained "ultimate principles" (T Intro.10, SBN xvi), so also must the ultimate principles of the mind be left unexplained. Any "hypothesis" that philosophers might attempt to introduce on the basis of what they claim to be *a priori* reasoning should be "rejected as presumptuous and chimerical" (T Intro.8, SBN xvii).

Hume supports this conception of science, both moral and natural, in Book 1 of the *Treatise*, "Of the understanding," where he uses the experimental method to explore the sources of our beliefs and other ideas. Its first part addresses the "elements" (T 1.1.4.7, SBN 13) of his system, including the identification of mental states with what he calls "perceptions." We come by our most basic perceptions, simple impressions, in two different ways, either by sensation or through emotional responses to what we sense and think. We form ideas when we think of what our senses and feelings deliver or when we form complexes out of this material. And compounding ideas from prior ideas or copying them from prior simple impressions is, with a small set of exceptions (see §2.4), the *only* way we form ideas. This is Hume's empiricism: All thoughts must ultimately have their origins in prior sensations or emotions.

Hume uses this "first principle" (T 1.1.1.12, SBN 7) throughout the *Treatise* in order to debunk philosophers' claims to have special insight into the ultimate nature of reality. He shows that we have no impressions that would allow them to form the ideas they would need even to think of their claims. Hume then goes on to reconstruct our actual beliefs about the phenomena in question on the basis of our experiences. Our ideas are traced back to their ultimate impression sources.

In Part 2 of Book 1, Hume uses this method to consider both how our sensory experiences come in a spatiotemporal order without space or time themselves being objects of sensation, and how our experiences of the world relate to objects that are independent of experience. Part 3 examines our capacity to reason, and to secure either knowledge or probable beliefs. Because he takes causation to be the central relation in probabilistic reasoning (T 1.3.2.3, SBN 74), he spends almost all of this part considering it. Our idea of a cause and its effect requires that they be necessarily connected, but it is far from obvious how we come by this idea. What impression is its source? We cannot use demonstrative reason to discern intrinsic necessary connections between objects, nor do we have a sense organ that gives us direct experience of them. It turns out that we end up believing that a cause and an effect are necessarily connected because our ideas of them are associated on the basis of our having regularly experienced prior conjunctions of similar objects. The impression of necessity that yields the idea of necessary connection is an inner feeling that accompanies the association of ideas, rather than the discovery of a special quality in the objects that links them together. With this reformed understanding of causation in hand, Hume offers us a set of "rules by which to judge of causes and effects" (T 1.3.15), thus codifying the methods that moral and natural scientists should use. He does not, in this Part, worry about possibly sceptical implications of his treatment of causation.

Hume postpones some of his most fundamental explorations of human cognition for Part 4, "Of the sceptical and other systems of philosophy." There he offers a defence of his model of the mind as "nothing but a bundle or collection of different perceptions, which succeed each other with an inconceivable rapidity, and are in a perpetual flux and movement" (T 1.4.6.4, SBN 252). There is no unifying subject that stands over these perceptions, connecting them together by discerning rational connections between their objects or deciding whether to accept their portrayal of the world. Instead, we believe in the conclusions of reason when our ideas are associated together in the right way. We believe in the verdicts of the senses when our impressions are sufficiently coherent or constant for our imaginations to induce in us a sense that we are encountering independent objects in the world.

Hume also, in this Part—as its title leads one to expect—explores the human tendency to philosophize. As a "scientist of man," he recognizes that in order to explain the human mind, he must also explain why some people, including himself, are tempted to form "systems" that try to structure, challenge, or vindicate our fundamental beliefs. He thus explores why some people end up attracted to what he calls "false philosophy," where they posit entities that he takes to be literally unthinkable. And he is particularly interested in various kinds of sceptical philosophies, in part so that he can distinguish his preferred system—true scepticism—from them.

But why would Hume combine these two projects in Part 4—the presentation of some of the most basic features of his theory of mind and his investigation of the human tendency to philosophize? I argue in what follows that Hume recognizes that philosophy encounters a problem when it addresses its own fundamental commitments, such as his empiricist commitment to tracing our mental states back to their origins in experience. For how is experience to be understood? Depending on which model of the mind philosophers endorse, experience will play a different role in their theoretical systems. Hume sometimes seems to hold that he can simply look within to "observe" that the mind is bundle of perceptions without a unifying subject (T 1.4.6.3, SBN 252). But his opponents will reject this claim in part because they understand such observation differently. How, then, can a philosopher defend a model of the mind on the basis of experience without begging the question?

I argue in Chapters 1 and 4 (especially §§1.5 and 4.4; see also §7.5) that part of Hume's goal in his explorations of scepticism in Sections 1 and 2 of Part 4 is to show that only his model of the mind can make sense of our experiences in reaction to sceptical challenges. Although there is "no error" (T 1.4.1.8, SBN 184) in these arguments, no one actually believes them. As we shall see, he claims he can explain this disbelief as resulting from reflection's "so disturb[ing] the operation of my natural principles" (T Intro.10, SBN xix) as to undermine both the argument and the capacity it challenges. We merely create temporary confusion in ourselves, of a kind most vividly described in CtB's climax, when we address our core tendencies to believe. But his philosophical opponents have modelled the mind so that we should be able to accept the sceptic's conclusions. Our experience with disbelief is evidence against their models.

My elaboration and defence of this claim follows the path that Hume lays down for us in Part 4 of Book 1. Its first two Sections, "Of scepticism with regard to reason" (T 1.4.1) and "Of scepticism with regard to the senses" (T 1.4.2), share both similar titles and a common conclusion, applying to "[t]his sceptical doubt, both with respect to reason and the senses" (T 1.4.2.57, SBN 218). The former—my topic in Chapter 1— examines the attempt of "total" sceptics to undermine all rational belief entirely. The latter examines the attempt of "extravagant" sceptics to deny the existence of a world beyond our perceptions. Chapters 2 and 3 address Hume's explanation for the everyday belief in body that precedes his presentation of the sceptical challenge. In Chapter 4 I use my earlier interpretation of Hume's critique of "total" scepticism as a clue to interpreting his much more complex response to "extravagant" scepticism.

Hume ends the two sceptical Sections by stating:

> [W]hatever may be the reader's opinion at this present moment...an hour hence he will be persuaded there is both an external and internal world; and going upon that supposition, I intend to examine some general systems both ancient and modern, which have been propos'd of both, before I proceed to a more particular enquiry concerning our impressions.
>
> (T 1.4.2.57, SBN 218)

He here gives us the agenda for the next four Sections of Part 4 of Book 1, for the "more particular enquiry concerning our impressions" can only refer to Book 2's analysis of "secondary" impressions: namely, the passions (T 2.1.1.1, SBN 275). The exploration of ancient systems of the external world occurs in "Of the antient philosophy" (T 1.4.3), Hume's critique of substance-based metaphysics; the exploration of modern systems of the external world occurs in "Of the modern philosophy" (T 1.4.4), where he takes on the primary–secondary quality distinction that he says defines modernity (T 1.4.4.3, SBN 226). Since "Of the immateriality of the soul" (T 1.4.5) discusses the status of the soul *as a substance*, it seems that it must be Hume's exploration of ancient systems of the internal world. This would leave "Of personal identity" (T 1.4.6) as Hume's discussion of the modern system of the internal world. It opens by describing and then rejecting the view of "some philosophers" (whom Locke might come closest to; see §6.2) in which the mind is fundamentally self-conscious. In its final paragraph, he notes that we have only then "finish'd our examination of the several systems of philosophy, both of the intellectual and natural world" (T 1.4.6.23, SBN 263).

Thus I devote Chapter 5 to Hume's discussion of the ancient philosophy, including his critique of substance metaphysics and his seemingly contradictory endorsement of what appear to be very ambitious metaphysical principles that allow us to make claims about the world on the basis of our perceptions of it. I argue that Hume's metaphysical ambitions are far less robust than they at first appear, because he means his positive claims about the structure of the world to be restricted to the "appearances" of objects, rather than their "real nature and operations" (T 1.2.5.26n12.1–2, SBN 638–9). Chapter 6 addresses Hume's critique of modern systems of philosophy, especially his seemingly self-refuting rejection of the view in which self-consciousness is a component of every mental state (T 1.4.6.1–4, SBN 251–3). I argue that by connecting this rejection with his critique of the primary-secondary quality distinction, his argument is stronger than it first appears. I then focus on his subsequent endorsement of the bundle theory of the mind.

Hume follows his discussion of systems of philosophy with CtB, and its narration of a sceptical crisis, an escape from that crisis, and a return to philosophy as a true sceptic. I take this Section as the topic for Chapter 7. While in the earlier chapters I usually keep my discussion of others' interpretations to the footnotes, I use Chapter 7 for a particularly close comparison of my reading of Hume's scepticism with what I take to be the three leading alternatives: sceptical readings, such as those of Janet Broughton and Phillip Cummins; naturalist readings, such as those of Norman Kemp Smith and Don Garrett; and dialectical interpretations, such as those of Annette Baier and W. E. Morris.

Chapter 8 considers Hume's second thoughts about personal identity in the "Appendix" to the *Treatise*, published alongside Book 3 almost two years after the appearance of Books 1 and 2.

There might seem, however, to be two roadblocks to my interpretive approach to Part 4, each resulting from the suggestion that T 1.4.5 is meant as Hume's treatment of ancient internal systems. First, Hume includes a lengthy discussion of Spinoza (T 1.4.5.17–28, SBN 240–6) in T 1.4.5, and Spinoza certainly does not seem to be an ancient philosopher. Second, the titular topic of T 1.4.5, the immateriality of the soul, was a focus of intense debate among modern philosophers, especially in the early eighteenth century—much of it inspired by Locke's acknowledging the possibility of a purely material mind in *Essay* IV.iii.6.[9] Leibniz's *New Essays*, the exchange of letters

---

[9] See John Yolton, *Thinking Matter: Materialism in Eighteenth-Century Britain* (Minneapolis, MN: University of Minnesota Press, 1983).

between Anthony Collins and Samuel Clarke, and many other works addressed the issue. But in light of this contemporary debate about the immateriality of the soul, how can I suggest that Hume means T 1.4.5 to be an exploration of *ancient* systems of the internal world?[10]

The key for squaring the structure of Part 4 of Book 1, as given in Hume's statement at T 1.4.2.57 (SBN 218), quoted above, with the actual content of the Sections of that Part is in recognizing that he cannot be using 'ancient' and 'modern' as purely temporal designators. Berkeley, for example, is modern temporally, but he does not accept the primary–secondary quality distinction that would qualify his system as modern in Hume's sense (P 1.9–15); Democritus, as well as the Epicureans, on the other hand, while being from the ancient period, accept the 'modern' primary–secondary quality distinction.[11] It seems, then, that 'ancient' and 'modern' are meant to designate, not simply *when* a philosophical doctrine was most fully embraced, but *what* substantive doctrines it involves. And this means that Spinoza's seventeenth-century philosophical system can still count as ancient to Hume in that it relies on the substance–accident ontology; its "fundamental principle" includes "the unity of that substance, in which he supposes both thought and matter to inhere" (T 1.4.5.18, SBN 240).[12] Moreover, much of the eighteenth-century debate over the immateriality of the soul also turns on issues relating to the nature of

---

[10] Donald Livingston thus takes Hume to hold that ancient philosophy is concerned with the outer world, while modern philosophy is concerned with the inner. Livingston concludes that all of "Of the modern philosophy" (T 1.4.4), "Of the immateriality of the soul" (T 1.4.5), and "Of personal identity" (T 1.4.6) count as part of Hume's critique of modernity (*Philosophical Melancholy and Delirium: Hume's Pathology of Philosophy* [Chicago, IL: University of Chicago Press, 1998], 82–3). I find this suggestion hard to swallow, given Hume's statement at T 1.4.2.57 (SBN 218) that he will examine "general systems both antient and modern, which have been proposed of both [the internal and external worlds]," and his concern in T 1.4.4 about the modern conception of the *external* world as consisting only of primary qualities (T 1.4.4.5, SBN 227). Moreover, as I noted earlier, "Of the immateriality of the soul" is primarily concerned with the status of the soul as a *substance*.

[11] For Democritus, see Jonathan Barnes, *The Presocratic Philosophers* (London: Routledge and Kegan Paul, 1982), 370–7; for the Epicureans, see A. A. Long and D. N. Sedley, *The Hellenistic Philosophers*, I (Cambridge: Cambridge University Press, 1987), 52–7.

If I am right that Hume means "Of personal identity" to be his critique of the modern system of the internal world, Augustine might be a candidate for a philosopher who is ancient temporally, but modern in Hume's taxonomy. The Section starts with the description of a view of "some philosophers" who take the mind to include a fundamental self-consciousness of its unity (T 1.4.6.1, SBN 251). Hume rejects this view and replaces it with the bundle view, where we are not aware of ourselves as unified subjects. Roderick Chisholm suggests that the Augustinian view is the alternative to the Humean bundle view ("Notes on the Awareness of the Self," *The Monist* 49 [1965], 28–35), for Augustine says such things as: "I state that a man is able, when he tastes something, to swear in good faith that *he* knows whether it is sweet to his palate or the contrary, and no Greek trickery can beguile him from this knowledge" ("Against the Academicians," 3.12.26, in Peter King [tr. and intr.], *Augustine: Against the Academicians and The Teacher* [Indianapolis, IN: Hackett, 1995], 76).

[12] Note that a philosopher can subscribe to both ancient and modern systems, if he or she combines a substance ontology with the primary–secondary quality distinction. René Descartes, for example, does this, as does Spinoza, though it is not clear that Hume would take the latter's system to be modern in his special sense. For Hume understands the primary–secondary quality distinction that he takes to define modernity to mean that "colours, sounds, tastes, smells, heat, and cold" are "nothing but impressions in the mind,

substance. Opponents of the possibility of a material mind often argued that the unity of thought required a unified subject that only an immaterial, substantial soul could provide; a material entity would never exemplify the requisite unity.[13] Accordingly, Hume is entitled to view his discussion of the immateriality of the soul as speaking to ancient concerns, despite the contemporaneity of the debate on this topic.

0.3 Melancholia in Context

Though my strategy in this book is to approach Hume's true scepticism by a careful consideration of its context in the *Treatise*, it will be helpful, before I finish this Introduction, to develop a hint implicit in his use of the rhetoric of melancholia in his argument for true scepticism in CtB. We can assume that Hume was well aware of what he was implying when he relied on his personal experiences with the "disease of the learned" to defend his preferred system of philosophy.

The eighteenth century was a transitional period in medical science.[14] The humoral theory of Hippocrates and Galen that had dominated throughout the medieval period and the Renaissance still held sway among many physicians. But with the influence of the 'new science' of the seventeenth century, it was being

---

deriv'd from the operation of external objects, and without any resemblance to the qualities of the objects" (T 1.4.4.3, SBN 226). But, he says:

[t]he fundamental principle of the atheism of *Spinoza* is the doctrine of the simplicity of the universe, and the unity of that substance, in which he supposes both thought and matter to inhere. There is only one substance, says he, in the world; and that substance is perfectly simple and indivisible, and exists every where, without any local presence. Whatever we discover externally by sensation; whatever we feel internally by reflection; all these are nothing but modifications of that one, simple, and necessarily existent being, and are not possest of any separate or distinct existence. Every passion of the soul; every configuration of matter, however different and various, inhere in the same substance, and preserve in themselves their characters of distinction, without communicating them to that subject, in which they inhere."

(T 1.4.5.18, SBN 240–1).

Since Hume's Spinoza holds that what we "discover externally by sensation"—including presumably colours, sounds, tastes, smells, heat and cold—has a *real* existence, albeit as a modification of the world-substance, he does not need to demote these qualities to the level of mere impressions in mind, in the manner of the moderns.

The fact that Spinoza himself held a version of the primary–secondary quality distinction ("Letter 6," *Collected Works of Spinoza*, Vol. 1, ed. and tr. E. Curley [Princeton, NJ: Princeton University Press, 1985], 178) does not require us to suppose that Hume would attribute it to him. For Kemp Smith has suggested that Hume knew Spinoza's work only through his reading of Bayle's article on him (T 1.4.5.22n, SBN 243n)—an article in which the distinction does not appear (*The Philosophy of David Hume* [London: Macmillan, 1941], 325). Richard Popkin agrees with Kemp Smith in "Hume and Spinoza," *Hume Studies* 5 (1979), 65–93. Wim Klever has argued against Kemp Smith's suggestion in "Hume Contra Spinoza?" *Hume Studies* 16 (1990), 89–106, and "More about Hume's Debt to Spinoza," *Hume Studies* 19 (1993), 55–74. See §5.5.

[13] See Ben Lazare Mijuskovic, *Achilles of Rationalist Arguments: The Simplicity, Unity and the Identity of Thought and Soul from the Cambridge Platonists to Kant: A Study in the History of Argument* (The Hague: Martinus Nijhoff, 1974). See also Thomas Lennon and Robert Stainton (eds.), *The Achilles of Rationalist Psychology* (Dordrecht: Springer, 2008).

[14] My discussion here is indebted to Stanley W. Jackson, *Melancholia and Depression: From Hippocratic Times to Modern Times* (New Haven, CT: Yale University Press, 1990).

challenged, supplemented, or replaced by mechanical and chemical theories. In the humoral theory, melancholy—black bile—is one of the four fundamental constituents of the human body. Disease occurs when these constituents are out of equilibrium, with melancholia being the result of an excess of black bile. Its symptoms included aversion to food, despondency, sleeplessness, irritability, restlessness, and prolonged fear or depression.[15] And because melancholy was supposed to have a special affinity for the spleen, melancholia was thought to produce various disorders in the trunk of the body. Thus *hypochondria*—a syndrome involving various disorders in the stomach and bowels—was taken to be intimately connected with melancholia; its psychological symptoms were supposed to have been caused by the "vapours" that would emanate from accumulated black bile in the system. (For women, *hysteria*—a similar syndrome involving a loose congeries of symptoms—was also paired with melancholy.)

Medical theorists, from the Greeks onwards, linked scholarliness to melancholia. The Aristotelians supposed that "those who have become eminent in philosophy or politics or poetry or the arts are clearly of an atrabilious temperament"—of a temperament in which the black bile is predominant; and because of their temperament, people in these fields were more susceptible to melancholic diseases.[16] Rufus of Ephesus, a physician of the early second century AD, took this point one step further. Rather than following the Aristotelian view that academics had a temperamental *predisposition* to melancholic diseases, he claimed that the special kind of mental activity involved in intellectual labour was *itself* responsible for their tendency towards melancholia.[17] Similar theories continued until well into the seventeenth century. Robert Burton, in his encyclopedic *Anatomy of Melancholy*, lists "overmuch Study" as one of the causes of melancholia, and includes a section on the "Love of Learning... [and] the Misery of Scholars."[18]

Even with the rise of mechanist medical theories, melancholy and the associated syndromes of hypochondria and hysteria continued to be understood in terms of an accumulation of black bile in the stomach and spleen. Now, however, the mechanism of the disease was more often understood in terms of animal spirits—the very fine substance through which the nervous system was thought to operate. But the link between melancholia and scholarliness remained. Bernardino Ramazzini, an early-eighteenth-century medical writer, says that

scholars, even when endowed by nature with a jovial temperament, gradually become saturnine and melancholic. Hence it is often said that the melancholic are talented, but perhaps it

---

[15] See Jackson, *Melancholia*, 30.

[16] Although Aristotle's authorship of this work is disputed, the quotation is from *Problems* 953a10–12, in E. S. Forster's translation in *The Complete Works of Aristotle*, ed. Jonathan Barnes, Vol. 2 (Princeton, NJ: Princeton University Press, 1984).

[17] Jackson, *Melancholia*, 37.

[18] Section 2, Member 3, Subsection 15 of the first Partition of the *Anatomy of Melancholy*, ed. F. Dell and P. Jordan-Smith (London: George Routledge and Sons, 1931).

would be nearer the mark to say that the talented become melancholic; this is because in mental work the more spiritious part of the blood is used up, whereas the more foul and earthy part is left in the body.[19]

Despite changes in the aetiology of melancholy and hypochondria, treatment for and prophylaxis against it remained fairly constant. Selective purging and bloodletting were usually prescribed, but, more importantly, patients were told to change their diets and their habits; scholars, in particular, were told to spend less time at their books, to exercise regularly, and to socialize more frequently.[20]

The eighteenth century brought with it the popularization of diagnoses of melancholia, hysteria, and hypochondria. Cheyne, who might have been the physician to whom Hume was writing in 1734, wrote a popular book on hypochondria called *The English Malady* (1733), the title of which points to the prevalence of the diagnosis in England in the early eighteenth century. He says that "[t]hese *nervous* Disorders [are] computed to make almost *one third* of the Complaints of the People of *Condition* in *England*."[21]

We can expect, then, that Hume would have known of a general link between melancholy, hypochondria, and the life of study from a variety of sources, both popular and more specialized. Wright suggests that Bernard Mandeville's *Treatise on the Hypochondriack and Hysterick Diseases*[22] is the probable source for the phrase 'disease of the learned,' quoted by Hume when reporting his doctor's diagnosis in the 1734 letter.[23] Like Ramazzini, Mandeville attributes scholars' melancholia to

---

[19] The quotation is preceded by: "Almost every student who devotes himself seriously to the pursuit of learning complains of weakness of the stomach. For while the brain is digesting what is supplied by the passion of knowledge and the hunger for learning, the stomach cannot properly digest its own supply of food. [Lacking sufficient animal spirits for digestion,] indigestion, severe flatulence, pallor, and emaciation of the whole body result...." (Bernardino Ramazzini, *Diseases of Workers* (1700), tr. Wilmer Cave Wright, intr. George Rosen [New York, NY: Hafner Publishing Company, 1964], 381).

[20] Jackson, *Melancholia*, 131–2.

[21] George Cheyne, *The English Malady: Or, A Treatise of Nervous Diseases of all Kinds; as Spleen, Vapours, Lowness of Spirits, Hypochondriacal and Hysterical Distempers, &c.*, 2nd edn. (London: George Strahan and J. Leake, 1734), ii.

[22] Mandeville's book is in the form of three dialogues: the first two between Misomedon, who suffers from chronic hypochondria, and Philopirio, an empiricist physician; the third between these two characters and Polytheca, Misomedon's wife, who has had hysteria for many years. The general point of the dialogues is to raise questions about overly theoretical approaches to medicine and to stress that changes in diet and lifestyle are the best treatments for hypochondria. Philopirio argues that only by following what experience shows to be useful in curing diseases (and by tailoring particular remedies for each patient) will people be able to recover from their illnesses. Theory, he argues, tends only to lead people to ignore what experience tells them. Mandeville has his physician-mouthpiece, Philopirio, suggest that scholars can avoid the disease "if they commit no Excess in those things that exhaust the finer Spirits, but divert themselves daily with Hunting, the Tennis-court, or other brisk Exercises." Special remedies should be taken with care, however, in that these more often cause more harm than they provide benefit (*A Treatise on the Hypochondriack and Hysterick Diseases* (1730), intr. Stephen H. Good [Delmar, NY: Scholars' Facsimiles & Reprints, 1976], 138).

[23] The full title of the first edition (1711) is *A Treatise of the Hypochondriack and Hysterick Passions, Vulgarly call'd the Hypo in Men and Vapours in Women; in which the Symptoms, Causes, and Cure of those Diseases are set forth after a Method interily new. The whole interspers'd, with Instructive Discourses on the*

interference in the proper functioning of the stomach brought about by the loss of animal spirits through excess study. Moreover, Mandeville's mouthpiece in this dialogic work says:

> I'll add, that [hypochondriacs] are oftner Men of Learning, than not; insomuch, that the *Passio Hypochondriaca* in High-Dutch is call'd *Der Gelahrten Kranckheydt*, the Disease of the Learned; because they are more subject to it than other People....Men of Sense, especially those of Learning, are guilty of Errors, that, unless they are of a very happy Constitution, will infallibly bring the Disease upon them, such as Blockheads can't commit; for all Men that continually fatigue their Heads with intense Thought and Study, whilst they neglect to give the other Parts of their Bodies the Exercise they require, go the ready way to get it....So that softheaded People are no otherwise exempt from this Disease, than the grand Seignor's Eunuchs are from Claps, by being uncapable of performing what may occasion it.[24]

I am unsure about whether Wright is correct about Mandeville's significance for Hume's and his physician's use of this phrase. While it is true that Hume does refer to Mandeville in the "Introduction" to the *Treatise* as one of the "late philosophers in *England*, who have begun to put the science of man on a new footing" (T Intro.7, SBN xvii), the connection between scholarliness and mental illness was common enough at this time to make pinpointing a definitive source impossible.[25]

My suggestion is that Hume deploys the rhetoric of melancholia in CtB in order to draw on the idea that it is a condition brought on by excessive study's interfering with the body's proper functioning. For I think that he recognizes that there is something about philosophy itself that leads it, in particular, to interfere with the proper functioning *of the mind*.

Consider the methodology of Humean "scientists of man." They attempt to "explain the nature and principles of the human mind" (T 1.1.2.1, SBN 8) by turning their minds inward so as to observe what occurs there as they go about their lives. There is a problem, however. As Hume notes in the "Introduction," reflective self-observation is different from the observations that play a role in the other natural sciences, because in self-observation the observer and the object observed are one and the same person. Thus there is always the possibility that "reflection and premeditation would so disturb the operation of [the observer's] natural principles, as must render it impossible to form any just conclusion from the phaenomena" (T Intro.10, SBN xix). I call this problem *reflective interference*. And in Chapters 1 and 4 I argue that part of Hume's reactions to sceptical arguments can be seen to spring from problems connected with reflective interference.

Real Art of Physick it self; And Entertaining Remarks on the modern Practice of Physicians and Apothecaries: Very useful to all, that have the Misfortune to stand in need of either. In Three Dialogues.

[24] Mandeville, *Treatise*, 107. See also 212–13, 216, 219.

[25] Wright claims, in contrast, that other texts on hypochondria in this era do not point to excessive reflection as a cause, *The Sceptical Realism of David Hume* (Minneapolis, MN: University of Minnesota Press, 1983), 236n10.

In each of "Scepticism with regard to reason" and "Scepticism with regard to the senses," Hume reflects on the operations of one of his core cognitive capacities. In both cases he learns that some of our most fundamental beliefs depend on seemingly arbitrary principles of the imagination. And in both cases, though officially eschewing a radical sceptical rejection of the beliefs in question, he nonetheless finds himself losing touch with them: "The attention is on the stretch: The posture of the mind is uneasy; and the spirits being diverted from their natural course, are not govern'd in their movements by the same laws, at least not to the same degree, as when they flow in their usual channel" (T 1.4.1.10, SBN 185). The result is a momentary loss of both our reflective investigation of the capacity and the capacity itself. They are "destroy'd by their subtility" (T 1.4.1.12, SBN 186). Our natural propensities can then reassert themselves, and, "an hour hence" (T 1.4.2.57, SBN 218), we will be fully re-engaged with the processes of reasoning and sensing.

Hume's sceptically-minded interpreters see him as showing here merely that we are irrational in our incapacity to embrace our reflective conclusions; the so-called "naturalist" interpreters see him as revealing a non-rational source—Nature—for the normative endorsement of our fundamental propensities. But I argue that Hume is instead drawing our attention to reflective interference. Given that our reflective investigations are the same in kind as the natural propensities they study, reflection itself can be interrupted when the propensities become the focus of study. And thus we are to learn from Hume's investigations of scepticism, not that we should try to reject our rational or sensory verdicts, nor that we should embrace them because of their naturalness; rather, we should recognize that our investigations so disturb the propensities in question that we should come to see that philosophy can say nothing further about them, either in their favour or in rejection. Just as melancholia is the result of the scholar's studies interfering with his normal constitution, the philosopher's reflections interfere with her mental life, yielding the upheaval in which we are tempted to give up on both our fundamental beliefs and the reflections by which we investigate them. It turns out that philosophy cannot accomplish some of the tasks it sets itself. As true sceptics, we must learn to accept that we "cannot defend ...our reason [or the senses] by reason" (T 1.4.2.1, SBN 187).

Hume repeatedly describes his project as an "anatomy of mind" or an "anatomy of human nature" (T 2.1.12.2, SBN 326; see also T 1.4.6.23, 2.1.8.7, 2.1.12.2, 3.3.6.6, Abs.2, SBN 263, 301, 325, 620–1, 646; L 1.32–3). But anatomy proper, like Hume's "science of man," suffers from methodological problems: in cutting open an animal to discern its inner features, scientists might obscure the very features they are interested in knowing more about. Indeed, there might be some features of an animal that are so dependent on their unimpeded operation that any anatomists who use dissection or vivisection will misunderstand or mischaracterize them. That is to say that anatomy proper must confront the fact that its method puts limits on what can be known by means of it—just as I have suggested is the case with Hume's philosophy, where reflective interference puts some questions beyond the domains in which philosophers "can expect assurance and conviction" (T 1.4.7.14, SBN 273). More-over, Hume was sure to have known that anatomy has the methodological problem that I have suggested also afflicts his approach to philosophy. For Cicero—Hume's exemplar of a true sceptic[26]—made just this point in his *Academica*:

We do not know our own bodies, we are ignorant of the positions of their parts and their several functions; and accordingly the doctors themselves, being concerned to know the structure of the body, have cut it open to bring its organs into view, yet nevertheless the empiric school [*viz.* physicians who subscribe to a sceptical view] assert that this has not increased our knowledge of them, because it is possibly the case that when exposed and uncovered they change their character.[27]

We must always be careful that the steps we take to make observation possible—incision or reflective introspection—do not interfere with the operations of the physical or mental system that we want to investigate.

Thus far, of course, I have provided only hints and suggestions in favour of the interpretation of Hume's true scepticism that I have adumbrated here. The chapters that follow fill out the details.

0.4 Some Preliminaries

Before I start that task, I would like to draw attention to two choices I have made in constructing my argument. First, I have restricted my interpretive focus almost entirely to the *Treatise*, even though Hume revisits the topics I discuss here in the first *Enquiry*, especially in "Of the Academical or sceptical philosophy" (EU 12), and the *Essays*, most notably in "The Sceptic." But recent interpreters have rightly emphasized that each of these works is best understood as having its own aims and arguments, despite their thematic and argumentative overlap with the *Treatise*.[28]

Consider, for example, how Hume presents his consideration of causal reasoning in the *Enquiry*: he raises "sceptical doubts" (EU 4) followed by a "sceptical solution" (EU 5). But the same topic is addressed in Book 1 Part 3 of the *Treatise* with its present-ation of rules for causal reasoning (T 1.3.15) and only one, seemingly incidental mention of scepticism (T 1.3.13.12, SBN 150), and as if he were oblivious to possible sceptical

---

[26] In the "Letter from a Gentleman" Hume points to Cicero as a model for his scepticism (LG, 24). He also mentions "devouring" the works of Cicero in his youth (MOL, xxxiii). See Thomas Olshewsky, "The Classical Roots of Hume's Scepticism," *Journal of the History of Ideas* 52 (1991), 269–87, for a discussion of Cicero's influence on Hume.

[27] H. Rackham (tr.), *'De Natura Deorum' and 'Academica'* (Cambridge, MA: Harvard University Press, 1933), II, xxxix, 122.

[28] See especially Stephen Buckle, *Hume's Enlightenment Tract: The Unity and Purpose of an Enquiry Concerning Human Understanding* (Oxford: Oxford University Press, 2001), and the essays in Peter Millican, *Reading Hume on Human Understanding: Essays on the First 'Enquiry'* (Oxford: Clarendon Press, 2002). For the *Essays*, see Christopher Williams, *A Cultivated Reason: An Essay on Hume and Humeanism* (University Park, PA: Pennsylvania State University Press, 1999).

consequences of the view. In fact, in the *Treatise*, Hume restricts his consideration of scepticism almost entirely to Part 4 of Book 1—the Part to which my discussion is devoted. In addition to the one reference from Part 3, already noted, he uses the term (and its cognates) only two other times: once in the "Introduction" (T Intro.3, SBN xiv) and once in an important footnote that he included in the "Appendix" to the *Treatise* with the instructions that it was to be appended to his earlier treatment of the idea of the vacuum (T 1.2.5.26n12, SBN 638–9; I discuss this footnote in §§3.2.1 and 5.1). Thus it would be a mistake to assume that passages and ideas from the *Enquiry* can be incorporated into an interpretation of the *Treatise* without significant contextualization.

Similarly, Hume's essay "The Sceptic" is meant to be read in conjunction with the three other philosophical character sketches, "The Epicurean," "The Stoic," and "The Platonist." He clearly takes the views he expresses in the former to be bound up with his literary purposes in these linked pieces. Accordingly, because the focus of my discussion is the *Treatise*, I make only occasional and brief reference to his other works. My goal is to understand Hume's scepticism *in the 'Treatise,'* not his commitment to this position in some broader sense.[29]

A second preliminary point concerns my discussion of Hume's philosophical forebears when offering interpretations of his arguments. I frequently discuss John Locke (see §§2.1, 4.3.1, and 6.1), René Descartes (see §§1.2 and 5.3), the ancient sceptics (see §§1.2 and 4.1), and others (such as Pierre Bayle, Nicolas Malebranche, and George Berkeley). My goal is not to make claims that properly belong to the history of ideas, where the concern is the causal influence of one thinker on another (and where the evidence in support of a claim to such influence would require, for example, the memoranda of one from her or his reading of the other). Instead, my goal falls within the history of *philosophy*, where the interest lies in the *arguments* that an author makes, and how she or he might be responding to possible objections as revealed in other philosophers' *arguments*. I also do not pause to fully defend my readings of the philosophers I take Hume to be arguing against. I assume that Hume would have been open to those readings and that his views should have the resources to address the objections those readings contain (sometimes implicitly).

In privileging a particular set of philosophical interlocutors, I am guided by Hume's letter of 1737 (to Michael Ramsay), written shortly after he had left La Flèche, having completed much of the *Treatise*. He says:

I shall submit all my Performances to your Examination, & to make you enter into them more easily, I desire of you, if you have Leizure, to read once over La Recherche de la Verité of Pere Malebranche, the Principles of Human Knowledge by Dr Berkeley, some of the more metaphysical articles of Bailes Dictionary, such as those [. . . of] Zeno, & Spinoza. Des-Cartes

---

[29] Hume indicates in "My Own Life" that he takes his later presentation of his views to involve only a change in the "manner," not the "matter" (MOL, xxxv). In a longer study it would be possible to test the interpretation of scepticism in the *Treatise* that I develop here against its presentation in his other works.

Meditations would also be useful but don't know if you will find it easily among your Acquaintances[.] These Books will make you easily comprehend the metaphysical Parts of my Reasoning....[30]

Though Locke is not included in this list, I take Hume's familiarity with his *Essay* to be signalled in the "Introduction" to the *Treatise* (T Intro.7, SBN xvii). In fact, I take much of Book 1 to be Hume's attempt to forge a more fully empiricist account of mind than the one offered by Locke, who retains without argument some scholastic metaphysical baggage, such as a substance-mode ontology.

---

[30] Included in R. Popkin, "So, Hume did Read Berkeley," *Journal of Philosophy* 61 (1964), 775; the interpolations are Popkin's.

1

Total Scepticism and the Challenge to Reason

Hume's first engagement with scepticism[1] as a "system of philosophy" occurs in "Of scepticism with regard to reason" (T 1.4.1, hereafter 'SwR'), where he presents an argument purporting to show that "all the rules of logic require a continual diminution, and at last a total extinction of belief and evidence" (T 1.4.1.6, SBN 183). The result would be "*total* scepticism" (T 1.4.1.7, SBN 183). But, he notes, no one is actually persuaded by this argument, despite there being "no error" (T 1.4.1.8, SBN 184) in it. "Nature, by an absolute and uncontroulable necessity has determin'd us to judge as well as to breathe and feel" (T 1.4.1.7, SBN 183). In the "Abstract" to the *Treatise*, Hume summarizes the argument by saying: "[W]e assent to our faculties, and employ our reason only because we cannot help it. Philosophy would render us entirely *Pyrrhonian*, were not nature too strong for it" (T Abs.27, SBN 657).

The challenge for the interpreter is to make sense of Hume's attitude towards the sceptic's argument. How can he avoid its outcome if it is not in error? Even if nature might cause us to ignore the negative verdict on reason, is this not simply a case of our being *irrational*? What does Hume hope to accomplish in his first consideration of a system of philosophy?

After clarifying the structure of the sceptical challenge in §1.1, I offer my answers to these questions. I take my clue from what Hume declares to be his "intention" in presenting "the arguments of that fantastic sect," namely:

to make the reader sensible of the truth of my hypothesis, that all our reasonings concerning causes and effects are deriv'd from nothing but custom; and that belief is more properly an act of the sensitive, than of the cogitative part of our natures . . . If belief . . . were a simple act of the thought, without any peculiar manner of conception, or the addition of a force and vivacity, it must infallibly destroy itself, and in every case terminate in a total suspense of judgment. But as experience will sufficiently convince any one, who thinks it worth while to try, that tho' he can find no error in the foregoing arguments, yet he still continues to believe, and think, and reason

---

[1] This chapter is largely taken from "Hume's Scepticism and Ancient Scepticisms," in Jon Miller and Brad Inwood (eds.), *Hellenistic and Early Modern Philosophy* (New York, NY: Cambridge University Press, 2003), 251–73.

as usual, he may safely conclude, that his reasoning and belief is some sensation or peculiar manner of conception, which 'tis impossible for mere ideas and reflections to destroy.

(T 1.4.1.8, SBN 183–4; emphasis in original)[2]

In §1.2, given the clarification in the "Abstract" that the "fantastic sect" is Pyrrhonism, I explore their model of the mind, where belief is construed as a "simple act of the thought." After sketching Hume's theory of belief in §1.3, I argue in §1.4 that Hume uses our inability to embrace the Pyrrhonian conclusion as a reason to reject this model of belief. For if we did have to make an act of assent in order to have a belief, we would be able to embrace the conclusion.[3] Instead, we naturally embrace the conclusion of our reasoning without any need for assent, even if such reflective consideration is always possible.

But it is not possible to reflect always; our nature leaves us in a default position of accepting the verdicts of reason. In §1.5 I consider the role of 'nature' in Hume's argument. Our nature stops us from following the sceptic to his conclusion, but this does not mean that we are irrational. Instead, I argue that, when our capacity to reflect is deployed for special philosophical purposes, it ends up undermining both reason and itself. So I understand Hume's point to be that certain kinds of philosophical investigation of the mind can serve to obscure those of its features that were originally of interest. The proper response is to recognize that philosophy is unable to answer some of the questions it poses for itself. This is a problem for philosophy, but not for our everyday reasoning and believing.

I conclude this chapter by, in §1.6, suggesting that Hume's argument in SwR sets the stage for understanding his considerations of sceptical challenges to the senses in "Of scepticism with regard to the senses" (T 1.4.2, hereafter 'SwS'). My consideration of the latter Section spans the three following chapters, with Chapter 4 devoted to spelling out the argument in SwS that I take to be parallel to the argument in SwR discussed here.

---

[2] As Donald Baxter pointed out to me, Dugald Stewart says, after quoting the italicized portion of this passage: "The distinction here alluded to between the *sensitive* and the *cogitative* parts of our nature (it may be proper to remind my readers) makes a great figure in the works of Cudworth and of Kant. By the former it was avowedly borrowed from the philosophy of Plato. To the latter, it is not improbable, that it may have been suggested by this passage in Hume" (*Dissertation on the Progress of Philosophy*, excerpts from which are reprinted in James Fieser [ed.], *Early Responses to Hume's Metaphysical and Epistemological Writings*, II, 2nd edn. [Bristol: Thoemmes Press, 2005], 219).

[3] By taking Hume's admitted intentions as the focus of my interpretation, I am aligned with W. E. Morris ("Hume's Scepticism about Reason," *Hume Studies* 15 [1989], 39–60) and Annette Baier (*A Progress of Sentiments* [Cambridge, MA: Harvard University Press, 1991], ch. 1), each of whom argues that Hume aims in this Section to reject intellectualist and rationalist theories. Where I differ from them is that they suggest that Hume thinks that the sceptic's argument depends on a conception of reason that Hume does not share. But Don Garrett correctly notes that Hume uses 'reason' here as he does throughout the *Treatise*, and thus Morris and Baier cannot be right in their seeing Hume as targeting only a narrow conception of reason in SwR (*Cognition and Commitment in Hume's Philosophy* [New York, NY: Oxford University Press, 1997], 84–5). Using the historical background of Hume's argument as my support, I argue in what follows that Hume's target is what he takes to be an *incorrect model of belief*, where it is treated as the outcome of a faculty different in kind from that which generates reasoning. For Hume, reasoning's nature is to produce beliefs.

1.1 An Argument against Rational Belief

The sceptical argument in SwR asks us to take our fallibility seriously. Briefly, it tells us that, because we know that we have erred in the past, sometimes even in the simplest cases of reasoning, we should reduce our confidence in our beliefs. And because that reduction is itself a case of reasoning, the requirement to reduce our confidence iterates until we are left with no beliefs at all. The argument is notorious. D. C. Stove calls it "not merely defective, but one of the worst arguments ever to impose itself on a man of genius," largely because he takes Hume merely to misunderstand the nature of probability.[4] I argue below that once we understand what Hume means by 'probability,' the argument is much more compelling (though, as I show in §§1.3 and 1.4, still dependent on some assumptions that should be rejected).

For Hume, reasoning works to discover relations (T 1.3.1.2, SBN 73), and he thinks that it does so in two ways. On the one hand, reasoning can yield "knowledge" when we "demonstrate" that a relation must hold between two objects simply in virtue of their own qualities. The only way that the relation could not obtain were if the objects were "chang'd"; equivalently, leaving the objects unchanged but denying the relation yields a contradiction (T 1.3.1.1, SBN 69). Thus arithmetic truths admit of knowledge (as do relations of resemblance, qualitative comparisons, and contrarieties [T 1.3.1.2, SBN 70]).[5] On the other hand, reasoning yields "probability" when the grasp on a relation depends on features extraneous to the relata (T 1.3.1.1, SBN 69). It is thus possible to conceive of the relation's not obtaining by varying the extraneous features. For example, our belief that a throw of the dice is most likely to yield a seven depends on our prior experience with how dice behave. But we could conceive of other outcomes by supposing the dice to be loaded or for them to start landing only on their edges rather than their faces (or for the course of nature itself to change, so that when tossed they turn into flowers or evaporate into thin air). And, more generally, all true causal beliefs count as cases of probability (as do relations of identity and spatiotemporal comparisons [T 1.3.2.1, SBN 73]).[6]

In the sceptical argument, Hume says that because we have doubts about our demonstrative reasoning "knowledge degenerates into probability" (T 1.4.1.1, SBN 180), and that similar doubts about our probabilistic reasoning means that the likelihood of any claim ultimately suffers from a "continual diminution" until it disappears entirely, leaving "all... uncertain" (T 1.4.1.6–7, SBN 183). If this means that our knowledge that, say, 15 per cent of 35 is 5.25, is reducible to the point where

---

[4] D. C. Stove, *Probability and Hume's Inductive Scepticism* (Oxford: Clarendon Press, 1973), 132. I owe thanks to David Owen for drawing this statement to my attention.

[5] Thus such relations are known to hold *a priori*—simply by considering the relata jointly without needing to consult experience—and to hold certainly.

[6] The need to consult objects beyond those being related makes our grasp of probabilistic relations *a posteriori*.

all we can say is that P(0.15 × 35 = 5.25) = 0, it is indeed a bad argument.[7] How could a purported demonstration have a probability at all? It either is true or false with certainty, and so is not the kind of claim to which our notion of probability applies. Recent interpreters have clearly shown that this cannot be Hume's point. After all, P(0.15 × 35 = 5.25) = 0 is quite clearly a belief, and it would enable us to conclude with total confidence that P(0.15 × 35 ≠ 5.25) = 1. But Hume says that the outcome of the sceptic's argument should be a "total extinction of belief" (T 1.4.1.6, SBN 183).[8]

Instead, the proper way to understand Hume's argument has to do with the stance we take towards our reasoning; it only indirectly touches on the objects of our reasoning such as mathematical claims like '15 per cent of 35 is 5.25.' He seems to be relying on the fact that 'reasoning' can mean two things. It can name a process that takes place within us when we try to discover how (broadly speaking) things are—let us call this the *psychological* sense of reasoning. Or 'reasoning' can name a normatively laden activity that we succeed in only when we manage to get at the truth of things (again broadly speaking) in the right manner—let us call this the *authentic* sense of reasoning (T 1.3.13.12, SBN 150). Thus when you try to figure out the appropriate 15 per cent tip on a $35.00 dinner, you are psychologically reasoning, no matter what result you come up with. But you only reason authentically when you correctly recognize that the tip should be $5.25.

The question at the centre of the sceptical argument of SwR asks how you can tell whether your psychological reasoning is authentic reasoning. Why should you give your psychological reasoning "authority" (T 1.4.1.5, SBN 182) over your beliefs? Your psychological reasoning is the cause of your belief, and your experience tells you that psychological reasoning produces truth only some of the time. Since we err not infrequently (especially when calculating the tip after a nice meal), before we should be confident in the outcome of a stretch of psychological reasoning—before we should treat it as authentic—we should check it in light of our acknowledged capacity for error. Is our first reckoning of the tip *really* correct? Hume thinks that this checking process involves us in a different kind of reasoning. In figuring out the tip, we were using demonstrative reasoning in an attempt to achieve knowledge, but in checking on whether our psychological reasoning is authentic, we are making a probabilistic judgement about the likelihood that we erred.

This might at first seem to be an odd claim about how we check our mathematical judgements. When I want to find out if I have correctly calculated a tip, I usually continue to use demonstrative reasoning by simply recalculating to see if I get the same result as at first. Or I might ask someone else to do the arithmetic; Hume himself says that the mathematician looks to the "approbation of his friends" and for "universal assent" to his proofs (T 1.4.1.2, SBN 180). But he is right in saying that

---

[7] See Robert Fogelin, *Hume's Skepticism in the 'Treatise of Human Nature'* (London: Routledge and Kegan Paul, 1985), 14–18.

[8] See especially David Owen, *Hume's Reason* (Oxford: Oxford University Press, 1999), ch. 8.

checking in this manner does involve causal, probabilistic reasoning, for the second calculation will count as a *check* of the first only if I assume that it would be highly unlikely for my or my friends' psychological reasoning to misfire twice in the same way. And, if the second calculation differs from the first, I will have to enter into more complicated reasonings—perhaps calculating for a third or fourth time to see if our psychological reasoning converges on one result, which will then be treated as authentic.[9]

The nature of the checking process is what leads Hume to assert that "all know-ledge degenerates into probability" (T 1.4.1.1, SBN 180). This is not to say that an authentic demonstration stops being a demonstration; it means that our confidence that we have succeeded in a demonstration can only ever be probabilistic, as in 'I'm almost wholly confident that I'm right on this, but it is conceivable that I'm wrong.' Recall that our being able to conceive of something's not being the case is a sign that we can only ever grasp that relation probabilistically (T 1.3.1.1, SBN 69).

The sceptical argument gets its force because the process of checking iterates. Our estimation of the likelihood that we were initially right might itself not be authentic; for we might have erred in assessing the possibility that we erred in the first place, say by overestimating the reliability of our tip-calculations. And our assessment of the overestimation will itself be subject to a further correction, and so on until there is a "total extinction of belief and evidence" (T 1.4.1.6, SBN 183). It is important to be clear on what he means here. It is possible that some of our reflective assessments of the reliability of our reasonings are positive (as in 'I'm almost wholly confident that . . .'), but this is not enough to avoid the loss of evidence. For 'evidence' here has its eighteenth-century sense of 'evidentness' or subjective certainty.[10] And even if a round of checking has a positive verdict, it still puts us one step back from our initial verdict; it distances us from the initial claim. As David Owen has reminded us, it was a commonplace of early-modern logic to hold that the certainty of an argument was inversely proportional to its length and complexity.[11] Hume's sceptical argument is meant to show that every argument should be infinitely complex, and thus we should have no faith in the verdicts of our reason.

But of course we do. No one can really succumb to the "*total* scepticism" (T 1.4.1.7, SBN 183) that involves the abandonment of all beliefs. For, as we saw previously, Hume thinks that nature has constructed us so that we cannot help but judge.

---

[9] Fred Wilson points out that testimony offers a parallel case (*Hume's Defense of Causal Inference* [Toronto, ON: University of Toronto Press, 1997], 250), but he overstates the comparison. The crucial point in SwR is that we treat *our own* reasoning as if it were the reasoning of someone else. We can do this, of course, but we can never do this *fully*: in assessing someone else's testimony we rely on our own reason, so in assessing our own reason we must also continue to rely on our own reason. We can never fully get it in view so as to treat it as we do testimony.

[10] Garrett, *Cognition*, 228; Owen, *Hume's Reason*, 86n4, 185. Kevin Meeker disagrees with this reading of 'evidence' in "Hume's Iterative Probability Argument: A Pernicious Reductio," *Journal of the History of Philosophy* 38 (2001), 224.

[11] Owen, *Hume's Reason*, 184–8, 195.

Though we can follow the first few iterations of the checking process, we soon give up the argument, surrendering to our natural inclination to believe our reasoning. The question that has mystified Hume's interpreters is what he wants us to think of all this.

1.2 Sceptics, Ancient and Modern

In the passage where he announces his intentions in SwR, we saw that Hume suggests that total sceptics think that they can sustain their argument because of their conception of belief as a "simple act of the thought" (T 1.4.1.8, SBN 184). What is this conception of belief and how would it, if it were true, enable the sceptical conclusion? Using Hume's identification of the total sceptics with the Pyrrhonians in the "Abstract" to the *Treatise*, I answer these questions below by considering ancient Pyrrhonism.

Hume was likely aware of this "sect" primarily through the reports of Sextus Empiricus and Diogenes Laertius.[12] And we find something like the argument of SwR in two of the batteries of arguments—the ten Modes of Aenesidemus and the five Modes of Agrippa—that they describe the sceptics as having prepared in order to challenge the doctrines of their opponents. The fourth Mode of Aenesidemus involves drawing attention to how our judgements, especially those relating to sensory experience (*phantasiai*), are affected by the circumstances (*peristateis*) of judgement.[13] Sextus points out that when we prefer the judgement in one circumstance over that occurring in another, we must rely on a criterion (*kritērion*). But what justifies the criterion? If it is used without proof, it is arbitrary, but if a proof is given, that proof must itself rely either on the same criterion—rendering it circular—or a different one, setting one on an infinite regress.[14] The second Mode of Agrippa has a similar structure. Sextus says of it: "[W]e assert that the thing adduced as a proof of the matter proposed needs a further proof, and this again another, and so on *ad infinitum*, so that the consequence is suspension [*epochē*], as we possess no starting-point for our argument" (PH i 166). Diogenes' version of this argument runs: "And in order that we may know that an argument constitutes a demonstration

---

[12] For discussions of Hume's use of the ancient sceptics, see, T. M. Olshewsky, "The Classical Roots of Hume's Skepticism," *Journal of the History of Ideas* 52 (1991), 269–87; Richard H. Popkin, "Sources of Knowledge of Sextus Empiricus in Hume's Time," *Journal of the History of Ideas* 54 (1993), 137–41; and, especially, Peter Fosl, "The Bibliographic Bases of Hume's Understanding of Sextus Empiricus and Pyrrhonism," *Journal of the History of Philosophy* 16 (1998), 93–109.

[13] As Julia Annas and Jonathan Barnes note, this argument has little to do with circumstances, and indeed little to do with sense impressions, applying more generally to any judgement whatsoever; *The Modes of Scepticism: Ancient Texts and Modern Interpretations* (Cambridge: Cambridge University Press, 1985), 90.

[14] "For the proof always requires a criterion to confirm it, and the criterion also a proof to demonstrate its truth; and neither can a proof be sound without the previous existence of a true criterion nor can the criterion be true without the previous confirmation of the proof" (PH i 116).

[*apodeixis*], we require a criterion; but again, in order that we may know that it is a criterion we require a demonstration; hence both the one and the other are incomprehensible [*akatalēpton*], since each is referred to the other" (DL ix 91). In each of these Modes we find the general pattern of Hume's argument in SwR: what allows us to tell whether a purported (that is, psychological) judgement is an authentic one? We either must dogmatically assert that it is, or enter into an infinite regress.

But, despite the similarity of these arguments to the argument of SwR, it is hard to equate the ancient Pyrrhonians with Hume's total sceptics. The latter hold that "all is uncertain, and that our judgment is not in *any* thing possest of *any* measures of truth or falsehood." They think that they can "forbear viewing certain objects in a stronger and fuller light" even if experience has suggested that they always accompany another kind of objects (T 1.4.1.7, SBN 183).

Pyrrhonian sceptics, however, are not nearly this extreme.[15] Sextus describes their motivation as primarily ethical. They eschew positive doctrines [*dogmata*], instead cultivating

an ability, or mental attitude [*dunamis*], which opposes appearances to judgements in any way whatsoever, with the result that, owing to the equipollence of the objects and reasons thus opposed [*isostheneia*], we are brought firstly to a state of mental suspense [*epochē*] and next to a state of "unperturbedness" or quietude [*ataraxia*].   (PH i 8)

These sceptics have learned that attempts to formulate doctrine almost always lead to frustration either because there are no decisive arguments in support of the doctrine in question that defeat all of its competitors, or because holding to the doctrine is itself a source of anxiety given the opposition to it from others and from the world. And so they have decided that a life without doctrine is the best means to achieving a peaceful, unperturbed life. Note that they do not even hold these claims as doctrine; they are rather the expressions of what appears to them to be the case (*ta phainomena*) (PH i 15). It is on the basis of this appearance that they respond to their rivals' attempts to formulate doctrine by showing that any argument in favour of it can be balanced by an equally plausible argument against it. Hence they think that suspending judgement on the issue is the best option, even while they remain open to the possibility of a resolution (*skeptos*, after all, means investigator, and they also call themselves *zētētikai*, or seekers [PH i 7]).

The Pyrrhonians were well aware that their view struck others as implausible. It seemed to many that it would be impossible to live after having suspended judgement on all things. Diogenes makes this criticism vivid by recounting one story about Pyrrho, the fourth- and third-century-BC namesake of the later Pyrrhonians:

He led a life consistent with this doctrine, going out of his way for nothing, taking no precaution, but facing all risks as they came, whether carts, precipices, dogs or what not,

---

[15] Julia Annas thus concludes that Hume did not understand ancient scepticism correctly ("Hume and Ancient Scepticism," in Juha Sihvola [ed.], *Ancient Scepticism and the Sceptical Tradition*, Acta Philosophica Fennica 66 [Helsinki: Societas Philosophica Fennica, 2000], 271–85).

and, generally, leaving nothing to the arbitrament of the senses; but he was kept out of harm's way by his friends who, as Antigonus of Carystus tells us, used to follow close after him.

(DL ix 62).

The problem is that, as Diogenes immediately goes on to say, this description of Pyrrho is likely apocryphal, disseminated by those who wanted to discredit the Pyrrhonians. Diogenes reports that Aenesidemus, who revived Phyrrhonian scepticism in the first century BC, says that it was only Pyrrho's "philosophy that was based upon suspension of judgement, and that he did not lack foresight in his everyday acts. He lived to be nearly ninety" (DL ix 62). Sextus, moreover, repeatedly confronts the objection that sceptical suspension leaves one unable to lead a normal life, responding that even though he gives up doctrine, he continues to accept appearances (*phainomena*); in particular the directions of nature, the affections, customs, and the arts are sufficient as guides for life (PH i 23). And included amongst the directions of nature are those causal appearances brought about by experience of the constant conjunction of particular kinds of objects (PH ii 100–2). Thus, unlike Hume's total sceptics who try to free themselves from even these associatively-induced beliefs, the ancient Pyrrhonians refrain only from making claims about the non-evident (*adēla*) structure underlying the appearances (PH i 13), while continuing to breathe and feel *and judge* about how things *seem* to them.[16]

---

[16] There has been much debate in the past thirty-five years over how best to understand ancient Pyrrhonism. The issue turns on whether their target is merely philosophical and quasi-scientific doctrine, or all beliefs whatsoever. A parallel issue concerns the appearances to which the sceptics remain committed. Are they just everyday, non-technical beliefs? Or are they some non-belief-like, non-judgemental mental state? Michael Frede has staked out the conservative interpretation. See his "The Skeptic's Beliefs" and "The Skeptic's Two Kinds of Assent and the Question of the Possibility of Knowledge" in *Essays on Ancient Philosophy* (Minneapolis, MN: University of Minnesota Press, 1987), 179–200, 201–22. The radical interpretation has been defended by Myles Burnyeat in "Can the Sceptic Live his Scepticism?" in M. Schofield, M. Burnyeat, and J. Barnes (eds.), *Doubt and Dogmatism* (Oxford: Clarendon Press, 1980), 20–53; "Idealism and Greek Philosophy: What Descartes Saw and Berkeley Missed," *Philosophical Review* 91 (1982), 3–40; and "The Sceptic in his Place and Time," in R. Rorty, J. B. Schneewind, and Q. Skinner (eds.), *Philosophy in History* (New York, NY: Cambridge University Press, 1984), 225–54. See also Jonathan Barnes, "The Beliefs of a Pyrrhonist," *Proceedings of the Cambridge Philological Society* 208, NS 28 (1982), 1–29. I will try to stay neutral on this debate.

Donald Baxter uses the recent debate over how best to understand the ancient sceptics to motivate his interpretation of Hume's scepticism (*Hume's Difficulty: Time and Identity in the 'Treatise'* [New York: Routledge, 2008], ch. 1). He suggests that Hume is a Pyrrhonian as this position is interpreted in Michael Frede's essays. Attempts to actively assent to any position must fail, but we can nonetheless assent passively, by how things feel to us. We manage to "forget the difficulty" that our active engagement with our cognitive propensities causes, such as the upheaval at the climax of the "Conclusion of this book" (T 1.4.7; see *Hume's Difficulty*, 10). Baxter thus falls into what in §7.2 I call the "sceptical" school of interpreters. My concern with Baxter's reading as it applies to SwR is that he assimilates too easily Hume's reaction to the sceptical argument against reason to the ancient sceptic's suspense in the face of equipollent considerations. In §1.6 I argue that Hume wants us to learn that philosophy turns out to be impotent when it tries to give an ultimate justification for our reasoning because our reflections interfere with its operations.

We should not, however, be too surprised that Hume's total sceptics are not a direct match for the ancient Pyrrhonians. For, as Richard Popkin masterfully demonstrates, philosophers in the early-modern period often revived Pyrrhonian arguments for many different purposes, especially in connection with the religious foment brought on by the Reformation. Catholics argued that the impotence of reason meant that one should follow the customs of one's society—and the Catholic church—while Protestants said that it meant that one should follow whatever religious appearances one felt within.[17] And so Hume would have been familiar with many contemporary versions of Pyrrhonism. Pierre Bayle's *Dictionary*, for example, contains arguments akin to that of SwR without the nuance that accompanies Sextus's presentation of the ancient view (HCD, "Pyrrho," 194–209).

But consideration of the ancient sources helps us to see why Hume thinks that a view of belief as a "simple act of the thought" makes one susceptible to Pyrrhonian arguments. Of course, this conception of belief is not the Pyrrhonians' own—they eschewed doctrine. But it is the view of belief held by their primary interlocutors and targets, the Stoics, who in their epistemology held that belief results from an act of assent. We stand over our impressions, as it were, and are able to withhold our assent to any of them unless it forces itself upon us; the criterion of judgement is what they call a cognitive impression (*phantasia kataleptike*). The Pyrrhonians' challenge was that for any purported such impression, there was another one indistinguishable from it that failed to present us with the truth. Putting it in the terminology I used in §1.1 to recount the sceptical argument of SwR, the ancient Pyrrhonians argued that any assent to a purported cognitive impression would be merely psychological, and thus would need to be authenticated by means of a higher level act of assent. The Stoics developed sophisticated responses to this challenge, largely in terms of a complex story of cognitive development whereby in the natural course of our upbringing we acquire the capacity to assent only to cognitive impressions (even if only the Sage actually uses this capacity properly).[18]

Hume seems uninterested in the details of this historical debate, presumably because just as Pyrrhonism had undergone a revival in the early-modern era, so too had Stoic epistemology. René Descartes, most famously, and following him, Nicolas Malebranche, made belief an act of the will, and introduced their own version of cognitive impressions, namely clearly and distinctly perceived ideas (AT VII, 56; ST I.2).[19] So long as there is a separation of that feature of mind by means of which we entertain various thoughts from that by means of which we form beliefs, the

---

[17] Richard Popkin, *The History of Scepticism from Erasmus to Spinoza* (Berkeley, CA: University of California Press, 1979).

[18] See Michael Frede, "Stoics and Skeptics on Clear and Distinct Impressions," *Essays on Ancient Philosophy* (Minneapolis, MN: University of Minnesota Press, 1987), 151–76.

[19] As Peter Kail points out, Malebranche is, "in many ways, Hume's antithesis" ("Hume's Ethical Conclusion," in M. Frasca-Spada and P. J. E. Kail [eds.], *Impressions of Hume* [Oxford: Clarendon Press, 2005], 129).

argument of SwR can get a grip.[20] For the sceptic can ask: how can I be sure that this would be an authentic assent, rather than a merely psychological assent?

Descartes and Malebranche, like the Stoics, could try to escape the regress by arguing that there are some ideas to which we cannot help but assent, so that there would be no cognitive space into which the sceptic's question could be lodged. We are *passive* in such cases, unable to do anything but to believe.[21] This would allow them to escape the sceptic's threatened regress, but it is not clear that they are entitled to this move. The point is clearest with Malebranche. He says that the understanding presents to us perceptions of connections between things, and that the will must either consent to this perceived connection to yield a judgement, or direct the understanding to continue considering other information to see if the perceived connection remains plausible. When all such considerations are exhausted, we are "obliged to rest with what the understanding has already represented" (ST I.2, 8). "But to the extent that there is something obscure in the subject we are considering, or that we are not entirely certain that we have discovered everything needed to resolve the question . . . , we are free not to consent" (ST I.2, 8). Indeed, Malebranche holds we *should* not consent, because we are culpable for our errors, and they are the cause of our misery (ST III.ii.9, 249). So even though we are passive in our consenting when the understanding presents us with an indubitable connection, Malebranche leaves himself vulnerable to the sceptic's argument—that we should always withhold our consent given that the understanding has previously presented objects as con-nected that turned out ultimately to be separate from one another.[22]

1.3 Hume's Model of Belief

Hume says in the passage where he announces his intentions in SwR that his conceptions of belief and causal reasoning as deriving from "custom" and the "sensitive" part of our nature allow him to escape the force of the sceptical argument. Recall that his treatment of these topics starts with the problem of

---

[20] Even those, like John Locke, who do not accept some of the basic tenets of Cartesian rationalism, still model the mind in such a way that we stand over our ideas, acquiring knowledge when we perceive their agreement or disagreement, forming opinions when we judge them to agree or disagree for the most part. It is unclear whether this leaves Locke susceptible to the argument of SwR. On the one hand, he says we are wholly passive in perceiving the agreement or disagreement in the case of ideas; we cannot have the ideas without perceiving their (dis-)agreement (E IV.xx.16). On the other hand, he says that, in judgements of probability, we can continue to search out for evidence that might influence our view. Moreover, "Manifest Probabilities may be evaded, and the Assent withheld, upon this Suggestion, That *I know not yet all that may he said on the contrary side*. And therefore though I be beaten, 'tis not necessary I should yield, not knowing what Forces there are in reserve behind" (E IV.xx.14). This suggests that the sceptic would have cognitive room to raise the doubts that get the regress going. See Owen, *Hume's Reason*, 54–61.

[21] Consider Descartes's claim about his assent to the *cogito*: "[A] great light in the intellect was followed by a great inclination in the will" (AT VII 47).

[22] Malebranche leaves himself especially open to the sceptical argument of SwR when he says that we should always "heed the weakness and limitation of [our] own minds" (ST III.ii.9, 249).

how we are able to recognize the necessary connections between causally related objects. We do not have direct insight into such connections because it is always possible to conceive of the objects apart from one another. Even if we have always experienced objects of similar types conjointly, we still cannot directly discern that objects of those types will continue to be so conjoined; nature could change. It is only because our experience leads us to associate together our ideas of the relevant types of objects that we come to believe that an instance of one will always accompany an instance of the other (T 1.3.6). Belief, then, is not the outcome of a "simple *act* of the thought," but a *passive* event in our minds brought about by how our experiences impact on our associative propensities. Causal reasoning involves *feeling* that objects belong together, rather than actively recognizing their connection (see T 1.3.8.12, SBN 103).

So what happens when we raise the questions of SwR about the authority of reason? Why should I believe the verdict given to me by my associative propensities? On Hume's view, these questions are no longer quite as pressing, for his conception of causal reasoning leaves us in a default position of accepting its authority. A causal inference is an association that has a vivacious idea as its outcome, and the vivacity of an idea *just is* the psychological manifestation of its having authority with us. The objects of such ideas "strike upon us with more force; they are more present to us; the mind has a firmer hold of them, and is more actuated and mov'd by them. It acquiesces in them; and, in a manner, fixes and reposes itself on them" (T App.3, SBN 624). There is no need, then, for some act of assent, separate from the process of reasoning itself, in order for us to accept the verdict of our causal reasoning. It *starts* from a position of authority by its very nature, and so we normally rest contented with what our reason tells us.

We normally *will* rest contented, but *should* we? There are obviously cases where we do feel the need to take a second look at our reasoning in order to be sure of its verdict. Consider the mathematician who thinks that she has solved an outstanding problem, and so asks herself whether her purported demonstration really is a demonstration. Or the backgammon player who thinks that his position in the game is strong enough to merit doubling the stakes, but who then reassesses the situation just to be sure. These are ordinary enough occurrences, and ones that any philosophical account of reason and belief should have room for.

Hume acknowledges this point in the case of causal reasoning when he says that the authority of any stretch of it is not "entire" (T 1.3.1.5, SBN 182); belief is the outcome of causal reasoning, but the belief is not so strong as to block our reconsidering the matter under investigation. This point applies even to the mathematician, who engages in demonstrative, not probabilistic, reasoning. Since Humean demonstrative reasoning is an exploration of the limits of conceivability, her doubts about her reasoning arise with the recognition that even though she might not be able to conceive of the denial of her purported mathematical theorem, someone else might be able to. Her belief in her demonstration turns out to be based on the causal inference that others will, like her, be similarly unable to conceive of the idea in question.[23]

We can now see the crucial difference between Hume and the Stoics and their early-modern descendants discussed above. For Hume, the question posed by the sceptic in SwR comes *after* we have formed a belief. We start out fully *engaged* by our reasoning, carried along by it into a state of belief. Thus a paradigm piece of causal reasoning for Hume is our instinctively stopping at the edge of a river because of our expectation that we would sink were we to continue (T 1.3.8.13, SBN 103–4). In order to call it into doubt we have to step back from it by means of a new mental act, a "reflex act of the mind" (T 1.4.1.5, SBN 182) that separates us from our reasoning allowing us to evaluate it. Even then, we will be engaged by our reflections, believing whatever outcome they lead us to, and it would take ongoing "reflex judgements" (T 1.4.1.8, SBN 184) to drive us into the sceptic's regress. Self-conscious reasoning where we actively evaluate whether we should accept the initially perceived connection is the exception, not the rule.

Hume does not spend time in SwR explaining how his opponents end up embracing a false account of belief, but I think we can construct one on his behalf. He says in another context that "there appears a great resemblance between the sects of the Stoics and Pyrrhonians, though perpetual antagonists; and both of them seem founded on this erroneous maxim, That what a man can perform sometimes, and in some dispositions, he can perform always, and in every disposition."[24] That is, the Stoics think that, since we *can* reflect on our thought in order to assent to or reject its verdict, this is the posture that the mind is *always* in—standing over its mental processes, deciding whether to accept them. Where Hume models belief on the basis of our unreflective thinking, the Stoics and their early-modern descendants take the opposite approach, modelling belief on the self-conscious reasoning we undertake when trying to be sure to get things right. And so they treat what Hume calls the "reflex act of the mind," whereby we consider whether a perceived connection should be accepted, not as an option that we sometimes exercise, but as necessary in every belief.[25]

---

[23] As Owen points out, Hume's response to total scepticism hinges on our incapacity to follow through on probabilistic checks on our reasoning. Thus the initial challenge to *demonstrative* reasoning, where we make the first probabilistic assessment of the likelihood of error, is not addressed in Hume's response (*Hume's Reason*, 182–3).

[24] *Dialogues Concerning Natural Religion*, ed. Norman Kemp Smith (Indianapolis, IN: Bobbs-Merrill, 1947), 133. The quoted statement is Cleanthes', though Philo, usually thought to best reflect Hume's own views, agrees with it.

[25] Locke is an interesting case here. He holds that such "reflex" acts are built into the very structure of the mind. In perceiving an idea, we perceive that we are perceiving (E II.xxvii.9), and it is because of this self-consciousness that we can be held responsible for our deeds—and perhaps also for our thoughts—in that we could have delayed acting until all the relevant factors were properly considered (E II.xxi.47). Consider also Samuel Clarke's definition of consciousness: "*Consciousness*, in the most strict and exact Sense of the Word, signifies...the *Reflex Act by which I know that I think, and that my Thoughts and Actions are my own and not Another's*" (*A Letter to Mr. Dodwell*, 6th edn. [London: James and John Knapton, 1731], 149). See §§2.3 and 4.3.1.

Moreover, Descartes in particular emphasizes that the faculty of mind responsible for assent, in his case the will, is different in kind from and superior to the understanding (AT VII, 57). Hume, I think, would say that he misinterprets the capacity to reach a verdict from the reflective perspective. For Hume holds that, when reasoning psychologically, our default stance—in everyday and *reflective* reasoning—is to assume the authenticity of our verdicts. It takes reflection to make the psychological constitution of reasoning evident. The Cartesians notice this authenticity at the level of our reflective judgements and then assume that it must arise from a special faculty (the will) different in kind from the faculty that processes ideas (the understanding).

Descartes also follows the Stoics in thinking that, in principle, all error is avoidable (by the Sage, or by the one who uses his will rightly). Given that he takes us to be as it were superintendents of our mental processes, where the superintendent is different in kind and superior to that which it oversees, he holds that we always have the ability to withhold our cognitive commitments until all the considerations have been properly taken into account. Thus, unlike Hume, Descartes and those who adopt similar views leave themselves open to the sceptic's attack—taking all considerations into account means taking human fallibility seriously, and this means that they will never exhaust all the relevant considerations for belief, leaving them unable to consent to anything.

1.4 "Philosophy wou'd render us entirely Pyrrhonian..."

Two problems with Hume's alternative account of belief still need to be addressed. First, while I noted that Hume wants to allow for the possibility of reflective consideration of our initial instinctive causal verdicts, how does his account of causal reasoning makes proper room for this? Second, why does Hume emphasize that there is no error in the sceptic's argument?

Taking up the first question first, Hume should and does want to make room for the possibility of our treating causal facts as objective, true independently of what we happen to feel. He wants to be able to say that someone might think that 'eating cheese causes headaches' and be wrong about it even if, given her experience, her ideas of cheese and of headaches are associated. For it might be the case that she only eats cheese when also drinking copious amounts of red wine; and it is the wine that *really* causes the headache. But how can Hume's account of causation allow for this? There is no fact of the matter, an intrinsic necessary connection between the wine and the headache, waiting to be discovered.

He responds to this problem by introducing certain "general rules"

form'd on the nature of our understanding, and *on our experience of its operations in the judgments we form concerning objects*. By them we learn to distinguish the accidental circumstances from the efficacious causes; and when we find that an effect can be produc'd without the concurrence of any particular circumstance, we conclude that that circumstance makes not a part of the efficacious cause, however frequently conjoin'd with it.

(T 1.3.13.11, SBN 149; emphasis added)

That is, our experiences include cases of dashed causal expectations, where kinds of objects, previous instances of which were experienced conjointly, surprised us when we encountered instances of them independently of one another. So we learn that there is a difference between our causal beliefs and the causal facts, namely those objects that will be conjoined not just when we happen to experience them, but *always* (T 1.3.14.31, SBN 170). In order to increase our confidence in a causal belief we can vary the circumstances in which the cause and effect are found (for example, try eating cheese without drinking wine). Hume lists eight general rules that we should follow to avoid falling prey to causal errors, to increase the probability that our beliefs will track the actual course of nature (T 1.3.15). He says that these rules constitute "all the LOGIC I think proper to employ in my reasoning" (T 1.3.15.11, SBN 175).

Note, however, that even if all these rules are followed, the causal belief still remains merely probabilistic; it is still conceivable that the two kinds of objects are merely accidentally conjoined, and that there will be cases in the future where instances of them occur independently of one another. Hume's argument that we are unable to grasp intrinsic connections between objects still stands, and so these rules are not going to give us that. For the corrective "general rules" are not different in kind from the lower-level, association-engendered causal inferences that we would like to correct. Thus, in the quoted paragraph, he points to our *experience* of the operations of the understanding as standing behind the corrective rules. And we expect the mind to continue as it has in the past—associating ideas together on the basis of the experience of constant conjunctions, mistaking accidental connections for causal ones, and the like—only as a result of our associating together the relevant ideas. The corrective rules, like the unreflective causal judgements they correct, are codifications of our associative tendencies (T 1.3.13.12, SBN 150).

This is why our corrective reflections automatically have authority with us when we are fully engaged by them, just as our unreflective judgements have authority with us when we are fully engaged by them. And just as the authority of our unreflective judgements is not "entire," neither is the authority of our reflective judgements. Hume says:

[T]he sceptics[26] may here have the pleasure of observing a new and signal contradiction in our reason, and of seeing all philosophy ready to be subverted by a principle of human nature [our tendency to generalize on the basis of experience], and again sav'd by a new direction of the

---

[26] In my Introduction I noted that this is Hume's only invocation of scepticism in his treatment of causation in the *Treatise*.

very same principle. The following of general rules is a very unphilosophical species of probability, yet 'tis only by following them that we can correct this, and all other unphilosophical probabilities.   (T 1.3.13.12, SBN 150)

In SwR, the total sceptic tries to exploit this fact about our causal reasoning in order to get his regress going. At each stage we can legitimately ask whether the reasoning at the previous stage is authentic. Since the corrective rules are not different in kind from our less reflective judgements, it is always possible to ask whether the initial authority they bear should be accepted. So the sceptic is at least in part right. There is "no error" in his "arguments" (T 1.4.1.8, SBN 184). "[A]ll the rules of logic" do "require a continual dimunition, and at last a total extinction of belief and evidence" (T 1.4.1.6, SBN 183), where 'logic' refers to the general rules for causal reasoning listed at *Treatise* 1.3.15.

There is still, however, a *motivational* question that needs to be considered. As we have seen, unlike the Stoics and the early moderns who were inspired by them, for whom belief is a "simple act of the thought," we do not, for Hume, *need* to give a reflective verdict on our reasoning in order to form a belief. Instead, reasoning by its very nature produces a belief, even if its authority is not entire. This means that we need a *reason* to reflect on our reasoning; we are not compelled into the regress simply by our attempt to reach a conclusion. Consider again the mathematician and the backgammon player. The former is motivated to reflect on her reasoning because she worries that her reputation will be harmed if she declares something to be inconceivable that others can conceive without too much trouble; or she is moved simply by "curiosity" or the "love of truth" (T 2.3.10) to care about the mathematical realm. The backgammon player might have a competitive personality, or given that he has money on the game he could worry about his potential loss. Moreover, even if someone is moved to check her reasoning, the motivational question reappears after the first round of checking, for it too yields a belief, the authority of which is not entire. Why reflect again? Presumably the number of iterations of checking will be determined by the relative weight of the various motivations at work in the person in question. After a few rounds of checking, the mathematician or backgammon player will rest in her or his verdict, and move on to the next thing in her or his life.

The sceptic, however, claims to be driven by different motives. In presenting the argument of SwR, Hume says that the possible unreliability of our reason "is a doubt, *which immediately occurs to us, and of which, if we wou'd closely pursue our reason*, we cannot avoid giving a decision" (T 1.4.1.6, SBN 182; emphasis added). He also says that "we are *oblig'd* by our reason" (T 1.4.1.6, SBN 182; emphasis added) to try to correct our reasoning reflectively. But what can Hume mean by this? In his official discussion of motivation in Book 2 of the *Treatise* he famously declares that reason has no power to obligate us; it "is, and ought only to be the slave of the passions" (T 2.3.3.4, SBN 415). And, as we have seen, normally we are motivated by a desire to discover mathematical truths or to win money at backgammon; reasoning is one component of those activities, and to the extent that our motive dominant at the time requires it, we will accept or reflectively correct our reasoning as needed. What would it be, then, to "pursue our reason" independently of any other motivation?

The best clue for answering this question is the first clause of Hume's summary statement of SwR in the "Abstract" to the *Treatise*: "[P]hilosophy wou'd render us entirely *Pyrrhonian*..." (T Abs.27, SBN 657; first emphasis added). While he does not expand on this point himself, I think we can extrapolate a bit. He seems to be hinting that it is a peculiarly philosophical state of mind that drives us into the regress. Unlike the backgammon player or mathematician, who has extrinsic motivations for checking his or her reasoning, the philosopher is motivated by a curiosity about the status of reason itself. Are its verdicts justified? Should we trust the beliefs that reason automatically instills in us? Why? These are legitimate questions, and the philosopher will (try to) apply them to any stretch of reasoning, continuing to (try to) apply them until she comes up with a wholly unimpeachable answer.[27] But Hume thinks that the Pyrrhonian is right in saying that such a justification will not be forthcoming; our reasoning is always fallible. And this means that

[t]his sceptical doubt...with respect to reason...is a malady, which can never be radically cur'd, but must return upon us every moment, however we may chace it away, and sometimes may seem entirely free from it. 'Tis impossible upon any system to defend...our understanding...; and we but expose [it] farther when we endeavour *to justify [it] in that manner.* As the sceptical doubt arises naturally from a profound and intense reflection on [this] subject, it always encreases, the farther we carry our reflections, whether in opposition or conformity to it. (T 1.4.2.57, SBN 218; emphasis added)[28]

Thus any attempt to "justify" reason in this philosophical "manner," any attempt to show that its verdicts are ultimately grounded, serves only to push us into the sceptic's regress. The philosopher "cannot defend his reason by reason" (T 1.4.2.1, SBN 187) because, insofar as he engages in "profound and intense reflection" on the status of reason, he will never rest content with the not-fully-entire authority that our reasoning has by its very nature. He will (try to) continue undertaking those "reflex acts of the mind" (T 1.4.1.5, SBN 182) whereby our reasoning is viewed as merely psychological, in need of some further authentification.

---

[27] 'Unimpeachable' here does not mean indubitable. Probabilistic assessments are unimpeachable when they actually capture the causal facts. Our experience with error in our probabilistic assessments means that we can ask whether a given such assessment is correct.

[28] This passage comes from the final paragraph of "Of scepticism with regard to the senses" (T 1.4.2), and it applies to "[t]his sceptical doubt, both with respect to reason and the senses" (T 1.4.2.57, SBN 218). The ellipses in the quotation come from my excising its references to scepticism about the senses. See §4.8 for a discussion of this passage in its proper context.

1.5 "...were not nature too strong for it"

Of course, Hume holds that the sceptic cannot maintain the philosophical state of mind whereby we prescind from our natural commitment to the verdicts of our reason: Nature is too strong for him. In the passage stating his intentions in presenting the sceptical argument, Hume suggests that our incapacity to adopt total scepticism indicates that his preferred model of belief is correct. That is, he uses the empirical fact of our reactions to the sceptical challenge—our "experience" (T 1.4.1.8, SBN 184) of maintaining belief—as a piece of evidence in favour of his model of the mind. If, as Hume's opponents hold, we stood over our reasoning, having to decide whether to accept its verdicts, we should be able to embrace the sceptic's conclusion. The fact that we continue believing shows that we are instead immersed in our reasoning, and it is not in need of some further act of assent.

Before we can accept this conclusion, however, we have to consider what *causes* us to continue believing, especially given Hume's emphasis that there is "no error" in the sceptic's argument. Though our nature is such as for us to maintain our belief, Hume's opponents might say that this is not evidence in favour of a different model of belief, but rather evidence that we (usually) fail to think rationally. In what sense is nature too strong for us?

Sometimes Hume makes it sound as if it is a mere fact that is true of us. When we engage in long and complex reasoning, we get confused, lose the thread, are no longer persuaded by our considerations:

[A]s the action of the mind becomes forc'd and unnatural, and the ideas faint and obscure; tho' the principles of judgment, and the ballancing of opposite causes be the same as at the very beginning; yet their influence on the imagination, and the vigour they add to, or diminish from the thought, is by no means equal. Where the mind reaches not its objects with easiness and facility, the same principles have not the same effect as in a more natural conception of the ideas; nor does the imagination feel a sensation, which holds any proportion with that which arises from its common judgments and opinions.   (T 1.4.1.10, SBN 185)

If this were the whole of Hume's story, he could not use our incapacity to follow the sceptic to the "total extinction of belief" as evidence in favour of his preferred model of belief. Instead, it would seem to be evidence that we cannot follow reason's demands, that we are fundamentally irrational. While some interpreters do reach this conclusion,[29] I think that charity demands that we recognize that Hume must have more in mind here. Not only would this interpretation undermine his statement of his intentions, it would also leave him in an extremely uncomfortable position. Why should we continue to engage in a philosophical project with Hume if we are

---

[29] Hume's point would then be that we ought not to believe the verdicts of reason, even if we cannot follow this prescription. See, for example, Robert Fogelin, *Hume's Skepticism*, ch. 2; and Wayne Waxman, *Hume's Theory of Consciousness* (Cambridge: Cambridge University Press, 1994), 277.

fundamentally irrational—and would have no beliefs at all if we were more fully rational?[30]

A second reading—that of the "naturalist" interpreters—continues to take our incapacity to follow the sceptic as a merely natural fact about us. But they take Hume's emphasis on our natural tendency to believe to mean that our incapacity has *normative* force. We *should* not follow reason in this case because it conflicts with our natures. Norman Kemp Smith, for example suggests that, for Hume, reason "has no rightful jurisdiction" over our fundamental tendencies to believe: reason's support for or rejection of a belief counts for nothing if it is not seconded by our primitive belief-involving instincts.[31] While a full assessment of the naturalist interpretation will have to await Chapter 7, it has at least three problems as an interpretation of SwR.

First, how can Hume continue to treat reason as a critical capacity if our nature is meant to trump its verdicts? When reason dictates, for example, that we ought not to believe a claim, we are left waiting to see whether this prescription does or does not affect us: if it does not, it should not; if it does, it should. That is to say that, on the naturalist reading, Hume leaves us only with what we *do* do, not what we *ought* to do. Moreover, given that this reading leaves the sceptical argument intact, it leaves us in a position where reason's particular verdicts are supposed to be given some credence, even while we hold that we ought not to accept its general verdict against itself.

Second, the naturalist interpretation fails to comport with Hume's stated intention of making readers "sensible" of his view of belief. For treating our natural tendencies as normative does not require that one abandon a conception of belief as an "act of the thought" (T 1.4.1.8, SBN 184). Rather, it introduces a second principle that could guide a reasoner's assent. She could thus look for what reason urges or for what nature urges, whichever is stronger.[32] Hume's point, however, is that our natural

---

[30] Philip Cummins calls this the "integration problem" ("Hume's Diffident Skepticism," *Hume Studies* 25 [1999], 43–65). I discuss it in more detail in Chapter 7.

[31] Norman Kemp Smith's *Philosophy of David Hume* (London: Macmillan, 1941) is the classic statement of the naturalist interpretation; the quotation is from 108. See also Garrett, *Cognition*, ch. 10; Wilson, *Hume's Defense*, ch. 3; and Owen, *Hume's Reason*, ch. 9. Owen's statement of the naturalist view is especially clear: "Reason's hold on us is limited, and a good thing too. If its influence were unlimited, it would entirely destroy itself. It is only because its influence is limited by other aspects of our nature that it can have any influence at all. We can be rational only if we are only partly rational. This is not a new theory of reason; it is a new theory of how reason plays only a limited role in belief formation" (*Hume's Reason*, 195).

[32] Don Garrett—the leading contemporary naturalist interpreter—uses what he calls the "Title Principle" to specify its core commitment. It is based on Hume's statement from the "Conclusion" to Book 1: "Where reason is lively, and mixes itself with some propensity, it ought to be assented to. Where it does not, it never can have any title to operate upon us" (T 1.4.7.11, SBN 270). Garrett describes Hume's reconsideration of the sceptical argument of SwR in the "Conclusion" (where it is integrated with other sceptical arguments to create a "dangerous dilemma" at T 1.4.7.6, SBN 267), in these terms: "Because the elaborate and refined reasoning by which the probability of causes undermines all belief is not lively but strained, and mixes itself with no propensity or interest, it may, according to the Title Principle, be ignored. Other reasoning, however, ought still be *assented to*; and since even the most elaborate and refined philosophical reasoning turns out to mix itself with the propensities of curiosity and ambition, this includes philosophical reasoning. In effect, the Title Principle excises from *the domain of assent-worthy reasoning*

response to the sceptical challenge is supposed to show that belief does not require an act of assent.

Third, the naturalist interpretation overlooks how Hume accounts for the natural interruption of the sceptic's regress. It is not a brute fact, but rather the result of the self-referential nature of the inquiry that the philosopher tries to pursue—"defend[ing] his reason by reason" (T 1.4.2.1, SBN 187). Hume actually makes this point twice, first by relying on his analysis of reasoning as constituted from the imagination's associative tendencies and second by considering reason's normative force.

Consider the passage quoted above where Hume describes our mental processes as we attempt to follow the sceptic. His point is not just that our nature is recalcitrant, as it might be with any long and complex argument, but rather that, because reason is attacking reason, the very structures that the philosopher wants to investigate start to crumble. Thus the passage continues: "The attention is on the stretch: The posture of the mind is uneasy; and the spirits being diverted from their natural course, are not govern'd in their movements by the same laws, at least not to the same degree, as when they flow in their usual channel" (T 1.4.1.10, SBN 185). Philosophical reflections on our reasonings *interfere* with the proper workings of the mind; they *distort* it; they *alter* its normal economy.

The potential for the mind to interfere with itself while it is investigating itself philosophically is a theme throughout the *Treatise*. In the "Introduction," for example, he says that purposeful experimentation is of little help in the 'science of man' because "reflection and premeditation would so disturb the operation of my natural principles, as must render it impossible to form any just conclusion from the phaenomenon" (T Intro.10, SBN xix).[33] Hume recognizes that sometimes the mind-under-investigation has a different shape from the mind-while-not-being-investigated. And it is the latter he wants to know more about, even though he must investigate it to find out about it. Hume seems to think that the reflections urged by the sceptic have a similar distorting effect on the mind. Causal reasoning, our propensity to associate ideas in an orderly fashion, starts to break down when the reflective gaze on it starts

---

precisely the reason-undermining iterations of the probability of causes that were the original source of the dangerous dilemma, while leaving other reasoning intact" ("Hume's Conclusions in 'Conclusion of this book'," in S. Traiger (ed.), *Blackwell Guide to Hume's 'Treatise'* [Malden, MA: Blackwell, 2006], 169; emphases added). He makes it clear that for him, Hume is interested in which mental principles are worthy of assent, rather than, as I suggest, leaving behind the assent-based conception of belief.

[33] As I discuss in Chapter 7, in the "Conclusion" to Book 1 the philosophical interference with the mind becomes so intense that Hume describes himself as suffering what appears to be a nervous breakdown: "The *intense* view of these manifold contradictions and imperfections in human reason has so wrought upon me, and heated my brain, that I am ready to reject all belief and reasoning, and can look upon no opinion even as more probable or likely than another. Where am I, or what? From what causes do I derive my existence, and to what condition shall I return? Whose favour shall I court, and whose anger must I dread? What beings surround me? and on whom have I any influence, or who have any influence on me? I am confounded with all these questions, and begin to fancy myself in the most deplorable condition imaginable, inviron'd with the deepest darkness, and utterly depriv'd of the use of every member and faculty" (T 1.4.7.8, SBN 268–9).

to iterate. Recall that the authority of reason was a product of the vivacity of its associatively produced conclusions. But as we are forced farther and farther back in the regress, we no longer have had the relevant experiences needed to get our associations off the ground. Thus we are less and less able to reach rational conclusions and, having less and less vivacity, they are less and less authoritative with us.

Hume recapitulates this point in the final paragraph of SwR, only this time emphasizing its normative dimension. The context is his consideration of how his response to the sceptic differs from the traditional response, where the argument's status as a piece of reasoning means that reason must have "some force and authority;" so that even if the sceptic is right about reason's limitations, his doubts "can never be sufficient to invalidate all the conclusions of our understanding" (T 1.4.1.12, SBN 186). Hume rejects this "expeditious" solution and instead describes how the sceptical arguments are "destroy'd by their subtility:"

Reason first appears in possession of the throne, prescribing laws, and imposing maxims, with an absolute sway and authority. Her enemy, therefore, is oblig'd to take shelter under her protection, and by making use of rational arguments to prove the fallaciousness and imbecility of reason, produces, in a manner, a patent under her hand and seal. This patent has at first an authority, proportion'd to the present and immediate authority of reason, from which it is deriv'd. But as it is suppos'd to be contradictory to reason, it gradually diminishes the force of that governing power, and its own at the same time; till at last they both vanish away into nothing, by a regular and just diminution. The sceptical and dogmatical reasons are of the same kind, tho' contrary in their operation and tendency; so that where the latter is strong, it has an enemy of equal force in the former to encounter; and as their forces were at first equal, they still continue so, as long as either of them subsists; nor does one of them lose any force in the contest, without taking as much from its antagonist.   (T 1.4.1.12, SBN 186–7)

The sceptic's argument, by using reason to attack reason, ends up undermining both reason and itself. In attempting to make a rational argument against believing the verdicts of reasoning, he merely causes confusion within himself. This is not Pyrrhonian equipollence, where reason equally supports the two sides of the argument; it is instead the mutual destruction of reason and its investigator. The regress fails ultimately to grip us because, even though each of its steps is under-taken in the 'pursuit' of reason, reason (temporarily) leaves us when we reflect on it too intensely.

So it is not just that we are psychologically unable to stick with the philosophical mindset necessary for the sceptic's argument; it is that the sceptic's use of the philosophical mindset undermines his capacity to continue investigating and also undermines that feature of the mind he is most interested in vindicating—reason's authority. Recall the earlier quotation about the upshot of SwR: "'Tis impossible upon any system to defend . . . our understanding . . .; and we but expose [it] farther when we endeavour to justify [it] *in that manner*" (T 1.4.2.57, SBN 218; emphasis added).

We learn from the failure of the sceptic's regress to grip us not that the instinctively given authority of reason is spurious or that it is vindicated. Rather we learn that philosophy cannot pass either verdict on reason because the activity of reflecting on reason "in that manner" leaves us without the very thing we were putting on trial.

What we must do is learn to accept our incapacity to give a final verdict on our reason: "Carelessness and in-attention"—a refusal to take the "reflex act" whereby the psychological constitution of our reasoning is made evident to us—"alone can afford us any remedy" (T 1.4.2.57, SBN 218). In the "Conclusion" to Book 1, Hume calls someone who "studies philosophy in this careless manner" a "true sceptic," in that he is "diffident of his philosophical doubts, as well as of his philosophical conviction; and will never refuse any innocent satisfaction, which offers itself, upon account of either of them" (T 1.4.7.14, SBN 273). I address this Section in detail in Chapter 7, but at this point we can already see that, unlike the total sceptic, who thinks that he can abandon reason entirely, the true sceptic accepts that reasoning yields belief, even while recognizing its fallibility. Philosophy cannot vindicate it, but that does not mean that we should try to live without it (whatever that would mean). Rather we should come to accept that philosophy cannot accomplish everything. As Hume says in describing the aims of his philosophy: "I may contribute a little to the advancement of knowledge, by giving in some particulars a different turn to the speculations of philosophers, and pointing out to them more distinctly those subjects, where alone they can expect assurance and conviction" (T 1.4.7.14, SBN 273). Speculating about the reliability of our reasoning, simply for its own sake rather than in the service of some extrinsic motivation, turns out not to be a fruitful topic for philosophers; we cannot expect "assurance and conviction" on this topic because our speculations interfere with the very object of our speculations.

1.6 Scepticism with Regard to Reason and the Senses

The passage I quoted earlier as summarizing what Hume wants us to learn from SwR actually appears at the end of the Section immediately following it: SwS. He clearly wants these two Sections to be read together. Not only do they have parallel names, but SwS starts with a conjunctive adverb that links his conclusion from SwR with what he is setting out to address in SwS:

Thus the sceptic still continues to reason and believe, even tho' he asserts, that he cannot defend his reason by reason; and by the same rule he must assent to the principle concerning the existence of body, tho' he cannot pretend by any arguments of philosophy to maintain its veracity.   (T 1.4.2.1, SBN 187)

We will see in Chapters 2, 3, and 4, where I examine SwS in detail, that Hume ends up making things significantly more complicated than this initial statement suggests.

Nonetheless, SwS ends by connecting the two sceptical Sections in the passage I quoted earlier, when I omitted the references to beliefs stemming from the senses:

This sceptical doubt, *both with respect to reason and the senses*, is a malady, which can never be radically cur'd.... 'Tis impossible upon any system to defend *either our understanding or senses*; and we but expose them farther when we endeavour to justify them in that manner.

(T 1.4.2.57, SBN 218; emphases added)

I argue in Chapter 4 that SwR and SwS also share a common argument.

In order to set the stage for that chapter, it will be helpful to break down my interpretation of SwR into the following eight steps.

(1$_R$)   Deployment of an argument from the ancient sceptics to argue that we should not believe the verdicts of reason.

(2$_R$)   Observation that no one believes the sceptical conclusion in (1$_R$). Our nature is to believe our reasonings.

(3$_R$)   Recognition that the argument in (1$_R$) depends on reflection on our reasoning that makes its fallible, psychological nature manifest to us.

(4$_R$)   Argument that Hume's model of belief as the outcome of experience-engendered association best explains our incapacity to accept the sceptical conclusion.

(5$_R$)   Diagnosis of opponents' model of belief as an "act of the thought" in terms of their failure to recognize that reflection is optional and that reflective verdicts depend on experience-engendered association.

(6$_R$)   Acknowledgement that, given (3$_R$), there is a legitimate *philosophical* question to be asked about whether we should believe the verdicts of reason.

(7$_R$)   Recognition that, because of reflective interference, philosophers are unable to answer the legitimate question in (6$_R$).

(8$_R$)   Acceptance of the "true" scepticism, where we continue to use our reason without being able to give it a fundamental justification.

Note that, in SwR, step (5$_R$) is not made explicitly, though I suggested in §1.3 that it is implicit in Hume's discussion.

In Chapter 4 I offer an interpretation of SwS that embodies these same eight steps. In this case, the starting point is our belief in the verdicts of our senses. But, in analogy to (1$_R$), Hume borrows from the ancient sceptics by presenting an argument suggesting that we should not believe the verdict of the senses; we do not have sensory access to a mind-independent world. But, as was the case with reason in (2$_R$), so also in the case of the senses: no one, no matter what they might say, can actually embrace the "extravagant" scepticism that denies the world (T 1.4.2.50, SBN 214). Hume recognizes, however, that just as the sceptic's argument against reason depended on reflection, (3$_R$), so also does the sceptic's argument against the senses. He then, as in (4$_R$), uses this point to argue that our incapacity to believe the sceptic's conclusion is best explained by his own preferred model of the mind, where we are carried along by our associations to believe in an independent world, rather than one in which we stand over our sensory perceptions having to decide whether they match the world. Moreover, Hume does explicitly in SwS what I suggested was implicit in (5_R) of SwR: he shows that his opponents' model of the mind actually presupposes his own preferred model, both in its retaining a world that our perceptions might match and in its presupposition that we have special access to our perceptions. Though Hume's model does not *require* us to reflect, we *can* as philosophers, reflect nonetheless; we can ask whether our sensings should be accepted, just as he considered in (6_R) whether our reasonings should be accepted. But the reflective interference that I emphasized in (7_R) reappears in SwS, and we turn out to be unable to answer the question philosophy poses for us. As we challenge the verdicts of our sensings, we are simultaneously challenging the verdicts of our introspectings, and thus each undermines the other. Ultimately, the conclusion of SwR, (8_R), is brought together with the conclusion of SwS in the passage I quoted previously. We recognize that we can continue believing our reason and our senses even though no philosophical vindication of them is possible.

There are also, however, three notable differences between the two sceptical Sections. First, where SwR starts off with the sceptical challenge to reason, the sceptical challenge in SwS does not occur until the 44th and 45th of its 57 paragraphs, leaving only one quarter of the Section for Hume to assess and diagnose it. The difference here, I suggest, is due to the fact that, by the time Hume reaches SwR, he has already given a full explanation of the understanding, namely the detailed discussion of knowledge and probability in Part 3 of Book 1. But Hume starts SwS without yet having provided an explanation of the mechanisms involved in our sensory beliefs. Thus he devotes the first 43 paragraphs of the Section to accounting for how we come to believe in the independent existence of the objects that we sense. I explore the details of this account in Chapters 2 and 3 before returning to the sceptical portion of SwS in Chapter 4.

Second, Hume spends far more time in SwR developing the sceptical argument than he does in SwS. As we saw in §1.1, in SwR he slowly takes us through the various steps whereby we seem required by "all the rules of logic" (T 1.4.1.6, SBN 183) to abandon our beliefs. But in SwS, he emphasizes how easy it is to reach the sceptical conclusion: it takes "a *very little* reflection and philosophy" (T 1.4.2.44, SBN 210; emphasis added) or "a *little* reflection" (T 1.4.2.50, SBN 214; emphasis added) for us to recognize the mind-dependence of our sensations.

The third difference between SwR and SwS I take to be related to the second. In the former Section, Hume focuses mainly on the fact that we do not follow the sceptic as he tries to extinguish all belief. In the latter, where the sceptical challenge is so easily available, his primary concern is the philosophical attempt to retain both the sceptical conclusion and the belief in the objective world by means of the "double existence" theory. Thus, where step (5_R) in the argument of SwR was left merely implicit, its analogue in SwS, (5_S), is a focus of Hume's discussion (see §4.5).

2

The Phenomenology of Sensory Experience

Hume starts the *Treatise* seemingly taking for granted that we encounter such things as apples, chambers, Paris, the sun, children, pineapples, and so on (all of these are examples from T 1.1.1).[1] We sense these things, and others sense the same things. We live in a shared world of public objects. Throughout most of Book 1, especially while investigating the general features of our perceptions (in Part 1) and the structure of reason (in Part 3), Hume does not pause (or not often) to investigate the principles of mind responsible for our taking ourselves to have sensory access to the world. Instead, he mostly postpones this task until "Of scepticism with regard to the senses" (T 1.4.2, hereafter 'SwS'), the longest and most complex Section of the *Treatise*, though Part 2's investigation of the spatiotemporality of our experiences also does address the issue to some extent.

SwS is notoriously difficult to interpret, in part because Hume undertakes at least five different tasks in it, and does not always bother to note their differences from one another. First, he offers an interpretation of our unreflective or "vulgar" sensory experiences that emphasizes our sense of immersion in a world of persisting, public objects (most obviously in T 1.4.2.1–2, SBN 187–8, but also intermittently throughout the Section). For Hume, we move through the world with a default, background assumption that we have access to things that that our senses reveal to us. One problem for him is how this assumption can be characterized, given his view that

---

[1] Norman Kemp Smith says that Hume starts the *Treatise* using "naively realistic" language, and only later in "Of scepticism with regard to the senses" (T 1.4.2) distinguishes between "impressions as being objects of immediate awareness and independently existing bodies as being the objects of belief" (*Philosophy of David Hume* [London: Macmillan, 1941], 113–14, 212–13, 450–8).

Note that we need to distinguish between a characterization of the vulgar as (naively) believing that they encounter objects directly, and the *philosophical thesis* of naive (or direct) realism, where, in the philosophical analysis of the mind, perceptions are taken to present independently existing objects. I suggest in what follows that Hume interprets the vulgar as experiencing the world naively. In Parts 1 and 3 of Book 1, however, he sounds like a naive realist in the philosophical sense, in that he takes the vulgar's naive beliefs at face value, leaving their full analysis for "Of scepticism with regard to the senses" (Part 2 sets the stage for this discussion). Of course, in this Section the appearance of naive realism is quickly dissolved.

beliefs, as vivacious ideas, must be occurrent.[2] The vulgar sense of immersion in the world, in contrast, is not an occurrent belief, but rather an unstated set of attitudes toward and commitments about what we perceive, or as Hume says, "a point, which we must take for granted in all our reasonings" (T 1.4.2.1, SBN 187). Some of the difficulty in interpreting SwS, I suggest in §2.2, arises from Hume's having to make these implicit attitudes and assumptions explicit, in order to have a viable explanandum. He (and his interpreters) sometimes ends up attributing the explicit beliefs to the vulgar, rather than recognizing that they are the philosophical articulation of a more primitive attitude towards the world as our senses present it to us.

Hume's second task in SwS is to explain the principles responsible for the vulgar attitudes towards the sensory world. He considers which faculties are involved in our beliefs about bodies (T 1.4.2.3–14, SBN 188–93), and argues that the imagination ultimately contributes the most. He then offers two accounts of the relevant mechanisms of the imagination—one that starts from sensations that cohere with one another (T 1.4.2.15–22, SBN 194–8), the other from sensations that are constant (T 1.4.2.23–43, SBN 198–210).

Third, Hume assesses the vulgar sensory beliefs from a philosophical point of view and seems to suggest that they are false (T 1.4.2.44–5, SBN 210–11). Fourth, he explains how philosophers have responded to this verdict by forming systems such as "extravagant scepticism," which tries to deny the existence of any objects beyond our perceptions (T 1.4.2.50, SBN 214), or representational realism (the theory of "double existence"), where we are taken to have special access to a realm of inner representations from which we infer the public world (T 1.4.2.46–55, SBN 211–18). Fifth, he assesses these philosophical systems in light of his own considered view, though his verdict here is particularly obscure (T 1.4.2.56–7, SBN 218).

This chapter will be devoted to discussing Hume's execution of only the first of these tasks, what might be called his *phenomenology of sensory experience*.[3] By this phrase, I mean that he specifies what vulgar sensory experience is like so that he can then go on to explain how we come to experience the world in this characteristic manner. Chapter 3 examines his explanation in terms of the imagination's response to constant and coherent sensations. I postpone my examination of Hume's philosophical assessment of vulgar sensory beliefs until Chapter 4, where I use the analysis of his scepticism about reason that I offered in Chapter 1 to illuminate his scepticism about sensory experience.

Hume's phenomenology of sensory experience emerges in the first three quarters of SwS, and a proper understanding of it is crucial for making sense of his treatment

---

[2] Louis Loeb argues against the suggestion that Humean belief must be occurent in *Stability and Justification in Hume's 'Treatise'* (Oxford: Oxford University Press, 2002), 65–74.

[3] Edmund Husserl says that in the *Treatise*, Hume "gives the first systematic sketch of a pure phenomenology" ("Author's Preface" to W. R. Boyce-Gibson's English translation of *Ideas* [London: George Allen and Unwin, 1931], 23).

of the philosophical responses to our sensory beliefs in the final quarter, including his own sceptical position. I approach this topic by considering two interpretive puzzles. First, Hume characterizes the vulgar belief about external objects as involving two elements: objects *continue* to exist when unperceived, and they exist *distinctly* from our occurrent perceptions of them. He goes on to say that these two beliefs stand or fall together. The puzzle, frequently noted in the secondary literature, is that the two beliefs seem not to be so linked. Most commentators argue that, while an object's continued existence entails its distinct existence, the converse need not hold: an object could exist independently from our sensing of it while we have an occurrent sensation, but might then cease existing along with our sensation of it. I suggest in §2.2, however, that these beliefs are independent in this way only if they are interpreted in a more sophisticated fashion than Hume intends. If we pay proper attention to his characterization of the vulgar as having a sense of immersion in the world—as implicitly taking themselves to be in direct contact with the objects around them—the two beliefs do operate together.

The second puzzle (detailed in §2.3) arises because Hume's account of the structure of sensation seems to conflict with his phenomenology of sensory experience. In particular, he holds that the mind is transparent to itself so that "all sensations are felt by the mind, such as they really are" (T 1.4.2.5, SBN 189); they "are known to us by consciousness, [and] ... must necessarily appear in every particular what they are, and be what they appear" (T 1.4.2.7, SBN 190). Yet he also repeatedly tells us throughout Book 1 of the *Treatise* that sensations are image-like. Given the claims about mental transparency, it seems as if we should recognize our impressions as images and thus reject the suggestion that the vulgar take themselves to have immediate access to everyday objects. Instead, Hume denies that our impressions present themselves as images (T 1.4.2.4–11, SBN 189–92). In resolving this puzzle in §2.4, I use Hume's account of general ideas to show that he distinguishes between the content of perceptions when taken in isolation and their content when our associative response is taken into account. Sensations, I suggest, have imagistic content in isolation (in one sense of 'imagistic'), but when caught up in the imagination's associations in the right way, afford us the vulgar sense of immersion in the world.

Before I delve into these two interpretive puzzles, it will be helpful to briefly review John Locke's treatment of our knowledge of the external world. We see in what follows that many of Hume's arguments are probably meant as responses to Locke. Having a summary of Locke's view on the table also sets the stage for my discussion of the final quarter of SwS in Chapter 4 (see especially §4.5). For his representational realism is a version of what Hume calls the "system of a double existence" (T 1.4.2.52, SBN 216)—his chief target in his critique of philosophical accounts of sensory experience.

2.1 Locke on Sensitive Knowledge

Locke uses the term 'idea' to stand for "whatsoever is the Object of the Understanding when a Man thinks" (E I.i.8), where thinking, in its most general sense, just is the perception of ideas (E II.ix.1). Thus thinking, along with willing, is one of the "two great and principal Actions of the Mind" (E II.vi.2). As an empiricist, Locke holds that we can acquire new simple ideas only by sensation, when the world's impact on our sensory organs causes an idea in us, or by reflection, when we turn our mind on itself in order to observe its operations. Given that my concern in this chapter is limited to sensory beliefs, I postpone my discussion of Locke's treatment of reflection and Hume's reaction to it to Chapter 4 (§§4.3.1 and 4.3.2).

Though Locke argues that sensation is the only means by which we can gain access to the world around us, he suggests that we cannot do so directly:

> For, since the Things, the Mind contemplates, are none of them, besides it self, present to the Understanding, 'tis necessary that something else, as a Sign or Representation of the thing it considers, should be present to it: And these are *Ideas*.   (E IV.xxi.4)

Thus, though there is some controversy in the secondary literature over how best to interpret Locke's treatment of ideas,[4] I think he is best understood as identifying ideas with inner "images" or "pictures"[5] that portray objects in the external world. These two elements of his account of ideas—their being inner and their being imagistic—require comment.

I am using 'inner' here to indicate that ideas, for Locke, are not merely mental phenomena, but are recognized to be mental phenomena. Everyday objects, in contrast, count as external because they are, and are taken to be, non-mental. Thus Locke says that, in perceiving an idea, "the Mind" has an "intuitive" knowledge of it (E IV.i.4), and this includes recognition of its mentality: "There can be nothing more certain, than the *Idea* we receive from an external Object is in our Minds" (E IV.ii.14). At the same time as we recognize ideas to be mental in this way, Locke thinks that we also grasp their representative qualities. In the case of simple ideas, "the Mind supposes" that they are "taken from" "Archetypes . . . which it intends them to stand for, and to which it refers them" (E II.xxxi.1). When we are "invincibly conscious" to ourselves that the idea in us is the result of occurrent sensation, "we can thence certainly inferr the existence of [the] . . . thing without us, which corresponds to that *Idea*" (E IV.ii.14). Locke takes the grasp of the conformity of an idea to the external object that both causes it and is represented by it to fall into one of the four "sorts" of knowledge (E IV.i.3). But, in the case of everyday objects, this grasp has less certainty

---

[4] See John Yolton, *Perceptual Acquaintance from Descartes to Reid* (Minneapolis, MN: University of Minnesota Press, 1984), ch. 5; Michael Ayers, *Locke: Epistemology* (London: Routledge, 1991), Part 1; and Vere Chappell, "Locke's Theory of Ideas," in V. Chappell (ed.), *Cambridge Companion to Locke* (Cambridge: Cambridge University Press, 1994), 26–55.

[5] For explicit comparisons of ideas to images see E II.i.15, II.i.25, II.x.5, II.xiv.9. For ideas as pictures, see E II.viii.5, II.x.5, II.x.7, II.xi.2, II.xi.17, II.xxiv.1, II.xxv.6, II.xxix.8 (ideas are "as it were, the Pictures of Things"), II.xxxi.6, III.iii.7, IV.vii.16, IV.xi.1. Note, however, that in his discussion of the primary-secondary quality distinction, he distinguishes between those ideas that, by resembling their objects, are properly called images of them (the primary qualities) and those that are not the "likeness" of something existing outside of us (E II.viii.7; see also II.xxx.2).

than the intuitive knowledge involved in recognizing our own existence (E IV.ix.3) or the demonstrative knowledge involved in knowing God (E IV.x). Nonetheless, our access to objects that ideas of sensation afford us qualifies as what Locke calls "Sensitive Knowledge" (E IV.ii.14). Thus, for Locke, our sensing an object in the world is akin to our recognizing that we are seeing an object by means of a mirror image. We are aware of the image, and by means of it we are aware of an actually existing object beyond the mirror that is indirectly being made available to us (E II. i.15, II.i.25, II.viii.16).[6]

Note, however, that Locke limits sensitive knowledge to the existence of the object at the time it is or was sensed. It does not assure us of the object's continuation in existence when we are not sensing it:

Thus, seeing Water at this instant, 'tis an unquestionable Truth to me, that Water doth exist: . . . as it will also be equally true, that a certain number of very fine Colours did exist, which, at the same time, I saw upon a Bubble of that Water: But being now quite out of sight both of the Water and Bubbles too, it is no more certainly known to me, that the Water doth now exist, than that the Bubbles or Colours therein do so; it being no more necessary that Water should exist to day, because it existed yesterday, than that the Colours or Bubbles exist to day, because they existed yesterday. (E IV.xi.11)

He thinks instead that we have merely probable "opinions" or "beliefs" (E IV.xv.3) about objects' continuing to exist while we no longer sense them, based on our understanding of the typical behaviour of the object in question. Thus in the case of the water and bubble, he says: "[I]t be exceedingly much more probable [that the water still exists]; because water hath been observed to continue long in existence, but bubbles, and the colours on them, quickly cease to be" (E IV.xi.11).

Interpreters have always had difficulty understanding Locke's analysis of sensitive knowledge. His official definition of knowledge restricts it to the "perception of the connexion and agreement, or disagreement and repugnancy of any of our Ideas" (E IV.i.2). He stresses: "Since *the Mind*, in all its Thoughts and Reasonings, hath no other immediate Object but its own *Ideas*, which it alone does or can contemplate, it is evident, that our Knowledge is only conversant about them" (E IV.i.1). But sensitive knowledge requires us to go *beyond* our ideas, by recognizing how the objects that they represent conform to them. Indeed, given that we do not have a grasp of external objects except by means of ideas that represent them (E IV.xxi.4), it seems hard to see how Locke thinks it is even possible for us to compare an idea with its object.[7] George Berkeley famously rejects the coherence of this possibility and thus

---

[6] Locke will even say that visual ideas are two-dimensional, "as is evident in Painting" (E II.ix.8).

[7] Locke defends himself in the correspondence with Edward Stillingfleet: "In the last place, your lordship argues, that because I say, that the idea in the mind proves not the existence of that thing whereof it is an idea, therefore we cannot know the actual existence of any thing by our senses: because we know nothing, but by the perceived agreement of ideas. But if you had been pleased to have considered my answer there to the sceptics, whose cause you here seem, with no small vigour, to manage; you would,

concludes that the world is nothing but ideas and the minds that sense them. In Chapter 4 I show that in the final quarter of SwS Hume levels a version of this criticism at philosophical accounts of our sensory beliefs that, like Locke's, suppose that we grasp an inner representation from which we then infer an external object.

Despite Hume's criticism of Lockean systems in the latter portions of SwS, many interpreters nonetheless assume that his basic theory of mind is more or less equivalent to Locke's,[8] though obviously there is the verbal change when Hume uses 'perception' rather than 'idea' as the name for the basic mental item. He reserves 'idea' for one of the two kinds of perception, thoughts, while "sensations, passions and emotions" are what he calls "impressions" (T 1.1.1.1, SBN 1). I argue in what follows, however, that in the early parts of SwS Hume also shows that his account of sensory impressions is very different from Locke's account of ideas of sensation. Humean sensations, though imagistic (at least in one sense of the term), are not recognized as images, nor are they thought to be inner by those who are aware of them (even if philosophers rightly recognize them as mental). In Chapter 6 I show that Locke is in fact one of Hume's main targets in his account of the mind and perceptions.

2.2 What do the Vulgar Believe?

What exactly do we normally believe about the objects around us that we sense? This question is surprisingly tricky to answer, in that it is easy to over-intellectualize what

---

I humbly conceive, have found that you mistake one thing for another, *viz.* the idea that has by a former sensation been lodged in the mind, for actually receiving any idea, i.e. actual sensation; which, I think, I need not go about to prove are two distinct things, after what you have here quoted out of my book. Now the two ideas, that in this case are perceived to agree, and do thereby produce knowledge, are the idea of actual sensation (which is an action whereof I have a clear and distinct idea) and the idea of actual existence of something without me that causes that sensation. And what other certainty your lordship has by your senses of the existing of any thing without you, but the perceived connexion of those two ideas, I would gladly know" (*Works*, Vol. 4 [London: T. Tegg *et al.*, 1823], 360).

The secondary literature on this issue is voluminous. For a useful summary on the interpretive assumptions that create problems for Locke's readers, see especially Lex Newman, "Locke on Sensitive Knowledge and the Veil of Perception—Four Misconceptions," *Pacific Philosophical Quarterly* 85 (2004) 273–300. Other recent interventions in the debate are: Martha Brandt Bolton, "Locke on the Semantic and Epistemic Roles of Simple Ideas of Sensation," *Pacific Philosophical Quarterly* 85 (2004), 301–21; Samuel Rickless, "Is Locke's Theory of Knowledge Inconsistent?" *Philosophy and Phenomenological Research* 77 (2008), 83–104; and Lex Newman, "Locke on Knowledge," in L. Newman (ed.) *The Cambridge Companion to Locke's 'Essay concerning Human Understanding'* (New York, NY: Cambridge University Press, 2007), 313–51.

[8] Norman Kemp Smith, for example, says that "Hume is unshaken in his adhesion to Locke's doctrine of ideas" (*Philosophy of David Hume*, 11). Terence Penelhum says that "in certain key respects [Hume] merely takes over the central doctrines of the Lockean 'way of ideas' and uses them for his own sceptical purposes...He accepts that the human mind is occupied, in all its activities with what Locke calls ideas, which come to it from 'experience'....The term that Hume uses in place of Locke's 'ideas' is 'perceptions'" (*Hume* [London: Macmillan, 1975], 28–9). Barry Stroud says that Hume "adopts without criticism" the theory of ideas that is given "[i]ts most detailed formulation in Locke's *Essay*" (*Hume* [London: Routledge and Kegan Paul, 1977], 17). See also Don Garrett, *Cognition and Commitment in Hume's Philosophy* (New York, NY: Oxford University Press, 1997), 14.

is in many ways a very primitive stance towards things. I sit at *my desk*, look at *the table*, feel *the computer keys* under my fingers. Most of the time, I do not think about the bookshelf behind me, or my house here in Toronto a few blocks away, or Paris across the Atlantic, but if I were to do so I would believe them to exist. Most of the time, though, my thought is fully engaged by the objects in my vicinity and whatever else happens to be on my mind. And should someone else be here with me, we would take ourselves to encounter the same objects, not acknowledging our different perspectives on them. We rarely think about the *sensations* that we take to give us access to these public objects, nor do we normally think about our *taking* our sensations to give us the world. We are immersed in the world that our senses make present to us without giving the sensations any mind; they are transparent to us. As Hume puts it at one point, we have a "blind submission" (T 1.4.7.10, SBN 269) to our senses; the ongoing, independent existence of body is something "we take for granted" (T 1.4.2.1, SBN 187). The challenge for a philosopher interested in understanding our sensory beliefs about the world is to make these beliefs precise without attributing to the vulgar thinker an overly sophisticated understanding of her or his situation.

In SwS, Hume does not spend as much time as one might like in articulating his interpretation of vulgar sensory experience. Instead, he presents his explanandum rather quickly and without much in the way of clarification or motivation. He says he will investigate: "Why we attribute a continu'd existence to objects, even when they are not present to the senses; and why we suppose them to have an existence distinct from the mind and perception" (T 1.4.2.2, SBN 188). And, he tells us, our beliefs in the continued and distinct existence of objects

are intimately connected together. For if the objects of our senses continue to exist, even when they are not perceiv'd, their existence is of course independent of and distinct from the perception; and *vice versa*, if their existence be independent of the perception and distinct from it, they must continue to exist, even tho' they be not perceiv'd.   (T 1.4.2.2, SBN 188)

A puzzle arises because it can easily seem that the two beliefs are not connected in this way. Thus many interpreters suggest that, though an object that continues to exist while unperceived must thereby exist distinctly from our perceptions, it is possible for a distinctly existing object not to continue in existence when it is no longer perceived.[9] It might pop in and out of existence at the same time as we happen to have perceptions of it.[10] Indeed, we have already seen that Locke distinguishes

---

[9] For example, see H. H. Price, *Hume's Theory of the External World* (Oxford: Clarendon Press, 1940), 18; Jonathan Bennett, *Locke, Berkeley, Hume* (Oxford: Clarendon Press, 1971), 315; Stroud, *Hume*, 259n2; Henry Allison, *Custom and Reason in Hume* (Oxford: Clarendon Press, 2008), 231; and Robert Fogelin, *Hume's Skeptical Crisis* (New York, NY: Oxford University Press, 2009), 59.

[10] Georges Dicker argues that if objects and perceptions varied in this way, they would be causally related, and so not ultimately distinct. Thus he concludes that distinct existence does entail continued existence ("Three Questions about *Treatise* 1.4.2," *Hume Studies* 33 [2007], 115–53). I think that his argument does not work, for at least two reasons.

between sensitive knowledge, where we recognize the distinct existence of objects, and the merely probable belief that the object continues to exist when no longer perceived.

To resolve this puzzle it will help to clarify exactly how these interpreters understand the explanandum's beliefs. Consider their construal of the belief in distinct existence. Given that they suggest that it does not require continued existence, they must hold that the content of the belief is limited to a claim about the object *while it is being sensed*. That is to say, these interpreters suppose that the vulgar have an awareness of the fact that they are *sensing* the object, and hold a belief about it that is accordingly restricted. In this interpretation, then, Hume would be following Locke, who emphasizes that we have sensitive knowledge only when we have a "perception and Consciousness . . . of the actual entrance of *Ideas*" (E IV.ii.14) from external objects by means of the senses. A similar reading can be given to the belief in continued existence by including recognition that we have previously sensed the object in its scope. Because this interpretation of the explanandum requires the vulgar to understand that their access to the world is mediated by their sensations, I call it the *sophisticated interpretation*. It can be summarized as follows:

(C$_s$)   The belief that an object (say, a table), not currently being sensed but having been sensed earlier, exists.

(D$_s$)   The belief that an object (the table) currently being sensed exists distinctly from the impression of it.

Given that Hume often cashes out the belief in continued existence as a belief in the identity of an object across interrupted perceptions, we could add the following to this first interpretation:

(I$_s$)   The belief that an object (the table now) currently being sensed is the same as an object (the table then) sensed previously.

First, I think that the distinctness in which Hume is interested here is best understood as mind-independence, and that kind of independence is compatible with a causal relation between the impression and the object, whether the impression is thought to be the cause of the object (as Dicker suggests) or *vice versa* (a possibility that strikes me as equally conceivable). For Hume is clear at T 1.4.2.2n (SBN 188n) that he is working with a conception of "external" objects that he has previously introduced in "Of the idea of existence, and of external existence" (T 1.2.6), where they are understood as differing from perceptions in "relations, connexions and durations" (T 1.2.6.9, SBN 68). While the object and the impression would have equal durations in this construal, it could nonetheless be true that they differ in connexions and relations. Consider a momentary bubble the existence of which is coincident with the impression of it. The bubble would be on the water, while the impression would not so float; the bubble might cause a bird to dive at it (when the bird takes it to be a fish), but the impression would not cause the bird's diving.

Second, even if Dicker were right that objects that exist only when they are perceived are thereby causally related in such a way that the object no longer qualifies as a having a distinct existence, it does not follow that the person with the perception must *believe* such an object to lack distinctness. For the belief in causal dependence would require the observation of the impression and of the object (and a concomitant association of their ideas). And, as I urge in what follows, we do not normally *observe* impressions unless we are introspecting. Dicker's paraphrase of the vulgar beliefs in distinct and continued existence effaces their being *beliefs*, with the opacity of context they bring in their wake. See "Three Questions," 116.

In this interpretation, the vulgar have beliefs that directly concern the objects of their impressions, *considered as such*; the perceptions are included within the scope of the beliefs. The vulgar recognize that they *sense* the table, and hold that the table *that they sense* exists independently of them.

Note that interpreters who favour this construal of the beliefs should argue that neither distinct nor continued existence implies the other. For not only could we sense a distinctly existing object that might not persist beyond our sensing of it, we could also believe that an object we have sensed earlier continues to exist even if, when we sense it, we take its existence to depend on our sensing of it. On a certain interpretation of Berkeley, for example, objects continue to exist when not perceived by the subject because God perceives them. Nonetheless, they are dependent on the subject's mind for their existence when she or he perceives them.[11]

Though the sophisticated interpretation conflicts with Hume's claims about the links between the explanandum's beliefs, it sometimes does sound as though it accurately captures his conception of vulgar experience. Thus, in the course of giving his first explanation for the vulgar belief in the continued existence of objects, he says: "I suppose that the door still remains, and that it was open'd *without my perceiving it*" (T 1.4.2.20, SBN 196–7; emphasis added). Similarly, "When we are absent from [an object], we say it still exists, but that *we do not feel, we do not see it*. When we are present, we say *we feel, or see it*" (T 1.4.2.38, SBN 206–7; emphases added).[12] Also:

[W]e may observe that when we talk of real distinct existences, we have commonly more in our eye their independency than external situation in place, and think an object has a sufficient reality, when its Being is uninterrupted, and independent of the *incessant revolutions, which we are conscious of in ourselves*.   (T 1.4.2.10, SBN 191; emphasis added)[13]

---

[11] For example, Berkeley argues that our ideas must exist in God when not perceived by us (D 2.212, 214–15), and it is not obvious that the objects we perceive are numerically different from those God perceives.

[12] Preceded by: "'Tis certain, that almost all mankind, and even philosophers themselves, for the greatest part of their lives, take their perceptions to be their only objects, and suppose, that the very being, which is intimately present to the mind, is the real body or material existence. 'Tis also certain, that this very perception or object is suppos'd to have a continu'd uninterrupted being, and neither to be annihilated by our absence, nor to be brought into existence by our presence" (T 1.4.2.38, SBN 206–7).

[13] In another passage that might seem to support the sophisticated interpretation, Hume says: "Since all impressions are internal and perishing existences, *and appear as such*, the notion of their distinct and continu'd existence must arise from a concurrence of some of their qualities with the qualities of the imagination; and since this notion does not extend to all of them, it must arise from certain qualities peculiar to some impressions. 'Twill therefore be easy for us to discover these qualities by a comparison of the impressions, to which we attribute a distinct and continu'd existence, with *those, which we regard as internal and perishing*" (T 1.4.2.15, SBN 194; emphases added). I take it, however, that Hume is here in the process of giving his *explanation* of our vulgar beliefs, rather than characterizing the explanandum.

Note also the contradiction between the first sentence of the passage, where Hume says that all impressions "appear" as "internal and perishing existences," and its last sentence, where he says that we only "regard" a subset of our perceptions "as internal and perishing." I take it that the first sentence gives Hume's verdict as a philosopher, who is introspectively investigating his mind. From that perspective, impressions do appear as "internal and perishing existences." The final sentence gives how the introspecting philosopher characterizes the vulgar belief.

Hume here seems to say that the vulgar have some sort of consciousness of their changing perceptions (though, as we shall see briefly in §2.3, and in more detail in §§4.3.2 and 6.6, the meaning of both 'consciousness' and 'perception' is less than clear), and that they believe an object to have distinct existence when they take it not to participate in those changes. This passage makes it seem as if the vulgar have the awareness of their perceptions that is characteristic of the sophisticated interpretation.

But I think it unlikely that Hume really wants to characterize vulgar sensory experience in these terms. First, given Locke's having distinguished between the beliefs in distinct and in continued existence, it would be surprising for Hume to have asserted their "intimate connexion" (T 1.4.2.44, SBN 210) unless he interpreted them differently from Locke. Second, elsewhere in SwS, when explicitly addressing how to describe what the vulgar believe, Hume emphasizes that we take that which we perceive to be the ordinary objects we find around us, not recognizing the perceptions that afford us our awareness of them. Thus, "the vulgar confound perceptions and objects, and attribute a distinct continu'd existence to the very things they feel or see" (1.4.2.14, SBN 193). And, most notably:

Now we have already observ'd, that however philosophers may distinguish betwixt the objects and perceptions of the senses; which they suppose co-existent and resembling; yet this is a distinction, which is not comprehended by the generality of mankind, who as they perceive only one being, can never assent to the opinion of a double existence and representation. Those very sensations, which enter by the eye or ear, are with them the true objects, nor can they readily conceive that this pen or paper, which is immediately perceiv'd, represents another, which is different from, but resembling it. In order, therefore, to accommodate myself to their notions, I shall at first suppose; that there is only a single existence, which I shall call indifferently *object* or *perception*, according as it shall seem best to suit my purpose, understanding by both of them what any common man means by a hat, or shoe, or stone, or any other impression, convey'd to him by his senses.   (T 1.4.2.31, SBN 202)

Hume insists here that the vulgar take themselves to encounter the pens, paper, hats, shoes, and stones of the everyday world—not realizing that they are in fact aware only of what, in his philosophical investigation of our vulgar beliefs, he now realizes are impressions. He acknowledges what I have been calling the vulgar's sense of immersion in the world.

Accordingly, though there is some textual support for the sophisticated interpretation, I think that Hume is best understood in terms of what I will call the *naive* interpretation of the vulgar's beliefs. It does not attribute to them any claims *about* their perceptions, but rather makes them as it were blind to the perceptual mediation of their experience. Their beliefs are solely about the *objects* of their perceptions without any reference to their being the objects *of perceptions*:[14]

---

[14] My phrasing here is influenced by Kenneth Winkler's in his "Hume on Scepticism and the Senses," in D. C. Ainslie and A. Butler (eds.), *Cambridge Companion to Hume's 'Treatise'* (New York, NY: Cambridge University Press, 2015), 135–64.

(C_n)   The belief, of an object (say, a table) that has been sensed but is not currently being sensed, that it (the table) exists.

(D_n)   The belief, of an object (the table) that is currently being sensed, that it (the table) exists.

The identity version of (C_n) is:

(I_n)   The belief, of an object (the table now) currently being sensed and of an object (the table then) that was previously sensed, that it (the table) is one continuing object.[15]

In this interpretation the scope of the vulgar's beliefs does not encompass the impressions by means of which the table is sensed; the beliefs concern only the table itself. The vulgar do not have opinions *about* their perceptions, only about the *objects* that their perceptions present to them. Thus they do not openly recognize that their objects are mind-independent; rather, because the contents of their beliefs make no mention of the mind or its perceptions, their beliefs embody a commitment to the mind-independence of their objects without its being explicitly articulated.[16]

Note that the belief in the distinct existence of sensory objects, D_n, becomes somewhat attenuated on this reading: the belief's overt content is distinct from, and makes no reference to, the fact that we are sensing the object. But Hume himself emphasizes that the belief in continued existence has priority over the belief in distinct existence: "'Tis the opinion of a continu'd existence, which first takes place, and without much study or reflection draws the other along with it, wherever the mind follows its first and most natural tendency" (T 1.4.2.44, SBN 210). Indeed, the fact that the sophisticated interpretation leaves D_s on a par with C_s suggests that it misconstrues Hume's intentions.

Moreover, we saw above that the sophisticated interpretation of the explanandum failed to accord with Hume's claim that they are "intimately connected" (T 1.4.2.2, SBN 188). But reading the vulgar's beliefs as C_n and D_n does allow him to say that they are closely linked, for their overt contents are identical: the table exists. How Hume ultimately understands tables and other such objects will be postponed to §3.3.

---

[15] Why not: "The belief, of interrupted impressions with resembling table-like content, that they are the table" (here I have run together the belief in continued existence, distinct existence, and identity, though they could be distinguished easily enough)? This gloss might seem to capture Hume's claim, when summarizing his explanation of the vulgar outlook, that we have a "propension to bestow an identity on our resembling perceptions" that yields the fiction of a continued existent (T 1.4.2.43, SBN 209). But because this interpretation attributes to the vulgar a *de dicto* belief about their perceptions (that they are the table), it ends up as a variant of the sophisticated interpretation, with its concomitant problems that I have just canvassed.

[16] As will become important in §4.5.3, the philosopher who offers this interpretation of vulgar belief relies on the vocabulary of everyday objects (tables, and so on) in addition to the vocabulary of perceptions. As Hume emphasizes in the latter parts of SwS, philosophical systems of the external world are parasitic on our vulgar beliefs about the world (T 1.4.2.46, SBN 211).

If Hume is committed to the naive interpretation of the explanandum's beliefs, what are we to make of the passages that conform with the sophisticated interpretation? I think that one of the reasons that SwS is so difficult to interpret is that he does not do a very good job of distinguishing several different levels of analysis.[17] We have seen that the distinction between the naive and sophisticated interpretations of the explanandum turns on how much of Hume's preferred philosophical vocabulary of 'perception' and the like is properly attributed to the vulgar. The sophisticated interpretation takes the vulgar to have some sort of grasp of it (though it need not be exactly in Hume's terms) in all of their dealings with the world. They have a pervasive sense that they are *sensing* the world, and they make claims about that which they recognize themselves to be *sensing*. The naive interpretation, in contrast, while *using* the perceptual vocabulary to *describe* the vulgar beliefs, does not attribute a grasp of it to them, at least not in their ordinary dealings with everyday objects. This interpretation does not preclude that the vulgar might *on occasion* think about their sensations or thoughts ("I was *smelling* the rose, when all of a sudden I *remembered* that I had left the stove on"—where the smelling and remembering are the focus of my thoughts, rather than the rose or the stove [see T 1.3.8.15–17, SBN 105–6; I discuss this passage in detail in §4.3.2]). But the point of the naive interpretation is that the vulgar's outlook is normally directed only to the *objects* of their sensations, without any reference to their being the objects *of sensation*. The problem is that Hume makes it difficult for his readers to keep these interpretations separate.

There are two related obstacles. First, Hume is frustratingly ambiguous about the fundamental item in his theory of mind: perceptions.[18] Sometimes, as in most of SwS, he equates perceptions with the content of which we are aware when having a thought or sensation (T 1.4.2.46, 50, 53; SBN 211, 213, 216; see also T 1.4.2.36, 38, 43, 56; SBN 205, 206, 209, 218). Those interpreters I noted earlier, who take Hume to have taken over Locke's theory of ideas, though with an obvious change of terminology, point to passages such as these in support of their reading. But I show in §2.3 (and in Chapters 4 and 6) that Hume in fact rejects core elements of Locke's theory. A further problem for a Lockean reading of Humean perceptions is that Locke not only treats ideas as mental objects, but also has a theory of the mental activity— perception (E II.ix)—by means of which we are aware of those ideas: for Locke, we perceive ideas. If Humean perceptions are mental objects like Lockean ideas, Hume is

---

[17] Dicker accuses Hume of a "penchant for reading his own metaphysical views into what he presents as the ordinary views of humankind" ("Three Questions," 135).

[18] See Catherine Kemp, "Two Meanings of the Term 'Idea': Acts and Contents in Hume's *Treatise*," *Journal of the History of Ideas* 61 (2000), 675–90; and Annette Baier, "A Voice, as from the Next Room," in *Death and Character: Further Reflections on Hume* (Cambridge, MA: Harvard University Press, 2008), 212. Dicker attributes to Hume "a genuine collapsing of the distinction between" perceptual episodes and their objects ("Three Questions," 129). Allison notes "Hume's lamentable inattention to (or perhaps exploitation of) the *perceived–perceiving* ambiguity" (*Custom and Reason*, 243).

left without an account of our awareness of those objects. The mind, for him, is merely a bundle of perceptions, not a bundle of perceptions and in addition a set of awarenesses of those perceptions (T 1.4.6.3, SBN 252). Thus sometimes Hume treats perceptions not as mental objects, but as unified act-and-object packages: mental states or episodes of awareness. In §6.6 I argue that this latter conception of perception makes better sense of his core claims about perceptions, even if he does repeatedly fall into the habit of equating perceptions with their contents—that of which we are aware when having a perception understood as a state of awareness— when, as in SwS, theorizing about the objects of our beliefs. Thus, in what follows I try to be clear about whether I take Hume to be using 'perception' to indicate the content of which we are aware or the broader state of awareness itself.

The second obstacle to keeping the naive interpretation of the explanandum in view when reading SwS is related to Hume's ambiguous use of 'perception.' His goal in the *Treatise* is a theory of the mind's principles, an account of "which of the impressions and ideas are causes, and which effects" (T 1.1.1.7, SBN 4). If perceptions are, as in the Lockean interpretation, mental objects, then there is a sense in which we always already have perceptions under observation, and must merely pay appropriate attention in order to discover their causal principles. But, on my preferred interpretation where perceptions are mental episodes, the vulgar do not, in having a perception, have any kind of awareness of *it*, even while it affords them an awareness of its *content*. We must introspect or reflect on the mind before we become aware *of the perception*. Introspection is thus crucial to the philosophical project of understanding the mind. And, throughout the *Treatise*, Hume himself emphasizes that he relies on introspection to reach his conclusions. He describes it as a process of "entering most intimately" into himself in order to "observe" his perceptions (T 1.4.6.3, SBN 252). We are to change the "point of view, from the objects [of the perceptions] to the perceptions" (T 1.3.14.29, SBN 169) themselves. "Reflection" allows us to "consider" a perception not "as the representation of any absent object, but as a real perception in the mind, of which we are intimately conscious" (T 1.3.8.15, SBN 106).

While a full account of Humean introspection must be postponed until §4.3.2, note here that he allows for several different 'grades' of introspection. In the lowest grade, we retain our vulgar grip on the world at the same time as we observe the perceptions that are involved in producing it. At one point, Hume likens this stance to what we would have if "we cou'd see clearly into the breast of another, and observe that succession of perceptions, which constitutes his mind or thinking principle" (T 1.4.6.18, SBN 260). In this quasi-third-personal introspection, our grasp on, say, a hat is not called into question; but we are now also aware of the perceptions of the hat that occur when the person we are observing thinks or senses it. The directedness of the observed perceptions towards the hat is recognized by means of our ongoing vulgar grasp of it as observers of both the hat and the other person's mind. As Kemp Smith rightly notes, most of Hume's investigations of the mind prior to SwS take place at this level of introspection.[19] For example, he says: "To give a child an idea of scarlet or orange, of sweet or bitter, I present the objects, or in other words, convey to him these impressions" (T 1.1.1.8, SBN 5). "We cannot form to ourselves a just idea of the taste of a pine-apple, without having actually tasted it" (T 1.1.1.9, SBN 5). We continue to take ourselves to be in direct contact with oranges and pineapples at the same time as we investigate the mind's perceptions of these objects.

In the next higher level of introspection, Hume no longer takes for granted our vulgar beliefs about the world. Instead, as in SwS, he turns his attention to the mental principles that are responsible for producing them. It now becomes difficult to separate the naive and sophisticated versions of the explanandum. For I have suggested that the vulgar take themselves to be immediately aware of the independently existing objects that furnish the world, even if, in so taking, they do not form an explicit belief (the only kind Hume allows) about their access to the world. The introspecting philosopher realizes that they are aware only of the content of sensations (ultimately sensory images; see §2.3). So the philosopher could, as in the sophisticated interpretation, characterize the vulgar as believing *that* the objects of their sensations exist independently. The sophisticated interpretation is a correct description of what the introspecting philosophers learns to be *true of* the vulgar. The mistake is in thinking that the vulgar's belief includes this philosophical knowledge. In this second level of introspection, the philosopher observes the perceptions that embody the vulgar's unstated assumptions about the world. The challenge for the philosopher is to retain an accurate characterization of the assumptions while excavating how the reflectively uncovered perceptions are responsible for them.

I find Hume's tactic for resolving this challenge to be hopelessly inadequate. In the central passages of SwS that describe the psychological mechanisms responsible for producing the vulgar beliefs about body (T 1.4.2.31–45, SBN 202–11), he "accommodates" himself to their "notions" by using 'object' and 'perception' interchangeably, "according as it shall seem best to suit my purpose" (T 1.4.2.31, SBN 202). Much of the difficulty interpreters have with SwS stem from this accommodation, as it obscures the relationship between the explanandum and the explanans.

Hume also allows for an even higher level of introspection. In both the first and second levels, philosophers "observe" the mind's perceptions. Most of the time, Hume takes this observation for granted, not bothering to explain how it is possible for philosophers to observe perceptions. But sometimes he does investigate this question—reflecting on the *introspecting* mind, as it were, in order to discover how it works. His answer, briefly, is that we become introspectively aware of the mind's perceptions by forming what he calls "secondary ideas" (T 1.1.1.11, SBN 6) of them (I offer a full interpretation of this notion in §4.3.2). And, as we will see in §6.5, just as Hume explains the vulgar belief in the unity of everyday objects in terms of the

[19] See fn. 1.

association of ideas of them, he also explains philosophers' belief that the minds they observe are unified in terms of the association of such secondary ideas.

2.3 Sensory Images

I have already hinted that Hume thinks that the introspecting philosopher discovers that our sensations are images as of external objects—literally so in the case of our visual and tangible impressions, and metaphorically so in the case of our other sense modalities. The puzzle here is to square this claim about the imagistic nature of sensations with the naive interpretation of the explanandum, where the vulgar take themselves to be aware of hats, shoes, and stones, rather than images of them. This puzzle becomes even more difficult when Hume seems also to commit himself to some theses about mental transparency, so that we cannot be in error about our sensations, nor overlook them when we have them. How then can he also hold that the vulgar take themselves to be in contact with the world?

In solving this puzzle, I focus my interpretation on the early portions of Hume's positive treatment of the explanandum's beliefs, where he considers which mental faculty is responsible for them: reason, the senses, or the imagination. Hume's argument against the senses is especially telling for our purposes, because here he openly addresses the manner in which sensations are imagistic, starting the task that he will not finish until the later Sections of Part 4 of Book 1: namely, an account of the nature of perceptions. I show that Hume breaks with Locke's imagistic conceptions of sensory representations by holding that recognition of their being images in not part of our everyday experience, but is revealed only in moments of reflection.

Hume's argument against reason as the source of the explanandum's beliefs is brief and unremarkable, basically relying on the fact that "children, peasants, and the greatest part of mankind" (T 1.4.2.14, SBN 193) subscribe to them despite never having encountered any of the purported arguments for the existence of objects that philosophers have offered. Moreover, the philosophical arguments tend to yield conclusions that are in conflict with what the vulgar believe. As we have seen, they take themselves to be in direct contact with objects; philosophers, in contrast, argue that we are in direct contact only with imagistic perceptions, which are "interrupted, and dependent on the mind" (T 1.4.2.14, SBN 193), while the objects that exist are independent of us. Finally, philosophers typically[20] restrict the belief in the independent existence of objects to their primary qualities; the vulgar believe both primary and secondary qualities to exist independently of them (T 1.4.2.12–13, SBN 192). It follows that the vulgar's beliefs cannot arise from reason. The philosophical analysis of the belief in body is one of Hume's chief concerns in the final quarter of SwS. I return to it in Chapter 4.

---

[20] Hume is something of an exception (T 1.4.4); see §§6.3 and 6.4.

Hume offers a more detailed and more interesting discussion of whether the senses can be the source of the beliefs in the explanandum. The question is how to understand sensation. In the first paragraph of the main text of the *Treatise*, Hume says that all sensations should be classified as impressions—those perceptions that "strike upon the mind, and make their way into our thought or consciousness ... with most force and violence" (T 1.1.1.1, SBN 1). But in so striking, do sensory impressions on their own suffice for the belief in the independence of their objects? Hume is quick to dismiss the possibility that sensation yields the belief in continued existence, C_n. Here he agrees with Locke's point about the bubble on the water that we saw earlier (§2.1). The senses serve only to deliver impressions, and once we are no longer sensing an object, they are no longer operating with respect to it. Accordingly, they cannot produce the belief that an object *not being sensed* continues to exist (T 1.4.2.3, SBN 188–9).

Hume also argues against the suggestion that the senses are responsible for the belief in the distinct existence of an object, D_n. He first rejects the possibility that they secure the belief by "present[ing] their impressions ... as images and representations" (T 1.4.2.3, SBN 188–9). I think Hume means to capture here something like Locke's view.[21] We saw in §2.1 that Locke argues that we recognize that an idea of sensation is an inner image or representation, and thus our perception of it involves the awareness of (at least[22]) two things: the idea/image and that which it portrays. Hume dismisses the Lockean view as follows:

That our senses offer not their impressions as the images of something *distinct*, or *independent*, and *external*, is evident; because they convey to us nothing but a single perception, and never give us the least intimation of any thing beyond. A single perception can never produce the idea of a double existence, but by some inference either of the reason or imagination. When the mind looks farther than what immediately appears to it, its conclusions can never be put to the account of the senses; and it certainly looks farther, when from a single perception it infers a double existence, and supposes the relations of resemblance and causation betwixt them.
(T 1.4.2.4, SBN 189)

Hume rejects the Lockean double-existence model because, in his analysis, the vulgar "suppose their perceptions to be their only objects, and never think of a double existence internal and external, representing and represented" (T 1.4.2.36, SBN 205). Accordingly, impressions do not, by themselves, "intimate" anything beyond their content. Sensation is a case of an impression's "appearing" or being "offered" to the

---

[21] At least, Hume is arguing against the traditional representationalist reading of Locke. See fn. 4.

[22] In fact, Locke thinks that every perception of an idea also involves a grasp of ourselves as the one perceiving it: "In every Act of Sensation, Reasoning, or Thinking, we are conscious to our selves of our own Being" (E IV.ix.3). And: "[C]onsciousness ... is inseparable from thinking, and it seems to me essential to it: It being impossible for any one to perceive, without perceiving, that *he* does perceive. When we see, hear, smell, taste, feel, meditate, or will anything, we know that *we* do so" (E II.xxvii.9; emphases added). Locke thus gives a tripartite analysis of thinking: we perceive an image-like idea, "suppose" that which the idea portrays, and recognize ourselves as the one who is perceiving.

mind—locutions which presumably mean that we become aware of the impression or its content. Hume has not denied that there might be a sense in which we are aware of more than simply the impression when believing in the distinct existence of sensory objects. But he will not accept Locke's attempt to build the "supposition" of, "reference" to, or "inferring" of an external object into sensation itself, let alone the suggestion that we also thereby recognize the resemblance and causal connection between object and impression.

One problem with Hume's argument is that, up until this point, he has repeatedly equated sensory perceptions with images. How, then, does his view differ from Locke's treatment of ideas as images? Hume sometimes uses image-talk in connection with his fundamental empiricist principle, that (almost[23]) all simple ideas are copies or "images" (T 1.1.1.1, 1.1.1.6, 1.4.6.18, 2.1.11.8, 2.2.5.3, 2.3.6.5, 2.3.10.5; SBN 1, 6, 260–1, 320, 358, 426, 450) of prior simple impressions. By 'image' here he means that the content of a simple idea must have appeared previously as the content of a simple impression, with the difference between them lying in their vivacity—the "manner" in which this content is conceived—where impressions have more vivacity than ideas. More worrying, however, is his willingness, both before and after the anti-Lockean passage in SwS, to say that sensory impressions are themselves images. In the "Abstract" to the *Treatise*, for example, he describes his view by saying: "When we ... have the images of external objects conveyed by our senses; the perception of the mind is ... an *impression*" (T Abs.5, SBN 647). In the *Treatise* proper, we find such passages as:

Put a spot of ink upon paper, fix your eye upon that spot, and retire to such a distance, that at last you lose sight of it; 'tis plain, that the moment before it vanish'd the *image or impression* was perfectly indivisible.   (T 1.2.1.4, SBN 27; emphasis added)

Nothing can be more minute, than some ideas, which we form in the fancy; and *images, which appear to the senses*; since there are ideas and images perfectly simple and indivisible. The only defect of our senses is, that they give us disproportion'd *images* of things, and represent as minute and uncompounded what is really great and compos'd of a vast number of parts.

(T 1.2.1.5, SBN 28; emphasis added)

The very *image, which is present to the senses*, is with us the real body; and 'tis to these interrupted images we ascribe a perfect identity.   (T 1.4.2.36, SBN 205; emphasis added)[24]

---

[23] The missing shade of blue is an exception (T 1.1.10, SBN 6; see §2.4).

[24] See also T 1.1.7.6, 1.1.7.10, 1.2.3.7, 1.3.5.5, 1.3.9.9, 1.3.9.16, 1.3.10.2, 1.3.10.5, 1.3.11.13, 1.3.12.10–11, 1.3.12.22, 1.3.12.24, 1.4.2.33, 1.4.2.38, 1.4.5.15, 1.4.7.3, 2.2.4.4, 2.2.5.5; SBN 20, 22, 35, 85, 110, 116, 119, 121, 129, 134–5, 140, 141, 203, 207, 239, 265, 353, 359. On occasion, Hume borrows mental imagery language from the optical science of his day, as at T 1.3.9.11, SBN 112: "'Tis universally allow'd by the writers on optics, that the eye at all times sees an equal number of physical points, and that a man on the top of a mountain has no larger an image presented to his senses, than when he is coop'd up in the narrowest court or chamber. 'Tis only by experience that he infers the greatness of the object from some peculiar qualities of the image; and this inference of the judgment he confounds with sensation, as is common on other occasions. Now 'tis evident, that the inference of the judgment is here much more lively than what is usual in our common reasonings, and that a man has a more vivid conception of the vast extent of the ocean from the image he receives by the eye, when he stands on the top of a high promontory, than merely from

And since ideas ultimately inherit their content from prior simple impressions, where the difference between these two kinds of perceptions only concerns their vivacity, or the manner in which the content is conceived, sensory ideas also are imagistic.[25]

To understand how Hume can both identify sensory perceptions with images and reject Locke's conception of ideas as images, it will be helpful to take a step back, and to consider more generally the different ways we can be aware of an image. Take our awareness of an image properly speaking, say, to adapt Locke's mirror analogy, the image in a mirror of the dog on the other side of the room. In being aware of this mirror image, we might be said to be aware of one (or more) of four different things:

(a) a pattern of coloured patches on a flat expanse;
(b) a piece of reflective glass that bears the image as of the dog;
(c) the dog as she is depicted in the image—her left flank, with the sun shining on her shoulder, as from the reversed perspective of a few feet away; and
(d) the dog herself, on the other side of the room.

If sensory perceptions are or involve the awareness of an image, then we must decide which of these four ways of being aware of an image Hume intends.

Locke analogizes the mind to a mirror so that ideas are images in sense (b). In it, we are both aware of the image in the mirror and recognize that it is a mirror image portraying something beyond it (the dog). Similarly, in perceiving a Lockean idea, we are aware of the idea itself, as an inner representation, and of the object represented by the idea (what we "refer" it to or "suppose" it taken from). Hume's rejection of the Lockean double-existence model in the paragraph quoted earlier means that he cannot be taking impressions to be images in this sense.

My argument in §2.2 that Hume is committed to capturing the vulgar sense of immersion in the world might suggest that when he speaks of sensation as being imagistic, he is using 'image' in sense (d), where it is merely the means by which we directly encounter the objects around us. He would then be following Antoine Arnauld, who says: "[W]hen one sees oneself in the mirror, it is oneself that one sees, and not the image."[26] As Hume puts it, that would mean the senses would

---

hearing the roaring of the waters. He feels a more sensible pleasure from its magnificence; which is a proof of a more lively idea: And he confounds his judgment with sensation; which is another proof of it. But as the inference is equally certain and immediate in both cases, this superior vivacity of our conception in one case can proceed from nothing but this, that in drawing an inference from the sight, beside the customary conjunction, there is also a resemblance betwixt the image and the object we infer; which strengthens the relation, and conveys the vivacity of the impression to the related idea with an easier and more natural movement" (a related passage is T 2.2.8.3–4, SBN 372–3). It is unlikely, however, that Hume actually endorses the equation of impressions and images in these latter passages, in that the judgement-based view of the optical scientists that he describes is in conflict with his own imagination-based analysis of our belief in body.

[25] Hume does not describe non-sensory impressions, such as passions, in imagistic terms. And thus the ideas that copy them, "idea[s] of reflection" (T 1.2.3.10, SBN 37), are also not imagistic.

[26] Antoine Arnauld, *Of True and False Ideas*, tr. and intr. S. Gaukroger (Manchester: Manchester University Press, 1990), 62.

"present their impressions...as these very distinct and external existences" (T 1.4.2.3, SBN 189).

Somewhat surprisingly, perhaps, Hume rejects this option. Because he treats impressions as mental items, he takes this view to require that the senses "convey the impressions as those very existences, by a kind of fallacy and illusion" (T 1.4.2.5, SBN 189). And he does not think that the senses by themselves have the capacity to create this kind of illusion. Instead, it turns out that the vulgar assumption of direct contact with objects is the result of the workings of the imagination. But why is he so sure that the senses themselves cannot put us in touch with objects?

It is at this point that Hume's commitment to a version of the transparency of the mental becomes relevant. He tells us that "all sensations are felt by the mind, such as they really are" (T 1.4.2.5, SBN 189) and that they do not, by themselves, pretend to make us aware of independently existing objects:

[E]very impression, external and internal, passions, affections, sensations, pains and pleasures, are originally on the same footing; and that whatever other differences we may observe among them, they appear, all of them, in their true colours, as impressions or perceptions. And indeed, if we consider the matter aright, 'tis scarce possible it shou'd be otherwise, nor is it conceivable that our senses shou'd be more capable of deceiving us in the situation and relations, than in the nature of our impressions. For since all actions and sensations of the mind are known to us by consciousness, they must necessarily appear in every particular what they are, and be what they appear. Every thing that enters the mind, being in *reality* a perception, 'tis impossible any thing shou'd to *feeling* appear different. This were to suppose, that even where we are most intimately conscious, we might be mistaken. (T 1.4.2.7, SBN 190)

There are at least three points about this passage that need to be addressed.

First, consider the sense in which Hume endorses the transparency of the mental here. The thesis has two components. On the one hand, we are never in error about the contents of our minds[27]—Hume's "where we are most intimately conscious" we cannot be "mistaken." On the other hand, there can be no mental content of which we are not aware[28]—"all actions and sensations of the mind are known to us by consciousness." It might seem surprising that Hume could subscribe to the transparency thesis, given that his eventual explanations for C_n and I_n involve our making a series of mistakes and errors about our perceptions. Also, when he first introduces his theory of impressions and ideas, he notes that we sometimes mistake the latter for the former, as in dreams (T 1.1.1.1, SBN 2); and his account of motivation includes the claim that we all tend to mistake those impressions that are calm passions for reason-involving ideas (T 2.3.3.8, SBN 417).[29]

---

[27] Daisie Radner, in her discussion of related ideas in Descartes, calls this the "incorrigibility thesis" ("Thought and Consciousness in Descartes," *Journal of the History of Philosophy* 26 [1988], 439–52).

[28] Radner calls this the "evidence thesis" ("Thought and Consciousness").

[29] Hume makes a similar claim about our moral self-knowledge: "Our predominant motive or intention is, indeed, frequently concealed from ourselves, when it is mingled and confounded with other motives,

The tensions between these claims and the assertions about mental transparency arise because Hume has not yet told us what consciousness is. And we should keep in mind that the term was used in a variety of ways in this period. Samuel Clarke, for example, points to five different meanings: the reflexivity whereby all thoughts declare themselves to belong to their subject ("the strict and properest Sense of the Word"), the act of thinking, the power to think, simple sensation, or the capacity to determine motion by the will.[30] As I discuss in more detail in §4.3.2, Hume sometimes uses 'consciousness' to describe the awareness that he takes to characterize perceptions as a matter of course, as in the first paragraph of the *Treatise*, where we are told that impressions and ideas "make their way into our thought or consciousness" (T 1.1.1.1, SBN 1).[31] But sometimes he uses 'consciousness' to mean something like introspection or what Locke calls 'reflection,' where we turn our attention inwards, to observe our mental "operations" (E II.i.4). Thus in the "Appendix" to the *Treatise*, Hume clarifies that "consciousness is nothing but a reflected thought or perception" (App.20, SBN 635).

Hume, I take it, is using 'consciousness' in the quoted passage in the first of these two senses. But given this usage, the transparency theses are fairly innocuous. To say that we are always conscious of our perceptions is just to say that perceptions *are* states of awareness; it is not possible for perceptions to be in the mind and for us not thereby to be conscious of their content. And to say that we are not in error about our perceptions in this consciousness of them is to say that there is no space between our awareness of the perception and the perception itself into which error could fall. The consciousness of the perception constitutes a mental episode as being the state of awareness it is;[32] the consciousness does not consist in a higher-order claim *about* the perception, whereby the perception might have properties that are overlooked or misunderstood. Thus Hume takes himself to have shown that the senses, by themselves, cannot be responsible for the belief in the distinct existence of body because impressions do not contain any content adverting to their being so distinct. In particular, they do not contain within themselves anything that announces that the object is distinct from the self. For if they did, we would be conscious of it and

---

which the mind, from vanity or self-conceit, is desirous of supposing more prevalent" (EM App.2.7, SBN 299).

[30] "[E]ither the Reflex Act, by which a Man knows his Thoughts to be his own Thoughts; *(which is the strict and properest Sense of the Word;) or* the Direct Act of Thinking; *or* the Power or Capacity of Thinking; *or (which is of the same Import,)* simple Sensation; *or the* Power of Self-Motion, or of beginning Motion by the Will" (*A Letter to Mr. Dodwell*, 6th edn. [London: James and John Knapton, 1731], 177n).

[31] Wayne Waxman argues that Hume thus has a theory of consciousness in addition to an account of perceptions (*Hume's Theory of Consciousness* [Cambridge: Cambridge University Press, 1994]). I find this interpretation hard to square with Hume's claim that the mind is nothing but a bundle of perceptions.

[32] See T 2.1.5.4, SBN 286, where Hume says of the passions that "their sensations, or the peculiar emotions they excite in the soul…constitute their very being and essence"—a fact he takes to be an "original quality" of these perceptions.

philosophers would not need to have "recourse to the most profound metaphysics" when arguing over the status of the self (T 1.4.2.5–6, SBN 189–90).

Once the transparency thesis is understood in this light, the appearance of a conflict between it and his positive explanation of our belief in body is dissolved. For though in a *single* episode of sensing, taken in isolation, we are conscious or aware of it for what it is, we do not normally have sensations in this kind of isolation. Normally, sensations are accompanied by the imagination's associative response; and it is this response that leads us to mistake our consciousness of a perception for our being in cognitive contact with the world. Consider how hard it is to prescind from our normal engagement with the world so that we recognize that we only see it from our limited perspective. It is not easy to step back from the belief, say, that I am working at a rectangular table in order to make it palpable to myself that my vision yields only a trapezoidal image as of a table.

The second point to note about the passage is that Hume is here introspectively examining what goes on in the mind when we have sensations. He is not describing how we normally experience things. Instead, as my table example suggests, he has looked within to "observe" exactly what impressions are like in isolation from our associative responses,[33] and he is reporting on what he has found them to be "in their true colours" (T 1.4.2.7, SBN 190). What gives Hume confidence that his introspective investigation of the mind gets things right? A second transparency thesis seems to be in play here, this time in terms of *philosophers'* capacity to accurately report on the workings of the mind when they introspect. Given that, later, Hume will explain philosophers' beliefs about the unity of the mind when they reflect on it in terms of their *mistaking* the bundle of perceptions for a single ongoing entity (T 1.4.6.15–22, SBN 259–63), we will need an explanation of his confidence in his introspective results in SwS. I return to this issue in §4.3.2.

The third point from the passage concerns what Hume finds when he introspects. Though Hume does not emphasize this point in SwS, his earlier analysis of our spatiotemporal perceptions in Part 2 of Book 1 of the *Treatise* shows that our perceptions of body present merely an array of finitely many coloured and tangible indivisible points (T 1.2.1, 1.2.3), along with various qualities (smell, taste) that have no obvious links to the spatially located body (T 1.4.5).[34] Impressions would then be images in sense (a) in the analysis of image-awareness given above. But then why think that impressions are *images* at all? The very language of 'image' suggests that something is being portrayed; Hume himself says that "an image necessarily resembles its object" (T 1.4.6.18, SBN 260). How does the pixelated, coloured, tangible

---

[33] As Hume says, philosophers "abstract from the effects of custom" when investigating perceptions (T 1.4.3.9, SBN 223).

[34] For simplicity's sake, I will focus hereafter on our sensations of objects' spatial qualities. I discuss the non-spatial sensations in §5.6.

expanse that the vulgar are aware of portray something as mundane as the hat, shoe, or stone that Hume tells us the vulgar take themselves to encounter?

In answering this question, Hume appeals to the imagination. As I discuss in more detail in Chapter 3, the coherence and constancy of our sensory impressions cause us to associate our ideas in such a way as to believe in the continued existence of everyday objects. So while a sensory impression taken in isolation presents merely an array of coloured tangible points, an impression taken in its associative context seems to present an everyday object. Thus I think, for Hume, insofar as impressions are images, they are images in sense (c) above: we are aware of whatever is portrayed in the image *as it is portrayed*. Hereafter I will call this the *image-content* of an impression (or of the idea that copies it). In the case of the dog in the mirror, the sense-(c)-image reveals only one side of her, as seen from a particular (reversed) perspective. But, where Locke's mirror analogy assumes that we *know* that we are aware of a mirror-image, and thus are aware of both the image and the dog it depicts, Hume rejects the idea that sensation involves awareness of two things. I think that the crucial difference is that he wants to preserve the vulgar assumption that they encounter objects directly. The analogy would be a case where we do not realize that we are looking in a mirror, and thus assume that we are encountering the dog herself.[35] Thus this analysis also differs from Arnauld's analysis that relies on (d), where the role of the mirror image is effaced entirely, and we are taken simply to be in direct cognitive contact with the dog. In (c), we are still *in fact* aware only of the *image* as of the dog, how she appears from our particular perspective, even if the imagination leads us to overlook this fact in favour of an assumption about the dog.

The question, then, is how the imagination can do the trick Hume requires of it. How can our awareness of an array of coloured tangible points, an image in sense (a), be converted into a perspective on an object (an image in sense [c]), which perspective we routinely overlook, thus yielding our vulgar sense that we are in touch with the world around us? Before I detail Hume's answer to this question, it will help to indicate that he has already in the *Treatise* suggested that the imagination can convert an awareness of one thing into an awareness of something else. For in his discussion of abstract or general ideas (T 1.1.7), he shows that a perception's content is not exhausted by whatever it presents to us in isolation; when the imagination's associative response is taken into account, the perception can count as having a different content. An idea of a particular can represent a class or collection when the imagination responds to it in the right way. In §2.4 I detail Hume's account of the psychological mechanism that makes general thought possible, and in Chapter 3 I suggest that it provides a framework for understanding his account of the vulgar belief in the independent existence of objects.

---

[35] Consider also a case of being taken in by a *trompe l'oeil* painting.

2.4 General Ideas and Other Fictions

I noted previously that Hume's fundamental empiricist principle—often called the "copy principle" in the secondary literature—holds that simple ideas acquire their content from prior simple impressions (T 1.1.1.7, SBN 4), where impressions are equated with "sensations, passions and emotions" (T 1.1.1.1, SBN 1).[36] Although he sometimes uses this principle to dismiss the intelligibility of certain kinds of objects—particularly metaphysical entities such as substantial forms or occult qualities (T 1.4.3)—he also is willing to apply it with a fair degree of flexibility.[37] He signals this willingness immediately after he first establishes the copy principle, when he allows that were we to confront a display of all the shades of blue in the spectrum except for one that we had never previously sensed, our imaginations could nonetheless form an idea of the missing shade of blue necessary to fill the gap, even without having had a prior impression.[38] Although Hume dismisses the missing-shade-of-blue example as "so particular and singular, that 'tis scarce worth our observing, and does not merit that for it alone we should alter" (T 1.1.1.10, SBN 6) the copy principle, it does show that, right from the start, his empiricism allows that the imagination has a capacity to generate novel content.

Hume exploits this capacity in his discussion of general ideas. In his adaptation of Berkeley's criticism of Locke (P Intro.7–24), Hume argues that we never have perceptions whose contents lack a particular size, shape, and so on (T 1.1.7.6, SBN 19–20). So we do not have an idea of, say, dogs in general, by having a perception that portrays neither a Golden Retriever, nor an Airedale, nor a mutt, but that somehow captures all these options all at once. Given that we manifestly are able to think general thoughts, the Berkeleyan point seems to create a "paradox": "[S]ome ideas are particular in their nature, but general in their representation" (T 1.1.7.10, SBN 22). Hume resolves the paradox by distinguishing between the content an idea has in isolation, and the content it acquires by means of the imagination's response to it. Ideas of particular objects "become general in their representation" (T 1.1.7.6, SBN 20) if accompanied by our associative propensities in the right way. First, there must be an idea of a particular object, such as a particular Golden Retriever. Second, we must be disposed to associate our ideas of the particular dog with our ideas of other

---

[36] I build here on an argument I first presented in "Adequate Ideas and Modest Scepticism in Hume's Metaphysics of Space," *Archiv für Geschichte der Philosophie* 92 (2010), 49–51.

[37] Here I follow Garrett, *Cognition and Commitment*, ch. 2. See Eric Schliesser's "Hume's Missing Shade of Blue Reconsidered from a Newtonian Perspective" (*Journal of Scottish Philosophy* 2 [2004], 164–75) for an interesting exploration of problems with the empirical assumptions that inform Hume's discussion of the missing shade.

[38] In §4.3.2 I point out that Hume also notes a second "limitation" to the copy principle immediately after giving the example of the missing shade of blue. He says that, when introspectively examining the mind, we can form secondary ideas by means of which we think of other ideas, even though we do not have prior introspective impressions of ideas. Nonetheless, because the secondary ideas are of ideas that are copied from impressions, he suggests that they too can be appropriately tied back to experience (T 1.1.1.11, SBN 6–7).

dogs. If I am inclined to think that 'all dogs are golden,' my idea of the particular Golden Retriever is immediately replaced by an idea of a particular Airedale or a particular Poodle, thus revealing to me that my generalization was in error. Third, there must be a name that triggers the associative propensity.

Wayne Waxman has suggested that this last linguistic element is not strictly necessary to Hume's story.[39] My dog, for example, could think of dog biscuits in general, by remembering the previous one she ate and being disposed to think of other such biscuits, all without having any linguistic abilities. But Hume's insistence on the role of language in general thinking suggests that he has something else in mind. Though he has little interest in the philosophy of language or such topics as meaning or reference, he does recognize that language, like justice, is a rule-governed artifice or convention, something that for its intelligibility depends on the mutual coordination of people's behaviour (T 3.2.2.10, SBN 490). There is a social and normative dimension to language use. I think that Hume's insistence on the role of language in our general thinking is an attempt to introduce a social and normative dimension into his account of ideas.[40] For, thus far in the story, there is nothing stopping people from having radically different associative reactions from one another. When thinking of a dog, one person might be disposed to think of Hurricane Katrina, the Eiffel Tower, a stick of butter, and so on, while another might be disposed to think of Lassie, Santa's Little Helper, Asta, and Benji. Although our common human nature means that most people tend to be influenced by their associative propensities similarly, there is no guarantee that there are not deviant cases. The general term 'dog,' however, has been enmeshed in a series of conventions so that the latter set of associations is appropriate and the former inappropriate.[41]

It follows from Hume's account of general ideas that a single idea of a particular object can end up yielding different general thoughts. I can think of a particular Golden Retriever, along with the word 'dog,' thus triggering the appropriate associative disposition for my thinking of dogs in general. Or I can think of the same particular dog, along with the word 'mammal,' thus triggering a different associative disposition that yields the thought of mammals in general. Or I can think of the same dog, along with the word 'animal' to think of animals in general (T 1.1.7.9, SBN 21). And it is not necessary for us to start actually associating the idea of the particular dog with ideas of other dogs or mammals or animals, as the case may be. The

---

[39] Waxman, *Theory*, 105–15.

[40] See Páll Árdal, "Convention and Value," in G. Morice (ed.), *David Hume: Bicentenary Papers* (Austin, TX: University of Texas Press, 1977), 51–68; and Fred Wilson, *The External World and our Knowledge of It* (Toronto, ON: University of Toronto Press, 2008), ch. 1.

[41] Indeed, it cannot be said that the person with the radically deviant associations is thinking of dogs at all. If she has the word 'dog' in mind, the best we would say is that she has *attempted* to think of dogs. Jerry Fodor, in *Hume Variations* (Oxford: Clarendon Press, 2003), misconstrues Hume's theory by supposing that we think of concepts by means of particular ideas, thus overlooking the role of a public language in his analysis of mind.

disposition to so associate is sufficient to convert the thought of the particular dog into the thought of dogs or mammals or animals (T 1.1.7.7, SBN 20–1).

The moral of Hume's account of general ideas is that even though it is impossible for us to have an idea that, taken in isolation, represents a class of objects, our imagination's response to our ideas of particulars can *constitute* such a class as an object of thought.[42] Hume does not give us enough detail to really be clear on some issues here, but I think that he would not want the ideas that an individual person might be disposed to think of to play this constitutive role *by themselves*; rather our shared, linguistically trained reactions would together constitute the class *for us*. As such, if I have a slight idiosyncrasy in my imaginative propensities for the kind, insect, by sometimes associating ideas of black widow spiders with those of ants, bees, fleas, and the like, I will still be thinking of insects when my thought of a particular ant is accompanied by my slightly deviant imaginative reactions. I am less clear of how Hume would deal with more pervasive errors of classification. If we all associate ideas of particular whales with ideas of particular goldfish, eels, seahorses, and the like, would he say that we have a kind that includes whales among the fish, or that we are all systematically mistaken in our classifications of whales? I suspect the latter, in that we can use the philosophical relation of resemblance to eventually acquire *knowledge* of how goldfish, eels, and seahorses resemble (T 1.3.1), thus ruling whales out as members of the kind. What is important for our purposes here is that, in thinking of a particular in the right imagination-involving way, we are thereby thinking of the universal, even though it cannot be thought of by means of a single perception, taken by itself.

In the discussion of spatiotemporal ideas in Part 2 of Book 1 of the *Treatise*, Hume says that any time we think of something that is not directly derived from the impressions that the idea copies, we engage in a *fiction*: "Ideas always represent the objects or impressions, from which they are deriv'd, and can never without a *fiction* represent or be apply'd to any other" (T 1.2.3.11, SBN 37; emphasis added). Thus, though he does not himself apply the label 'fiction' in his account of general ideas, they do satisfy the definition, in that an idea of a particular is used not to represent the content of the impression from which it is derived, but rather to represent a class. Hume, I take it, does not mean this label to import an epistemic assessment of the idea, as if fictions always involve falsehood (though sometimes they do).[43] Instead, he means only to draw on the sense of 'fiction' found in its Latin root, *fingere*, so that a

[42] Don Garrett seems to overlook this point in his "Hume's Naturalistic Theory of Representation," *Synthese* 152 (2006), 301–19. He argues that, for Hume, "things represent other things by playing a significant part of their causal and/or functional roles, through reliable indication and/or modeling, by the generation of mental effects and dispositions" (313). But this makes it seem as if the thing represented has causal or functional roles prior to being represented. For me, in contrast, Hume's point about general ideas is that the mind's dispositional reactions (when coordinated with others appropriately) are what make it the case that the particular represents a universal. Garrett puts it differently: "The...general idea...takes on the functional roles of all of the members of the kind together" (314).

[43] See Saul Traiger, "Impressions, Ideas, and Fictions," *Hume Studies* 13 (1987), 381–99.

fiction is an "act of fashioning,"[44] in that the imaginative response to the proximate content constitutes or fashions the intended object.

In the Chapter 3 I suggest that this account of general ideas provides a model for the later fictions Hume discusses, such as the idea of the vacuum or the vulgar belief in the independent existence of sensory objects. We can distinguish four elements in this model:

Proximate Content
>   The content of an idea in isolation from the (relevant[45]) associative reactions of the imagination.

Revival Set[46]
>   Those ideas that the imagination associates with the idea that has the proximate content.

Linguistic Label
>   The words (as spoken or written) the ideas of which dispose the imagination to associate ideas from the revival set.

Intended Object
>   That which we think of when we respond to the proximate content and the linguistic term appropriately (as given by the rules established in the relevant language).[47]

---

[44] The *Oxford English Dictionary* lists this meaning first in its entry for 'fiction' (with a 1737 usage as its illustration). Samuel Johnson, in his *Dictionary*, gives "the act of feigning or inventing" as his first definition, and quotes Stillingfleet: "If the presence of God in the image, by a mere fiction of the mind, be a sufficient ground to worship that image, is not God's real presence in every creature a far better ground to worship it?" *A Dictionary of the English Language: The First and Fourth Editions*, ed. A. McDermott (Cambridge: Cambridge University Press, 1996). See Annette Baier, *A Progress of Sentiments* (Cambridge, MA: Harvard University Press, 1991), 103.

[45] The point of this qualification is to make room for Hume's practice of taking for granted that our perceptions yield an awareness of objects in the early portions of Book 1, while then going on, in SwS, to show that the imagination's reactions are in fact necessary for a proper understanding of this awareness. Thus the proximate content of the general idea of dogs might be a particular dog, but this idea of the particular itself depends on the appropriate imaginative associations as described in SwS (see Chapter 4).

[46] Garrett, *Cognition*, 24.

[47] I take this phrase from Hume's comment that "[b]efore those habits [of associating ideas from the revival set] have become entirely perfect, perhaps the mind may not be content with forming the idea of only one individual, but may run over several, in order to make itself comprehend its own meaning, and the compass of that collection, which it *intends* to express by the general term" (T 1.1.7.10, SBN 22; my emphasis).

My use of 'intended object' here differs from Donald Baxter's in *Hume's Difficulty* (London: Routledge, 2008). He defines the *intended object* of an idea as "what there is which an idea represents," as opposed to the *intentional object* of an idea, or "what the idea represents there as being" (51–4). My distinction between the proximate content of an idea and its intended object both fall within Baxter's conception of an intentional object. My claim is that Hume thinks what an idea represents there as being depends on whether it is taken in isolation, or in the context of our imaginations' reactions to it. The proximate content is what the idea represents there as being when taken in isolation. The intended object (in my sense) is what the idea represents there as being when the imagination's responses are taken into account.

Baxter's conception of intended object as what there is which an idea represents requires that we have some access to the world, whereby we can compare what there is with what the idea represents. Using the

In the case of the idea of dogs in general, the proximate content is the particular dog I happen to think of; the revival set contains whatever dogs I am disposed to think of when making claims about dogs in general; the linguistic label is 'dog'; and the intended object is the universal, dogs-in-general. But with a different proximate content and revival set, the intended object need not be a universal but could be some other fiction.

In SwS, for example, Hume emphasizes that the objects mentioned in the explanandum's C_n and I_n result from fictions (T 1.4.2.36, 1.4.2.42–3; SBN 205, 209). And in the earlier discussion of spatiotemporal ideas he has already shown himself willing to rely on something similar to the explanatory schema for general ideas when accounting for our beliefs about external objects. For example, he says:

When you tell me of the thousandth and ten thousandth part of a grain of sand, I have a distinct idea of these numbers and of their different proportions; but the images, which I form in my mind to represent the things themselves, are nothing different from each other, nor inferior to that image, by which I represent the grain of sand itself, which is suppos'd so vastly to exceed them. What consists of parts is distinguishable into them, and what is distinguishable is separable. But whatever we may imagine of the thing, the idea of a grain of sand is not distinguishable, nor separable into twenty, much less into a thousand, ten thousand, or an infinite number of different ideas.   (T 1.2.1.3, SBN 27)

Here ideas with the same image-content—an indivisible visual pixel—represent different objects: the grain of sand, its thousandth part, and its ten-thousandth part. This can only be possible if something more than an idea's image-content determines its content. The situation is structurally parallel to the "paradox" of general ideas, where ideas that, in isolation from our associative responses, have no intrinsic difference—the ideas of the same particular Golden Retriever—could, in light of our imaginations' responses to them, have different intended objects—dogs in general, mammals in general, or animals in general.

Hume's hints that a structurally parallel solution to the two paradoxes is also available, for he uses an example that is similar to the ideas of the grain of sand and its parts in order to motivate his discussion of general ideas:

[W]hen we mention any great number, such as a thousand, the mind has generally no adequate idea of it, but only a power of producing such an idea, by its adequate idea of the decimals,

---

three grades of introspection I distinguished in §2.2, in the first grade, we have access both to the object in the world and the perceptions in the mind that are responsible for our awareness of it. From this introspective posture, we can recognize the extent to which what there is in the world conforms to our representation of it—as Baxter would put it, we would have access to the intended object and in addition to the intentional object of the idea. As Hume goes on to take up the second (and eventually third) grade of introspection, it becomes difficult to secure access to what there is which an idea represents. Ultimately, I think, Hume's distinction between external objects taken as different in kind from perceptions and as the same in kind but different in "relations, connexions and durations" (T 1.2.6.8–9, SBN 67–8) gives us two ways to account for what there is which an idea represents. I discuss these two ways of thinking of external objects in §3.3.

under which the number is comprehended. This imperfection, however, in our ideas, is never felt in our reasonings; which seems to be an instance parallel to the present one of universal ideas.   (T 1.1.7.12, SBN 22–3)

Like Locke (E II.xxxi), Hume distinguishes between adequate ideas, which fully capture the objects they represent, and inadequate ideas, which leave out features of their objects. The paradox arises if we consider that an idea, taken in isolation, inherits all of its content from the impressions it copies. How can it represent something more than what that content contains? How can it indicate an object that its content somehow fails to fully characterize? In the quoted paragraph, he gives us an answer. We might think of the number, 1,000, by means of an idea with a (determinate) mass of points as its proximate content, along with the idea of the label 'one thousand' that is itself enmeshed in our arithmetic skills. If we use this idea simply in order to think of something large, this *inadequate* idea is sufficient. But if we need to be precise—say, to find the difference between 1,000 and 427—we call on those skills to make the proximate content adequate and thus to recognize the correct difference of 573. The ideas in the sand example are also inadequate ideas, in that they present as partless something that actually has parts. In this case, the same image-content serves as the proximate content for the idea of the grain and of its parts. But because of the different associative responses we have to the image-content, along with our "distinct" ideas of the numeric labels, the indivisible image-content can represent either the grain or one of its parts.

With this analysis in mind, we can return to Hume's explanation of our vulgar beliefs about the objects we sense. His claim is that a sensation "in its true colours"—that is, taken in isolation, in abstraction from our associative responses—presents us with nothing but an array of tangible and visible points (along with various sensations of pain, pleasure, smell, taste, and so on). But, to jump ahead in the story, insofar as we respond associatively to that array in the right fashion, being aware of that array just is being aware of something we take to exist independently of us. The array of points, an image in sense (a), becomes an image in sense (c) when the imagination's response constitutes an intended object other than the array. The vulgar thus are aware of the image, but in being so aware, they thereby think of a continuing, distinct object. They take the sensation to be a "hat, or shoe, or stone" because they do not encounter an impression in isolation. They are not aware of the impression as such, but rather are aware of what its image-content portrays. The challenge for Hume is to explain how the imagination effects this fiction. How can it constitute objects for perceptions other than image-contents? This is the topic of Chapter 3.

3

Coherence, Constancy, and the Belief in Continuing Objects

In §2.2 we saw that in "Of scepticism with regard to the senses" (T 1.4.2, hereafter 'SwS') Hume characterizes everyday sensory beliefs so that the vulgar manifest an attitude of immersion in a world of public objects. I also suggested that Hume is attempting to capture this attitude when he gives the explanandum for SwS as the belief in the continued and distinct existence of sensory objects, now understood as:

(C_n) The belief, of an object (say, a table) that has been sensed but is not currently being sensed, that it (the table) exists.

(D_n) The belief, of an object (the table) that is currently being sensed, that it (the table) exists.

(I_n) The belief, of an object (the table now) currently being sensed and of an object (the table then) that was previously sensed, that it (the table) is one continuing object.

Yet he also thinks that, from a philosophical point of view, we should say that sensory perceptions have imagistic content (§2.3). But then, given Hume's commitment to mental transparency, it seems that the vulgar would be aware of the imagistic nature of their experience and would not end up taking themselves to be directly in touch with objects in the world. I argued that this seeming tension could be resolved if we recognized that Hume distinguishes between the content that a perception has when it is in isolation and the content it has when the imagination's reactions are taken into consideration (§2.4). For example, an idea that is of a particular in terms of its own distinctive content might nonetheless serve as a general idea when the imagination reacts to it appropriately. In this chapter I examine Hume's account in SwS of how the imagination, in its reactions to sensory impressions with "constant" (T 1.4.2.18, SBN 194) or "coherent" (T 1.4.2.19, SBN 195) imagistic content, yields our vulgar sense of immersion in the world.

The account, unfortunately, can seem tedious, consisting almost entirely of one *ad hoc* psychological mechanism after another. H. H. Price perhaps understates the case when he says that it is "somewhat difficult to follow," with "a good deal of needless tortuousity about its details."[1] Part of this problem arises because, throughout SwS, Hume calls on various mental principles that he has developed earlier in the *Treatise* to account for other phenomena, such as the idea of the vacuum or of a perfect equality. SwS has more footnotes to other portions of the *Treatise* than any of its other Sections. My discussion below is thus forced to take what might seem to be a somewhat digressive path, as I backtrack to explain Hume's prior discussions of some of these topics.

I start in §3.1 by considering the first of Hume's two attempts to explain how the imagination produces the vulgar belief in the continued existence of objects (C_n). He suggests that when our sensations are coherent, we imaginatively extend the coherence beyond what we immediately sense so that objects are taken to exist even when we are not sensing them. After expanding on how the imagination executes this extension for several paragraphs, Hume unexpectedly abandons it, saying: "[W]hatever force we may ascribe to this principle, I am afraid 'tis too weak to support alone so vast an edifice, as is that of the continu'd existence of all external bodies" (T 1.4.2.23, SBN 198–9). He does not elaborate. And thus it is a puzzle why Hume finds it too weak and, given its weakness, why he bothers to present the coherence explanation in the first place. I suggest in what follows that the weakness ultimately stems from its presupposing too much from his earlier accounts of general ideas and causal association; nonetheless, it can supplement our beliefs in continued existence based on constancy.

I address these latter beliefs in §3.2: namely, beliefs in continuing objects that arise from constant experience. Given that Hume's explanation of these beliefs appeals to his earlier explanation of our belief in the identity of an unchanging object, and it in turn draws on his explanation of our idea of a vacuum, I make a long detour in the middle of my discussion to explore his earlier views. I particularly focus on the accusation that his account of these phenomena is circular, and I argue that although it has various flaws, it is not circular in a problematic fashion.

In §3.3 I explore the conceptions of objects at work in the vulgar's belief and in Hume's philosophical system. And in §3.4 I suggest that though Hume accounts for the vulgar's beliefs about objects in terms of the imagination's making various mistakes, the beliefs are not as such in error, even if they do embody a *philosophical* error in their unarticulated assumption of direct access to objects. I postpone further discussion of the philosophical assessment of the vulgar belief for Chapter 4.

3.1 Coherent Experience and the Belief in Continuing Objects

Hume describes the coherence of experience as follows:

Bodies often change their position and qualities, and after a little absence or interruption may become hardly knowable. But here 'tis observable, that even in these changes they preserve a

---

[1] Henry H. Price, *Hume's Theory of the External World* (Oxford: Clarendon Press, 1940), 37.

coherence, and have a regular dependence on each other; which is the foundation of a kind of reasoning from causation, and produces the opinion of their continu'd existence. When I return to my chamber after an hour's absence, I find not my fire in the same situation, in which I left it: But then I am accustom'd in other instances to see a like alteration produc'd in a like time, whether I am present or absent, near or remote.   (T 1.4.2.19, SBN 195)

As I mentioned in §2.2, Hume explicates the vulgar belief in continued existence in terms of their belief in the *identity* of an object through interruptions in our awareness of it, where this belief is interpreted sufficiently naively, as in I_n: I believe of the fire that I had previously seen in full flame and of the ashes I now witness, that they are both part of one ongoing fire. Because my prior experience with fires has involved witnessing their gradually burning down from flames into ashes, I then fill in, as it were, what I have missed on this occasion, and suppose that the fire continued to exist in conformity to my prior experiences even though I did not observe it: I "suppose the continu'd existence of objects, in order to connect their past and present appearances, and give them such an union with each other, as I have found by experience to be suitable to their particular natures and circumstances" (T 1.4.2.20, SBN 197).

Hume notes that although causal associations are involved in the production of this coherence-based belief in the continued existence of objects, they play an "indirect and oblique" role (T 1.4.2.21, SBN 197). The problem is that, on the face of it, interrupted experience of what we take to be a continuous object should contradict our causal expectations, rather than induce our conviction in the object's continuity. If my experience has included observations of ashes arising only gradually as a fire burns down, then the abrupt appearance of ashes, without the prior observation of the hot embers (and before that, of the low flames, preceded by higher flames, and so on), should serve only to undermine my causal expectations for ashes. Hume argues in his treatment of probable reasoning that "as 'tis frequently found, that one observation is contrary to another, and that causes and effects follow not in the same order, of which we have had experience, we are oblig'd to vary our reasoning on account of this uncertainty, and take into consideration the contrariety of events" (T 1.3.12.4, SBN 131). We then adjust our causal expectations in light of the level of regularity in our experience, yielding beliefs that are merely probabilistic in the strict sense that Hume uses when there is real uncertainty whether a particular effect will follow on a particular cause (T 1.3.11.2, SBN 124).

So why do we react to the ashes, not by revising our expectations for fires, but rather by supposing that the fire existed unobserved during our absence from it? Hume's answer is that the imagination wants to extend the coherence of objects beyond what we directly experience until it becomes "as compleat as possible" (T 1.4.2.22, SBN 198).[2] He uses the analogy of inertia: "[T]he imagination, when

---

[2] Hume refers us at this point to his earlier discussion of how we form the idea of "exact equality" (T 1.2.4.24, SBN 48). On the one hand, we recognize that any measurement leaves room for error, especially

set into any train of thinking, is apt to continue, even when its object fails it, and like a galley put in motion by the oars, carries on its course without any new impulse" (T 1.4.2.22, SBN 198). We thus come to posit the existence of an unobserved object that conforms to our causal expectations for things of that kind. We believe that there must have been a fire in the hearth all along, burning down steadily, even though we see only the ashes.

It is at this point that Hume expresses his puzzling dissatisfaction with his explanation. It is "too weak to support alone" (T 1.4.2.23, SBN 198–9) all of our beliefs about the continuity of objects. Though he does not give reasons for his reservations, I have three suggestions.[3]

First, the coherence-based explanation of the continued existence of body seems to start too late in the game: namely, with such things as my experience as of ashes or as of the blazing fire. But we saw in §2.3 that Hume thinks that sensory impressions are ultimately arrays of coloured and tangible points (along with non-located smells, tastes, sounds). How do we end up thinking that our awareness of such arrays is the awareness as of ashes or flames?

Second, we saw that Hume's explanation depended on our grasp of what would be "suitable to...the nature and circumstances" of the object that we take to have continued existence. How do we acquire a grasp of the nature of something like a fire? Hume cannot intend that we somehow already understand the nature of the particular fire we are encountering, for it might be *sui generis*, unlike anything we have encountered before. Instead, we group this fire as a member of the kind, fires, and thus rely on a general idea—an idea of a previous particular fire, along with a linguistically triggered disposition to think of others when appropriate. The problem is that if we rely on the general idea in order to recognize the continued existence of fires when unobserved, how do we acquire the general idea? We need to have had prior experience of fires as being the kind of things that persist through interrupted observation in order to count the ashes we experience as the final stage of a fire that continued even when we were absent.

---

given that "sound reason convinces us that there are bodies vastly more minute that those, which appear to the senses" (T 1.2.4.24, SBN 48); the addition or removal of any such minute particle would undermine the supposed equality of the bodies even if we could not recognize it. On the other hand, our practices of remeasuring and checking our initial claims of equality accustom us to improving our provisional judgements. Thus we form the "fiction" of exact equality, where all possible corrections have been made, including those for minute bodies. "But tho' this standard be only imaginary, the fiction however is very natural; nor is any thing more usual, than for the mind to proceed after this manner with any action, even after the reason has ceas'd, which first determin'd it to begin" (T 1.2.4.24, SBN 48). As in the coherence-based account of the supposition of continued existence, the imagination's inertia leads it to posit a kind of structure in the world that outstrips what we directly experience.

[3] Louis Loeb, in contrast, takes Hume not really to be dissatisfied with his coherence account, but rather wanting to supplement it by considering experiences that are constant, rather than coherent. He goes on to argue that Hume could (and should) have relied on the coherence account by treating constancy as a special case of coherence (*Stability and Justification in Hume's 'Treatise'* [Oxford: Oxford University Press, 2002], 191, 207–14).

It might seem that Hume could escape this criticism by suggesting that we acquire the general idea of fire from those cases where we have an uninterrupted experience of fires, and then rely on it to make sense of interrupted cases. But this response understates the pervasiveness of interruptions in our experience. As he himself admits, "the turning about of our head, or the shutting of our eyes" (T 1.4.2.21, SBN 198; see also T 1.4.2.18, 1.4.2.35; SBN 194, 204) suffices to put a gap in our experience as of the fire. How then do we come to understand how fires typically behave?

This point can be generalized into the third possible reason for Hume's thinking that the coherence-based explanation of C_n is ultimately too weak for his purposes. I noted in §2.2 that, prior to SwS, Hume mostly takes for granted that our impressions reveal the world to us. Thus his accounts of both general ideas and causal association are developed presupposing that sensory objects persist while unperceived. And, just as the coherence-based explanation relies on prior general ideas that capture the natures of such things as fires, it also relies on a prior grasp of the causal properties of fires, considered as mind-independent entities. But he also appeals to our beliefs in these causal properties in order to explain our belief in the mind-independence of fires. Too much of what Hume uses in his first explanation of C_n requires that we already believe our objects to continue when unperceived.

In light of what he admits to be the inadequacy of his coherence-based explanation, Hume goes on to offer an explanation for C_n and I_n in light of the constancy of our experience. I suggest in §3.2.5, however, that the coherence-based explanation, with its presupposition of both general ideas and causal association, can be grafted onto the constancy-based explanation. Thus, even though it is not successful on its own terms, it is not thereby otiose.

3.2 Constant Experience and the Belief in Continuing Objects

I describe Hume's explanation of how constant experience yields the belief in the independent existence of objects in §§3.2.1–3.2.4. My central concern is whether the explanation of C_n and I_n in terms of our reactions to sensations that display constancy can escape the circularity that I suggested infected his coherence-based account. Barry Stroud and Henry Allison each suggest that it cannot.[4] Allison in particular traces the root of this circularity to Hume's explanation of how an "unchangeable" (that is, unchanging[5]) object can nonetheless be thought of as

---

[4] Barry Stoud, *Hume* (London: Routledge and Kegan Paul, 1977), 100; Henry Allison, *Custom and Reason in Hume* (Oxford: Clarendon Press, 2008), 240–6.

[5] I use 'unchanging' for Hume's 'unchangeable.' Given that he equates the unchangeable with the "stedfast" (T 1.2.3.11, SBN 37), I take him not to be intending the modal connotation in 'unchangeable.' I sometimes wonder, however, if Hume uses 'unchangeable' to indicate not just that the object in question is unchanging for me, but also (conceived of) as unchanging for others who might perceive it.

temporal. I argue, in §3.2.2, that Allison's criticism misses its mark, even if Hume's explanation is not wholly unproblematic. In §3.2.3 and 3.2.4 I sketch the mechanism that Hume takes to produce I_n and C_n, and in §3.2.5 I show how it can be extended to encompass the coherence explanation.

I should note at the outset of this section that my discussion here in particular takes an indirect path. The central element of Hume's constancy-based explanation of C_n and I_n is what I call the *idea-substitution mechanism*, where the imagination inserts one idea in the place of another without our realizing it.[6] He first introduces this mechanism in his explanation of our idea of the vacuum (empty space), in the course of his larger exploration of our spatiotemporal perceptions in Part 2 of Book 1 of the *Treatise*, "Of the ideas of space and time." Hume then models his explanation of the idea of the unchanging on his explanation of the idea of the vacuum. And, in SwS, the account of the unchanging becomes a central element of his constancy-based explanation of the vulgar belief in continued existence. Accordingly, in §§3.2.1 and 3.2.2 I delve into the sometimes obscure corners of Hume's discussion of space, time, and our perceptions of them. I use the details I uncover there both to guide the interpretation of the constancy-based mechanism in §3.2.3–3.2.5, and especially, in §3.4, to make sense of Hume's conflicted attitude towards the epistemic value of the vulgar belief.

Hume characterizes constancy in experience as involving the repetition of impressions that are qualitatively identical, especially in the brief interruptions—blinking and the like—that created one of the problems for his coherence-based explanation of C_n:

These mountains, and houses, and trees, which lie at present under my eye, have always appear'd to me in the same order; and when I lose sight of them by shutting my eyes or turning my head, I soon after find them return upon me without the least alteration. My bed and table, my books and papers, present themselves in the same uniform manner, and change not upon account of any interruption in my seeing or perceiving them.   (T 1.4.2.18, SBN 195)

Hume offers a four-stage explanation of how this constancy in experience produces C_n. The first two stages focus on an explanation of I_n, the belief of an object, such as the bed, seen before and after our blinking, that it is one bed. In stages three and four, Hume shows that, even when we are not perceiving it, we believe that the bed continues to exist.

Hume's explanation of I_n can be summarized as follows. Because the occurrence of interrupted qualitatively identical sensations feels like the uninterrupted experience of an unchanging object, we mistake the one for the other. We thus take the resembling sensations to be experiences of one and the same continuing object.

---

[6] I take this label from T 1.2.5.21, SBN 62: "We use words for ideas, because they are commonly so closely connected, that the mind easily mistakes them. And this likewise is the reason, why we *substitute the idea* of a distance, which is not consider'd either as visible or tangible, in the room of extension, which is nothing but a composition of visible or tangible points dispos'd in a certain order" (emphasis added).

The details of this account are less easy to pin down, mostly because Hume at this point invokes the brief and puzzling treatment of the unchanging.

There, the difficulty arises because Hume argues that we do not have a discrete impression of time, different from our impressions of various objects. Rather, the idea of time is an abstraction from the successiveness of our experiences; it "arises altogether from the manner, in which impressions appear to the mind, without making one of the number" (T 1.2.3.10, SBN 36). Because our experience of temporality just is the successiveness of our experiences, Hume concludes that we cannot directly experience an unchanging object by itself as having duration. We would instead have one unchanging perception and, without any change in it being experienced, we would not have anything from which to abstract the successiveness that is essential to the Humean idea of time (T 1.2.3.10–12, SBN 36–7).

Nonetheless, Hume tells us, we *think* we can understand the duration of an unchanging object, and he relies on his explanation of this "fiction" (T 1.2.3.11, SBN 37) in the first step of his constancy-based explanation of C_n and I_n in SwS. In keeping with his strategy throughout Part 2 of Book 1, where he takes space and time to admit of parallel accounts (T 1.2.2.4, 1.2.3.7, 1.2.3.17; SBN 31, 35, 39), Hume approaches the idea of a temporal and yet unchanging object by considering what he takes to be a parallel spatial case, the idea of a vacuum. As I noted earlier, Hume's explanation of the idea of the vacuum also serves to introduce the idea-substitution mechanism, the crucial element in his constancy-based account of our vulgar beliefs. For these two reasons, it is worthwhile to examine this explanation in some detail.

3.2.1 The Idea-Substitution Mechanism and the Idea of a Vacuum

Just as we do not have a discrete impression of time, so also we do not have a discrete impression of space. Instead, as was the case with time, our idea of space is an abstraction of the manner in which objects appear—their (simultaneous) arrangement alongside one another. Though some commentators suggest that Hume here begs the question by explaining the *experience* of space in terms of prior *spatial* arrangements of objects, I think this criticism is misplaced.[7] Just as it is not begging the question to explain our *experience* of apples in terms of properties of *apples*, so

---

[7] Allison, for example, says: "[W]hen Hume talks about a determinate extension as a 'disposition of points' or a 'manner of appearance,' this must already be understood in spatial terms, say as contiguous or as located at a certain distance from each other, from which it follows that it cannot be the source of our idea of extension..." (*Custom and Reason*, 60). But Allison seems to assume that our experience can have *a spatial character* only if we already have the *idea* of space. Hume denies this assumption, instead arguing that the spatial character of our experience yields the idea of space, as its cumulative effect allows us to abstract this character from it. Donald Baxter (*Hume's Difficulty* [London: Routledge, 2008], 20) makes a similar response to Alexander Rosenberg, who makes the parallel objection to Hume's account of time as an abstraction from the successiveness of our experience of objects ("Hume and the Philosophy of Science," in D. F. Norton [ed.], *Cambridge Companion to Hume* [Cambridge: Cambridge University Press, 1993], 83). For other responses to the accusation of circularity in Hume's account of the ideas of space and time, see Lorne Falkenstein, "Hume on Manners of Disposition and the Ideas of Space and Time," *Archiv für Geschichte der Philosophie* 79 (1997), 179–201; and Donald Baxter, "Hume's Theory of Space and Time," in

also in the case of space.[8] And his point is that space is not a feature of the world that we encounter in any other way than by finding objects arranged in it. Space is not, by itself, an object of experience.

At first, Hume concludes from his analysis of the idea of space as an abstraction of the disposition of objects that we have no idea of a vacuum. If an idea is to be of something spatial, it must be of *objects* that are spread out in relation to one another; thinking of empty space is impossible (T 1.2.3.16, SBN 39). Hume's discussion becomes more complex than this initial sketch might suggest when he considers the objection that we must have the idea of a vacuum given the early-modern scientific debate over whether a vacuum exists (T 1.2.5.2, SBN 54).[9] Even if there might be no vacuums in nature, the suggestion runs, we clearly have an *idea* of one. Hume responds both by clarifying the sense in which he rejects the idea of a vacuum and by explaining the idea that operates in the scientific debate. It turns out that although we cannot directly experience a vacuum, we can think of one by means of a fiction.[10]

He points out that his denial of the idea of a vacuum does not preclude, say, the idea of two "luminous bodies ... whose light discovers only these bodies themselves, without giving us any impression of the surrounding objects" (T 1.2.5.8, SBN 56). He allows that we can recognize the distance between these bodies, but our awareness of the "invisible" distance separating them does not count as the idea of empty extended

---

D. F. Norton and J. Taylor (eds.), *Cambridge Companion to Hume*, 2nd edn. (Cambridge: Cambridge University Press, 2009), 134–5.

Allison goes wrong, I think, in part because he takes Hume to be in the proto-Kantian business of giving not only an account of the *idea* of space but an account of *space itself*. Thus, in the paragraph following the one just quoted, Allison says that "the first part [of Hume's system; that is, finite divisibility] construes *space and time* as compound ideas that track compound impressions, while the second [part of Hume's system; that is, the ideas of space and time as abstractions from our cumulative experiences of objects] considers them as manners of appearing ... " (60; emphasis added). But Hume never says that space and time are *themselves* compound ideas. The closest he comes to saying anything substantive about space and time themselves is in *Treatise* 1.2.2, where he argues that "the most minute parts" of space must conform to our ideas of them (T 1.2.2.1, SBN 29); but this argument still presupposes a distinction between *ideas* of the parts of space and *space itself* (see my "Adequate Ideas and Modest Scepticism in Hume's Metaphysics of Space," *Archiv für Geschichte der Philosophie* 92 [2010], 39–67). As the title to Part 2 of Book 1 clearly indicates, Hume's primary business there remains "the *ideas* of space and time" (emphasis added).

[8] Indeed, Hume emphasizes that part of the novelty of his treatment of causation is that it reverses the normal explanatory order. Rather than accounting for our perceptions of a phenomenon in terms of features of the phenomenon, he explains the nature of necessary connection in terms of our impression of it (T 1.3.6.3, 1.3.14.26–7; SBN 88, 167–8).

[9] See Edward Grant, *Much Ado About Nothing: Theories of Space and Vacuum from the Middle Ages to the Scientific Revolution* (Cambridge: Cambridge University Press, 1981).

[10] Though Hume never explicitly uses the word 'fiction' in connection with his discussion of the vacuum, he defines it when explaining the idea of the "unchangeable" (T 1.2.3.11, SBN 37)—an explanation that is openly modelled on his explanation of the idea of the vacuum (see §3.2.2). I take it then that the idea of the vacuum can also be seen as resulting from a fiction. Just as his discussion of the unchangeable invokes a "fictitious duration" (T 1.2.5.29, SBN 65), his account of the vacuum invokes a "fictitious distance" (T 1.2.5.23, SBN 62).

space (T 1.2.5.16, SBN 59).[11] The reason is that the idea of the two luminous bodies has only two components, the two simple ideas of the bodies (supposing, that is, that the bodies are thought of as indivisible). We have no "positive" (T 1.2.5.5, SBN 55) idea of the distance between them because we cannot distinguish it from the two objects in such a way that we could form a separate idea of it. For one of Hume's core principles holds that objects are different from one another if and only if they can be distinguished from one another; and they can be so distinguished if and only if they can be separated in thought (T 1.1.7.3, SBN 18).[12] In the case of the luminous bodies, we can distinguish the bodies from one another, but not the empty space from either of them (T 1.2.5.11, SBN 57).[13]

Hume's claim hinges on his commitment to all sensory perceptions' having image-content. Without there being something that would yield such content, we, like the blind, are unable to perceive anything visually, rather than having perceptions of nothing:

A man, who enjoys his sight, receives no other perception from turning his eyes on every side, when entirely depriv'd of light, than what is common to him with one born blind; and 'tis certain such-a-one has no idea either of light or darkness. The consequence of this is, that 'tis not from the mere removal of visible objects we receive the impression of extension without matter; and that the idea of utter darkness can never be the same with that of vacuum.

(T 1.2.5.5, SBN 55–6)

In thinking of the two separated luminous bodies, then, our perceptions will have a spatial *element*, in that the two objects are disposed in an appropriately spatial manner. But this element is not a third component of the idea.[14] In order to think

---

[11] Note the contrast with René Descartes and John Locke here. Descartes takes extension to be the principal attribute of body, and distance to be a mode of extension. Accordingly there can be no distance without body (AT VIIIA 49–50). Locke allows for the possibility of empty space (E II.iv.3), and conceives of distance as the linear measure between two points in space (E II.xiii.3); for him, there can be distance without body, but not without space. Hume splits the difference between Descartes and Locke. He takes the idea of space to be an abstraction from the manner in which we experience bodies, and thus follows Descartes in holding that we cannot conceive of space without body (at least not directly). Nonetheless, Hume, like Locke, thinks that we can have an idea of distance even when there is no body, the difference being that Hume denies that the thought of this "invisible" distance between the separated luminous bodies can be separated out as the thought of a vacuum.

[12] This principle is itself somewhat obscure, and Hume does not take the time to defend it. It can seem like a surprisingly metaphysical principle for an empiricist, in that it asserts an isomorphism between objects in the world and our powers of conception. Why assume that all the objects in the world are in principle cognizable by us? And why assume that our capacity to make distinctions matches up with the real differences in the world? I address these questions in detail in §§5.3 and 5.4.

[13] Hume makes a parallel point about tangible objects. To simplify my exposition I restrict my attention to the visual case.

[14] Allison, in contrast, argues that "Hume's explanation of the ... fictitious idea of a vacuum ... involves a *petitio principii*. ... In the case of the vacuum, Hume attempted to explain how, due to certain resemblances, we tend to conflate our idea of an imaginary empty space with a real filled one (constituted by an array of colored or tangible points); and the problem is that the possibility of this conflation presupposes that we already have an idea of such an empty space, which is the very thing Hume wants to deny being

of the space between the two objects—say, the mid-point of the invisible distance separating them—we must first concretize the invisible distance by using our imagination to fill it in with sensible objects. We are able to think of the mid-point only because we insert something there to be thought of (T 1.2.5.16, SBN 59).

Hume argues that the scientific debate over the existence of the vacuum has depended on exactly this kind of substitution of one idea for another. When the debate focuses on the *emptiness* of the empty space, the idea in play is of invisible distance, conceived by means of an idea such as that of the two separated luminous bodies. When the debate focuses on the *spatiality* of the empty space, the idea in play is of the two bodies with other visible bodies inserted between them. The problem is that those engaged in this debate have failed to recognize that they are relying on two ideas here, not one. Thus they "falsely imagine" that they "can form ... an idea" of a vacuum (T 1.2.5.14, SBN 58).

Hume cannot mean to suggest here that those arguing about the vacuum have (false) opinions *about* which ideas they can form; they are arguing about the universe, not the mind.[15] Rather, in the same way that the vulgar beliefs, C_n, D_n, and I_n, embody a commitment to the mind-independence of their objects without its being explicitly articulated, the physicists arguing about the vacuum *take themselves* to be thinking about empty space when in fact their ideas are of two bodies separated by imperceptible distance or the perceptible space between them when that distance is filled with body. They do not notice the change in their ideas and instead continue in their reasoning as if they have been thinking about one thing all along. Similarly, Hume eventually argues in SwS that the vulgar, without realizing it, substitute the thought of an unchanging object for their interrupted qualitatively identical sensations. They take themselves to be encountering a continuing object when in fact their perceptions are different from one another (see §3.2.3).

Hume explains the phenomenon whereby we unknowingly substitute one idea for another by offering a speculative argument that appeals to the neuroscience of his day, though he also suggests that, even if his speculations are in error, the phenomenon of mistaking one idea for another is real (T 1.2.5.19, SBN 60). The claim is that the contents of ideas are stored in various brain cells; when we conceive an idea, "animal spirits run" to the appropriate cell and "rouze up" its content (T 1.2.5.20, SBN 60). But sometimes the animal spirits end up awakening the content from a cell different from the one we had intended. Hume suggests that when objects of experience are connected by the natural relations of resemblance, contiguity, or causation, the contents of their ideas are stored in neighbouring brain cells. And so when we try to form one such idea, the animal spirits are particularly likely to

possible" (*Custom and Reason*, 57). But Allison is being uncharitable here, in that Hume is clear that the idea of the two luminous bodies cannot be decomposed to yield an idea of empty space.

[15] See Baxter, "Hume's Theory," 138.

"turn a little to the one side or the other . . . falling into the contiguous [brain] traces" and thus

present other related ideas in lieu of that, which the mind desir'd at first to survey. This change we are not always sensible of; but continuing still the same train of thought, make use of the related idea, which is presented to us, and employ it in our reasoning, as if it were the same with what we demanded.   (T 1.2.5.20, SBN 61)

Hume goes on to suggest that this process of idea substitution is especially apt to occur with the relation of resemblance. For in such a case, not only are the related objects resembling, "but the actions of the mind, which we employ in considering them, are so little different that we are not able to distinguish them" (T 1.2.5.21, SBN 61). Hume's acknowledgement here that mental states involve "actions" as well as objects will prove significant both in his later use of the idea-substitution mechanism in SwS and in my argument in §6.6, where I consider how he ultimately understands the "internal world" of perceptions.

Hume thinks that idea substitution can lead to error. It "is the cause of many mistakes and sophisms in philosophy" (T 1.2.5.20, SBN 61), "there being nothing more common, than to see men deceive themselves in this particular; especially when by means of any close relation, there is another idea presented, which may be the occasion of their mistake" (T 1.2.5.22, SBN 61). Thus suppose I am wondering which sweater to wear this evening, and I consider my blue one, only to dismiss it because I think it has a hole. In fact, however, it is my grey sweater that has the hole, and the blue one is still intact. Hume's diagnosis would be that the resemblance between the sweaters has meant that the idea of the grey sweater took the place of the idea of the blue sweater in my deliberations, without my realizing it. My rejection of the blue sweater occurs because of an idea substitution. The error here is obvious: I come to believe that my blue sweater has a hole, when in fact it does not. The standard for determining that an error has occurred is set by the condition of the object of my thought.

Hume also suggests that the idea-substitution mechanism is at work in connection with language. Words as experienced (aurally or visually) are, he thinks, causally linked to the ideas they stand for (T 1.3.6.14–15, SBN 93), and thus "'tis usual for men to use words for ideas, and to talk instead of thinking in their reasonings. We use words for ideas, because they are commonly so closely connected, that the mind easily mistakes them" (T 1.2.5.21, SBN 61–2). Hume does not elaborate on this claim, but he must mean for the phenomenon to be quite different from the kind of idea substitution involved in the sweater example. In that case, the content of the substituted idea (the grey sweater with the hole) was mistakenly taken to be a feature of the content of the idea it replaced (the blue sweater). But in the case of linguistic idea substitution, Hume clearly does not mean to suggest that we take the content of the idea of the word and mistakenly apply it to the idea of the thing that the word stands for: we do not come to believe that the apple has five letters when the idea of the word 'apple' is substituted for the idea of the apple! His point is rather that sometimes we will end up forming beliefs about the apple without forming the idea of it, instead simply associating our idea of the word 'apple' with other ideas, such as the idea of the word 'red.' Thus Hume argues that it is "usual, after the frequent use of terms, which are really significant and intelligible, to omit the idea, which we wou'd express by them, and to preserve only the custom, by which we recal the idea at pleasure" (T 1.4.3.10, SBN 224). So unlike the idea substitution in the case of the sweaters, linguistic idea substitution need not yield error. If the apple is red, then our belief is true whether or not it is a result of our ideas of terms or ideas of apples and of other red things. Of course, thinking only of the word, 'apple,' and not the thing itself, might also lead us into error *indirectly*. If, for example, the apple is in fact dull, we might nevertheless believe that it is shiny simply because of an association of the words 'apple' and 'shiny.' As we saw in §2.4, linguistic terms can import a kind of generality into our thought, and thus relying on linguistic ideas rather than ideas of things might cause us to overlook the particularity of a given object.

Hume's real concern about linguistic idea substitution, however, is that a term that is "wholly insignificant and unintelligible" (T 1.4.3.10, SBN 224) might be used as if it had a meaning. He gives the examples of 'faculty' and 'occult quality,' which philosophers bandy about frequently enough for them to form what they take to be beliefs about real phenomena. In fact these terms are empty, but because we are accustomed to thinking by means of linguistic labels rather than by means of the ideas for which the terms stand, the philosophers do not realize that they are talking nonsense. So linguistic idea substitution is a *direct* cause of error when we use meaningless terms (see §5.1).

The case of the vacuum offers yet another use of the idea-substitution mechanism. Here, we think of the word, 'vacuum,' in conjunction with either the idea of the two objects separated by an invisible distance, or the idea of that distance now concretized with space-filling objects. These two ideas are related to one another in three ways. First, the separated bodies in the first idea affect the senses in the same way as the bodies connected by extension in the second idea (T 1.2.5.15, SBN 58–9). Second, the separated bodies can receive bodies between them without themselves undergoing any change: "That is, in other words, an invisible and intangible distance may be converted into a visible and tangible one, without any change on the distant objects" (T 1.2.5.16, SBN 59). And third, the separated bodies have the same effects on other bodies as similar bodies connected by extension (T 1.2.5.17, SBN 59). Thus the ideas that are substituted for one another in connection with the word 'vacuum' are related both by resemblance (in the first and third case) and causation (in the second). We will accordingly overlook the change of ideas and take ourselves to be thinking of one phenomenon (T 1.2.5.21, SBN 62).

Is there an error here?[16] Unlike the case of the sweaters, where the facts about the blue sweater were the standard against which we measured our thinking, here we do

---

[16] Baxter assumes that fictions are "evident falsehoods." He describes Annette Baier's claim that "Humean fictions are not false, simply unverifiable" (*A Progress of Sentiments* [Cambridge, MA: Harvard

not have a clear-cut object of thought, facts about which establish a standard. It is not that we are trying to think of the separated luminous bodies and mistakenly make claims *about them* based on the substitution of the idea of concretized distance between them; rather, we are making claims about the invisible distance thought of by means of the substituted idea of the filled-in space. Nor is there an error here akin to the linguistic error arising from empty terms, such as 'faculty' or 'occult quality.' For the idea of the term 'vacuum' does have ideas connected with it. The problem is that the idea substitution means that 'vacuum' is associated with two different ideas, the difference between which we overlook. The error is in assuming we can think of empty space *directly*, without the intervention of the imagination and the idea-substitution mechanism.

Most of us, however, will not make overt assumptions about *how* we think of the vacuum (if indeed we bother to think of it at all). Instead, our "discourses and reasonings" (T 1.2.5.19, SBN 60) will manifest a commitment to the vacuum as a single object of thought, when in fact it is a fiction of the imagination. Hume allows that we can reason successfully despite this mistaken commitment. Thus he considers what would happen were every object in a room to be annihilated, leaving only the walls standing. Would there be a vacuum in the room? Or would the walls, though themselves not moving, somehow meet one another at a point, given that there is no longer body remaining between them?[17] Hume's final verdict—a passage from the "Appendix" that was to be inserted as a footnote into the body of Part 2—is as follows:

Thus if it be ask'd, whether or not the invisible and intangible distance [between the walls in the room] be always full of *body*, or of something that by an improvement of our organs might become visible or tangible, I must acknowledge, that I find no very decisive arguments on either side; tho' I am inclin'd to the contrary opinion, as being more suitable to vulgar and popular notions. If *the Newtonian* philosophy be rightly understood, it will be found to mean no more. A vacuum is asserted: That is, bodies are said to be plac'd after such a manner, as to receive bodies betwixt them, without impulsion or penetration. The real nature of this position

University Press, 1991], 103) as "an attempt to save Hume from himself, [rather] than an attempt to take him at his word" (*Hume's Difficulty*, 103n17). Although I do not accept Baier's version of the point, I too argue that fictions need not yield falsehoods—in part because I take Hume's words to be more ambiguous on this issue than Baxter supposes.

[17] See Descartes, AT VIIIA, 50, for his version of this problem. He argues that, given that extension is the principal attribute of body, the removal of all body from the inside of a vessel would mean that its sides would have to be in contact. Locke offers his version at E II.xiii.21, where he argues that God could put all of the matter in the universe at rest, and then remove "this Book, or the Body of him that reads it." Given that all the body is at rest, the result would be a vacuum where the body or book had been. David and Mary Norton, in their annotations to the critical edition of the *Treatise*, point also to Pierre Gassendi, Jacques Rohault, Nathaniel Fairfax, John Keill, Walter Charleton, and Jean-Baptiste de Boye, Marquis d'Argens, as having discussed versions of this thought experiment ("Editors' Annotations," in David F. Norton and Mary Norton [eds.], *Hume, A Treatise of Human Nature: A Critical Edition*, Vol. 2, *Editorial Material* [Oxford: Clarendon Press, 2007], 723).

of bodies is unknown. We are only acquainted with its effects on the senses, and its power of receiving body.   (T 1.2.5.26n12, SBN 638–9)

Thus Hume is willing to countenance talk of the vacuum *when it is properly understood* in terms of what we think of when the mind substitutes ideas for one another.

It will be helpful to compare Hume's position here with his discussion of general ideas. In §2.4 we saw that we think of a class of objects by thinking of a particular member of the class (the *proximate content*) and the name for the class (the *linguistic label*), whereby we are disposed to think of other members of the class as needed (the *revival set*). I suggested that this schema yields a fiction that constitutes the class as the *intended object* of thought. Most of us, however, overlook this structure, not recognizing the role that the imagination plays in constituting the thought of the class. And, as I argue in Chapter 5, philosophers tend to posit mind-independent objects that conform to our fictional constructions. In this case, for example, they might make the Platonic mistake of thinking that we encounter universals directly. Because we can *think* of classes they assume that *classes* exist apart from the mind's activities. Though the philosophical interpretation of our cognitive situation is wrong, it does not follow that our being in that situation—our thinking general thoughts—is somehow out of order or to be avoided. Fictional thoughts are not *ipso facto* errors.

The case of the vacuum can thus be taken to be analogous to general ideas, though the fiction of the imagination at work in our thought of it is different. We have a label, 'vacuum,' connected with ideas that we substitute for one another as needed. Whereas with general ideas we often recognize the substitution of one member of the revival set for another, with the vacuum we overlook the differences between the elements of the relevant set. But I suggest that the fiction constitutes the vacuum as our intended object of thought, even as the proximate content remains that given by either one of the mutually substituted ideas. Hume can countenance the Newtonian claims about the vacuum in the quoted passage because he has shown how the component ideas operate in our thought of it. Philosophers go wrong when they overlook the role of the imagination in this process and take us to encounter vacuums directly, as if they were wholly mind-independent objects.

In §3.4 and Chapter 4 we see that Hume's use of the idea-substitution mechanism to explain the vulgar beliefs about objects has the same moral. It does not *ipso facto* render them in error; rather, their error is a kind of implicit misunderstanding about their relation to their intended objects of thought—in this case the tables and beds and fires with which they take themselves to have direct contact.

3.2.2 The Idea of a "Stedfast" Object

Hume suggests that our thinking of an unchanging or "stedfast" (T 1.2.3.11, SBN 37) object in time is analogous to the idea of the vacuum (T 1.2.5.28, SBN 65). It is only by means of a "fiction [that] we apply the idea of time, even to what is unchangeable, and suppose, as is common, that duration is a measure of rest as well as of motion" (T 1.2.3.11, SBN 37). Hume's explanation of this fiction is compact, though the general point is clear enough: While the unchanging object, thought of in isolation, does not yield an idea of temporality, the fact that we are aware of it as surrounded by changing objects allows us to treat it as if it were changing and thus in time.

I find the details, however, to be confused. Hume suggests that the fiction takes the form of an idea substitution:

> For we may observe, that there is a continual succession of perceptions in our mind; so that the idea of time being for ever present with us; when we consider a stedfast object at five-a-clock, and regard the same at six; we are apt to apply to it that idea in the same manner as if every moment were distinguish'd by a different position, or an alteration of the object. The first and second appearances of the object, being compar'd with the succession of our perceptions, seem equally remov'd as if the object had really chang'd. To which we may add, what experience shews us, that the object was susceptible of such a number of changes betwixt these appearances; as also that the unchangeable or rather fictitious duration has the same effect upon every quality, by encreasing or diminishing it, as that succession, which is obvious to the senses. From these three relations we are apt to confound our ideas, and imagine we can form the idea of a time and duration, without any change or succession.   (T 1.2.5.29, SBN 65)

Hume wants us to rely here on his prior explanation of the imagination's fiction of the idea of the vacuum. The consideration of the unchanging object at five o'clock and at six o'clock is meant to be akin to the idea of the two luminous bodies separated by an "invisible distance" in the account of the idea of the vacuum, though in this case the five-o'clock object and six-o'clock object are separated by an unchanging duration. But, because we are aware of other objects that do change during this time, we can conceive the object as also having changed between the appearances, just as we could fill the invisible distance between the luminous bodies with visible objects. Analogues to the three relations that we saw earlier (§3.2.1) support the imagination's fiction of the idea of a vacuum are also in place here. First, the five-o'clock and six-o'clock consideration of the object affect us similarly whether or not any change occurs between them—they are "equally remov'd." Second, the object could have changed between the two appearances, and thus the idea of the object at the two times could be converted into the idea of a changing object between those times. And third, the objects at five o'clock and six o'clock have the same effects on other qualities whether or not change occurs between them. Thus we substitute the two ideas for one another, thinking of the object as at five o'clock and as at six o'clock with unchanging duration separating them when we want to emphasize the steadfastness of the object, and thinking of the changes during this time when wanting to emphasize the temporality of the steadfast object.

Stroud and Allison both contend that Hume's explanation here presupposes what it tries to explain—the possibility of our recognizing the temporality of an unchanging object. He says, for example, that in its first step we are to "consider a stedfast object at five-a-clock, and regard *the same* at six" (T 1.2.5.25, SBN 69; emphasis added). But surely our capacity to regard something unchanging as the same at two times is exactly what is in question.[18] Allison puts the point this way:

A feature of Hume's account of identity, which has been emphasized by Stroud, is its circularity.[19] According to Hume, we acquire this idea [of the unchanging] by imagining a change in time without imagining any variation in the object. This would be fine if we really had an invariable impression (or perceived an unchanging object); for, as Hume points out, we could still note the passage of time through the observation of changes in *other* objects or our perceptions and, therefore, form the idea of *this* object remaining identical throughout a stretch of time. The problem is that for Hume we have no such impression, since perceptions are perishing existences, lacking any temporal thickness. Indeed, if we did have such an impression the idea of identity would not be a fiction, since it would be copied from it.[20]

I think, however, that Allison makes things more difficult for Hume than is necessary in at least two ways.

First, as Donald Baxter has argued, we do not need to make Allison's assumption that Hume takes all perceptions to lack temporal thickness—what Baxter calls the "brevity assumption."[21] Of course, Hume does say that perceptions

succeed each other with an inconceivable rapidity, and are in a perpetual flux and movement. Our eyes cannot turn in their sockets without varying our perceptions. Our thought is still more variable than our sight; and all our other senses and faculties contribute to this change; nor is there any single power of the soul, which remains unalterably the same, perhaps for one moment.   (T 1.4.6.4, SBN 252-3)[22]

---

[18] It is important to distinguish this criticism of circularity from the criticism of circularity I noted in fn. 7, where Hume is said to beg the question by explaining the idea of time in terms of the temporal (that is, successive) manner in which objects appear. But Hume can legitimately appeal to the element of successiveness in our experience of objects when accounting for our *idea* of time, so long as we do not need to *think of* that element in order to perceive the objects. As Baxter puts it: "[T]his charge of circularity is misguided. A certain point of resemblance might intrude on our attention if we are naturally susceptible to the intrusion" (*Hume's Difficulty*, 20).

The criticism of circularity in Hume's account of the idea of the unchangeable is different. The concern here is that he presupposes our having an *idea* of the unchanging object existing at different times (at five o'clock and at six o'clock) in his explanation of why we believe the unchanging object to persist through time.

[19] Allison here refers to Stroud, *Hume*, 103-4.

[20] *Custom and Reason*, 240.   [21] *Hume's Difficulty*, 33.

[22] Baxter suggests that this passage does not require the brevity assumption, and speaks more to the fact that there is an "inconceivably small gap, if any, between perceptions" (*Hume's Difficulty*, 34). Moreover, Hume's analogy of the mind to a theatre, which immediately follows this passage, requires the rejection of the brevity assumption. Perceptions are meant to be analogues of actors, whose appearance on the stage is, of course, not momentary (*Hume's Difficulty*, 34). A similar point can be made about Hume's other crucial analogy for the mind, the "republic or commonwealth," where citizen-perceptions live full lives so as to "give rise to other persons" or perceptions, and thus "propagate the same republic" (T 1.4.6.19, SBN 261).

But in Book 2 he allows that some impressions of reflection—in particular, passions such as compassion and malice—are defined by their whole, temporally thick, "bent and tendency" (T 2.2.9.2, SBN 381). The passions are "slow and restive" (T 2.3.9.12, SBN 441) and can become enduring, "settled principle[s] of action" (T 2.3.4.1, SBN 419). Even in his discussion of spatiotemporal perceptions, Hume emphasizes that when we are focused on an object, our awareness of time—of successiveness—ceases (T 1.2.3.11, SBN 37): we can get lost in our thoughts. Thus there is nothing stopping him from allowing that our sensation of an unchanging object can give us "one constant and uninterrupted perception" (T 1.4.2.35, SBN 204), even while we have other changing perceptions. Hume's point is that, in the absence of such extraneous changes, the one uninterrupted perception would not afford us an awareness of time.[23]

Allison thinks, however, that a temporally thick perception would mean that Hume could appeal to it directly to get the idea of identity: there would be no need for a fiction. My second objection to Allison is that this point misunderstands the nature of Humean fictions. Recall the definition I quoted in §2.4: "Ideas always represent the objects or impressions, from which they are deriv'd, and can never without a fiction represent or be apply'd to any other" (T 1.2.3.11, SBN 37). An impression that is unchanging can be copied into an idea of the (unchanging) content of that impression, but it cannot by itself yield an idea of the unchanging *as temporal*. Without the successiveness that is essential to our awareness of time, the unchanging awareness of an object yields only the idea of one thing, a unity, rather than a Humean identity—a thing persisting the same *in time* (T 1.4.2.26–8, SBN 200). Thus a fiction is needed in order to bring the successiveness of our other perceptions into contact with the perception of a unity. We need to go beyond the perception itself in order to apply the idea of time to its object. Hume's definition of 'fiction' does apply.

I noted above that in explaining this fiction, Hume seems to beg the question by presupposing that we could think of the *same* unchanging object at five o'clock and at six o'clock. But my response to Allison helps to show that Hume can defend himself from this charge by saying that until the fiction has taken place, we have only concurrent ideas, one of the single object and the others of, say, the successive moving hands on the clock. However, when the imagination leads us to unknowingly replace the idea of the single object with the compound idea of the object in question *and* the changing clock, then we take ourselves to be thinking of the unchanging object *in time*. The point is that the idea-substitution mechanism allows us to think of the unchanging *as persisting through time*, rather than merely thinking of the one

---

[23] A mind such as "one reduc'd even below the life of an oyster," with only "one perception, as of thirst or hunger" at a time (T App.16, SBN 634), would accordingly have no awareness of time while each perception occurs. The perceptions would be successive but would not afford the sub-oyster an awareness of their successiveness.

unified object *along with* some changes (say, of the clock). We take the unity to "participate of the changes of the co-existent objects, and in particular of that of our perceptions" (T 1.4.2.29, SBN 201).

Even if Hume can defend himself from Stroud's and Allison's criticisms, I think that he nonetheless overstates the similarities between the idea of the unchanging and of the vacuum. Our ideas of space and time are both abstractions of a manner in which objects appear, either alongside one another or successively to one another. A non-fictional idea of a vacuum as empty space, were it possible, would thus be an idea of *the manner of appearance of objects* (alongside one another) in the *absence of objects*. The temporal parallel would be a case of having an idea of the manner of appearance of objects (successively to one another) in the absence of objects. This is not the idea of an unchanging object, but rather the idea of the temporality of nothingness—say the idea of time before the creation.[24] Conversely, a non-fictional idea of an enduring and yet unchanging object, were it possible, is an idea of an *object* in time *without the manner of appearance* (successiveness) that yields the idea of time. The spatial parallel would then be the idea of a visible or tangible object in space without the manner of appearance (its being alongside other objects) that yields the idea of space. This is not the idea of a vacuum, but rather the idea of a single indivisible (and thus unextended) and yet spatial object.[25]

In the case of the vacuum and its temporal analogue, we try to have an idea of the *manner of appearance* relevant to space or time *without objects* so appearing.[26] In the case of the unchanging object and its spatial analogue, we try to have the idea of an *object* in space or time *without the appropriate manner of appearing*. When the idea of the vacuum is properly distinguished from the idea of the unchanging, it becomes clear that Hume cannot assume that his prior account of the former can easily be transformed into an account of the latter. Consider these two differences.

First, the two fictions generate their intended objects by different means. The fiction of the idea of the vacuum relies on the mutual substitution of the idea of the two luminous bodies separated by an invisible distance and the idea of those bodies with objects arrayed between them. The proximate content in each case is of something spatial, and the intended object retains the spatiality of this proximate

---

[24] Or if God's pre-existing creation means that we conceive an object even in this case, perhaps a secularized example would be better. A temporal parallel to the vacuum would then be the time before the big bang.

[25] Baxter argues that "there is no spatial analogue to a steadfast object" (*Hume's Difficulty*, 41). Briefly, he sees the steadfast object as an object lacking temporal parts that coexists with a temporal succession. The spatial parallel then would be an object lacking spatial parts coexisting with objects that are spread out with respect to one another. I am not sure, however, why an indivisible object would not satisfy this definition. A single perception of it would not yield an idea of space, but in the context of other perceptions it would be spatial.

[26] Baxter usefully reminds us that for Hume we only have ideas of such manners by having ideas of objects arrayed appropriately, from which we then generalize in light of its similarity to other ideas whose objects display analogous arrangements (*Hume's Difficulty*, 21).

content, though now *emptied* of content. The fiction of the unchanging relies on the mutual substitution of the idea of a single object by itself (an idea of unity) and the compound idea of the single object along with a concurrent succession such as the moving hands of the clock. The proximate content in the second idea is the compound of the single object *and* a temporal succession; the proximate content of the first idea is one component of this compound idea, the single object taken in isolation. Whereas both ideas involved in the fiction of the idea of the vacuum were spatial, only the second idea in the fiction of the unchanging is temporal (and only one of this second idea's components involves a succession). And whereas the intended object in the fiction of the idea of the vacuum *empties* the mutually substituted ideas of their content, the intended object in the fiction of the unchangeable object *melds* the content of the two components of the second idea. The unchanging is thought to be in time.

Second, the ingredient ideas in the two fictions are significantly different from one another. We do not ever come across two luminous bodies separated by an invisible distance, though an idea of them provides the proximate content for the thought of the vacuum. Even when we look at two stars on a cloudless moonless night, we have impressions of the blackness between them, as if we were looking at a dark screen in the sky. We can *imagine* the separated luminous bodies, but this thought is unlikely to occur to anyone not inclined to speculate on, say, the velocity of two falling bodies unhindered by air resistance. The idea of the vacuum is thus abstruse, relevant to scientific thought, but not part of our everyday experiences. The ingredient ideas in the thought of the unchanging, in contrast, are ubiquitous. We have ideas of unities all the time, whenever we keep our thought focused on discrete content. If we are not so engaged by this content that we lose ourselves in it, becoming oblivious to changes in the environment and in ourselves, we will also have the concurrent experience of successive objects.[27] The fiction of the idea of the unchanging is thus a commonplace. Moreover, Hume *needs* this fiction to be ubiquitous for it to play the role he gives it in his explanation of the vulgar belief in the continued existence of body. Given these differences between the fictional ideas of the vacuum and of the unchanging, I find it surprising that he chooses to explain the latter in terms of the former, rather than *vice versa*.

In SwS, Hume refers us back to the account of the unchanging from T 1.2.5 (T 1.4.2.29n37, SBN 200n), and reasserts the need for a fiction when confronting the seemingly paradoxical relation of identity.[28] It is not the self-sameness of an object in

---

[27] Here I disagree with Stefanie Rocknak, who says that because "our impressions seem to be constantly changing in light of the fact that we seem to be constantly moving through the world," the vulgar only rarely encounter the unchanging ("The Vulgar Conception of Objects in 'Of Skepticism with regard to the Senses,'" *Hume Studies* 33 [2007], 75).

[28] Hume is not as clear on this point as one would like, but I think he uses 'identity' here differently from his first introduction of it as one of the seven "philosophical" relations (T 1.1.5.4, SBN 13). Because reason, for Hume, is defined as the faculty that discovers such relations (T 1.3.2.2, SBN 73), I call this the *rational*

abstraction from time, which Hume calls "unity" (T 1.4.2.26, SBN 200), but rather the sameness of an object through time. The problem is that if we emphasize that the object at one time is to be the same as an object at another, we end up with what appear to be two objects, and thus the idea of "number" rather than identity (T 1.4.2.27–8, SBN 200). So it seems "utterly impossible" to think of an unchanging object in time (T 1.4.2.28, SBN 200).

Hume's solution is the fiction of the steadfast object. The two ideas that provide the proximate content for the fiction each yields one of the contrasting options. The unchanging object thought of in conjunction with a succession is an idea of number; the unchanging by itself is the idea of unity. But when these ideas are mutually substituted for one another, we end up with something unchanging and yet temporal as our intended object. The unchanging object is thus experienced as "a medium betwixt unity and number; or more properly speaking, is either of them, according to the view, in which we take it: And this idea we call that of identity" (T 1.4.2.29, SBN 201). The idea substitution constitutes the thought of identity. Hume concludes that "the principle of individuation is nothing but the *invariableness* and *uninterrupted-ness* of any object, thro' a suppos'd variation of time, by which the mind can trace it in the different periods of its existence, without any break of the view, and without being oblig'd to form the idea of multiplicity or number" (T 1.4.2.30, SBN 201).

3.2.3 *The Belief in the Identity of Unchanging Objects of which we have Interrupted Experience (I_n)*

Hume is quick to extend the mechanism explaining the belief in steadfast objects to the case where our experience of the unchanging object is interrupted—or, to put it

conception of identity. This relation is in play when, say, I think of the chair in front of me and actively consider whether it is the same as the chair that was located there yesterday. Hume holds that our determination of this relation is at best probabilistic. Though I take the chair to be one chair that has persisted since yesterday (and has a history extending well before then), it is conceivable that someone rearranged the furniture overnight and that the chair there now merely resembles the prior one (it is now two over to the left, say). It depends on whether there was any causal interference in the chair's spatiotemporal path and how objects of that "species" typically behave:

We readily suppose an object may continue individually the same, tho' several times absent from and present to the senses; and ascribe to it an identity, notwithstanding the interruption of the perception, whenever we conclude, that if we had kept our eye or hand constantly upon it, it wou'd have convey'd an invariable and uninterrupted perception . . . Whenever we discover such a perfect resemblance, we consider, whether it be common in that species of objects; whether possibly or probably any cause cou'd operate in producing the change and resemblance; and according as we determine concerning these causes and effects, we form our judgment concerning the identity of the object.   (T 1.3.2.2, SBN 74)

Of course, Hume also holds that the identity we recognize in "an invariable and uninterrupted perception" is itself less than clear cut, and is ultimately dependent on the imagination's fiction of the idea of the unchangeable. There is thus a parallel here between Hume's account of the causal relation and his account of the identity relation: our rational recognition of each ultimately results from how our imaginations react to patterns in our experience. (My thoughts on Hume's treatment of the rational conception of identity have been influenced by Abraham Roth's "The Psychology and 'Language' of Identity in the *Treatise*: Unity, Number, or Something In Between?" presented at the 41st International Hume Conference [Portland, OR, July 2014].)

more exactly, where we have interrupted qualitatively indistinguishable sensations. He thinks that because the latter experience feels like the former experience, we mistake the one for the other and treat the object of which we have interrupted experience as if it were unchanging. He again invokes the idea-substitution mechanism. Not only does the idea of the object after the interruption resemble the idea of the object previously, but the "act[s] or operation[s] of the mind" in having these ideas are similar (T 1.4.2.32, SBN 203). Thus the imagination reacts as if we had experienced a steadfast object. As in I_n, we believe of the object that we had perceived previously and of the object that we now perceive, that it is one steadfast object.

Hume sometimes uses the vocabulary of "perfect" and "imperfect identity" to describe his view.[29] In having uninterrupted experience of an unchanging object, we take it to have a "perfect identity" (T 1.4.2.24, 1.4.2.31, 1.4.2.33, 1.4.2.36, 1.4.2.39, 1.4.2.40, 1.4.6.6, 1.4.6.8; SBN 199, 202, 203, 205, 207, 208, 254, 255), though only by means of the fiction of the steadfast object. In having an interrupted experience of qualitatively indistinguishable objects, we treat them as if they were two portions of one steadfast object, which accordingly displays "imperfect identity" (T 1.4.6.9, SBN 256). As we will see in §3.2.5, Hume will go on to extend his account of imperfect identity to apply also to those cases where we have interrupted experiences the contents of which are not qualitatively indistinguishable, but rather resembling, contiguous, or causally related.

3.2.4 The Belief of an Object not Currently Sensed that it Exists (C_n)

In stages three and four of his four-step argument for the belief in the continued existence of sensory objects, Hume moves from focusing on the identity claim, I_n, to C_n, where we believe of an object not currently being sensed that it exists.[30] The source for this belief is a tension that arises from I_n. We have seen that in believing of an object, say a hat, sensed previously and sensed now that it is the same hat, we substitute the fiction of an unchanging object for the ideas of the hat arising from our sensing it currently and in the past. And yet the fiction of an unchanging object is of an object that we remain *aware of* through the passage of time, while we are *not* aware of the hat in the periods when it is neither sensed nor thought of. Hume suggests that we resolve this tension by supposing the existence of a continuing and yet unsensed object.[31] We engage in the "fiction of continued existence" (T 1.4.2.36, SBN 205), where 'fiction' is to be understood as described in §2.4—as the fashioning

---

[29] L. Ashley and M. Stack. "Hume's Theory of the Self and its Identity," *Dialogue* 13 (1974), 239–54.

[30] Rocknak takes the transition here to be from one vulgar perspective to a new one ("Vulgar Conception," 78). But I think that Hume wants the four-stage exposition to be addressed to one phenomenon: the vulgar belief in continued existence. The transition to stage three instead involves moving from the belief of objects that we re-encounter that they are the same (I_n) to the beliefs of objects that we are not encountering at all that they exist (C_n).

[31] It would be better, but more awkward, to rephrase this supposition so that it retains the vulgar sense of immersion in the world, where their sensing (or not sensing) objects is not within the scope of the belief (see §2.2): we suppose, of an object we are not sensing, that it continues to exist.

of an object of thought different from what can be directly copied from impressions (and given that the steadfast object is itself the product of a fiction, the fiction of continued existence involves a double fiction). Though we were not aware of the hat between our sensings of it, we suppose that it was, like the unchanging object, continuing to exist. When we think of the hat between our sensings of it, the mind responds by producing a steadfast conception of it that connects it with our most recent sensing of it, so that we take it to persist ongoingly.

This fiction will end up as a *belief* of the hat not being sensed that it exists when the vivacity of the hat-impression that triggers the idea substitution overflows into the substituted ideas, thus enlivening them to the appropriate level (T 1.4.2.41, SBN 208). Moreover, our memories of re-encountering objects that exemplify constancy and supposing that they continued to exist while unperceived means that we apply this expectation of continued existence even to novel situations that resemble those we have encountered previously. The vivacity of the memories, in these cases, enlivens the fiction of continued existence to yield a belief (T 1.4.2.42, SBN 209).

I think that Hume's point here can be cashed out using the vocabulary we developed in connection with general ideas, where the imagination's linguistically structured response to the proximate content (in that case, a particular) constituted a class as the intended object of thought (§2.4). In the case of continued existence, the proximate content is the image-content as of the hat, given to us either in an impression when we re-encounter it, forming the belief that it is the same hat as the one there previously, or in an idea when, while not sensing it, we take the hat to continue existing. In each case, the intended object of awareness is not the image. Rather, the imagination's disposition to substitute the fiction of a steadfast object means that we take ourselves to be aware of a persisting object. As we saw in §2.3, Hume is clear that the relation between the image-content and the intended object is not be understood on the model of a "double existence internal and external, representing and represented" (T 1.4.2.36, SBN 205), though I show in Chapter 4 (§4.5) that he thinks that philosophers tend to misinterpret it in these terms. Rather, I suggest, we should see the relation between image-content and intended object as in the treatment of general ideas, that is as *constitutive*. Being aware of the image-content in the right way—with the imagination's tendency to substitute the fiction of the steadfast object—*is what it is* to be aware of a continued existence. And, as I discuss in more detail in §3.3, the continued existence *is* what we are aware of when responding imaginatively to constant experience in this way. As in the treatment of general ideas, the 'we' here needs to be taken socially, so that two (or more) people can rightly be said to encounter the *same* objects and so that idiosyncrasies in imaginative response do not suffice to undermine access to such shared objects.

3.2.5 Integrating the Coherence Account into the Constancy Account

I emphasized in my interpretation of Hume's account of general ideas (§2.4) that it was the reliance on language—the need for a term to trigger the associative disposition that made the thought count as general—that enabled him to introduce the social and normative element into our conceptual life. There are rules that determine which generalizing associations are correct. Though I have suggested that the mental structure that makes general thought possible is analogous to the structure involved in the belief in continued existence, the linguistic element in Hume's analysis of general ideas has not yet reappeared in his account of object awareness. But I think we can see him implicitly relying on a linguistic element if we integrate his earlier coherence account of the belief in continued existence into the constancy account. And I think he points to such an integration both, briefly, in "Of the antient philosophy" (T 1.4.3) and, in more detail, in "Of personal identity" (T 1.4.6), when he elaborates on and extends the account of our identity beliefs, I_n, from SwS. I discuss the details of his account as it applies to persons or minds in Chapter 6, but he approaches this topic in "Of personal identity" by first considering our beliefs about the identity through time of natural objects, artifacts, plants, and animals, "there being a great analogy betwixt [these], and the identity of a self or person" (T 1.4.6.5, SBN 253).[32]

He extends there the account of the belief in the unchanging object that persists in time (§3.2.2) to explain how we believe that a changing object remains identical through time:

We have a distinct idea of an object, that remains invariable and uninterrupted thro' a suppos'd variation of time; and this idea we call that of *identity* or *sameness*. We have also a distinct idea of several different objects existing in succession, and connected together by a close relation; and this to an accurate view affords as perfect a notion of *diversity*, as if there was no manner of relation among the objects. But tho' these two ideas of identity, and a succession of related objects be in themselves perfectly distinct, and even contrary, yet 'tis certain, that in our common way of thinking they are generally confounded with each other. That action of the imagination, by which we consider the uninterrupted and invariable object, and that by which we reflect on the succession of related objects, are almost the same to the feeling, nor is there much more effort of thought requir'd in the latter case than in the former. The relation facilitates the transition of the mind from one object to another, and renders its passage as smooth as if it contemplated one continu'd object. This resemblance is the cause of the confusion and mistake, and makes us substitute the notion of identity, instead of that of related objects.   (T 1.4.6.6, SBN 253–4)

---

[32] In the passage that I have quoted Hume restricts the analogy to the identity-beliefs about "plants and animals" and about persons or minds. But he then goes on to use examples such as a mass of matter (T 1.4.6.8, SBN 255), a planet (T 1.4.6.9, SBN 256), and a ship (T 1.4.6.11, SBN 257), making it clear he wants the analogy to be broader than he states. As I discuss in more detail in Chapter 6, Hume here is breaking with Locke, who thinks we need distinct accounts of identity for different categories of things—non-living natural objects, artifacts, plants and animals, and persons. Hume also breaks with the "antient" philosophers who treat these different categories similarly, in terms of an ontology of substance, whereby a continuing unchanging form preserves the identities of things despite the changes in their accidents (T 1.4.3).

We respond to the related objects of which we have ongoing experience as if we were encountering a steadfast object. Similarly, when our experience of related objects is interrupted, it feels sufficiently like the experience of interrupted qualitatively identical objects, and we respond to the former as we do to the latter by assuming that we are encountering the same object, despite the interruptions and changes. We "boldly assert these different related objects are in effect the same, however interrupted and variable" (T 1.4.6.6, SBN 254). Our responding in this manner means that the object of which we have interrupted experiences has imperfect identity, as opposed to the perfect identity exemplified by the unchanging object of which we have uninterrupted experience.

Thus we can see Hume, in "Of personal identity," as extending the four-step account from SwS to apply not only to cases of constantly experienced objects, but also to *coherently* experienced ones. In the former case, our experiences are qualitatively indistinguishable, and thus the natural relation of resemblance associates our ideas, causing us to overlook the changes in our experiences. But resemblance can extend beyond qualitative indistinguishability, and contiguity and causation are natural relations in addition to resemblance. These other relations also associate our ideas in such a way that we overlook the changes in our experiences. Hume gives a series of examples, each involving an increase in the diversity of our experience, where we nonetheless find objects to be imperfectly identical.

First, we continue to find an object the same even while it changes when the change is proportionally small relative to the whole, such as the "addition or diminution of a mountain ... to a planet" (T 1.4.6.9, SBN 256). Second, we continue to find imperfect identity when an object changes "gradually and insensibly" (T 1.4.6.10, SBN 257). Third, we tolerate more significant changes when such changes are oriented towards a "common end or purpose," such as a ship (T 1.4.6.11, SBN 257). Fourth, we accept even more dramatic changes—an acorn growing into an oak—while still finding imperfect identity, when the parts have a "mutual dependence" or "sympathy" with one another, as in a plant or animal (T 1.4.6.12, SBN 257). Fifth, we often treat things the same in kind as if they were one imperfectly identical thing, as when we say that the church newly constructed after the fire is the same as the one it replaced (T 1.4.6.13, SBN 258). And finally, sixth, Hume allows that pretty much any change whatsoever can be tolerated while we continue to find imperfect identity, so long as it is taken to be "natural and essential" to things of that kind, such as the ongoing changes in a river (T 1.4.6.14, SBN 258). In this case, the changing object must be seen in light of our linguistically structured concepts, as described in §2.4.[33] Thus there is a sense in which questions of identity are not metaphysical, but rather "grammatical" or "verbal," ultimately

---

[33] Thus at T 1.3.2.2 (SBN 74), when explaining how we can use reason to actively investigate the identity of objects (as opposed to the non-rational, instinctive belief that is the focus of SwS), he explicitly notes that we consider "whether [interruptions and changes] be common in that *species* of objects" (emphasis added).

dependent on our conventions for tolerating change in an object (T 1.4.6.21, SBN 262).

I think that we should see Hume here as subsuming the coherence-based explan-ation of I_n in the constancy-based one.[34] As I noted in §3.1, he relies on our expectations for kinds of objects when explaining why we believe that objects that change coherently persist even while unobserved. I raised three objections to the account. First, it starts too far along in the process, taking our experiences to involve image-contents as if of objects ('image' in sense [c] that I distinguished in §2.3) rather than the most primitive kinds of images that involve merely a patterned array of colours and feels (sense [a] in §2.3). Second, the reliance on general ideas in the coherence-based account presupposes our already having developed conceptions of objects as falling into kinds that persist beyond our perceptions of them. Third, Hume relies on causal association in this account, but his explanation of causal association took for granted that our experience is as of mind-independent objects. With the explanation of imperfect identity across interrupted experiences, Hume has the beginnings of a response to these objections.

In particular, I think that Hume can be seen as providing the rough outlines of a developmental story about how we respond to our experiential input. At first, as infants, we are given merely the pixelated array of coloured and tangible points (along with the non-spatial sensations such as smells and tastes) that pre-exist the fictions of the imagination—an image in sense (a) from §2.3. The fiction of the steadfast object emerges when, say, we stare unblinkingly at the red spot on the toy suspended over the crib for a few moments. The impression of red during this period is unchanging, but we continue to be aware of the Jamesian "blooming, buzzing confusion" that our senses otherwise afford us.[35] The ingredients for the belief that the red object is one thing throughout these changes are in place. We start to have a feel for the experience of the unchanging as persisting in time. Of course, we also have frequent interruptions in our experience of the red spot:

[W]e shut [our] eyes, and afterwards open them; and find the new perceptions to resemble perfectly those, which formerly struck [our] senses. This resemblance is observ'd in a thousand instances, and naturally connects together our ideas of these interrupted perceptions by the strongest relation, and conveys the mind with an easy transition from one to another

(T 1.4.2.35, SBN 204).

Now, despite the interruptions in our experiences, we come to believe that the red spot is the same because our experience feels so similar to that which occurs when we are staring. This belief in the identity of an object across very brief interruptions

---

[34] This interpretation is the opposite of Louis Loeb's. He thinks that Hume could have treated constancy as the minimal case of coherence, and thus used the coherence-based inertia explanation to address the constancy-based beliefs (*Stability and Justification*, ch. 6). Loeb is here following Price (*Hume's Theory*, 60–5).

[35] William James, *Principles of Psychology* (Cambridge, MA: Harvard University Press, 1981), 462.

presumably is extended as we become accustomed to various regularities in our experience, so that we come to allow for changes in perspective caused by a movement of the eyes or the head, as well as for longer and longer interruptions. We come to think of very simple objects as continuing identically while unperceived, and thus start to develop a conception of a world of stable objects.

With the six extensions of this basic mechanism, Hume seems to be gesturing at how we refine this basic conception, allowing for more complex kinds of objects as we become accustomed to different kinds of regularities in experience. And of course at the same time as we are developing the habits essential to the fiction of continued existence, we also develop the habits involved in causal beliefs and in general ideas. The linguistic element in general ideas is especially important, for as we are trained by our parents and others to match signs (gestural, verbal, or written) with ideas, we also become more skilled at finding meaningful resemblances between things. We *learn* "what is natural and essential to any thing" (T 1.4.6.14, SBN 258), as we are told what an acorn is and which trees are oaks. As Hume says in a 1767 letter to William Mure, "the continual Application of the Words and Phrazes teaches us at the same time the Sense of the Words and their Reference to each other" (L 2, 157).[36]

The three objections to the coherence account I noted in §3.1 can be avoided if Hume can successfully make out the developmental story sketched here. The pixelated array of coloured and tangible points becomes an image in sense (c)—an image as of an object—when the imagination develops the habits that constitute our believing that things, of various level of complexity, persist in an objective world around us. The reliance on kind terms and causal notions in his original coherence-based account of the belief in continued existence is unproblematic if Hume can show that all of these habits arise in tandem. Once we develop a fairly stable conception of a world of continuing objects of various kinds, then the coherence-based explanation can do its work.

It is striking, however, that Hume himself never mentions—or even hints at—a developmental story of this sort.[37] There are no indications that SwS should be read developmentally, even though such an approach seems not only plausible, but altogether mandated for someone who thinks that mental habits are at the root of

---

[36] See Claudia Schmidt, *David Hume: Reason in History* (University Park, PA: Pennsylvania State University Press, 2003), 39. She also notes there that in a letter of 1754, Hume goes so far as to say: "'Tis certain we always think in some language, viz. in that which is most familiar to us; and 'tis but too frequent to substitute words instead of ideas" (L 1, 201).

[37] Peter Strawson sees the absence of "empirical psychology" that investigates such things as "infantile development" as a sign that Hume backs away from a "more thoroughgoing naturalism" (*Skepticism and Naturalism: Some Varieties* [New York, NY: Columbia University Press, 1985], 12). Janet Broughton worries that Hume's neglect both of the question of "*when* the productive sequences of events" occur that yield the belief in body and of a possible answer that appeals to infant development, reveals a "relatively narrow notion of explanation" based merely in causal links between perceptions and the habits they engender ("Hume's Explanation of Causal Inference," in Paul Hoffman, David Owen, and Gideon Yaffe [eds.], *Contemporary Perspectives on Early Modern Philosophy* [Peterborough, ON: Broadview Press, 2008], 303–4).

the explanandum's beliefs, and that such habits are acquired in experience. Interestingly, Hume does point to a role for a developmental story in his treatment of causal beliefs. He notes that our causal expectations must develop incrementally:

The probabilities of causes are of several kinds; but are all deriv'd from the same origin, *viz. the association of ideas to a present impression.* As the habit, which produces the association, arises from the frequent conjunction of objects, it must arrive at its perfection by degrees, and must acquire new force from each instance, that falls under our observation. The first instance has little or no force: The second makes some addition to it: The third becomes still more sensible; and 'tis by these slow steps, that our judgment arrives at a full assurance.... 'Tis worthy of remark on this occasion, that tho' the species of probability here explain'd be the first in order, and naturally takes place before any entire proof can exist, yet no one, who is arriv'd at the age of maturity, can any longer be acquainted with it.   (T 1.3.12.2–3, SBN 130–1)

Hume admits that, as adults, we sometimes encounter novel objects and are unsure how they will behave. But nonetheless, our years of experience with regularities in objects have already primed us to believe in the uniformity of nature. A similar point could be made about our belief in an objective world. Though we sometimes encounter novel objects, and are unsure how they behave when unobserved, our experience hitherto has primed us to expect a world of mind-independent objects. We try to fit the novel object into the categories with which we are familiar: the ephemeral, like Locke's bubbles on the water; the short-lived, like a flower's bloom; the relatively long-lasting, like a tree; and the nearly indestructible, like a rock or a star.

When Hume does consider what it would be like to experience the world without the pre-existing expectation that nature will be uniform, he turns not to infants, but to Adam, "created in the full vigour of understanding, without experience" (T Abs.11, SBN 650), who is unable to infer that the collision of one billiard ball with another will cause the second to move. Hume does not pause to note, however, that until Adam had developed the appropriate associative habits in his imagination, he would be unable to recognize that such a ball is one continued item even when he blinks or turns his head.[38]

One reason that Hume might have shied away from presenting an openly developmental account of the explanandum's beliefs could be the difficulty of acquiring the right kind of evidence for it. We saw in Chapter 2 (§2.2) that his approach to the "anatomy of mind" requires that he introspect in order to observe the operation of his mental principles. How can he observe the emergence of the habits involved in our belief in continuing, mind-independent objects?[39] As an adult he is already fully accustomed to the vulgar sense of immersion in the world.

---

[38] Perhaps by saying that Adam is in the "full vigour of the understanding," Hume means to suggest that he has developed sufficiently to take himself to move in an objective world.

[39] In §4.3.2 I suggest that Hume believes that the same associative reactions that constitute the vulgar sense of immersion in the world are also involved in the philosopher's introspective beliefs about the

But recall that Hume sometimes analogizes introspection to the observation of perceptions in "the breast of another" (T 1.4.6.18, SBN 260); I called this the first grade of introspection in §2.2. Thus it might seem possible to theorize about mental development by using such third-personal observation of an infant. But, because he also acknowledges that this kind of introspection is a mere thought experiment, where the findings are the result of analogical reasoning from one's own reflective investigations, it could not be used to shed light on infant experience; the analogy is not in place. Moreover, Hume was familiar, and probably unimpressed, with other early modern philosophers who did offer developmental stories—what Locke calls "conjecture[s] concerning things not very capable of examination" (E II.ix.5). Malebranche, for example, describes the experiences of the infant as it leaves the birth canal, and is shocked by the brightness of the sun (ST II.i.8, 125–6).[40] The reasoning here is sufficiently unpersuasive that Hume might have thought it was better simply to avoid an analysis of infant experience. The human being develops into someone who believes in the independent existence of objects, and at that point the mechanisms Hume describes in SwS are operative in her or him.

3.3 Objects

I argued in §2.2 that Hume understands the vulgar beliefs about body that he takes as his explanandum in SwS to explicitly concern only objects, and not the vulgar's impressions of them: they believe, of the table of which they have impressions, that it (the table) exists. But I left how best to understand objects, such as the table, as an open question. We can now return to that issue.[41] In my presentation of Hume's explanation of the belief in the continued existence of objects (§§3.2.3–3.2.5), I have emphasized that, though a sensation in isolation merely presents an image-content,

---

mind—that the perceptions they observe within exist independently of their being introspected. Thus it is *impossible* for an anatomist of mind to observe the mind prior to the emergence of the propensities that produce the explanandum's beliefs, C_n and D_n. The propensities must already be in place for introspection to be possible.

[40] See also ST II.i.7, 117, 119–20.

[41] One problem here is the multiple ambiguity in Hume's use of the term 'object.' First, it can refer to the table, pens, hats, and stones that the vulgar take themselves to encounter. Second, philosophers redescribe these vulgar objects as "external" objects, where their externality is glossed as mind-independence in two different ways, as their being either "specifically different" from perceptions or the same in kind as perceptions while differing in "relations, connexions and durations" (T 1.2.6.9, SBN 68). Third, philosophers also use 'object' generically, to mean something like 'object of awareness,' so that perceptions or their image-contents count as mental objects. Fourth, the interpretation of Hume's theory of mind that I have developed here distinguishes between the proximate content in a state of awareness—such as a particular in the case of a general idea, or the image-content in the case of a sensory perception—and the intended object, such as a universal or an object in the second sense. Fifth, in Book 2 Hume introduces yet another sense of 'object' in terms of the ultimate focus of attention in the indirect passions, a person, either oneself (in the cases of pride and humility; T 2.1.2.2, SBN 277) or another (in the cases of love and hatred; T 2.2.1.2, SBN 329). My focus in this section is primarily on the first two of these senses. See the catalogue of Hume's usage in Marjorie Grene, "The Objects of Hume's *Treatise*," *Hume Studies* 20 (1994), 163–77.

the imagination responds to constant and coherent sensations to yield the thought of an intended object that is taken to have a temporal duration typical of things of its kind. In having, at one particular moment, an impression with an image-content as of the table, I think of the table as something that was built some time ago and will end when it is burned or crushed or collapsed. My intended object is not the table-as-seen-by-me-at-this-moment, but the table as a public object that has a determinate history and a probable future and that others can also encounter. When I sense unfamiliar things, I rely on their resemblance to those things I have previously encountered in order to (fallibly) construct a temporal path for them.

In this explanation, Hume gives us an account of how we come to *think of* the everyday objects we encounter around us by means of our senses. But what *are* they?[42] Are they, as Berkeley insists, "congeries" of ideas (D 3, 249)? Or are they, as realists such as Locke hold, something wholly mind-independent, best characterized by the sciences in terms of primary qualities? Hume's answers to these questions are less than straightforward in part because of his strategy of approaching such ontological questions by means of an investigation of how we think of the entities in question. Thus I start my discussion by considering the final three paragraphs of the Section "Of the idea of existence, and of external existence" (T 1.2.6, hereafter 'IEEE'), where Hume addresses the idea of external objects. His full answers to the ontological questions will emerge only after Chapter 4's discussion of the sceptical portions of SwS, Chapter 6's consideration of the "modern philosophy" (defined in terms of the primary–secondary quality distinction), and ultimately Chapter's 7's interpretation of Hume's final confrontation with scepticism in the "Conclusion of this book" (T 1.4.7).

In IEEE, Hume relies on his core empiricist, copy principle (§2.4) that, since (almost) all of our ideas must ultimately be copied from prior simple impressions, we can think only of things that were at some point directly experienced and objects compounded out of them. In particular, we cannot "form an idea of anything specifically different from ideas and impressions" (T 1.2.6.8, SBN 67):

The farthest we can go towards a conception of external objects, when suppos'd *specifically* different from our perceptions, is to form a relative idea of them, without pretending to comprehend the related objects. Generally speaking we do not suppose them specifically different; but only attribute to them different relations, connexions and durations. But of this more fully hereafter.   (T 1.2.6.9, SBN 68)

Hume appends a footnote to the final sentence, pointing us forward to SwS, and there he says that talk of objects, like tables, in C_n, D_n, and I_n, has to be understood with the tables being considered the same in kind, but different in "relations, connexions and

---

[42] Baxter distinguishes between "what an idea represents there as being" and "what there is which an idea represents" (*Hume's Difficulty*, 51ff). The vulgar's perceptions represent there as being continuing objects with which others can equally interact. The question I consider here concerns what there is which the vulgar perceptions represent.

durations." "For as to the notion of external existence, when taken for something specifically different from our perceptions, we have already shown its absurdity" (T 1.4.2.2, SBN 188). A footnote then directs us back to IEEE.

These related passages pose three difficulties. First, we have seen that Hume allows that, despite the limitations of the copy principle, fictions enable us to think of intended objects that can never be directly experienced (§2.4), and that the continuants that the vulgar take to exist themselves result from fictions (§3.2.5). How do they relate to the external objects described here? Second, what does it mean to distinguish between external objects that are taken to be "specifically different" from perceptions, and objects that are the same in kind as perceptions, but different in "relations, connexions and durations"? And, third, given that Hume does allow in IEEE that we can think of external objects in both of these ways, at least to some extent, why in SwS does he declare that taking objects as specifically different from perceptions is an "absurdity"? I address the first question in §3.3.1, and the other two in §3.3.2.

3.3.1 Vulgar Objects

As a starting point, it is important to note that in this portion of IEEE, Hume's topic is how *philosophers* can understand external objects. Hume's rejection of Locke's analysis of sensation means that the vulgar, being blind to the perceptual mediation of their experiences, will not conceive of their objects, such as a table, as *external*. Not being aware of the role perceptions play in affording them their awareness of the table, they do not take themselves to have some special *internal* relationship to their perceptions of the table, where it must then be considered as *external*. They are simply aware of the table, over there, beside the window. It is the introspecting philosophers who recognize that the vulgar experience of objects is mediated by perceptions. Hume introduces his discussion of the idea of external existence by saying:

We may observe, that 'tis universally allow'd *by philosophers*, and is besides pretty obvious of itself, that nothing is ever really present with the mind but its perceptions or impressions and ideas, and that external objects become known to us only by those perceptions they occasion.
(T 1.2.6.7, SBN 67; emphasis added)

When philosophers make their characteristic introspective moves, they recognize perceptions as mental entities, and thus can interpret the vulgar as holding that ordinary objects, like the table, are external in the sense of being mind-independent. (Hume's claim that the perceptual mediation of our awareness of objects is "pretty obvious of itself" will be echoed in the latter portions of SwS, where he says that it take "a very little reflection and philosophy" [T 1.4.2.44, SBN 210] or "a little reflection" [T 1.4.2.50, SBN 214] to undermine vulgar belief; I consider Hume's repeated emphasis on the ease of this kind of reflective move in §4.5.)

The challenge for Hume is to explain how an introspecting philosopher can characterize the content of the vulgar belief when interpreted in these terms. The first difficulty I noted above stems from Hume's empiricist requirement that all ideas acquire their content from prior impressions. If impressions are internal entities, how is it possible for us, as philosophers, even to *think* of external entities?

> Let us fix our attention out of ourselves as much as possible: Let us chace our imagination to the heavens, or to the utmost limits of the universe; we never really advance a step beyond ourselves, nor can conceive any kind of existence, but those perceptions, which have appear'd in that narrow compass.   (T 1.2.6.8, SBN 67–8)

Nonetheless, Hume immediately qualifies this point in the passage quoted above, admitting that there are two senses in which we can think of external objects, either as "specifically different" from perceptions, or as the same in kind but different in "relations, connexions and durations" from perceptions (T 1.2.6.9, SBN 68). The latter, Hume tells us, is how "generally speaking" we conceive of external objects, and it is this notion that he says, in SwS, fits with the vulgar's beliefs.

We have seen in §2.3 that the introspecting philosopher observes ideas and impressions with their image-contents, whereas the vulgar belief is not about them, but about the persisting thing. In the most basic form of introspection that I identified in §2.2, philosophers simply retain their vulgar sense of immersion in the world, whereby they take for granted that there are such (intended) objects as the fire or the table at the same time as they observe perceptions of them. But once, as in SwS, they start to investigate sensory beliefs themselves, using what I called the second grade of introspection, they need some way to describe those objects appropriately without simply reverting to the vulgar immersion in the world.

Moreover, once philosophers start using introspection to investigate vulgar beliefs about objects, they learn that the image-content in the vulgar awareness of spatial objects is ultimately an array of coloured or tangible points. Thus far in my interpretation of Hume's explanandum in SwS (C_n, D_n, and I_n), I have de-emphasized his analysis of spatial impressions by suggesting that these beliefs concern the table of which we have impressions, as if impressions were *of tables* rather than merely presenting coloured and tangible arrays. In light of the explanation of C_n and I_n given in §3.2, however, we can modify the naive interpretation of the explanandum to incorporate Hume's more detailed analysis:

(C_n') The belief, of the image-content of prior impressions displaying constancy or coherence, that a persisting, public object (say, a table) exists.[43]

(D_n') The belief, of the image-content of occurrent impressions displaying constancy or coherence with prior impressions, that a persisting, public object (say, a table) exists.

---

[43] A further qualification could be added to this clause (and its analogues in D_n and I_n): a public object (such as the table) exists in a particular spatial location (say, under the window).

(I_n')   The belief, of the image-content of prior impressions that display constancy or coherence with occurrent impressions, that it is one continuing object (the table).

Whereas the original C_n, D_n, and I_n involved ascribing to the vulgar *de re* beliefs about such things as the table of which they have sensations (while *de dicto* their beliefs concerned the table itself, without reference to the sensations), the revised C_n', D_n', and I_n' make the *de re* ascriptions solely about the impressions, with the table showing up only in a *de dicto* ascription. The philosophers introspectively investigating the vulgar belief commit themselves existentially only to the perceptions.

I think that the revised analysis of the vulgar belief sheds light on Hume's claim in IEEE that the vulgar (all of us, "generally speaking") treat everyday objects as the same in kind as perceptions but differing in "relations, connexions and durations" (T 1.2.6.9, SBN 68). The philosopher both recognizes that the vulgar take such things as the table to be ongoing public objects and at the same time holds that ultimately their beliefs concern perceptual image-contents. For example, the vulgar might, in having constant or coherent impressions with brown trapezoidal image-content, have the table, over there, by the window, as their intended object. The intended object has different relations from the image-content, in that, for example, the table has a book on it, while its image-content does not. The intended object is connected differently from the image-content, in that the brown, trapezoidal image-content is essentially an object of one person's consciousness (in the sense of generic awareness I noted in §2.3), while the table can be encountered by others. And the intended object's duration, from when it was first constructed by the carpenter, until it is crushed in the earthquake or burns in the fire, is different from the duration of the image-content, which lasts only as long as the perceiver looks at the table from that one particular perspective. Nonetheless, the philosopher, in recognizing that the thought of the intended object results from the imagination's reactions to the image-content, can still make sense of it as arising from our impressions and ideas. And just as in §2.4, I suggested that our common reactions, when disciplined by linguistic rules, constitute universals, so also with external objects themselves. Thus the philosopher then can continue to describe the vulgar's intended object as not "specifically different" from perceptions. Let us call objects understood in this manner *vulgar objects*.

It is important to note that Hume does not mean this claim *metaphysically*: he is not asserting that the universe is made up of perceptions. Even if he will, on occasion, make bold claims about the physical world, especially earlier in Part 2 of Book 1 where he argues that space itself must be merely finitely divisible because our perceptions of it are only finitely divisible (T 1.2.2),[44] Hume's project is ultimately "to explain the nature and principles *of the human mind*" (T 1.1.2.1, SBN 8; emphasis

---

[44] See my "Adequate Ideas."

added). Thus his topic in IEEE is the *idea* of external existence, and his point is that philosophers can *think* of the vulgar's conception of external objects as being just like perceptual image-contents, only not necessarily fleeting or mind-dependent. The mechanism for the imagination's construction of intended objects shows that the vulgar are in fact aware of nothing other than image-contents when thinking of persisting tables, fires, and the like.

In order for the philosophers' claim to have metaphysical import, Hume would need to hold that their perspective is epistemically superior to that of the vulgar. The philosophers would then be able to assert what was *really* the case. I argue in Chapter 4, however, that Hume holds that while some philosophers do assert their superiority, they should ultimately recognize that their opinions *about perceptions* depend on the very same imaginative propensities as the vulgar opinions *about everyday objects*. So an attempt to use the philosophical perspective to usurp the vulgar perspective ends up also usurping the philosophical perspective. Instead, we should learn that the philosophers can describe the vulgar's external objects as the same in kind as perceptual image-contents, though persisting even when not sensed. I argue in Chapter 7 that Hume holds that "true sceptics" will recognize that the vulgar faith in the deliverances of the senses and of introspection is ineliminable. We do not have the vantage point we would need to reject the vulgar belief in body, even as we learn that our communal responses to sensory input causes this belief.

In the middle of SwS, Hume returns to this issue briefly, when he considers a possible objection to his constancy-based account of the vulgar belief in continued existence. Recall that we substitute the idea of a steadfast object when having interrupted, qualitatively identical impressions; but, because there is a tension between our thought of the persisting unchanging object and the interruptions in the impressions, we suppose that the steadfast object persists unperceived. At this point, Hume considers a possible Berkeleyan objection. The fiction of the steadfast object involves an unchanging *perception* over a period of time. The fiction of the continued existence is of something that continues while we are *not* aware of it. But "as the *appearance* of a perception in the mind and its *existence* seem at first sight entirely the same, it may be doubted, whether we can ever assent to so palpable a contradiction, and suppose a perception to exist without being present to the mind" (T 1.4.2.37, SBN 206).

As Norman Kemp Smith and others have pointed out, this is not a contradiction that the vulgar would find palpable.[45] They do not make ontological assumptions about perceptions and their mind dependence, in that the vulgar take themselves to be directly in touch with the world around them, and do not usually recognize that their experience is perceptually mediated. Philosophers, however, have been primed by Berkeley to believe that the *esse* of a perception is its *percipi* (P 1.3). In fact, this

---

[45] Norman Kemp Smith, *Philosophy of David Hume* (London: Macmillan, 1941), 478. See also Allison, *Custom and Reason*, 243.

way of putting the point is a bit awkward given that, for Hume, we do not *perceive* perceptions (unless the noun here is taken as an internal accusative—a nominalization of the mental activity). Using the framework we have been developing here, the Berkelyan point should be rephrased in terms of image-contents. As in the discussion of mental transparency in §2.3, the content of the image is simply whatever it is we are aware or "conscious" of, and thus the being of the image is constituted by our awareness of it.

But the vulgar, in being aware of the image-content, are at the same time carried along by the imagination's fiction of a continued existence, and thus they do not recognize the image *as an image*. Like the example of someone who sees a dog in a mirror without knowing that they are looking at a mirror (so that the image in the mirror is an image in sense [c] from §2.3), the vulgar take themselves to be directly in contact with a dog. And so, just as the dependency of the mirror-image on the one who unknowingly looks in the mirror is invisible to him, the dependency of the image-content on their awareness of it is invisible to the vulgar. Only a philosopher, who has temporarily suspended the imagination's associations and made a reflective look within, will recognize the image as an image and its dependency on her being aware of it. Hume pauses at this point to discuss two questions:

First, How we can satisfy ourselves in supposing a perception to be absent from the mind without being annihilated. *Secondly*, After what manner we conceive an object to become present to the mind, without some new creation of a perception or image; and what we mean by this *seeing*, and *feeling*, and *perceiving*.   (T 1.4.2.38, SBN 207)

As was the case with the idea of external existence in IEEE, the questions here arise for philosophers, and are in that sense somewhat incidental to Hume's goal in this part of SwS, where his focus is on the vulgar's beliefs. His concern is only to fend off the accusation that he has ascribed to the vulgar a belief that is literally unthinkable, that perceptual image-content could exist without simultaneously being perceived.

Hume's answers to these questions rely on both IEEE and his later discussion of how philosophers should properly understand the mind as a bundle—"a heap or collection"—of perceptions, lacking intrinsic unity at a time or across time (T 1.4.2.39, SBN 207; see T 1.4.6, towards which Hume points us in a footnote to T 1.4.2.36, SBN 206). While a full analysis of the bundle theory will have to wait until Chapter 6, Hume here emphasizes that we can conceive perceptions as existing apart from the bundle, and this capacity gives philosophers a way to understand how the vulgar conceive of external objects. As the discussion in IEEE indicates, they are just like the image-contents of which sensations make us aware, but with different "relations, connexions and durations" (T 1.2.6.9, SBN 68). Philosophers should thus model "seeing, and feeling, and perceiving" in terms of a vulgar object that is sometimes present to the mind and sometimes absent.

3.3.2 *Non-perceptual Objects*

In IEEE, Hume also allows that there is a very attenuated sense in which introspecting philosophers can think of external objects that are different in kind from perceptions—what I will call *non-perceptual objects*.[46] They can "form a relative idea of them, without pretending to comprehend the related objects" (T 1.2.6.9, SBN 68). But what does this mean?

Relations, for Hume, are complex ideas in which we recognize the relata to be connected in one of seven different ways: resemblance, identity, spatiotemporal relations, quantitative relations, qualitative relations, contrariety, and causation (T 1.1.5). Note that in keeping with Hume's treatment of general ideas (§2.4), particular instances of relations are prior to general versions of them. Consider, for example, the qualitative relation 'darker than.' We first find that *this* particular shade of blue relates in a certain manner to *that* particular shade of beige; we find that *this* particular moonless night relates in a similar manner to *that* particular cloudy day; and so on.[47] When we are suitably conditioned by the resemblances between these particular relatings, we form a general version of 'darker than' using one of these particular relations as the proximate content, and the others as part of the revival set.[48] With this preparation we could form a "relative idea" of a shade darker than a particular patch of green. The preexisting revival set would allow us to think of those objects that would satisfy the description.

In IEEE, Hume raises the possibility that we could think of non-perceptual objects in a similar fashion, even though we can otherwise think only of image-contents or vulgar objects. The problem is that the above sketch of relative ideas suggests that we must have prior instances where we successfully think of the relation in question before we can deploy our grasp of it in a relative idea. But we do not have that option available to us for non-perceptual objects. The relative idea would be the *only* means we could think of them. For example, in the final quarter of SwS, where Hume

---

[46] Daniel Flage uses this term similarly; "Relative Ideas Re-viewed," in R. Read and K. Richman (eds.), *The New Hume Debate* (London: Routledge, 2000), 139.

[47] Given Hume's views on general ideas, our initial encounters with a relation such as 'darker than' cannot be put in its terms. Instead, we find the objects to be related in a specific way, and we find the next pair to be related in a resembling specific way, with the resemblance between these relatings eventually causing us to form the general relation, 'darker than.'

[48] Michael Costa neglects that the ideas of pairs of objects in the revival set must themselves be *relatings*: cases of our comparing the objects in (a particularized version of) one of the seven different kinds of relations that Hume allows for at T 1.1.5. Costa instead takes the ideas of object-pairs in the revival set to be of objects that *are related* in the relevant way, though not *recognized* as such (the ideas in the revival set would thus be co-thinkings, rather than relatings). Such a view would not allow Hume to distinguish co-extensive relations such as 'having the same number of sides as' and 'having the same number of angles as' in comparisons of plane figures; or 'having more protons and neutrons than' and 'being heavier than' (and note that the latter relations are, for Hume, different types of relations, the former being quantitative and the latter being qualitative). See Michael Costa, "Hume on the Very Idea of a Relation," *Hume Studies* 24 (1998), 71–94.

interrogates philosophical responses to our sensory beliefs, he notes that we could not use causal relations to move from a perception to a non-perceptual object:

But as no beings are ever present to the mind but perceptions; it follows that we may observe a conjunction or a relation of cause and effect between different perceptions, but can never observe it between perceptions and objects.[49] 'Tis impossible, therefore, that from the existence or any of the qualities of the former, we can ever form any conclusion concerning the existence of the latter, or ever satisfy our reason in this particular.   (T 1.4.2.47, SBN 212)

A similar point should apply to all of the other relations.

Note, however, that Hume ends his initial presentation of relations by considering whether 'difference' should be added to his list of the seven relations: "But that I consider rather as a negation of relation, than as any thing real or positive. Difference is of two kinds as oppos'd either to identity or resemblance. The first is call'd a difference of *number*; the other of *kind*" (T 1.1.5.10, SBN 15). Accordingly, when we use a relative idea to think of a non-perceptual object—an object "specifically" different or different *in kind* from perceptions—we are really relying on our perceptually dependent grasp of resemblance in order to *negate* its application to a perception and the non-perceptual object. Whatever the non-perceptual object is, it is *not* like a perception. And that is all we can say of it: we cannot "pretend to comprehend the related objects," because any such attempt would introduce into them a resemblance to perceptions that would no longer leave them as specifically different.[50]

The third difficulty I noted in the conception of object at work in IEEE concerns Hume's attitude towards non-perceptual objects in SwS, where immediately after introducing the explanandum's beliefs, he says that the objects therein must be understood as vulgar objects, "[f]or as to the notion of external existence, when taken for something specifically different from our perceptions, [footnote to IEEE] we have already shewn its absurdity" (T 1.4.2.2, SBN 188). Given that he has allowed that we can (barely) conceive of non-perceptual objects in IEEE, I think his point must be that it would be absurd to interpret the objects that the vulgar take themselves to encounter as non-perceptual objects. The vulgar are not in the

---

[49] I argue that 'object' here should be taken to be referring to non-perceptual objects in §4.5.

[50] Hume harks back to this distinction in "Of the immateriality of the soul" (T 1.4.5), saying: "[A]s every idea is deriv'd from a preceding perception, 'tis impossible our idea of a perception, and that of an object or external existence can ever represent what are specifically different from each other. Whatever difference we may suppose betwixt them, 'tis still incomprehensible to us; and we are oblig'd either to conceive an external object merely as a relation without a relative, or to make it the very same with a perception or impression" (T 1.4.5.19, SBN 241). Though Allison does not discuss Hume's treatment of differences of kind, I think that he is right to interpret Hume's description of a non-perceptual object as "a relation without a relative" to mean that it is a "relative without a *relation*" (*Custom and Reason*, 255); we cannot specify a relation as obtaining between the non-perceptual object and a perception without thereby making it into a vulgar object.

introspective position of observing their perceptions and recognizing them as such, and so they cannot even begin to think of non-perceptual objects.

We will see in the following chapters, however, that introspecting philosophers do often try to make positive claims about non-perceptual objects, and accordingly fall into confusion. In particular, what Hume calls "false philosophy" emerges when philosophers take claims that apply only to vulgar objects and try to apply them to non-perceptual objects. The "true philosopher," in contrast, accepts that our access to non-perceptual objects is so limited as to preclude any substantive claims about them (T 1.4.3.9–10, SBN 222–4). They thus recognize that we have a limited, "human" perspective on nature—one that precludes our saying how things are in their "real nature and operations" independently of our understanding (T 1.2.5.26n12, SBN 638–9).

3.4 Are the Vulgar in Error?

In the preceding explanations of the psychological mechanism for our beliefs about the continued existence of body, Hume has repeatedly emphasized how we make *mistakes*. We believe *falsely* that the image as of the table that we are aware of one occasion is the same as the image as of it on another occasion:

This propension to bestow an identity on our resembling perceptions, produces the fiction of a continu'd existence; since that fiction, as well as the identity, is really false, as is acknowledg'd by all philosophers, and has no other effect than to remedy the interruption of our perceptions, which is the only circumstance that is contrary to their identity.   (T 1.4.2.43, SBN 209)

Does Hume thus hold that the vulgar are always in error when they have sensory beliefs? I think not, or, in light of the clear assertion in the passage, they are not in error in any straightforward way. A full argument for this claim will have to await Chapter 4, but I do want to point out here that although he relies on the language of error throughout his psychological explanation, he does not seem to think that those kinds of error suffice for *the vulgar* to recognize the falsity of their beliefs. Recall that I suggested that these beliefs (C_n, D_n, and I_n) should be construed naively, so that the vulgar remain blind to the perceptual mediation of their experience of objects. They manifest an attitude that embodies those beliefs without explicitly formulating them.

The naive construal of the beliefs might help to explain why he raises the sceptical challenge to them only *after* he has finished his explanation of the belief in continued existence, when he has turned to explain the supposedly equivalent belief in the distinct existence of body, D_n:

But tho' we are led after this manner, by the natural propensity of the imagination, to ascribe a continu'd existence to those sensible objects or perceptions, which we find to resemble each other in their interrupted appearance; yet *a very little reflection and philosophy* is sufficient to make us perceive the fallacy of that opinion. I have already observ'd, that there is an intimate connexion betwixt those two principles, of a *continu'd* and of a *distinct* or *independent* existence, and that we no sooner establish the one than the other follows, as a necessary consequence. 'Tis the opinion of a continu'd existence, which first takes place, and without much study or reflection draws the other along with it, wherever the mind follows its first and most natural tendency. But when we compare experiments, and reason a little upon them, we quickly perceive, that the doctrine of the independent existence of our sensible perceptions is contrary to the plainest experience.

(T 1.4.2.44, SBN 210; emphasis added in the first italicized phrase)

In the following paragraph, Hume goes on to detail the experiments, rooted in the Pyrrhonian tradition, that show the mind-dependence of sensations (I investigate these experiments in §4.1). It is only at this point in SwS that Hume seems to acknowledge what he now takes to be "the fallacy of that [vulgar] opinion." And this seemingly *new* recognition forces him to go "backwards upon our footsteps to perceive our error in attributing a continu'd existence to our perceptions" (T 1.4.2.44, SBN 210), as if he had realized only then, in light of "reflection and philosophy," that the belief in continued existence was false. But if the explanation for the belief in continued existence in body openly relied on mistakes and errors, why does Hume not dwell on its falsity when first presenting the argument?

In answer to this question, consider that Hume's explanations for C_n and I_n relied on the idea-substitution mechanism. As I noted in §3.2.1, although this mechanism can yield error—as when I make claims about my blue sweater on the basis of memories of my grey sweater—it need not—as when I believe that an apple is red while entertaining ideas only of the words and not the thing. Hume's attitude to the idea of the vacuum is of course the most telling analogue for understanding his assessment of C_n and I_n. I noted above that he is willing to countenance claims about the vacuum, *so long as it is properly understood*, in terms of the fiction whereby we think of "bodies ... plac'd after such a manner, as to receive bodies betwixt them, without impulsion or penetration" (T 1.2.5.26n12, SBN 638–9). The point is that, in this fiction, the proximate content that is involved in the idea substitution is not the focus of our thoughts. The fiction, when established within a linguistic community, constitutes an intended object differ-ent from the content of either of the substituted ideas. We can thus distinguish between *constitutive* and *epistemic* mistakes. In the latter we make false claims of an object that we already have in mind, such as the sweater, whereas in the former we come to think of a new object by means of an error at the level of proximate content. Compare what happens when we see the television screen with its pixelated array of coloured points. We do not see the points as such, but rather 'mistake' them for an image as of a news anchor or sitcom character. In seeing the points we see the images as of the anchor or character because of their cumulative effect on our imaginative propensities (and visual faculties). Of course, such mistakes are the whole point of televisual transmission. The technology exploits various limitations of human nature in order for us to see more than the array of pixels that is transmitted to us.

I think that Hume can describe the mechanisms that produce C_n and I_n as involving mistakes and errors, while nonetheless not wanting to reject them for this reason, because the mistakes here are constitutive. When taking the table that I am sensing in my office to be the same as the table I last saw there, my thought is focused not on the proximate content of the image-content as of the table, but on the intended object of the three-dimensional wooden structure that has an underside hidden from view, and a trajectory in time and space. In mistaking my awareness of that image-content for the awareness of a persisting object, I am not making a claim *about* that content but rather engaging in the fiction that yields the thought of the intended object. Recall that, as I emphasized in §§2.2 and 2.3, we are not even aware of the image-content-qua-image until we have introspectively withdrawn from our associations. Not being aware of images, considered as such, we cannot make the epistemic error of taking one image to be a different one. Rather, as is the case of the television set, we simply react naturally in each of the cases. In being aware of each image in the right associative context, we thereby become aware of the continuing thing, the same thing at different times.

Returning to the analysis of general ideas in §2.4, we can see a similar point. Suppose I am reasoning from 'All dogs are loyal' and 'This Poodle is a dog' to 'This Poodle is loyal.' In thinking of the first premise, I must have a particular dog in mind—say my Golden Retriever, with her particular loyalty—along with the appropriate associative dispositions and linguistic markers that allow this thought to function as a universal. But this does not mean that I am in error when I then apply the major premise to the Poodle. The fact that the mind can slide between the Poodle and the Golden Retriever is what, for Hume, constitutes their both belonging to the same kind. Sometimes the imagination's natural propensities can allow us to think beyond the limits of our perceptions when taken one by one.

Reading Hume's explanation of the belief in the continued existence of body as relying on constitutive rather than epistemic mistakes and errors means that it should not be construed as being essentially sceptical. The best recent interpretations of Hume's account of causation in the *Treatise* make analogous points. Thus David Owen and Don Garrett both argue that although Hume emphasizes that the transition from the impression of a cause to the idea of its effect is "determin'd" (T 1.3.6.12, SBN 92) by custom, not reason, it does not follow that we *ipso facto* make an error. Rather, Hume has anatomized probabilistic *reasoning*, showing that it is constituted out of some of our associative propensities.[51] So also, I suggest, in the first three quarters of SwS: Hume has anatomized our *sensing of objects*, showing that it is constituted out of some of our associative propensities. And just as the sceptical challenge to reason happens after he has anatomized it, when Hume asks in SwR why we should believe in the outcome of a stretch of reasoning, so also the sceptical challenge to sensing occurs only after he has anatomized it. If we are really aware of mental images, not independently existing objects, why believe that we are in touch with the world? Hume takes up that sceptical challenge in the final quarter of SwS, starting at T 1.4.2.44, SBN 210. His response to it is the topic of Chapter 4.

[51] Don Garrett, *Cognition and Commitment in Hume's Philosophy* (New York, NY: Oxford University Press, 1997), ch. 4; David Owen, *Hume's Reason* (Oxford: Oxford University Press, 1999), ch. 6.

4

Philosophical Reflection on Sensory Belief

As we have seen in Chapters 2 and 3, Hume spends the first three quarters of "Of scepticism with regard to the senses" (T 1.4.2, hereafter 'SwS') explaining the mental processes that produce our everyday, vulgar beliefs about body. How is it that from the meagre data that our senses provide, we end up taking ourselves to be living in a shared public world of independently existing bodies? How is it that we normally do not even recognize that our access to the world is mediated by the senses? Hume answers these questions by arguing that the imagination's responses to constant or coherent sensations serve to create the belief in what I have called vulgar objects—the pens, paper, hats, shoes, stones, and the like (T 1.4.2.31, SBN 202) that we find all around us (§3.3.1). We overlook the gaps in our experience or the changes in it that conform to our expectations: we *mistake* interrupted impressions for impressions of unchanging objects; we take the unchanging to be identical through time only because, without realizing it, we *substitute* the atemporal idea of an unchanging object for the experience of successions. Thus, as Hume notes in the paragraph summarizing his explanation of how the imagination produces the vulgar sense of immersion in the world, our everyday beliefs about body are "really false, as is acknowledg'd by all philosophers" (T 1.4.2.43, SBN 209).

I argued in §3.4, however, that we should take Hume's emphasis on *philosophers* here seriously. Because the imagination's operations serve to ensure that the vulgar are not thinking *about* their perceptions, the errors it induces in them are properly thought of as *constitutive*—merely *psychological* rather than *epistemic*. It is only when he turns to the belief that sensory objects exist distinctly from our sensations (D_n from, §2.2) at T 1.4.2.44 (SBN 210) that Hume considers how he should come to terms with vulgar beliefs about body from a philosophical point of view. Thus in the last quarter of SwS (T 1.4.2.44–57, SBN 210–18) he examines several possibilities—notably the "extravagant scepticism" that tries to deny the existence of body (T 1.4.2.50, SBN 214), the representational realist "hypothesis…of the double existence perceptions and objects" (T 1.4.2.52, SBN 215), and eventually his own ambivalent position on the topic (T 1.4.2.56-7, SBN 217–18). I offer my interpretation of this portion of SwS in what follows.

In Chapter 1 I suggested that Hume's argument in "Of scepticism with regard to reason" (T 1.4.1, hereafter 'SwR') provides a template for reading the much more complicated discussion in the final quarter of SwS. In §1.6 I provided an eight-step summary of my interpretation of Hume's treatment of the sceptical argument against rational belief. I show in what follows how those eight steps are recapitulated in Hume's treatment of the sceptical argument against sensory belief.

I start my discussion in §4.1 by comparing the argument against sensory belief that Hume offers in paragraphs 44 and 45 of SwS to its Pyrrhonian antecedents (the analogue to step $[1_R]$ in §1.6). As in step (2_R) of SwR, where he observes that no one actually embraces the "total" scepticism that the argument against rational belief entails, Hume in SwS argues that no one accepts the "extravagant," sceptical conclusion that we should abandon our belief in an external world (§4.2). It becomes clear that the Pyrrhonian "experiments" of SwS, similarly to the argument of SwR, involve first *reflecting* on our sensory beliefs and revealing the psychological propensities that constitute them (step $[3_R]$ in §1.6). I have previously gestured towards how I understand Humean reflection or introspection (§2.2), but it is now time to offer a full account of this capacity. I do so by first, in §4.3.1, reviewing both Locke's account of reflection as a form of inner sense and his treatment of consciousness as a form of inner awareness both more pervasive than and different from reflection. Then, in §4.3.2, I show how Hume breaks from Locke by taking reflection to be a form of inner *thought*, rather than sense, and by doing without consciousness as a second form of inner awareness.

In §4.4 I argue that, analogously to step (4_R) of my interpretation of SwR, Hume uses the fact that no one believes the Pyrrhonian conclusion as empirical evidence in favour of his model of the mind. Whereas I suggested that step (5_R) of SwR—an explanation of how those who take belief to be an "act of the thought" end up with their false model of reason—was left largely implicit, Hume puts considerable effort into the analogous task in SwS. Thus, in §4.5 I explore his treatment of double-existence theories of sensation—something like Locke's account of sensitive knowledge (§2.1)—in which we have a special intimate knowledge of our perceptions that allows us to infer the existence of resembling extramental objects as their causes. Hume suggests that his opponents help themselves *malgré eux* to the principles of the imagination that he takes to stand behind both our reflective beliefs about our perceptions and our vulgar beliefs about objects.

Step (6_R) in SwR involves Hume's considering what is now seen to be a distinctively philosophical question of whether we should believe the verdicts of reason, when reason is properly understood as an expression of our imaginative propensities. In Step (7_R) he realizes that because the reflective question depends on the same propensities as those it studies, philosophy is ultimately unable to answer it. Reflective interference means that the Pyrrhonian challenge to reason is "destroy'd by [its] subtility" (T 1.4.1.12, SBN 186). In §4.6 I argue that Hume poses the parallel question about the verdicts of the senses. Though we are not *required* to decide whether to believe them, there is a *philosophical* question of whether we should accept our instinctive faith in them. In §4.7 I show that because introspection depends on the same propensities as those responsible for the beliefs it studies, philosophy is ultimately unable to answer the question it has set for itself. Reflective interference leaves us losing both the sensory beliefs and the introspective beliefs necessary for posing it. I end this chapter (§4.8) by considering the shared conclusion of SwR and SwS (T 1.4.2.57, SBN 218). As I argued in Chapter 1 (step [8$_R$]), Hume ultimately wants us to make our peace with our instinctive tendency to believe our reasoning and our sensing despite philosophy's incapacity to offer a reflective endorsement of them.

The starting point for Hume's presentation of the Pyrrhonian challenge to our sensory beliefs is the positive explanation of the vulgar belief in the continued existence of body, as developed in the first three quarters of SwS. Using the vocabulary I deployed in my interpretation in Chapters 2 and 3, this explanation can be summarized as follows. In seeing, say, a table, I have an impression whose *image-content* has brown points arranged so that lighter ones are to the right and darker ones to the left in a trapezoidal pattern. My imagination responds to this image-content in light of the expectations I have developed from my experience in the world and my linguistic training. Thus the trapezoidal image-content serves as the *proximate content* that elicits the idea of the word, 'table,' and triggers the disposition to replace that content with image-content as of the table from the other side of the room or the image-content as of its feel to the touch, and so on, thus constituting a thought that has the three-dimensional, independently existing table as its *intended object*. In being aware of the image-content in this manner, I am thereby aware of the table. Hume thus tries to preserve the phenomenology of vulgar sensory experience in which we have direct access to a world of independent objects, while at the same time holding that the vehicles for this awareness are mental images.

At the core of this analysis is a fiction of the imagination. The *idea-substitution mechanism* leads us to substitute one idea for another without recognizing it. The image-content involved in our impression of the table is intersubstituted with image-contents from previous experiences with the table so as to yield the belief in the table's continued, identical existence. Though Hume uses the terms "error" (T 1.4.2.32; SBN 202), "mistake" (T 1.4.2.32, 34; SBN 202, 205), and "false" (T 1.4.2.43, SBN 209) throughout his explanation of our vulgar beliefs, he does not seem ready to dismiss the vulgar belief until he considers the belief in the distinct existence of our sensory objects. He then says, however, that

a very little reflection and philosophy is sufficient to make us perceive the fallacy of that opinion.... [W]hen we compare experiments, and reason a little upon them, we quickly perceive, that the doctrine of the independent existence of our sensible perceptions is contrary to the plainest experience.   (T 1.4.2.44, SBN 210)

I turn now to those experiments.

4.1 Pyrrhonian Experiments

In my interpretation of SwR, the first step of Hume's argument is:

(1$_R$)   Deployment of an argument from the ancient sceptics to argue that we should not believe the verdicts of reason.

In SwS, Hume borrows similarly from the Pyrrhonians to argue that our senses do not support belief in the mind-independence of objects. Thus step one is SwS can be characterized as:

(1$_S$)   Deployment of an argument from the ancient sceptics to argue that we should not believe the verdicts of the senses.

Hume offers three "experiments" in SwS to demonstrate the mind-dependence of our sensory impressions, though he also says that there is "an infinite number of other experiments of the same kind" (T 1.4.2.45, SBN 211).

   The first and third experiments have similar points, each bringing out the role of the body in producing our sensations. The first is as follows:

When we press one eye with a finger, we immediately perceive all the objects to become double, and one half of them to be remov'd from their common and natural position. But as we do not attribute a continu'd existence to both these perceptions, and as they are both of the same nature, we clearly perceive, that all our perceptions are dependent on our organs, and the disposition of our nerves and animal spirits.   (T 1.4.2.45, SBN 210–11)

Sextus Empiricus, in his version of the experiment as given in the First Mode of Aenesidemus, does not mention double vision, instead saying that "[w]hen we press the eyeball at one side the forms, figures and sizes of the objects appear oblong and narrow" (PH i 47). His goal is to make us recognize the relativity of our sensations to the human species. By pressing the eye, we are to realize that those animals with differently shaped eyes experience things differently. And we have no criterion by means of which to ratify the human way of experiencing things as privileged. The senses present merely how things appear to human beings, and cannot be trusted to reveal reality itself.

   Note then this difference between Hume and his Pyrrhonian sources. As we saw in Chapter 1, they want us to avoid making any judgements on how things really are, so that we live merely by the appearances. Hume, in contrast, wants us to recognize a truth about the structure of the mind: namely, that sensory objects (in this case, the image-contents our sensations afford) lack distinct existence. Unlike the Pyrrhonians, he does not use the eye-pressing experiment to compare human sensations with those of other animals, but instead uses self-induced double vision to help us recognize the dependence of impressions on the conditions of the body and its sense organs.

   The third experiment has a similar moral when it points to the "the changes in [objects'] colour and other qualities from our sickness and distempers" (T 1.4.2.45, SBN 211). Sextus, in the Sixth Mode of Aenesidemus, points out that "sufferers from jaundice see everything yellow, and those with blood-shot eyes reddish like blood" (PH i 126). (In fact, neither jaundice nor blood-shot eyes change the colours we see, though some kinds of eye disorders, such as cataracts, do interfere with normal vision.) And again, where Sextus's concern is to challenge our privileging of the reports of the senses when healthy over those when sick, Hume thinks that our recognizing the bodily dependence of our sensations will show us the error of our belief in the distinct existence of our sensory objects.

Annette Baier and Fred Wilson have each suggested that the emphasis on bodily dependence, rather than mind dependence, undermines Hume's argument, for his goal was to show that what we sense lacks distinct existence *from the mind*, not from the body. Indeed, the argument seems to presuppose the existence of sensory organs and the like.[1] Hume can respond to this criticism in two ways. First, earlier in SwS, he has already acknowledged that our beliefs about our own bodies are structurally identical to our beliefs about external objects:

[P]roperly speaking, 'tis not our body we perceive, when we regard our limbs and members, but certain impressions, which enter by the senses; so that the ascribing a real and corporeal existence to these impressions, or to their objects, is an act of the mind as difficult to explain, as that which we examine at present.   (T 1.4.2.9, SBN 191)

So the fact that the eye-pressing experiment and the changes from "sickness and distemper" make the bodily dependence of our sensations palpable to us, when we already recognize the questionable status of our beliefs about our bodies, could support the conclusion of mind-dependence, even if Hume does not spell out the details of such an inference.

A second and more significant response to Baier's and Wilson's objection can be found from a consideration of Hume's second experiment, which does not directly[2] invoke the conditions of our sensory organs. It, he tells us, "confirms" the results of the first, by drawing our attention to "the seeming encrease and diminution of objects, according to their distance; [and] ... the apparent alterations in their figure" (T 1.4.2.45, SBN 211). Again, we can find precedents from Sextus—in this case from the Fifth Mode of Aenesidemus:

[T]he same porch when viewed from one of its corners appears curtailed, but viewed from the middle is symmetrical on all sides; and the same ship seems at a distance to be small and stationary, but from close at hand large and in motion; and the same tower from a distance appears round, but from a near point quadrangular.   (PH i 118)[3]

---

[1] Fred Wilson, "Is Hume a Sceptic with regard to the Senses?" *Journal of the History of Philosophy* 27 (1989), 55–6; Annette Baier, *A Progress of Sentiments* (Cambridge, MA: Harvard University Press, 1991), 118–19.

[2] The reference to 'distance' in the experiment must be an invocation of the distance of the object *from our body and its sensory capacities*, and so this experiment does have an indirect reference to the embodied nature of human sensation.

[3] See also PH i 120.

Sextus then challenges us to find a reason to prefer the deliverances of the senses from one perspective over those from another. Crucially, in order to make this point, we need to *recognize* the perspectival nature of our sensations. But in Chapter 2 I showed that Hume thinks that the phenomenology of sensory experience normally leaves the vulgar unaware of the fact that they encounter the world through their perceptions and the points of view they encode. Instead, we take ourselves to simply be *given* the world. Only in unusual circumstances do we acknowledge that the senses in fact present mere images as of things. For example, tourists might take a picture of themselves from the islands in the Toronto harbour, so that the CN Tower on the shore some distance away seems to be held between their thumb and a forefinger. For Hume, this means we must prescind from our associative tendencies that lead us to believe that the Tower is a large structure across the harbour; we must step back from our normal sense of immersion in the world so that we can recognize the image-content as of the Tower *as* image-content. Similarly, in §2.3, I quoted the passage where Hume asks us to move away from an inkspot until the final moment before it disappears. The image-content of the spot-impression will, at that point, he tells us, be indivisible (T 1.2.1.4, SBN 27). Rather than being carried along by our imaginations, whereby we would continue to see the (divisible) spot, we refocus our attention inwardly so as to bring to light our awareness of the (indivisible) image-content. I am suggesting, then, that the invocation of the bodily dependence of sensations in the first and third experiments is something of a red herring. Hume's actual concern with the experiments is to help us step back from the imagination's reactions to our sensations so that we can see them for what they are.[4]

Hume thus later describes the transition from vulgar to philosophical awareness, as involving both introspection, where we make our perceptions, rather than their image-contents, into objects of awareness and "abstract[ion] from the effects of custom" (T 1.4.3.9, SBN 223). His point is that the association of ideas depends on relations of resemblance, contiguity, or causation between their contents; but when we focus on the ideas themselves, rather than their contents, the associations no longer will occur, in that we are no longer thinking of the contents that bear the relevant relations. The "very little reflection and philosophy" (T 1.4.2.44, SBN 210) involved in the Pyrrhonian reflections thus requires that we are no longer carried along by the associations that produce the vulgar sense of immersion, and instead recognize the image-contents of our sensory ideas as images.

Hume argues that once we recognize our perceptions as mind-dependent, the "necessary consequence" (T 1.4.2.50, SBN 214) of the argument is the rejection of the belief in mind-independent objects:

---

[4] Annemarie Butler has an astute analysis of Hume's argument here ("Vulgar Habits and Hume's Double Vision Argument," *Journal of Scottish Philosophy* 8 [2010], 169–87).

[T]he natural consequence of this reasoning shou'd be, that our perceptions have no more a continu'd than an independent existence.   (T 1.4.2.46, SBN 211)

But as a little reflection destroys this conclusion, that our perceptions have a continu'd existence, by shewing that they have a dependent one, twou'd naturally be expected, that we must altogether reject the opinion, that there is such a thing in nature as a continu'd existence, which is preserv'd even when it no longer appears to the senses.   (T 1.4.2.50, SBN 214)

Thus, just as in SwR the conclusion of the sceptical argument was meant to yield "a total extinction of belief and evidence" (T 1.4.1.6, SBN 183) in the verdicts of reason, the sceptical argument of SwS should yield a rejection of the verdicts of the senses.

But there is one obvious difference between the sceptical arguments in SwR and SwS that should be noted. Hume spends far more time developing the sceptical argument of SwR than he does the argument in SwS. In the former, he spends six paragraphs showing in some detail how the initial challenge to our reasoning iterates, driving us seemingly inexorably towards the sceptical conclusion. But in the latter, he suggests that we "quickly perceive, that the doctrine of the independent existence of our sensible perceptions is contrary to the plainest experience" (T 1.4.2.44, SBN 210); he rushes through the Pyrrhonian experiments in one paragraph. I will return to this point in §4.5, where I suggest that it lies behind Hume's greater interest in SwS than in SwR in explaining how philosophers come up with what he takes to be a false model of the mind. As my CN Tower example indicates, it is not entirely uncommon for the vulgar to recognize their sensations as such, even if they do not normally do so.

4.2 The Unbelievability of Extravagant Scepticism

In §1.6 I suggested that the second step of Hume's argument in SwR is:

(2$_R$)   Observation that no one believes the sceptical conclusion in (1$_R$). Our nature is to believe our reasonings.

Recall his claim that "neither I, nor any other person was ever sincerely and constantly of that opinion" whereby all belief is extinguished; that kind of "total scepticism" cannot be maintained (T 1.4.1.7, SBN 183). Hume makes a similar observation in SwS:

[R]ejecting the opinion of a continu'd existence upon rejecting that of the independence and continuance of our sensible perceptions . . . has been peculiar to a few *extravagant sceptics*; who after all maintain'd that opinion in words only, and were never able to bring themselves sincerely to believe it.   (T 1.4.2.50, SBN 214; emphasis added; see also T 1.4.4.6, SBN 228)

Thus we obtain:

(2$_S$)   Observation that no one believes the sceptical conclusion in (1$_S$). Our nature is to believe our sensings.

In both sceptical Sections, Hume is asserting what he takes to be an empirical fact. No philosophers really are total or extravagant sceptics, no matter what they say. We cannot stop ourselves from believing the verdicts of reason or our senses. I postpone my discussion of what Hume thinks we should make of this fact to §4.4.

4.3 Reflection

I suggested in §1.6 that the third step of Hume's argument in SwR involves recognizing the role of reflection in generating the sceptical argument against reason.

(3$_R$)   Recognition that the argument in (1$_R$) depends on reflection on our reasoning that makes its fallible, psychological nature manifest to us.

But in light of my analysis in §4.1 of Hume's invocation of the Pyrrhonian experiments, we can see that reflection is essential to his argument in SwS as well. In both SwR and SwS, we must *reflect* on our mental processes in order to raise the sceptical challenge. In SwR, a "reflex act of the mind" (T 1.4.1.5, SBN 182) allows us to see the merely psychological nature of what we instinctively take to be authentic reasoning. We must then confront the question of whether to accept the verdict of the reasoning process we witness within ourselves. In SwS, it takes "a very little reflection and philosophy" (T 1.4.2.44, SBN 210) or "a little reflection" (T 1.4.2.50, SBN 214) for us to recognize the mind-dependence of our sensations. By making our impressions into the objects of our introspection, we no longer are carried along by the associations that produce the vulgar sense of immersion in the world. Thus the analogue for (3$_R$) is:

(3$_S$)   Recognition that the experiments in (1$_S$) depend on reflection on our sensing that makes its reliance on mind-dependent perceptions manifest to us.

But how should we understand this kind of reflection?

I start my answer to this question in §4.3.1 by investigating its Lockian background. Locke's empiricism requires that all simple ideas be acquired either by sensation, when we interact with the world, or by "reflection"—when we make our mental operations themselves into our objects (E II.ii.4). Reflection, he argues, has the same structure as sensation. "And though it be not Sense, as having nothing to do with external Objects; yet it is very like it, and might properly be call'd internal Sense" (E II.i.4). Locke complicates matter when he introduces a second term for a kind of inner awareness, *consciousness*—"the perception of what passes in a Man's own mind" (E II.i.19). He argues that all ideas are conscious, and thus rejects the Cartesian theses that some ideas are innate and that the mind always thinks: if either thesis were true, we would be conscious of such ideas or such ubiquitous thoughts, but in fact this is not the case. Though both reflection and consciousness involve some kind of awareness of our inner states, I show below that Locke distinguishes between them: reflection requires us to direct our thoughts inwardly; consciousness, in contrast, is a special kind of grasp of ourselves as thinkers that accompanies every thought (and thus we should be careful not to assume that Locke or other early moderns use 'consciousness' in our contemporary sense, where it connotes only a generic kind of awareness). In §4.3.2 I show how Hume reacts to these Lockian theses about reflection. For him, it turns out that reflection involves a form of inner *thinking* by means of what he calls "secondary ideas" of perceptions, rather than a kind of internal *sensing*. And his theory of mind does not have space for a version of Lockian consciousness. In §4.4 I show that Hume's and Locke's differences over the nature of reflection can be linked to their different reactions to sceptical challenges like the Pyrrhonian experiments. Hume can account for the empirical fact of our retention of our sensory beliefs, while Locke has to resort to what Hume calls a "double existence" analysis of sensation (§4.5).

4.3.1 Reflection and Consciousness in Locke

Despite the fact that Locke's investigation of the understanding fundamentally relies on reflection, he says disappointingly little about how this capacity operates. We must instead follow up on his suggestion that it is a kind of internal sensation. Recall that, for Locke, we receive ideas of sensation when our sensory organs are so located as to be affected by signals from their distal causes: the scent of the rose reaches us when the particles interact with our noses; its colour and shape reach us when light of the right sort is reflected off the rose's petals and enters our eyes. These physical processes leave "impressions" that eventually reach the brain, at which point they cause us to perceive ideas of the relevant sensory quality. Locke leaves the nature of the causal link between matter and mind as an open question. Famously, he is willing to consider the possibility that the mental process is "superadded" to the material one in such a way that nothing but matter is involved in our sensory experience (E IV.iii.6).

Locke intimates that the same story applies to our reflective experience. Our mental operations leave behind impressions—physical or not—that interact with our minds, thus causing us to perceive reflective ideas of the operations (E II.i.8, 24). There is, however, one notable difference between sensation and reflection that Locke emphasizes. The impressions involved in sensation are often sufficient to "force the mind to perceive and attend to" the ideas they cause (E II.i.21). But, whereas our senses are always operative when we are awake, and thus we receive ideas of sensation all the time, we do not always occupy the mental posture needed for reflection. Only when we direct our attention inwardly will the impressions from our mental operations affect us. Thus many of us will reflect only intermittently or rarely. Locke claims that children in particular do not usually have ideas of reflection. They are too taken with the new objects that their senses are revealing to them to introspect (E II.i.8).

While in Book 2 of the *Essay* Locke is concerned to show how we acquire different kinds of ideas, in Book 4 he takes up the issue of how these ideas afford us knowledge.

We saw in §2.1 that Locke argues that sensitive knowledge, whereby we recognize the existence of the objects of our sensory ideas, exemplifies a kind of certainty that qualifies it as knowledge, though to a lesser degree than intuition or demonstration. I noted there that Locke notoriously seems to get himself into trouble at this point. Sensitive knowledge requires that the we perceive the "*actual real Existence* agreeing to any *Idea*" (E IV.i.7), while Locke elsewhere is clear that we can *never* perceive real existences directly, and instead perceive only ideas that represent them (E IV.xxi.4). How then can we grasp the external object in such a way as to compare it to the idea that represents it?[5] I show in §4.5 that Hume himself criticizes the philosophical system of double existence—a generic version of the Lockian view—for exactly this problem.

Somewhat surprisingly, Locke does not give us an account of how we can recognize the existence of those mental operations that are the objects of ideas of reflection. But I assume that he intends for us to carry the analogy between sensation and reflection through to knowledge. *Reflective knowledge* would then involve the perception of an agreement between an idea of reflection and the mental operation it represents. We would thus *know* that our minds were performing a mental operation when we reflected on it.

It might be objected, however, that we do not need to *reflect* on our minds to get this kind of knowledge. Thus Locke says: "[T]he Operations of our minds, will not let us be without, at least some obscure Notions of them. No Man, can be wholly ignorant of what he does, when he thinks" (E II.i.25).[6] Similarly, while arguing against the Cartesian view that the soul is essentially thinking, Locke says:

[A man] cannot think at any time waking or sleeping, without being sensible of it. Our being sensible of it is not necessary to any thing, but to our thoughts; and to them it is; and to them it will always be necessary, till we can think without being *conscious* of it.

(E II.i.10, emphasis added)

And, in his discussion of personal identity, Locke asserts that this kind of sensibility qualifies as knowledge:

[C]onsciousness... is inseparable from thinking, and as it seems to me essential to it: It be impossible for anyone to perceive, without perceiving, that he does perceive. When we see, hear, smell, taste, feel, meditate, or will any thing, we *know* that we do so.

(E II.xxvii.9; emphasis added)

Thus Locke clearly allows that we have a kind of immediate knowledge of our mental operations, and usually uses the term 'consciousness' to mark this kind of knowledge.

---

[5] See Chapter 2, fn. 7, for some of the secondary literature on this problem.

[6] Vili Lähteenmäki appeals to this passage as part of his case for construing ideas of reflection as accompaniments of every mental act ("The Sphere of Experience in Locke: The Relations between Reflection, Consciousness, and Ideas," *Locke Studies* 8 [2008], 78).

But what exactly is Lockian consciousness?[7] And might his introduction of it stand behind his shying away from a category of reflective knowledge?

As Mark Kulstad has shown, it is not easy to place consciousness into Locke's philosophy of mind.[8] I quoted above the clearest description that he gives of it: "[C]onsciousness is the perception of what passes in a Man's own mind" (E II.i.19). But this description creates at least two problems. First, we have just seen that in order to reject innatism, Locke says that every perception must be conscious. But if consciousness is itself a form of perception, then he has introduced an infinite hierarchy of perceptions. We would be perceiving that we perceive that we perceive that we perceive.... Second, the definition seems to assimilate consciousness to reflection, in that each involves an awareness of our mental states. Elsewhere, he equates our consciousness of our ideas with our observation of them within us (E I. i.3, II.i.4) and even describes consciousness as involving "a reflex Act of perception" that accompanies all thoughts (E II.xxvii.13). But, if consciousness were the same thing as reflection, how could Locke insist both that all of our perceptions involve consciousness and that reflection takes attention? How could he hold that children do not have ideas of reflection, even though they are presumably conscious of their perceiving ideas of sensation?

The solution, I think, is to see Locke as following the Cartesian tradition by treating consciousness as a form of perception that is different in kind from the garden-variety perception that Locke acknowledges could easily be identified with "Thinking in general" (E II.ix.1).[9] Rather, consciousness involves what Antoine Arnauld calls *réflexion virtuelle*[10]—a special kind of awareness of ourselves as mental subjects that accompanies all of our thoughts and volitions. As Locke puts it in his version of the *cogito*: "In every Act of Sensation, Reasoning, or Thinking, we are conscious to our selves of our own Being; and, in this matter, come not short of the highest degree of *Certainty*" (E IV.ix.3). This is not to say that we are self-obsessed, always dwelling on ourselves as the agents of our mental operations. Rather, I think

---

[7] I noted in §2.3 that 'consciousness' was a contested term in the early modern period. Locke was particularly influential in popularizing its use, though his readers struggled to understand what he meant by it. Pierre Coste, the French translator of the *Essay*, in an edition originally overseen by Locke himself, notes that he cannot find an appropriate French word for 'consciousness,' finally settling on '*con-science*' despite registering reservations about its appropriateness (*Essai philosophique concernant l'entendement humain*, tr. P. Coste, ed. G. J. D. Moyal [Paris: Vrin, 2004], 1005).G. W. Leibniz, in his response to Locke (*New Essays concerning Human Understanding*, tr. and ed. P. Remnant and J. Bennett [Cambridge: Cambridge University Press, 1996], 235n), introduces a French neologism, '*consciosité*,' out of a sense that '*con-science*' failed to capture the distinctive sense Locke intended. See Udo Thiel, "Hume's Notions of Consciousness and Reflection in Context," *British Journal for the History of Philosophy* 2 (1994), 75–115.

[8] See *Leibniz on Apperception, Consciousness, and Reflection* (Munich: Philosophia, 1991), ch. 3.

[9] Martha Bolton, "The Taxonomy of Ideas in Locke's *Essay*," in L. Newman (ed.), *Cambridge Companion to Locke's 'Essay concerning Human Understanding'* (New York, NY: Cambridge University Press, 2007), 85.

[10] Antoine Arnauld, *Of True and False Ideas*, tr. and intr. Stephen Gaukroger (Manchester: Manchester University Press, 1990), 53–4, 71.

Locke wants to allow that when sensing, say, an apple, our thought is focused on *the apple*, the idea of which we perceive; but at the same time, hovering in the background of our minds, we grasp ourselves as the ones perceiving this idea.[11] Kulstad worries that understanding consciousness in this way would conflict with Locke's fundamental empiricist thesis that identifies sensation and reflection as the only sources of ideas. But if consciousness is Locke's name for the special self-intimating quality of all of our mental acts, then he can suggest that it is special exactly in that does not involve the mediation of an idea (see E IV.xxi.4).[12] Instead, he can reserve 'idea' for those objects that are at the forefront of our thinking, "whatsoever is the Object of the Understanding when a Man thinks" (E I.i.8). Our awareness that we are the ones who are thinking thus does not involve the perception of an *idea*. As the perception of a *perception*, consciousness involves a kind of immediate grasp of its object that sets it apart from the representational forms of awareness that structure our access to the overt objects of thought.

If consciousness is understood in this way, we avoid the two problems that I noted above. First, there is no hierarchy of perceptions: Since consciousness *is* our implicit awareness of our undertaking mental operations, then we do not need to postulate a higher-level awareness of our consciousness in order to avoid the innatist's posit of ideas that are in the mind even though we are not aware of them. Second, children can be conscious of their mental operations without needing to reflect. In being conscious of their mental operations, children are not attending *to them*; their attention remains focused on the objects that they sense, even if they have an "obscure Notion" that they are sensing.[13]

We *can*, of course, reflect on a mental operation. We would then attend to the operation, overtly making it into the object of our thought. In these cases, we perceive an idea of reflection that represents the operation and we are conscious that we are perceiving this idea; but we are also conscious that we are the subjects of the mental operation that we are reflecting upon. Moreover, as Locke makes clear in his discussion of personal identity, where the capacity to reflect is said to be one of the defining features of persons, in being conscious both that we reflect and that we

---

[11] My thinking here is indebted to many conversations with Shelley Weinberg, whose dissertation focused on Locke's theory of consciousness. She argues for a conception of consciousness as the subject's proprietary awareness that she is thinking, where this consciousness is a constituent of every mental act. See "The Coherence of Consciousness in Locke's *Essay*," *History of Philosophy Quarterly* 25 (2008), 21–40. Angela Coventry and Uriah Kriegel argue for a similar position in "Locke on Consciousness," *History of Philosophy Quarterly* 25 (2008), 221–42.

[12] "For since the Things, the Mind contemplates, are none of them, *besides it self*, present to the Understanding, 'tis necessary that something else, as a Sign or Representation of the thing it considers should be present to it: And these are *Ideas*" (E IV.xxi.4; original emphasis on 'Ideas' only).

[13] Note that for this interpretation to succeed, the 'notion' Locke invokes here cannot be equated with an idea, despite his assertion that he uses 'idea' for "whatever is meant by *Phantasm, Notion,* or *Species*" (E I.i.8).

undergo the mental operation on which we reflect, we have a special immediate grasp of the identity of the reflecting subject with the one reflected upon (E II.xxvii.9).

We see here a fundamental difference between what I am calling reflective knowledge and Lockian sensitive knowledge. The latter is such a difficult category for interpreters because, given Locke's thesis that we only have access to external objects by perceiving ideas of them, it seems hopeless to say that we can perceive the agreement between the sensory object and our idea of it. When it comes to reflection, however, we have *two* ways of gaining access to our mental operations. We can *represent* them via ideas of reflection, and we are also always *conscious* of them in a direct way, immediately grasping ourselves as the subjects of the operations. It is no longer mysterious that we might then perceive the agreement between an operation as represented in an idea and as it is directly given to us in consciousness. Locke might have left reflective knowledge off the table in Book 4 of the *Essay* exactly because it is too obvious.

4.3.2 Humean Reflection

Hume's project, like Locke's, is an investigation of the mind and its operations. Like Locke, Hume thinks that introspection or observation of the mind is an essential component for this investigation. And, as we have seen in the Pyrrhonian experiments, Hume will sometimes call this kind of introspection 'reflection' in a Lockian sense (see also: T 1.1.1.12, 1.3.8.15, 1.3.14.6, 1.4.6.16, 3.1.1.26, App.15, 20; SBN 7, 106, 157, 260, 468, 634, 636), though he does not introduce it as a technical term. He also uses 'reflection' in an explicitly non-Lockian fashion, especially in connection with "impressions of reflection"[14]—desires, passions, and the like, that are caused by thoughts of sensory objects that we have previously experienced (T 1.1.2).[15] I am interested here only in the former sense—reflection as a form of observation of the mind. Unfortunately, Hume, even more than Locke, fails to provide a focused treatment of the nature and structure of this kind of introspection. In this subsection I try to fill in some of the blanks, focusing in particular on those passages where he makes a point of indicating that his account of the mind must include an explanation of how that account is possible. I suggest that on the one hand, Humean introspection is akin to Lockian reflection, as opposed to Lockian consciousness, in that our observing our mental operations is something we can do on occasion, not something that is always forced on us. On the other hand, Hume differs from Locke in that he

---

[14] Note that in the original edition of the *Treatise*, Hume uses both 'reflection' and 'reflexion,' with the latter spelling more prevalent when first introducing "impressions of reflexion" at T 1.1.2, though even there he uses both spellings. Mary and David Norton, in their editions of the *Treatise*, have standardized Hume's spelling, opting for the uniform use of 'reflection' (*David Hume, A Treatise of Human Nature: A Critical Edition*, Vol. 2, *Editorial Material* [Oxford: Clarendon Press, 2007], 636).

[15] Hume also uses 'reflection' in a third way, to indicate something like thoughtful investigation. For example, in his discussion of general ideas, he says: "And ... tho' the capacity of the mind be not infinite, yet we can at once form a notion of all possible degrees of quantity and quality, in such a manner at least, as, however imperfect, may serve all the purposes of reflection and conversation" (T 1.1.7.2, SBN 18).

does not take reflection to be a form of inner *sensation*. Introspection, for Hume, does not, like sensation, yield impressions, but rather ideas. Reflection is thus a form of inner *thought*.

Hume first makes his reliance on introspection explicit near the end of the first Section of the *Treatise*. He has established his first principle—that simple ideas normally inherit their content from prior simple impressions—and noted the counter-example of the missing shade of blue (see §2.4). He goes on to say:

> But besides this exception, it may not be amiss to remark on this head, that the principle of the priority of impressions to ideas must be understood with another limitation, *viz.* that as our ideas are images of our impressions, so we can form secondary ideas, which are images of the primary; as appears from this very reasoning concerning them. This is not, properly speaking, an exception to the rule so much as an explanation of it. Ideas produce the images of themselves in new ideas; but as the first ideas are supposed to be derived from impressions, it still remains true, that all our simple ideas proceed either mediately or immediately, from their correspondent impressions.   (T 1.1.1.11, SBN 6–7)

He admits here that a discussion of perceptions and their relations to one another must rely on "secondary" ideas of them (though this passage seems to be restricted to our thoughts about *ideas*,[16] he expands his point to include all of our perceptions at T 1.3.8.15–17, SBN 105–6, to be discussed shortly).[17] Note that, following Hume's usage here, I will call perceptions that are not themselves reflections on other perceptions *primary perceptions*. Hume's investigation thus far has shown that someone's tasting of, say, a pineapple amounts to the appropriate primary taste-impression's occurring in her mind; her thinking of the taste of the pineapple involves the occurrence of a primary idea that copies the first impression's content. The point in the passage is that his thinking of a pineapple-*idea* amounts to the occurrence of a secondary idea *of the pineapple-idea* in his mind. Insofar as philosophy, for Hume, involves an examination of the mind's perceptual economy,

---

[16] In fact, it might be possible to read this passage as discussing introspective thoughts of impressions—secondary ideas of (primary) impressions—in addition to secondary ideas of (primary) ideas. Given that Hume says that his point is supported by "this very reasoning concerning *them*," referring back to his claim that "our ideas are images of our impressions," it does seem that he has been relying on ideas of both ideas and of impressions. But later in the passage he says that "*ideas* produce the images of themselves in new ideas" (T 1.1.1.11, SBN 6; emphasis added), and thus seems to restrict his claim to the primary-*idea*–secondary-idea relationship. In any case, the claim that we can form secondary ideas of primary impressions is included in the discussion at 1.3.8.15–17, which ends with: "[A]fter this any one will understand how we may form the idea of an impression and of an idea, and how we may believe the existence of an impression and of an idea" (T 1.3.8.17, SBN 106).

[17] David Norton uses "secondary idea" in a non-Humean way in his "Editor's Introduction" to the student edition of the *Treatise*. Given Hume's suggestion that an idea of sensation can give rise to an impression of reflection, such as desire or aversion (T 1.1.2), and his later relabelling of impressions of reflection as "secondary impressions" (T 2.1.1), Norton suggests that the ideas that copy the secondary impressions might usefully be called secondary ideas ("Editor's Introduction," in *David Hume: A Treatise of Human Nature* [Oxford: Oxford University Press, 2000], I19). It is important to recognize that Hume's own usage of 'secondary idea' is quite different.

secondary ideas are the vehicles for philosophical thought. But, by putting intro-spective awareness into the category of secondary *ideas*, Hume has assimilated them to the category of thought, not sensation. Recall that he identifies thoughts with ideas and sensations with impressions in the opening paragraph of the *Treatise* (T 1.1.1.1, SBN 1). Thus, in what seems like an aside, he has simply abandoned the Lockian suggestion that introspection is best construed as inner sensation. Why?

A second puzzle in this passage arises when we take seriously that he pairs it with his discussion of the missing shade of blue—an admitted counter-example to his fundamental empiricist principle that simple ideas acquire their content from prior simple impressions. Secondary ideas are another "limitation" to this principle, for how do they acquire their content? His answer is that they copy primary perceptions in the same way that ideas copy impressions. This does not seem right. Primary ideas copy impressions by repeating their content, though with decreased vivacity (T 1.1.1.7, 1.1.7.5; SBN 5, 19). An impression of an apple and an idea-copy of it are both *of the apple*. Secondary ideas, however, copy primary perceptions by taking *them* as their content. The idea of the apple is *of the apple*, while the secondary idea of the idea-of-the-apple is *of the idea*.[18] To what extent is Hume's extension of the copy principle here legitimate? In resolving these two puzzles, consider four other places in Book 1 of the *Treatise* where Hume makes his reliance on secondary ideas in his philosophizing explicit.

Passage (1) The most significant such passage occurs at the end of his discussion of the causes of causal beliefs (T 1.3.8). His general claim is that in order for us to *believe* in the existence of a cause or effect, rather than merely *think* of it in a hypothetical manner, we need to have had a prior impression of the correlative effect or cause—we need to have *observed* it. But now he confronts a problem. His foundational empiri-cist claim assumes that simple ideas are caused by prior simple impressions. Suppose we introspectively observe an idea in ourselves—the idea of the scent of a papaya, say—but we have no memory of having ever actually smelled one. The foundational claim allows us to infer that we did in fact have a prior impression of the papaya's scent, despite our lack of memory. Thus, here we seem to infer an impression from an

---

[18] Consider the difference between two ways we might make a copy of the Mona Lisa. First, we might paint a picture that itself is of *la Gioconda*. Second, we could paint a picture showing the Mona Lisa *as a painting* on the wall in the Louvre where it is hung. The first kind of copying is analogous to the standard primary-idea–primary-impression relation, where the idea repeats the content of the impression. The second kind of copying is analogous to the secondary-idea–primary-perception relation, where the idea portrays the perception *as a perception*.

Those interpreters who take ideas to be *of impressions* because they are copies of them will overlook this point. Don Garrett, for example, takes ideas to copy impressions not by their having the same content, but rather by being *about* impressions (*Cognition and Commitment in Hume's Philosophy* [New York, NY: Oxford University Press, 1997], 66). Lorne Falkenstein says, similarly, that an idea "must always represent some antecedent impression" ("Hume and Reid on the Simplicity of the Soul," *Hume Studies* 21 [1995], 27). But then the distinction between primary and secondary ideas is lost.

idea, in contrast to Hume's suggestion that causal beliefs must have their source in prior impressions, not ideas.

[I]t may be ask'd, from whence are the qualities of force and vivacity deriv'd, which constitute this belief? And to this I answer very readily, *from the present idea*. For as this idea is not here consider'd, as the representation of any absent object, but as a real perception in the mind, of which we are intimately conscious, it must be able to bestow on whatever is related to it the same quality, call it *firmness*, or *solidity*, or *force*, or *vivacity*, with which the mind reflects upon it, and is assur'd of its present existence. The idea here supplies the place of an impression, and is entirely the same, so far as regards our present purpose... [paragraph on remembering a perception omitted].

After this any one will understand how we may form the idea of an impression and of an idea, and how we may believe the existence of an impression and of an idea.

(T 1.3.8.15, 17; SBN 106)

This is not an easy passage to interpret. Given the question that prompts it, his topic is clearly the structure of introspection—what happens when "the mind reflects upon" a perception, such as the idea of a papaya. We are thus no longer thinking of the *papaya*, but instead are thinking about our *idea* of the papaya and its causal source: We have a secondary idea of the primary idea of the papaya that has sufficient vivacity for us to *believe* that the primary idea exists. Hume at first claims that this secondary idea's vivacity is derived from the primary idea itself. Because we are "considering it" as a perception, it has enough vivacity to enliven the secondary idea into a belief; it "supplies the place of an impression."

There are two problems with this claim. First, why should we expect the primary idea to have sufficient vivacity to serve this role? The idea of the papaya might be very dim indeed; I might merely be idly fantasizing about my dream vacation in the tropics. Second, Hume here seems to repeat the same claim as we saw in the passage where he first introduces the notion of secondary ideas, where the relation between a secondary and a primary perception is analogized to the relation between a primary idea and the primary impression it copies in the normal, non-introspective case. But we have already noted that this does not seem right. In the normal case, ideas copy impressions by taking over their content, while in the introspective case the secondary idea copies the primary perception not by sharing its content, but by making it into its content. Before I offer my solution to these two interpretive problems, it will be helpful to consider the three other passages where Hume thematizes the role of reflection in his philosophy.

Passage (2) One of them occurs in the culmination of his discussion of causation, immediately before the presentation of his definitions of cause and effect. He attempts to bolster his case by "converting [his] present reasoning into an instance of it, by a subtility, which it will not be difficult to comprehend":

When any object is presented to us, it immediately conveys to the mind a lively idea of that object, which is usually found to attend it; and this determination of the mind forms the necessary connexion of these objects. But *when we change the point of view, from the objects to the perceptions*; in that case the impression is to be considered as the cause, and the lively idea as the effect; and their necessary connexion is that new determination, which we feel to pass from the *idea of the one* [that is, of the impression] to that *of the other* [that is, of the lively idea]. The uniting principle among our internal perceptions is as unintelligible as that among external objects, and is not known to us any other way than by experience.

(T 1.3.14.28–9, SBN 169; emphases added)

Hume here acknowledges that his strategy of investigating the causal relation indirectly, by focusing on how we make causal inferences, has meant that he has been making causal claims *about the mind* throughout his discussion. The experience of constant conjunctions *causes* the mind to associate its ideas of the cause and the effect; or, as the passage itself notes, once the mind has become accustomed to a causal regularity, the impression of the cause *causes* a lively idea of the effect. Hume here notes that these causal claims *about perceptions* require an identical analysis to the one he has given for causal relations between non-mental objects, only at one level higher in the perceptual hierarchy: We come to believe it by associating our secondary idea of the impression-of-the-cause with our secondary idea of the lively-idea-of-the-effect. And we will come to associate these secondary ideas only because of prior introspective experience of the impressions-of-causes conjoined with lively-ideas-of-effects.

Passage (3) The third of the four passages concerning secondary ideas can be found in Hume's discussion of the debate over whether the soul is a substance, where its perceptions would count as "abstract modes" or "actions" (T 1.4.5.26, SBN 244–5) that are merely rationally distinct from the soul. Hume responds:

As we conclude from the distinction and separability of their ideas, that external objects have a separate existence from each other; so when we make these ideas themselves our objects, we must draw the same conclusion concerning *them*, according to the precedent reasoning.

(T 1.4.5.27, SBN 245)

He here invokes his separability principles, which assert the mutual entailment of the difference of objects from one another, their being distinguishable in thought, and our being able to form separate ideas of them (T 1.1.7.3, SBN 18; see my discussion in §5.3). And he points out that these principles apply equally to perceptions and to external objects. The fact that we can form separate secondary ideas of perceptions shows that the primary perceptions are different from one another and thus do not depend on a substantial soul. I discuss Hume's argument against substance accounts of the soul in more detail in Chapter 5, but note here that, as in the previous passage, he emphasizes that his account of the mind's grasp of external world applies equally to the introspecting philosopher's grasp of the internal world.

Passage (4) The final set of passages where Hume openly discusses the structure of introspection can be found in his discussion of personal identity:

For my part, when I enter most intimately into what I call *myself*, I always stumble on some particular perception or other, of heat or cold, light or shade, love or hatred, pain or pleasure.

I never can catch *myself* at any time without a perception, and never can observe any thing but the perception.   (T 1.4.6.3, SBN 252)

Whereas in the second passage, Hume had described the introspective move as involving a change in perspective "from the objects to the perceptions," here he highlights how the observation of perceptions results from "intimate entry into" himself. And, though he does not emphasize the role of secondary ideas here, they are essential to his explanation of why we believe that the perceptions that we observe upon such intimate entry are unified:

[I]dentity is nothing really belonging to these different perceptions, and uniting them together; but is merely a quality, which we attribute to them, because of the union of *their ideas* [that is, secondary ideas of these different perceptions] in the imagination, *when we reflect upon them* [that is, the different perceptions].   (T 1.4.6.16, SBN 260; emphases added)

As I discuss in more detail in §6.5, Hume argues throughout his discussion of personal identity that just as our belief about the unity of a non-mental object is produced by the association of our ideas of its parts, so also our belief about the unity of the mind when we reflect upon it is produced by the association of our secondary ideas of its constituent primary perceptions. The resemblances and causal connections between our primary perceptions suffice for us to associate our secondary ideas of our perceptions together, making it feel to us as though the primary perceptions we observe are unified.

Note, then, that despite Hume's official rejection of the Lockian treatment of reflection as "internal" sensation, three of his discussions of secondary ideas *emphasize* the structural parallels between our sensory-based perception of external objects and our introspectively based perception of internal objects (passages [2], [3], and [4]). Indeed, in his treatment of personal identity, Hume declares that there is a "great analogy" (T 1.4.6.5, SBN 253) between our beliefs about the objects of sensation and about the mental.

With these passages now on the table, let us return to the two puzzles that I noted about his initial presentation of secondary ideas. Why treat introspection as a form of thinking—via secondary ideas—rather than as a form of sensing? And why think of secondary ideas as copies of primary perceptions, given that they have different contents? The key to resolving these puzzles is the paragraph on memory that I omitted in passage (1) when quoting it earlier:

Upon the same principles we need not be surpriz'd to hear of the remembrance of an idea; that is, of the idea of an idea, and of its force and vivacity superior to the loose conceptions of the imagination. In thinking of our past thoughts we not only delineate out the objects, of which we were thinking, but also conceive the action of the mind in the meditation, that certain *je-ne-scai-quoi*, of which 'tis impossible to give any definition or description, but which every one sufficiently understands. When the memory offers an idea of this, and represents it as past, 'tis easily conceiv'd how that idea may have more vigour and firmness, than when we think of a past thought, of which we have no remembrance.   (T 1.3.8.16, SBN 106)

So I can remember *a banana* (say, the one I left in the fruit bowl for breakfast tomorrow), but Hume notes that I can also remember *thinking of* a banana (say, when I was considering yesterday what I needed to buy at the supermarket). The former is the recollection of an *object* of experience (the banana), while the latter is the recollection of "the action of the mind" (my considering my shopping needs) and thus is the recollection of a *thought*. For Hume, then, there are two different ways memories can result from prior perceptions. Sometimes an idea copies an impression by acquiring its content from it, sometimes by representing the mental operation involved in our entertaining that content.

We can use Hume's point here to solve the second puzzle from the passage introducing secondary ideas, where he says that just as primary ideas copy primary impressions, secondary ideas copy primary ones. Given that he pairs this point with the missing shade of blue, it is clear that this claim is not as straightforward as it appears. But with his introduction of a second kind of copying relation between ideas and impressions, he can sidestep the apparent threat to his empiricism. The fact that we can remember either *episodes* of thinking (and sensing) or *objects* of thinking (and sensing) shows that secondary ideas are no threat to his fundamental principle that traces (almost) all ideas to simple impressions. Secondary ideas get their content "mediately" from impressions because we can only think of mental episodes that are either themselves impressions or that are ideas, "immediately" copied from impressions (T 1.1.1.11, SBN 7).

As for why, in a given instance, we remember via secondary ideas, rather than more directly, Hume holds, I take it, that it will normally depend on a panoply of incidental causes. We find ourselves remembering *thinking* of the banana rather than remembering *the banana* because that is where our associations take us. In our philosophical moments, however, we can use this capacity to observe our mental operations in a more disciplined fashion. Just as when shopping for groceries we can actively try to remember how many bananas remain in the fruit bowl, so also we can actively try to 'remember' our mental operations. With "intimate entry" into ourselves, we purposefully think about our perceptions as such.[19] We stop focusing on whatever objects our perceptions reveal to us, and instead think of the episodes of awareness themselves. And, just as memories have sufficient vivacity for them to ground causal inferences that yield belief (T 1.3.4), so also with our introspective quasi-memories of our perceptions, even if the primary perceptions themselves have relatively little vivacity, as in the idle fantasy of eating papaya on a tropical beach. Introspective thoughts of perceptions result in beliefs in the presence of the perceptions we observe in us. Thus my solution to the first puzzle arising from Hume's treatment of secondary ideas is that he does not simply *reject* Locke's "inner

---

[19] Of course, Hume ultimately has an extremely attenuated conception of action (T 2.3.1–3). Basically, I think, "intimate entry" into ourselves just means that the relevant secondary ideas do appear in the mind-bundle, along with an impression of willing.

sensation" model of introspection; he *replaces* it with a memory-based one, where reflection is a kind of thinking, yielding ideas, rather than a kind of sensation, yielding impressions.

There is one difference between Locke's and Hume's models of introspection that I do not think is particularly salient. Namely, sensation allows for present awareness of its objects, whereas memory only allows for awareness of objects in the past, and thus the difference between Hume and Locke might be cast in terms of their openness to our simultaneously being in a mental state and reflectively being aware of that state. Hume, it might seem, believes only in retrospection. This interpretation cannot be right, however. Note, for example, that the paragraph (in passage [1]) prior to the discussion of the memory of past mental operations concerns our being "assur'd of" a perception's "*present* existence." And his analogizing introspection to sensation in the other three passages we have examined suggests that Hume is disavowing the past-regarding elements of his memory model for introspection. Rather his point is that just as memory copies perceptions without violating empiricist principles, so also does reflection. There is no need to follow Locke by positing a non-sensory source for mental content.

Hume might also have a second reason for taking memory, rather than sensation, as his model for introspection. Consider how Locke demarcates perceiving an idea by means of sensation from perceiving an idea with the same content but in imagination or memory:

> For I ask any one, Whether he be not invincibly *conscious* to himself of a different Perception, when he looks on the Sun by day, and thinks on it by night; when he actually tastes Wormwood, or smells a Rose, or only thinks on that Savour, or Odour ... ? So that, I think, we may add to the two former sorts of *Knowledge*, this also, of the existence of particular external Objects, by that perception and *Consciousness* we have of the actual entrance of *Ideas* from them.... (E IV.ii.14; emphases added on 'conscious' and 'consciousness')

He thinks that the consciousness he takes to accompany the perception of every idea includes a grasp of how it arises in us—from sensation, from imagination, and presumably also, from reflection. Returning to Locke's mirror analogy, where an idea in the mind is compared to an image in a mirror (see §2.1), Locke thinks that, in the case of sensation, we know when we are *seeing* an image in the mirror, and not simply *envisioning* what we might see there.

For Hume, in contrast, sensations—impressions—are distinguished from thoughts—ideas—not by consciousness, but by vivacity. And I argue in §6.6 that the vivacity of a perception is best understood in terms of the extent to which we are able to resist entertaining its content. With sensations we are passive, and we end up with the relevant impressions whenever our senses are functioning properly with respect to the appropriate kinds of objects in our vicinity. Our thoughts, in contrast, are in our control to a much greater extent, though increases in the vivacity of the idea results in our finding it less and less easy to resist the thought. In causal beliefs, for example, we can conceive of things not happening as they have in the past and, to that extent, the idea can be resisted; but its high vivacity means that we find ourselves drawn to expect whatever accords with our prior experience. Similarly, memories present themselves with high vivacity, making it hard for us to think that things did not happen in the way that the ideas suggest.

I suggest that Hume uses memory as a model for introspection because our experience here lacks the irresistibleness characteristic of sensation. Recall Locke's point that reflection, in his technical sense, is optional, and rarely undertaken by those, like children, who focus primarily on the external world. So also with Humean introspection. We are not compelled to observe our perceptions in the same manner as when we passively receive sensations. There is not the robust causal link between our introspective posture and our mental operations that exists between our minds and the objects in the world that are within range of our sense organs. (Of course, Hume's analysis of the causal link between external objects and impressions is anything but straightforward: see §4.5.) Nonetheless, just as memories in particular can sometimes force themselves on us, the high vivacity of introspectively observed perceptions means that we have trouble turning our minds away from them when we are in a reflective mode (having already entered most intimately into ourselves). Thus Hume can be comfortable with the comparisons between introspection and sensation that we saw in passages (2)–(4), without making the Lockian move of treating introspection as a form of inner sensation.

We saw earlier that Locke introduces consciousness as a second and more pervasive form of reflective awareness, and I have emphasized here that he appeals to consciousness as a means for us to recognize the kind of mental operations we are undergoing when they occur in us. Hume does not appeal to consciousness to play this second role, instead appealing to the vivacity of perceptions to do the job. But does he nonetheless include something like Lockian consciousness in his model of the mind? The quick answer is 'no.' As I discuss in Chapter 6, the mind, for Hume, is merely a bundle of perceptions, not a bundle and in addition a set of consciousnesses of its constituent perceptions. Moreover, as I suggested in §2.3, Hume uses 'consciousness' ambiguously. Sometimes he uses it to describe the element in a perception that makes it into a state of awareness, as in the second sentence of the *Treatise* proper: "The difference betwixt [impressions and ideas] consists in the degrees of force and liveliness, with which they strike upon the mind, and make their way into our thought or *consciousness*" (T 1.1.1.1, SBN 1; emphasis added).[20] In this usage, 'consciousness' is akin to the Lockian perception of an idea, not the Lockian consciousness of our so perceiving. But in the "Appendix" to the *Treatise*, Hume

---

[20] This passage is in fact strange not only for the vague introduction of 'consciousness,' but also for its use of 'thought.' Given that he goes on, in the next sentence but one, to *identify* ideas with thoughts, it is surprising that he says here that both *impressions* and ideas "make their way into our thought" (T 1.1.1.1, SBN 1).

defines consciousness as "nothing but a reflected thought or perception" (T App.20, SBN 635), whereby consciousness seems to involve overt awareness of our mental states, as in Lockian reflection, though Hume, as we have seen, models introspection in terms of the formation of secondary ideas of primary perceptions.[21] Thus, where Locke introduces consciousness as a kind of reflective awareness different in kind from and more ubiquitous than reflection properly so called, Hume uses 'consciousness' to indicate his equivalent either of Lockian perception or Lockian reflection. There is no space for Lockian consciousness in his theory of mind.

I suggested earlier that Locke's introduction of consciousness as a form of inner awareness different from reflection might stand behind his omission of an account of reflective knowledge—a grasp of the existence of the mental operations that we reflect on akin to the grasp of the existence of external objects that is secured in sensitive knowledge. We can recognize the agreement between our ideas of reflection and the mental operations they portray because we have access to those operations, not just by representing them in ideas of reflection, but also by being conscious of them. If Hume, as I suggest, rejects the Lockian account of consciousness, how does he account for our default assumption, when reflecting on our minds, that things are as we observe?

In particular, we can ask questions about the introspective observation of the mind parallel to those that Hume asks in SwS about the sensory observation of the external world. Suppose, for example, I am observing my mind while I look at a table. My introspection reveals to me an impression as of a brown trapezoid. But why do I assume that such an impression continues in the mind even when I am not introspecting (supposing I continue to look at the table from the same perspective)? Or, to put it in analogy with C_n (the analysis of the belief in "continu'd existence" of an external object that I presented in §2.2), when we are looking at a table without simultaneously introspecting, we can nonetheless maintain:

(C_r) The belief, of a perception (say, an impression as of a table) that has been observed introspectively but is not currently being observed, that it (the impression) exists.

And why do I assume that the impression is in the mind distinctly from my reflective observation of it? For I take for granted that the impression would be in the mind,

<hr/>

[21] And this usage might also be present elsewhere in the main body of the text. For example:

[S]ince reason can never give rise to the idea of efficacy, that idea must be deriv'd from experience, and from some particular instances of this efficacy, which make their passage into the mind by the common channels of *sensation or reflection*. . . . If we pretend, therefore, to have any just idea of this efficacy, we must produce some instance, wherein the efficacy is plainly discoverable to the mind, and its operations obvious to *our consciousness or sensation*' (T 1.3.14.6, SBN 157–8; emphasis added).

The pairing of consciousness with reflection as an alternative to sensation as a source of perceptions is clear. He makes a similar pairing a few paragraphs later at T 1.3.14.10, SBN 161. I am unsure, however, whether he is using 'reflection' here in Locke's sense, to mean introspection, or to refer to impressions of reflection (passions and feelings).

when I am looking at the table, whether or not I introspectively observed it. Again, as in D_n, we get:

(D$_r$)   The belief, of a perception (the impression as of a table) that is currently being observed introspectively, that it (the impression of the table) exists.

Hume, unfortunately, never directly addresses these issues. The best we can do is work from the clues available to us, and gauge the success of the interpretation in light of its capacity to make sense of the text.

My suggestion is that we take the "great analogy" (T 1.4.6.5, SBN 253) between our beliefs about the identity of objects and the identity of the mind to mean that the mechanism responsible for our beliefs about the independence of external objects from our sensations of them is also responsible for our beliefs about the independence of internal objects from our introspective awareness of them. We saw in Chapter 3 that Hume explains our belief in the independent existence of, say, the table, by saying that when we have interrupted and changing sensations, each with image-contents as of the-table-from-various-perspectives in a constant or coherent fashion, the imagination responds so as to constitute the unchanging and uninterrupted table as our intended object. In being aware of image-content in the right manner, we take ourselves to encounter mind-independent objects. The analogous story for our beliefs about perceptions would say that in being aware of the image-content of the secondary idea in the right manner, we take ourselves to encounter an introspection-independent perception. I noted in §3.3.1 that the intended objects that we become aware of by means of this mechanism should be construed as *vulgar objects*, not specifically different from perceptions, but different in "relations, connexions and durations" (T 1.2.6.9, SBN 68). If my suggestion about our introspective awareness of perceptions is correct, then *perceptions themselves count as vulgar objects*.

It is not clear, however, that I am entitled to the suggestion that secondary ideas have image-content. After all, the image-content of a primary impression (and the primary idea that copies it) is an image as of the object of the perception—and ultimately (in the case of spatially located objects) is an array of coloured and tangible points. But Hume suggests in the crucial passage that analogizes introspection to memory that in forming a secondary idea of a perception we think of the mental operation involved in our being aware of that image-content: "[W]e not only delineate out the objects, of which we were thinking, but also conceive the action of the mind in the meditation, that certain *je-ne-scai-quoi*, of which 'tis impossible to give any definition or description, but which every one sufficiently understands" (T 1.3.8.16, SBN 106). It is by no means obvious that the secondary idea includes something like an *image* of the mental operation, even if the secondary idea also includes the image-content that the mental operation takes as its (proximate) object (we "delineate out . . . the object, of which we were thinking"). Recall, however, that Hume construes 'image' very widely, not merely in visual terms, so that every sense impression involves some kind of image. If we can take it to mean simply that a perception *portrays* something, then a secondary idea might well count as having image-content, in that it is a portrayal of the primary perception as an awareness-of-its-object. Thus the initial introduction of secondary ideas describes them as "*images* of the primary" (T 1.1.1.11, SBN 6; emphasis added), and Hume describes memory, which I have suggested he uses as the model for introspection, as "a faculty, by which we raise up the *images* of past perceptions" (T 1.4.6.18, SBN 260; emphasis added). In the first *Enquiry*, Hume even appeals to the mirror metaphor in describing our thoughts of prior mental states: "When we reflect on our past sentiments and affections, our thought is a faithful mirror, and copies its objects truly" (EU 2.2, SBN 18).

It might seem that Hume's assumption here that our introspective awareness gets the mind right speaks against the supposition that it is mediated by an image-content and our imaginative responses thereto. Recall that in §2.3 I noted his confidence in his reflective verdict that impressions "in their true colours" (T 1.4.2.7, SBN 190) appear as perceptions. Indeed, throughout the *Treatise* he takes his introspective investigation to yield the truth about the mind. At the same time, however, he also notes in the personal identity discussion (T 1.4.6) that, when reflecting on the mind, our secondary ideas are associated together in such a way that we overlook the diversity of the mind-bundle, and take it to be a unified entity, both at a time and across time (see §6.5). Elsewhere he writes:

It is remarkable concerning the operations of the mind, that, though intimately present to us, yet, whenever they become the object of reflexion, they seem involved in obscurity; nor can the eye readily find those lines and boundaries, which discriminate and distinguish them. The objects are too fine to remain long in the same aspect or situation; and must be apprehended in an instant, by a superior penetration, derived from nature, and improved by habit and reflection.   (EU 1.13, SBN 13)[22]

In the *Treatise*, in a passage immediately before the crucial passage on introspection, (1), Hume says that

'tis very difficult to talk of the operations of the mind with perfect propriety and exactness; because common language has seldom made any very nice distinctions among them, but has generally call'd by the same term all such as nearly resemble each other. And as this is a source almost inevitable of obscurity and confusion in the author; so it may frequently give rise to doubts and objections in the reader, which otherwise he wou'd never have dream'd of.
(T 1.3.8.15, SBN 105)

---

[22] Also: "[T]he finer sentiments of the mind, the operations of the understanding, the various agitations of the passions, though really in themselves distinct, easily escape us, when surveyed by reflection" (EU 7.1, SBN 60). Recall also the discussion in my Introduction of Hume's personal experiences with the difficulty of "bring[ing] the Idea he comprehended in gross, nearer to him so as to contemplate its minutest Parts & keep it steddily in his Eye, so as to copy these Parts in Order" (L 1,16).

What might explain Hume's seeming ambivalence about introspection, sometimes taking its verdicts to be especially veridical and sometimes acknowledging a more problematic structure?

If we take my interpretive suggestion, where the introspecting philosopher's access to the mind is analogized to the vulgar's access to the world (via the senses and memory), we see that, for Hume, the philosopher is *vulgar with respect to the mind*. Just as the vulgar typically take themselves to be immersed in the world, and are blind to the mental operations that afford them that awareness, so also introspecting philosophers typically take themselves to be immersed in the mind, and are blind to the mental operations that afford them that awareness. Hume himself, I think, sometimes embodies this un-self-conscious, 'vulgar' philosophical mindset by assuming introspection automatically gets the mind right, just as the vulgar-properly-speaking assume that their sensory observations get the world right. Thus we get the passages where he seems to embrace the verdicts of introspection without question.

But just as philosophers, when investigating the principles responsible for the vulgar sense of immersion in the world, show it to be more tenuous than the vulgar realize, so also philosophers can investigate the principles responsible for their *philosophical* sense of immersion in the mind that they reflectively observe, and show this sense of immersion to be more tenuous than philosophers normally realize. (In §2.2 I suggested that this kind of introspective investigation of *philosophical* beliefs about the mind requires a third level of introspection.) Thus Hume ends Book 1 of the *Treatise* with an acknowledgement that in the "most elaborate philosophical researches" it is "proper" that

we shou'd yield to that propensity, which inclines us to be positive and certain in *particular points*, according to the light, in which we survey them in any *particular instant*. 'Tis easier to forbear all examination and enquiry, than to check ourselves in so natural a propensity, and guard against that assurance, which always arises from an exact and full survey of an object. On such an occasion we are apt not only to forget our scepticism, but even our modesty too; and make use of such terms as these, *'tis evident, 'tis certain, 'tis undeniable*; which a due deference to the public ought, perhaps, to prevent.   (T 1.4.7.15, SBN 274)

He seems to acknowledge that his convictions about the structure of the mind are just as fallible as the vulgar's convictions about the world.

Note that in discussing Locke's and Hume's treatments of reflection, we have ended up with something of a reversal. Locke officially treats reflection on the model of sensation but, when it comes to reflective knowledge, his conception of consciousness introduces a disparity between our sensory access to the external world and our reflective access to the internal world. Our consciousness of the mental operations that are the objects of ideas of reflection allows for far greater epistemic security in the inner realm than in the outer. Hume, in contrast, models reflection on memory rather than on sensation: reflection allows us to *think* of perceptions via secondary *ideas*. But when it comes to the belief in the verdicts of introspection, he seems to fall back onto his account of our belief in the verdicts of sensation—each involving the association of ideas in the right manner so as to yield belief in the continued and distinct existence of their objects, be they inner or outer. I suggest in §4.7 that Hume's ultimate response to the Pyrrhonian challenge ends up relying on this parity between access to the inner and access to the outer.

4.4 Explaining the Resilience of Sensory Belief

How are we to decide between Locke's and Hume's accounts of reflection and its relation to sensation? As empiricists, each officially answers questions like this by appealing to what they discover when reflectively observing the mind. Locke would say that his observations show reflection to involve the perception of an idea that represents a mental operation, where both the perception and the operation that is represented by the idea are, in his special sense, conscious. Hume would say that his observations show reflection to involve secondary ideas of perceptions, the associations between which yield our belief in the introspection-independent existence of the primary perceptions. We seem to have reached an impasse. Each philosopher models reflection in such a way that observation of the mind yields an account of reflection in keeping with the model. How then is it possible to defend a model of the mind without begging the question?

The problem is especially difficult for empiricists who claim to appeal to *experience* to answer philosophical questions. When it comes to the foundational commitments of their understanding of the mind, such as how experience itself is to be understood—either the inner experiences given by introspection or the outer experiences given by sensation—empiricists seem to have left themselves without any independent source of evidence that would support one model of the mind over another. I suggest in this section, however, that one of Hume's goals in the discussion of scepticism in the final quarter of SwS is to resolve this problem.

Recall that we saw in Chapter 1 that, in SwR, Hume tells us why he has presented the sceptical challenge to reason despite its unbelievability:

My intention then in displaying so carefully the arguments of that fantastic sect, is only to make the reader sensible of the truth of my hypothesis, *that all our reasonings concerning causes and effects are deriv'd from nothing but custom; and that belief is more properly an act of the sensitive, than of the cogitative part of our natures.* . . . If belief, therefore, were a simple act of the thought, without any peculiar manner of conception, or the addition of a force and vivacity, it must infallibly destroy itself, and in every case terminate in a total suspense of judgment.

(T 1.4.1.8, SBN 183–4)

Accordingly, any philosophical system that treats belief as "a simple act of the thought"—either the Stoics or the early-modern inheritors of their assent-account of belief, such as Descartes and Malebranche—will be unable to explain why we cannot accept the sceptical challenge. Hume takes there to be "no error" in the sceptical argument (T 1.4.1.8, SBN 184), and this model of belief gives us no reason for thinking that we cannot follow it through to its conclusion. The model is thus disproved by the empirical fact of our incapacity to be total sceptics. In my reconstruction of Hume's argument in §1.6, this conclusion occurs as:

(4$_R$)   Argument that Hume's model of belief as the outcome of experience-engendered association best explains our incapacity to accept the sceptical conclusion.

Hume does not similarly declare his intentions in SwS, but I take it that we can read into it an argument parallel to that of SwR. He would then be using the empirical fact of our reaction to the Pyrrhonian challenge to sensory belief as evidence in favour of his model of sensation.[23]

Consider what happens when Locke is confronted with the Pyrrhonian challenge to sensory beliefs, keeping in mind Hume's emphasis on its dependence on reflection. How can Locke respond to the challenge, given that he allows for two different kinds of reflection: the "reflex Act" of consciousness that accompanies all mental states, and the observation of our mental operations that constitutes reflection in his technical sense? In §2.1 I emphasized Locke's analogizing the mind to a mirror so that perceiving an idea of sensation that represents an object is like seeing a mirror image of it. I also suggested there that Locke's use of the analogy requires that we *know* that we are seeing the object by means of a mirror-image. Consciousness is the mental analogue for this kind of knowledge: in being conscious of a thought, we know that we are perceiving an idea. It follows that, for Locke, we do not need to reflect, in his technical sense, in order to face the Pyrrhonian challenge. Every idea announces itself, as it were, as a mere image by means of our consciousness of our perception of it. And this means Locke has modelled the mind so that the question that the Pyrrhonian poses for us—should we believe that there is anything beyond the idea that we are conscious of?—is *always* posed for us. We have to *decide* whether to take our ideas to be veridical.

As I discuss in §4.5, Locke thinks that we can make this decision, and thus recognize the existence of external objects. But, as we saw in §4.2, Hume thinks that the "necessary consequence" (T 1.4.2.50, SBN 214) of the Pyrrhonian experiments is the extravagantly sceptical conclusion that "our perceptions have no more a continu'd than an independent existence" (T 1.4.2.46, SBN 211). Thus Hume holds that, if Locke is right about the structure of the mind, where we are always conscious

---

[23] Philip Cummins, in contrast, suggests that Hume's lack of an official statement saying that his intention in SwS is, as it was in SwR, to use the unbelievability of the sceptical conclusion as evidence for his model of the mind, to mean that the two sceptical Sections cannot be read in parallel, as I have done here ("Hume's Diffident Skepticism," *Hume Studies* 25 [1999], 52). He then struggles over how to understand the final paragraph of SwS (T 1.4.2.57, SBN 218; see §4.8), where Hume treats the sceptical challenge to reason and the senses as on a par ("Diffident Skepticism," 62–63n24).

of the mind-dependence of our ideas and needing to decide whether there are external objects beyond them, then we should be extravagant sceptics.

My suggestion, then, is that Hume uses the empirical fact of no one's believing the extravagantly sceptical conclusion about the external world, (2_S), as evidence against philosophical systems that model sensation in such a way that we recognize—or, as Locke puts it, are conscious of—the fact that our sensations give us merely images as of things, where the belief in the independent existence of objects results from our deciding that our images are sufficiently veridical. Hume's rejoinder is that, if we were so conscious, we would be able to draw the conclusion that the Pyrrhonians urge on us; we would be able to reject the belief in an external world entirely, and to remain in the position of accepting merely how things seem to us. Our inability to become extravagant sceptics shows that this model is inaccurate.

Hume's alternative model of the mind makes better sense of our reactions to the Pyrrhonian challenge. For Hume, we *can* reflect, but we are not *required* to reflect. Normally, we are carried along by our associations so as to believe in the independent existence of our sensory objects. But the Pyrrhonians are right to say that reflection reveals that the image-contents of perceptions are not distinct from our awareness of them. When we reflect we can suspend the associations productive of the belief in the sensory object, instead merely observing the perceptions within us. Hume points out, however, that this suspension is unsustainable:

There is a great difference betwixt such opinions as we form after a calm and profound reflection, and such as we embrace by a kind of instinct or natural impulse, on account of their suitableness and conformity to the mind. If these opinions become contrary, 'tis not difficult to foresee which of them will have the advantage. As long as our attention is bent upon the subject, the philosophical and study'd principle may prevail; but the moment we relax our thoughts, nature will display herself, and draw us back to our former opinion.[24]

(T 1.4.2.51, SBN 214)

Hume here makes it sounds as though our incapacity to maintain our philosophical reflections is simply a brute fact about us. Interpreters who attribute a strongly sceptical position to Hume take passages such as these as evidence that he holds that we *should* abandon our sensory beliefs, even if we are constitutionally incapable of adhering to what our philosophical analysis requires of us. Naturalist interpreters, in contrast, see Hume's emphasis here on our incapacity to give up our instinctive beliefs in the independent existence of sensory objects to mean that

---

[24] The passage continues: "Nay she has sometimes such an influence, that she can stop our progress, even in the midst of our most profound reflections, and keep us from running on with all the consequences of any philosophical opinion. Thus tho' we clearly perceive the dependence and interruption of our perceptions, we stop short in our carreer, and never upon that account reject the notion of an independent and continu'd existence. That opinion has taken such deep root in the imagination, that 'tis impossible ever to eradicate it, nor will any strain'd metaphysical conviction of the dependence of our perceptions be sufficient for that purpose" (T 1.4.2.51, SBN 214).

they are *justified*—not by reason, but by nature. I suggest in §4.7 that neither option gets Hume's position right. In particular, I argue that both are mistaken in supposing that he takes our incapacity to maintain the reflective posture to be merely a brute fact about us. I show that a clearer understanding of how he accounts for that incapacity allows for a different interpretation of his ultimate position.

Independently of how one understands Hume's analysis of the limitations of our reflections, we have seen that in SwS, as in SwR, Hume can be interpreted as using the empirical fact of our inability to accept the sceptical conclusion as evidence in favour of his model of the mind. Thus we have, in analogy with (4_R):

(4_S)   Argument that Hume's model of sensing as the outcome of experience-engendered association best explains our incapacity to accept the sceptical conclusion.

Just as we are not essentially reflectively aware of the mental processes involved in our reasonings so that we would need to make a special assent to our conclusions, we are also not essentially reflectively aware of the mental processes involved in our sensings, needing to decide whether our sensations give us the world.[25] Though we can, in moments of philosophical reflection, ask the Pyrrhonian question, we cannot ask it always. Our belief in the world is in that sense immunized from sceptical doubt.

---

[25]   This interpretation of Hume's use of the sceptical argument in the final quarter of SwS might seem to introduce unnecessary redundancy into the text. Recall that earlier in SwS, in a passage from his phenomenology of sensory experience that we explored in §2.3, Hume has already rejected the suggestion that we recognize our sensations as images simply in virtue of having them (T 1.4.2.4, SBN 189). Indeed, I suggested there that Locke was Hume's probable target, and emphasized that Locke's treatment of ideas as images differs from Hume's treatment of the image-contents of perceptions precisely because Locke claims that we always recognize—are conscious of—ideas as images. Why, then, would Hume offer the new argument, based on the unbelievability of extravagant scepticism in order to reject a Lockian model of sensation? One quick answer to this question might be that, just as he uses SwR to confirm his conclusion from Part 3 of Book 1 that causal reasoning is based in the "sensitive...part of our natures," he similarly means the sceptical argument at the end of SwS as a confirmation of what he has already established.

A second answer is that Hume has different targets in the two arguments. In the earlier rejection of ideas as images, his concern is how best to understand the *content* of our sensations. Hume here opposes Locke, and any other philosopher who takes sensations to present themselves as images. In the latter argument, Hume's target is the suggestion that a special kind of reflection—what Locke calls 'consciousness'—is built into every state of awareness. (In §6.2 we see that Hume also rejects the thesis, shared by Locke and others, that this consciousness is a kind of self-consciousness, so that we are always aware of ourselves as the subjects of our mental states.)

Ultimately, I think Hume returns to the issue of how best to model the mind in explaining sensation because his earlier rejection of the Lockian model was quite weak, consisting more in assertion than reasoning. He simply declares that it is "evident" that sensations are "single perceptions" that do not present the additional object that would make their being images palpable to us (T 1.4.2.4, SBN 189). He needs the later argument that draws on the unbelievability of extravagant scepticism to provide evidence in favour of what is otherwise a merely dogmatic assertion of his position.

4.5 Double-Existence Theories

Subscribers to a Lockian model could respond to Hume's argument in two different ways. First, they could argue that the Pyrrhonian experiments do not prove that sensations are mind-dependent. But, just as Hume suggests in SwR that there was "no error" (T 1.4.1.8, SBN 184) in the sceptical challenge to reason, he seems to think that the Pyrrhonian challenge to our sensing is well-founded. We are not, in fact, directly in contact with the external world (§2.3). I noted in §4.1 that Hume emphasizes the ease with which we recognize the lack of distinct existence for our sensations. He seems to take it that no one will seriously object to him on this front.

Hume's opponents' second possible response would be that they can have their cake and eat it too: namely, by adopting a version of Locke's conception of sensitive knowledge, where we both acknowledge the mind-dependence of every sensation and at the same time recognize mind-independent objects as their causes. In Hume's words, this model of the mind posits the "double existence of perceptions and objects" where "the former are suppos'd to be interrupted, and perishing, and different at every different return; the latter to be uninterrupted, and to preserve a continu'd existence and identity" (T 1.4.2.46, SBN 211). If this model can be sustained, then Hume cannot argue that the unbelievability of extravagant scepticism supports his account of sensory belief. For it could be that we recognize our sensory perceptions for what they are, and also recognize the objects beyond them that cause and, at least to some extent, resemble them.

Given the prevalence of such views in the early modern period—though I have emphasized Locke, suitably modified versions of it can be attributed to Descartes, Hobbes, and others—Hume has to take this possible rejoinder to his analysis of extravagant scepticism seriously indeed. Thus he devotes most of his discussion of sceptical arguments concerning sensory beliefs to responding to the double-existence theorists (T 1.4.2.46-55, SBN 211-17). He argues that their view is incoherent—mandated neither by reason nor by the imagination, or at least not directly. He suggests that philosophers have been attracted to it nonetheless because it is in fact parasitic on his own preferred explanation of the belief in the external world, even if the philosophers who offer it do not realize it.

Reason does not support the system of double existence because once we accept this system's starting point—the recognition that sensations present only how things seem to us—we cannot properly make an inference to a world beyond perceptions:

The only conclusion we can draw from the existence of one thing to that of another, is by means of the relation of cause and effect, which shews, that there is a connexion betwixt them, and that the existence of one is dependent on that of the other. The idea of this relation is deriv'd from past experience, by which we find, that two beings are constantly conjoin'd together, and are always present at once to the mind. But as no beings are ever present to the mind but perceptions; it follows that we may observe a conjunction or a relation of cause and effect between different perceptions, but can never observe it between perceptions and objects.

'Tis impossible, therefore, that from the existence or any of the qualities of the former, we can ever form any conclusion concerning the existence of the latter, or ever satisfy our reason in this particular.   (T 1.4.2.47, SBN 211–12)

As far as reason is concerned, we should be "extravagant sceptics," the untenability of which we have already discussed. Nor is the imagination directly responsible for the double-existence theory. For its normal workings produce the vulgar sense of immersion in the world where our associative responses to sensations are such that we take ourselves to encounter independently existing objects.

How then can the double-existence theorists still subscribe to their theory, given that it is mandated by neither reason nor the imagination? Hume's answer is that, without realizing it, they end up relying on the very processes that produce the vulgar belief in continued and distinct objects. Double-existence theorists are self-deceived:

[H]owever philosophical this new system may be esteem'd, I assert that 'tis only a palliative remedy, and that it contains all the difficulties of the vulgar system, with some others, that are peculiar to itself. . . . Were we not first perswaded, that our perceptions are our only objects, and continue to exist even when they no longer make their appearance to the senses, we shou'd never be led to think, that our *perceptions* and *objects* are different, and that our objects alone preserve a continu'd existence.   (T 1.4.2.44, SBN 211; emphasis added)

Though Hume dwells on the role of the imagination in producing the belief in the *objects* of the double-existence theory, note that he acknowledges here that it is in fact involved in its claims about *perceptions* as well. I first examine how Hume's claim applies to objects (§4.5.1), and then I turn to perceptions (§4.5.2). In §4.5.3 I consider whether Hume's own position should count as a double-existence theory.

4.5.1 Objects

Consider first the status of the external objects in the double-existence theory. We saw in Chapter 3 (§3.3) that Hume allows that there are two ways in which philosophers can describe external objects: as specifically different from perceptions, what I called *non-perceptual objects*; and as the same in kind but different in "relations, connexions and durations" (T 1.2.6.9, SBN 68) from perceptions, what I called *vulgar objects*. The latter result from the imagination's response to constant and coherent experience; the former result from philosophers' using the relation of resemblance to consider things that are absolutely unlike perceptions and their objects. He argues that while we can say almost nothing about non-perceptual objects, philosophers can characterize the objects that the vulgar take themselves to encounter as vulgar objects.

Although Hume is not as clear about this as one would like, I think that, in SwS, he suggests that double-existence theorists, like Locke, take themselves to posit non-perceptual objects. Consider the following passage:

Let it be taken for granted, that our perceptions are broken, and interrupted, and however like, are still different from each other; and let any one upon this supposition shew why the fancy, directly and immediately, proceeds to the belief of another existence, *resembling these percep-tions in their nature*, but yet continu'd, and uninterrupted, and identical; and after he has done this to my satisfaction, I promise to renounce my present opinion [that the double-existence theory does not arise directly from the imagination].... Whoever wou'd explain the origin of the *common* opinion concerning the continu'd and distinct existence of body, must take the mind in its *common* situation, and must proceed upon the supposition, that our perceptions are our only objects, and continue to exist even when they are not perceiv'd.[26]

(T 1.4.2.48, SBN 213; emphasis added on "resembling...")

He here *contrasts* the vulgar or "common" conception of external objects with the conception that the double-existence theorist uses. The vulgar take their perceptions to be external objects and to continue existing "even when they are not perceiv'd;" their external objects are vulgar objects. The double-existence theorist, in contrast, says that external objects *resemble* perceptions "in their nature," with the implication that they do not thereby *share* in that nature. They would thus be non-perceptual objects, or at least an *attempt* to posit non-perceptual objects, where these objects are nonetheless taken to be similar to vulgar objects.

The problem is that double-existence theorists want their objects to be non-perceptual, and yet they also want to give a positive characterization of them. But any attempt to characterize non-perceptual objects ends up relying on features that belong only to vulgar objects. Hume considers the double-existence theorists' sug-gestions that external objects cause and resemble our perceptions of them. In the case of causation, we saw in the passage quoted above, when considering whether reason supports the double-existence theory, that "we may observe a conjunction or a relation of cause and effect between different perceptions, but can never observe it between perceptions and objects" (T 1.4.2.47, SBN 211–12). We can point to, say, a tree as the cause of our impression as of a tree, but only if we return to the vulgar perspective where we take ourselves to have contact with such things as trees. That is, we can countenance a *vulgar* object as the cause of the impression. If, however, we try to posit a *non-perceptual* object as such a cause we get nowhere. We would end up combining two thoughts: the causal relation between the impression and its vulgar-object cause, and then the negation of resemblance between that vulgar-object cause and the non-perceptual object. This does not yield the causal connection between the non-perceptual object and the sensation that the double-existence theorists posit.

So also with their suggestion that objects resemble the perceptions that they are supposed to cause. Hume argues that this attempt to inject content into the double-existence theorists' objects ends up simply borrowing from the content of our perceptions: "We never can conceive any thing but perceptions, and therefore must make every thing resemble them" (T 1.4.2.54–5, SBN 216–17). In the penultimate paragraph of SwS, Hume concludes that the double-existence theorists' objects end

---

[26] The passage continues: "Tho' this opinion be false, 'tis the most natural of any, and has alone any primary recommendation to the fancy" (T 1.4.2.48, SBN 213).

up being merely another set of vulgar objects, products of their having remained under the influence of the vulgar tendencies of the imagination *malgré eux*:

> Philosophers deny our resembling perceptions to be identically the same, and uninterrupted; and yet have so great a propensity to believe them such, that they arbitrarily invent a new set of perceptions, to which they attribute these qualities. I say, a new set of perceptions: For we may well suppose in general, but 'tis impossible for us distinctly to conceive, objects to be in their nature any thing but exactly the same with perceptions.   (T 1.4.2.56, SBN 218)

We saw in §4.4 that Hume argues that we cannot maintain the introspective posture whereby we recognize our sensations as mere impressions (T 1.4.2.51, SBN 214). I take his point here to be that double-existence philosophers have in fact been switching between the vulgar perspective, where they take themselves to be in direct contact with objects—now acknowledged to be vulgar objects—and the introspective perspective, where they recognize their perceptions as mental phenomena:

> The imagination tells us, that our resembling perceptions have a continu'd and uninterrupted existence, and are not annihilated by their absence. Reflection tells us, that even our resembling perceptions are interrupted in their existence, and different from each other. The contradiction betwixt these opinions we elude by a new fiction, which is conformable to the hypotheses both of reflection and fancy, by ascribing these contrary qualities to different existences; the *interruption* to perceptions, and the *continuance* to objects. Nature is obstinate, and will not quit the field, however strongly attack'd by reason; and at the same time reason is so clear in the point, that there is no possibility of disguising her. Not being able to reconcile these two enemies, we endeavour to set ourselves at ease as much as possible, by successively granting to each whatever it demands, and by feigning a double existence, where each may find something, that has all the conditions it desires.[27]   (T 1.4.2.52, SBN 215)

Hume thus shows that his opponents, who try to model the mind so that something like Lockian sensitive knowledge is possible, are in fact relying on his own account of the mind. The only reason that they think that they have sensitive knowledge is that they have switched back to the vulgar sense of immersion in the world.

4.5.2 Perceptions

I noted above that Hume suggests that the double-existence theorist's view is parasitic on his own account of the mind not only in its treatment of objects but also in its treatment of *perceptions*. He does not follow up on this suggestion in SwS,

---

[27] The passage continues: "Were we fully convinc'd, that our resembling perceptions are continu'd, and identical, and independent, we shou'd never run into this opinion of a double existence; since we shou'd find satisfaction in our first supposition, and wou'd not look beyond. Again, were we fully convinc'd, that our perceptions are dependent, and interrupted, and different, we shou'd be as little inclin'd to embrace the opinion of a double existence; since in that case we shou'd clearly perceive the error of our first supposition of a continu'd existence, and wou'd never regard it any farther. 'Tis therefore from the intermediate situation of the mind, that this opinion arises, and from such an adherence to these two contrary principles, as makes us seek some pretext to justify our receiving both; which happily at last is found in the system of a double existence" (T 1.4.2.52, SBN 215–16).

but I think it is nonetheless worthwhile to explore what he might have had in mind. It will turn out that just as the objects in the double-existence theory turn out to depend on philosophers' retaining their vulgar sense of immersion in the world, the perceptions in the double-existence theory also depend on this vulgar sense of immersion.

Let us return to the Pyrrhonian experiments. They work by forcing us into the reflective posture where we focus on our perceptions as such, interrupting the associations of the imagination that produce our normal belief in the independent existence of our objects. But why, when we recognize sensory impressions for what they are, do we think of them as mind *dependent*? Recall from §2.3 that earlier in SwS, when exploring whether sensations were, by themselves, responsible for the vulgar belief in body, Hume considers whether sensory impressions present themselves as distinct from the mind. He asserts that "all sensations are felt by the mind, such as they really are" (T 1.4.2.5, SBN 189) and that "they appear, all of them, in their true colours, as impressions or perceptions" (T 1.4.2.7, SBN 190); "all impressions are internal and perishing existences, and appear as such" (T 1.4.2.15, SBN 194). He insists that sensations do not present themselves as distinct from the mind, for if they did they would need "to compare the object with ourselves" (T 1.4.2.11, SBN 192), and yet the self is not in fact part of their content. But, for the same reason that sensations do not present themselves as mind independent, they should not present themselves as mind dependent either. If they do not "compare the object with ourselves," their content should reveal neither mind independence *nor mind dependence*. Rather, it is only by contrast with the vulgar objects that the imagination leads us to believe have different "relations, connexions and durations" (T 1.2.6.9, SBN 68) from perceptions—it is only by contrast with public objects that persist when the sensations cease—that sensations count as mind dependent, private, and ephemeral.

A related point focuses on the sense in which the double-existence theory posits its "internal" object as "representing," while its "external" object is thereby "represented" (T 1.4.2.36, SBN 205). Recall from Chapter 2 that the starting point for Hume's explanation of our sensory beliefs is our awareness of a pixelated array of coloured and tangible points (the first of the four senses of 'image' distinguished in §2.3). This content counts as *imagistic*—as representing—only insofar as our associative responses to it lead us, in being aware of it, to believe that we are encountering a persisting object. Our reactions are such that, in being aware of the content, it is as if we are seeing an image in a mirror without realizing it. However, once we do realize that it is a mirror-image—or once we reflect on the mind—we can distinguish between the mirror or mental image and the object we take ourselves to be aware of by means of our awareness of the image. The point is that, once our perceptions are recognized as "interrupted, and perishing, and different at every different return," they can count as being *representations* of external objects only by reference to what we believe when we respond associatively to them in the normal ways. Impressions count as the "representing" element of a double existence because the vulgar reactions to their content yield the everyday belief in the "represented" second existent, a persisting public object.

My discussion, in §4.3.2, of Hume's account of reflection reveals a second way in which the internal half of the double-existence theory is parasitic on our vulgar imaginative responses. Double-existence theorists take themselves to distinguish between an inner realm of perceptions, to which we have immediate access, and the external world of objects that we can access only mediately, by means of the perceptions that represent and are caused by them. But I suggested above that Hume explains reflective awareness of perceptions in the same way as he explains sensory awareness of the world. In each case, we believe that what we perceive exists—either internal perceptions or external objects—only because of the appropriate association of ideas—secondary ideas in the former case and primary perceptions in the latter. So double-existence theorists are mistaken in their assumption of some kind of special immediate access to perceptions. There is no such thing as immediate access beyond the awareness of image-content that qualifies a sensory perception as a mental state (see §6.6). All awareness of *objects*, inner and outer, turns out to depend on the imagination.

In my interpretation of SwR (§1.3) I argued that Hume sees the systems of both total sceptics and dogmatic philosophers as springing from a common "erroneous maxim, That what a man can perform sometimes, and in some dispositions, he can perform always, and in every disposition."[28] Thus, in the case of reason, both the Stoics and their Pyrrhonian interlocutors mistakenly take the understanding to include the "reflex act" (T 1.4.1.5, SBN 182) by means of which we recognize the possibility of error as a fundamental feature of reasoning. But, for Hume, reflection on our reasoning is optional and, when it is undertaken, it has a structure that is the same in kind as the reasoning it examines. Thus, in my eight-step reconstruction of Hume's argument in SwR, we get:

(5$_R$)   Diagnosis of opponents' model of belief as an "act of the thought" in terms of their failure to recognize that reflection is optional and that reflective verdicts depend on experience-engendered association.

Double-existence theorists make a similar error in their analysis of how the mind relates to the world. Because we *can* reflect, so as to recognize the perceptual mediation of our sensory beliefs, they take it that we *always* recognize these perceptions: for Locke, we are always conscious of our mental states. But Hume argues that this recognition is itself mediated by our reflective, secondary ideas, and we do not normally reflect on them. Moreover, I suggested in §4.3.2 that the structure of reflection is similar to that of unreflective sensation. In each case, it is only because of the reactions of the imagination that we come to believe that the objects we observe

---

[28] *Dialogues Concerning Natural Religion*, ed. N. Kemp Smith (Indianapolis, IN: Bobbs-Merrill, 1947), 133.

(perceptions in the case of introspection, everyday objects in the case of sensation) have an independent existence. So, analogously to (5_R), in SwS, we have:

(5_S) Diagnosis of opponents' model of sensation as involving a double existence in terms of their failure to recognize that reflection is optional and that reflective verdicts depend on experience-engendered association.

I show in the discussion of personal identity in Chapter 6 that Hume allows that we can also reflect *on our reflections* by bringing those secondary ideas into focus, but the higher level perceptions—tertiary ideas—would themselves remain unreflective. We can never get all of our perceptions into view as objects of thought, because the perceptions that are the vehicles for this thinking would themselves be left out. We are, in this sense, irremediably vulgar.

Overall, then, Hume rebuts the challenge to (4_S)—what I have described as the use of the unbelievability of extravagant scepticism to support his conception of the mind as a mere bundle of perceptions, associations between some of which produce our belief in the independent existence of sensory objects. The attempt to offer something like a Lockian account of sensitive knowledge, where we always stand over our perceptions, recognizing them as mental representations, and at the same time grasping mind-independent non-perceptual objects, fails. The invocation of a mind-independent object turns out to depend on the belief in vulgar objects that Hume has shown to be produced by our associations. The claim that we always recognize our perceptions as *mental* representations turns out to depend both on the retention of a conception of the objective world against which we can count perceptions as mind-dependent representations, and on the associations of introspective secondary ideas that yield the belief in the existence of mind.

4.5.3 Hume as Double-Existence Theorist

To what extent does Hume himself count as a double-existence theorist? Not at all, given the definition of this view that I have been working with in this section, where it attempts to analyze *vulgar* sensory experience as involving the recognition of an inner mental representation and the grasp of a *non-perceptual* external object that both resembles and causes that representation. Hume, in contrast, treats vulgar beliefs about sensory objects in terms of a "single existence" (T 1.4.2.31, SBN 202; see also T 1.4.2.4, SBN 189). The vulgar simply have sensations, even if their associative response means that, in having them, they thereby think about public, temporally extended, vulgar objects. As I argued in Chapter 2, the vulgar take themselves to be immersed in the world and are thereby (mostly) blind to the perceptual mediation of their experience.

Hume's *philosophical theory* about the mind, however, does amount to a kind of double-existence theory. For he distinguishes between the image-content of the vulgar's sensations and intended objects of their thought. Unlike the Lockian double-existence theorists, however, Hume does not construe these objects as non-perceptual. Instead, as we saw in §3.3, intended objects are vulgar objects—the same in kind as perceptions, but different in "relations, connexions and durations" (T 1.2.6.9, SBN 68) from image-contents.

We have seen (§§4.5.1 and 4.5.2) that Hume's discussion of double-existence theories in the final quarter of SwS emphasizes their unwitting parasitism on the vulgar sense of immersion in the world. Hume's own philosophical version of this theory also displays this parasitism, though he makes no attempt to hide it from himself. Consider the three grades of introspection that, in §2.2, I suggested Hume relies on in his investigation of the mind: first, where he uses a quasi-third personal stance, allowing him to retain his vulgar grip on external objects and at the same time to observe the perceptions in the mind involved in his thinking and reasoning; second, when he examines the mind's capacity to have a vulgar grip on external objects, as in SwS; and third, where he observes his philosophical reflections in order to see how our beliefs about the mind arise, as in his discussion in "Of personal identity" (T 1.4.6). We now see that at each grade of introspection, Hume thinks that there is a sense that philosophers must retain their vulgar sense of immersion in the objects of their perceptions, be those the sensory perceptions that afford us the world, as in the first grade, or the reflective perceptions that make us aware of the mind, in the second and third grades. There is no philosophical stance that would allow us to transcend the mind's fundamental processes, including the imagination's tendency to associate ideas in such a way that we believe we are in contact with what we observe.

4.6 The Philosophical Question

I argued in Chapter 1 that Hume confronts the sceptical argument against reason in SwR twice—first as a means to support his conception of mind, and then as a challenge to reason once it is properly understood in Humean terms. Even if we cannot help but believe the verdicts of reason, *should* we? I argued there that this is a legitimate question—albeit one that, *contra* Descartes and others who hold an assent theory of belief, is not posed for us merely by the structure of the mind. It is thus a peculiarly *philosophical* question, asked only by those moved by their curiosity to discover whether our instinctive belief in reasoning is justified. Thus I suggested that step six of Hume's argument in SwR is:

   (6$_R$)   Acknowledgement that, given (3$_R$), there is a legitimate *philosophical* question to be asked about whether we should believe the verdicts of reason.

But Hume makes the same pivot in SwS. Although he starts the Section by taking the existence of body as a "point, which we must take for granted in all our reasonings" (T 1.4.2.1, SBN 187), he eventually comes to ask whether he should in fact believe the verdicts of the senses:

I begun this subject with premising, that we ought to have an implicit faith in our senses, and that this wou'd be the conclusion, I shou'd draw from the whole of my reasoning. But to be ingenuous, I feel myself *at present* of a quite contrary sentiment, and am more inclin'd to repose no faith at all in my senses, or rather imagination, than to place in it such an implicit confidence. I cannot conceive how such trivial qualities of the fancy, conducted by such false suppositions, can ever lead to any solid and rational system.   (T 1.4.2.56, SBN 217)

Even if, normally, we are carried along by our imaginations so that we have a sense of immersion in the world, his philosophical uncovering of the role of the imagination now leads him to question our sensory beliefs. Note that, as was the case in SwR, this is a distinctively *philosophical* question. Because we are normally blind to the mediation of our sensory beliefs by perceptions and our associative responses thereto, we do not *need* to decide whether to believe the verdicts of the senses. Nonetheless, we *can* reflect on the mind, discover how it is structured, and then ask whether our instinctive belief is justified. Thus, in parallel to SwR's (6_R), we have:

(6_S)   Acknowledgement that, given (3_S), there is a legitimate *philosophical* question to be asked about whether we should believe the verdicts of the senses.

Indeed, given that, as I have suggested, Hume holds that we are irremediably vulgar, dependent on the imagination's associations even in our philosophical moments, the question might seem particularly pressing.

4.7 Reflective Interference

I showed in Chapter 1 that even though the philosophical question of whether we should believe the verdicts of our reasoning is well-formed, we turn out to be unable to answer it. In reflecting on the mind, we interfere with the associative processes that Hume thinks constitute probabilistic reasoning. Rather than reaching a verdict on reasoning, this kind of *reflective interference* destroys that very capacity and, given that the sceptical question is itself based in reasoning, it destroys it too. They "they both vanish away into nothing, by a regular and just diminution" (T 1.4.1.12, SBN 187). Thus:

(7_R)   Recognition that, because of reflective interference, philosophers are unable to answer the legitimate question in (6_R).

With the sceptical challenge to reason thus silenced, our natural tendency to believe the verdicts of reasoning can reassert itself, and we continue on unharmed by our philosophical failure: We "reason and believe, even tho'...[we] cannot defend [our] reason by reason" (T 1.4.2.1, SBN 187). Philosophy turns out to be impotent when addressing whether our reasoning is worth believing. But because we do not need to reach a decision on this question when reasoning in everyday life, we can live with this philosophical impotence.

I think we can see the same pattern of reflective interference that we saw in SwR emerging in the penultimate paragraph of SwS. Philosophers reflect on the mind and reveal the perceptual mediation of our experience of external objects. They learn that the vulgar are mistaken in their attitude of immersion in the world, in that in fact our mental processes shape our access to things. But just as the reflective verdict in SwR depended on the very same features of mind as it was investigating, so also in SwS. As we saw in §4.3.2, philosophers' introspectively derived conclusions about sensing depend on their believing the verdicts of their reflections: they remain vulgar with respect to the mind. So if they are tempted to reject the vulgar beliefs about objects because of their dependence on the "trivial qualities of the fancy" (T 1.4.2.56, SBN 217), these philosophers should similarly reject the reflective conclusions that led to the initial rejection; they too depend on "trivial qualities of the fancy": "What then can we look for from this confusion of groundless and extraordinary opinions but error and falshood? And how can we justify to ourselves any belief we repose in them" (T 1.4.2.56, SBN 218)? Thus we get:

(7$_S$)   Recognition that, because of reflective interference, philosophers are unable to answer the legitimate question in (6$_S$).

As in SwR, the sceptical challenge undermines itself by attacking the mental processes on which it relies.

4.8 The Sceptical Malady and the Sceptical Remedy

Thus far I have suggested that the Pyrrhonian experiments of T 1.4.2.45 (SBN 210–11) serve to force us into a reflective posture, where we introspectively observe our perceptions, suspending the imagination's responses to their image-content, and thus leading us to temporarily lose our belief in enduring, public objects—what I have been calling vulgar objects (1$_S$). As a matter of fact, however, we cannot sustain this extravagant scepticism (2$_S$). The key to understanding this datum is Hume's model of reflection (3$_S$). It turns out that reflective beliefs about perceptions depend on similar principles of the imagination as vulgar beliefs about sensory objects. But this kind of reflection is optional, and thus there is no fundamental *requirement* that we *decide* whether to believe the verdicts of sensation. Lockian double-existence theorists, in contrast, model the mind so that the Pyrrhonian questions are *forced* on us because we always stand over—are conscious of—our sensory ideas. For them, there is nothing stopping us from embracing the extravagantly sceptical conclusion. Our incapacity to do so thus counts as evidence against this model of the mind and in favour of Hume's alternative (4$_S$). Indeed, he thinks that the double-existence model is the result of philosophers' taking the introspective posture for granted, not recognizing the role of the imagination in generating both their beliefs about inner perceptions and external objects (5$_S$). There is nonetheless still a legitimate *philosophical* question to be asked about our sensory beliefs. Once we recognize their dependence on the imagination, are we entitled to continue holding them (6$_S$)? This question is no longer forced on us by the mind's very structure, but it is still one we can ask when motivated by philosophical curiosity. But because the principles responsible for our reflective beliefs are the same in kind as those involved in our sensory beliefs, the investigation of the latter undermines the former, and we end up losing our grip on both (7_S). We are unable to answer the philosophical question.

Throughout my discussion I have emphasized the parallels between Hume's investigations of our belief in the verdicts of reason in SwR and our belief in the verdicts of the senses in SwS. In the former case, a Pyrrhonian argument is deployed to show that we ought not to accept any rationally generated beliefs (1_R). The empirical fact of our incapacity to accept "total" scepticism (2_R) is explained by the role of reflection in the generation of the argument, where reflective assessments of rational arguments turn out to be the same in kind as probabilistic arguments themselves, in each case yielding belief in its conclusion without the requirement of a further act of assent (3_R). Thus our incapacity to accept the sceptical conclusion is evidence in support of Hume's model of reasoning (4_R). The mistake of other philosophers is taking the reflective posture of the philosopher to be the fundamental structure of the mind, where rather than being carried along by our reasoning into belief, we must decide whether to accept its verdict (5_R). Hume allows that there is a legitimate philosophical question to be asked here (6_R), but it is not one that must be answered for us to continue reasoning successfully. When we try to answer the philosophical question, however, we face the problem of reflective interference. Because our reflective investigation of our reasoning is the same in kind as the unreflective reasoning we are exploring, the investigation ends up rebounding back on itself, undermining both our base-level reasoning and our reflective investigation (7_R).

In the final paragraph of SwS, Hume brings the two sceptical Sections together with a common conclusion:

This sceptical doubt, both with respect to reason and the senses, [a] is a malady, which can never be radically cur'd, but must return upon us every moment, however we may chace it away, and sometimes may seem entirely free from it. [b] 'Tis impossible upon any system to defend either our understanding or senses; and we but expose them farther when we endeavour to justify them in that manner. [c] As the sceptical doubt arises naturally from a profound and intense reflection on those subjects, [d] it always encreases, the farther we carry our reflections, whether in opposition or conformity to it. [e] Carelessness and in-attention alone can afford us any remedy. For this reason I rely entirely upon them; and take it for granted, whatever may be the reader's opinion at this present moment, that [f] an hour hence he will be persuaded there is both an external and internal world. . . .   (T 1.4.2.57, SBN 218)

I have distinguished six different claims in the paragraph, (a)–(f). The first four, (a)–(d), describe the sceptical malady: it cannot be "radically cur'd;" attempts to justify our faculties "in that manner" all fail; the malady arises "naturally" from a certain kind of reflection; and it only gets worse the more we reflect. The final two, (e) and (f), present Hume's remedy: "carelessness and inattention" that will restore our belief in the external and internal worlds. The challenge for the interpreter is to make sense of these claims, both serially and in conjunction with one another.

I noted in §4.4 that contemporary readers tend to take Hume here in one of two ways, each of which parallels an interpretive option that, in §1.5, we saw could also be applied to SwR. First, the *sceptical* interpreters take Hume in (a)–(d) to be embracing the sceptical conclusion, but with a caveat that our nature is too weak to follow it.[29] They take (e) and (f) to mean that our only option is to forget the conclusion we had reached previously. But rather than forgetting his conclusions about the mind's structure that he has established in SwS, Hume spends the following four Sections elaborating on their implications (see Chapters 5 and 6). The second interpretive option is the *naturalist* reading, where Hume is said not to reject the sceptical arguments against our sensory beliefs (hence [a] and [b]), but rather to hold that our natural tendency to accept the verdicts of the senses, (e)–(f), trumps any arguments against them.[30] In addition to saddling Hume with the problem I noted in Chapter 1 in connection with SwR—how to sort out the competing claims of what are seen as two sources of normativity in human nature—the naturalist interpretation faces a further problem here. For (c) and (d) make it clear that the sceptical doubt is just as natural as our beliefs in the verdicts of reason or the senses.

More could be said in evaluating the strengths and weaknesses of these interpretive options, but I will postpone further analysis of them until Chapter 7, where I examine Hume's final engagement with scepticism in the "Conclusion of this book" (T 1.4.7). At this point, however, I want to suggest that both styles of interpretation miss out on a crucial point in the argument. As I noted earlier when discussing our immunity to extravagant scepticism (§4.4), these readings take Hume to treat our incapacity to accept extravagant scepticism as a mere fact about us—a sign of our fundamental irrationality in the case of the sceptical interpreters, and a normatively laden fact in the case of the naturalist interpreters. I think that the incapacity should instead be seen as arising from reflective interference. Because Hume holds that reflective verdicts depend on the very same mental processes as our vulgar sensory beliefs, a challenge to the latter ends up inadvertently challenging the former as well. We end up believing neither the philosophical rejection of the vulgar belief nor the vulgar belief itself; rather, we create the moment of utter confusion that Hume illustrates so graphically for us in the climax to the "Conclusion of this book" (T 1.4.7.8, SBN 268–9; see Chapter 7). Because this momentary confusion undermines our reflections, our natural associative tendencies are able to reassert themselves, and we can return to the vulgar sense of immersion in the world. The recalcitrance of our natural tendencies in the face of philosophical reflection is not a brute fact, but a result of those reflections depending on the very tendencies they investigate.

---

[29] See especially Robert Fogelin, *Hume's Skepticism in the 'Treatise of Human Nature'* (London: Routledge and Kegan Paul, 1985); and Wayne Waxman, *Hume's Theory of Consciousness* (Cambridge: Cambridge University Press, 1994).

[30] See especially N. Kemp Smith, *Philosophy of David Hume* (London: Macmillan, 1941); and Garrett, *Cognition and Commitment.*

This interpretive suggestion conforms to the final paragraph of SwS as follows. First, in (a), Hume points out that the question of whether to believe the verdicts of reason and the senses is well-formed, but not amenable to a direct solution, a "radical cure" that answers it in its own terms. Second, though (a) describes the doubt as "return[ing] ... every moment,"[31] he notes in (c) that in fact it arises "naturally from a profound and intense *reflection*" (emphasis added). I take this to mean that the sceptical doubt is a problem *for philosophy*, as we reflectively stand back from our mental processes in order to understand their fundamental structures. And, as (d) emphasizes, once we start to question the verdicts of reason and the senses, we are on the road to the mutual destruction of both the sceptical doubt and the capacity it challenges. Recall the conclusion of SwR, where Hume says that "they [would] both vanish away into nothing, by a regular and just diminution," if our natural tendencies did not reassert themselves (T 1.4.1.12, SBN 187). But (e) reminds us that they do; because the reflections themselves are victims of their own attack, we return to the "carelessness and in-attention" whereby we are carried along by our mental processes so as to automatically believe in the outcomes of our reasonings and sensings, (f). We learn then, (b), that we cannot offer a philosophical "system" that would "defend either our understanding or senses" by "justify[ing] them *in that manner*" (emphasis added). We cannot get outside of our fundamental tendencies to believe in such a way as to show that they are justified or unjustified independently of those tendencies. Philosophy cannot accomplish all the tasks it sets for itself. Finally, as (f) makes clear, the acceptance of our fundamental tendencies to believe is not restricted to our vulgar moments, where we are oriented towards external objects; it applies just as much to our philosophical moments, when we investigate the "internal world." As I noted earlier, we are *irremediably* vulgar. Philosophers must learn to live with human nature, even if its fundamental capacities can neither be vindicated nor repudiated.

In my interpretation of SwR I suggested that the conclusion as it applies to reason can be summarized as:

(8$_R$) Acceptance of the "true" scepticism, where we continue to use our reason without being able to give it a fundamental justification.

(I imported the label, "true" scepticism, into SwR from the "Conclusion of this book" [T 1.4.7.14, SBN 273].) Not surprisingly, given that Hume openly presents the quoted passage as summarizing the outcome of both SwR and SwS, I take Hume's point to apply to sensory beliefs in a parallel fashion:

(8$_S$) Acceptance of the "true" scepticism, where we continue to use our senses without being able to give them a fundamental justification.

---

[31] Michael Williams suggests that Hume here engages in hyperbole ("The Unity of Hume's Philosophical Project," *Hume Studies* 30 [2004], 289).

5

Ancient Philosophy: Substances and Souls

In Chapters 1–4 we saw that Hume takes his task in the *Treatise* to be the explanation of not only vulgar beliefs and attitudes, but also the responses that philosophers have made to them. The title of Part 4 of Book 1 is thus "Of the sceptical and other *systems of philosophy*" (emphasis added), and in Sections 1 and 2 alone he has addressed "total" and "extravagant" scepticism, the system of "double existence," and his own preferred system. Hume ends "Of scepticism with regard to the senses" (T 1.4.2, hereafter 'SwS') by saying:

> I...take it for granted, whatever may be the reader's opinion at this present moment, that an hour hence he will be persuaded there is both an external and internal world; and going upon that supposition, I intend to examine some general systems both ancient and modern, which have been propos'd of both, before I proceed to a more particular enquiry concerning our impressions. This will not, perhaps, in the end be found foreign to our present purpose.
>
> (T 1.4.2.57, SBN 218)

I noted in my Introduction that he here sets the agenda for the following four Sections of the *Treatise*, leading up the "Conclusion of this book" (T 1.4.7). The "more particular enquiry concerning our impressions" is Book 2's discussion of those impressions of reflection that are passions.

He addresses ancient systems of the external world in "Of the antient philosophy" (T 1.4.3, hereafter 'AP'), where his focus is the commitment to substance ontology. I think that "Of the immateriality of the soul" (T 1.4.5, hereafter 'IS') should be seen as Hume's investigation of ancient systems of the internal world. Despite the fact that the debate he addresses in that Section featured such early moderns as Benedict Spinoza (whom he discusses at length; see §5.5), as well as John Locke, G. W. Leibniz, Ralph Cudworth, and others (see §§5.6 and 6.4), it nonetheless hinges on the question of whether and how the soul is a substance. Even though the ancients were the first to be tempted to posit substances as the deep structures underlying things, philosophers of the early modern period continued to be influenced by the same mental principles that moved the ancients.

Hume addresses modern systems of the external world, the defining thesis of which is the distinction between primary and secondary qualities, in "Of the modern philosophy" (T 1.4.4). In §§6.2–6.5 I argue that Hume's discussion of personal identity (T 1.4.6) should be seen as his response to the modern system of the internal world. Whereas such philosophers as René Descartes, Antoine Arnauld, and Locke take the mind to be characterized by a fundamental self-consciousness, so that in every mental act we are aware of ourselves as ongoing thinkers, Hume argues that perceptions do not include this reflective act. Our minds are thus nothing more than bundles of perceptions.

In the quoted passage, Hume tells us that the exploration of ancient and modern systems "will not be foreign to" his "purpose." My focus in this chapter and in Chapter 6 will be how he elaborates on his own conceptions of the mind and philosophy through his interrogation of his predecessors' systems. In §5.1 I show that Hume thinks that what he calls "false" philosophy, such as that endorsed by the ancients and the moderns, is defined by a desire to reach beyond the limits of our cognitive natures. Ancient philosophers try to get behind the world as it is presented to us in our perceptions, while modern philosophers assume that our access to the inner realm of perceptions is different in kind from and superior to our access to the outer world of objects. This diagnosis presents Hume with certain challenges. Given his conception of mind, how can false philosophers even begin to make the mistakes that he thinks they exemplify?

In the remainder of the chapter I use this analysis of false philosophy to address some of the interpretive challenges arising out of IS. It is a difficult Section—the second longest in the *Treatise*—that addresses a range of topics, from the relation between mind and body, to the spatial characteristics of perceptions, to the implications of Hume's philosophical conclusions for religion. In §§5.2–5.4 I restrict my focus to Hume's arguments against those systems that take the mind to be a substance. I examine the argument that perceptions themselves qualify as substances, and its reliance on various metaphysical principles that can seem surprisingly un-Humean. In §5.5 I try to make some sense of Hume's peculiar investigation of Spinoza and his critics. I finish my discussion in §5.6 with a brief examination of Hume's exploration of the possibility that even though perceptions do not *inhere* in minds, they might be literally contained *inside* of them.

5.1 True and False Philosophy

Hume's treatment of substance metaphysics in AP is, on its own terms, unexciting, in that it mostly revisits points he had made much earlier in the *Treatise*, in the short, three-paragraph, Section "Of modes and substances" (T 1.1.6). There he relied on his empiricist first principle that (almost all) ideas ultimately acquire their content from prior simple impressions to argue that the idea of a substance is the idea of a bundle or "collection" (T 1.1.6.1, SBN 16) of sensible qualities. In particular, Hume rejects the suggestion that the idea of substance includes a reference to an "unknown *something*, in which [the qualities] are supposed to inhere" (T 1.1.6.2, SBN 16).[1] We have no impression of such a subject of inherence, and thus we cannot have the idea of it either.

It might seem, however, that Hume's rejection of this conception of substance gets him into trouble. For he seems to be left with no explanation for our capacity to discover new features of an object. If its idea is limited to those qualities that we have sensed, then, when we find that the yellow-heavy-malleable-and-fusible gold is also soluble in *aqua regia*, we would seem to be dealing with a different bundle of qualities (yellow-heavy-malleable-fusible-and-soluble) rather than a new feature of the same one. But Hume sidesteps this objection by arguing that although we have "no idea of substance, distinct from that of a collection of particular qualities" (T 1.1.6.1, SBN 16), the idea represents more than those qualities. The imagination establishes a "principle of union" (T 1.1.6.2., SBN 16) for the bundle that allows it to continue the same as it gains and loses properties. As we saw in Chapter 2, Hume holds that the imagination's response to the content acquired in impressions can allow us to think of things not directly given in impressions. Applying the framework I developed in my interpretation of general ideas in §2.4, to the case of an idea of a substance, the original qualities serve as the proximate content for the idea, while its name triggers imaginative propensities that cause us to overlook the differences between those qualities and others that resemble, are contiguous, or cause them. Our intended object is thus the one ongoing substance with different modes.

Hume's recapitulates this argument in greater detail in AP, though he emphasizes there the belief that the bundle of qualities is simple at a time and identical through time. He returns to the mechanism he introduced in SwS, where the relations between image-contents cause us to associate their ideas and thus overlook the differences between them (T 1.4.2.24–35, 1.4.3.3–5; SBN 199–204, 219–21). But whereas Hume's original treatment of the belief in the unity of objects focuses on cases of constant experience, where interrupted impressions are qualitatively identical, I noted in §3.3.5, that in AP and (especially) "Of personal identity" (T 1.4.6) he extends the mechanism to include cases of coherent experience, where the image-contents of the perceptions are related by resemblance, contiguity, and causation. The imagination's associations cause us to believe that we are encountering a single unified object.

As the title to the section suggest, Hume's greatest concern in AP is how *philosophers* tend to respond to the imaginatively generated content. Because of the tension between the diversity in the proximate content and the unity of the intended object, they posit an intrinsically unified "substance, or original and first matter"

---

[1] Hume refers to this assumption of an "unknown *something*" as a "fiction"—the first appearance of this problematic term in the *Treatise*. Here it refers to the kind of philosophical fiction he will explore in AP, rather than to the kind of fiction that, in §2.4 and Chapter 3, I argued were constitutive of objects not directly experienced through sensation (such as vacuums, external objects, universals, and the like).

(T 1.4.3.4, SBN 220) that underlies the qualities. The "peripatetic philosophers" go so far as to

> assert the *original* matter to be perfectly homogeneous in all bodies, and considers fire, water, earth, and air, as of the very same substance; on account of their gradual revolutions and changes into each other. At the same time it assigns to each of these species of objects a distinct *substantial form*, which it supposes to be the source of all those different qualities they possess, and to be a new foundation of simplicity and identity to each particular species.
>
> (T 1.4.3.6, SBN 221)

Hume declares that the "whole system" is "entirely incomprehensible," but his point is that it nonetheless arises from natural principles (T 1.4.3.8, SBN 222).

In two crucial paragraphs, Hume uses the example of ancient substance metaphysics to sketch a general account of philosophical belief, both true and false:

> In considering this subject we may observe a gradation of three opinions, that rise above each other, according as the persons, who form them, acquire new degrees of reason and knowledge. These opinions are that of the vulgar, that of a false philosophy, and that of the true; where we shall find upon enquiry, that the true philosophy approaches nearer to the sentiments of the vulgar, than to those of a mistaken knowledge.   (T 1.4.3.9, SBN 222–3)

I take him here to provide a framework for understanding the arguments of Sections 3–6 of *Treatise* 1.4, and so I discuss it at some length. He presents what might be called an incipiently Hegelian, dialectical conception of philosophy.[2] The move from vulgar opinion into philosophy is marked by an increase of "reason and knowledge," though it turns out to be but a "false philosophy" and, oxymoronically, a "mistaken knowledge." The third stage, "true philosophy," emerges with the continued acquisition of "reason and knowledge," but in so doing it recovers and supersedes—one might say '*hebt auf*'—the truth that was hidden within the "sentiments of the vulgar." Thus, *developmentally*, one progresses from vulgar opinion, through false philosophy, to true philosophy. But, *epistemologically*, false philosophy is inferior to the vulgar consciousness, while true philosophy improves on both.

Hume illustrates this point by considering different ways of viewing the necessary connections between a substance's qualities. Consider, for example, the structure of a rose's petals and its scent. As I emphasized in §2.2, the vulgar take themselves to be immersed in the world. "[I]n their common and careless way of thinking" they

---

[2] See especially Donald Livingston, *Philosophical Melancholy and Delirium: Hume's Pathology of Philosophy* (Chicago, IL: University of Chicago Press, 1998), 12. In a similar vein, Amelie O. Rorty calls the *Treatise* "a British proto-version of [Hegel's] *The Phenomenology of Spirit*" ("From Passions to Sentiments: The Structure of Hume's *Treatise*," *History of Philosophy Quarterly* 10 [1993], 169). Annette Baier says: "I believe it is time that hindsight through the analytic empiricist tradition be supplemented with a more Hegelian look back at Hume's phenomenology of mind, *A Treatise of Human Nature*" ("Master Passions," in A. O. Rorty (ed.), *Explaining Emotions* [Berkeley, CA: University of California Press, 1980], 423n14). Henry Allison notes Hume's proto-Hegelian language in the final quarter of SwS, where he says that the philosophical system of double existence can be arrived at only through embracing the vulgar system (*Custom and Reason in Hume* [Oxford: Clarendon Press, 2008], 247–8).

remain focused on the contents of their perceptions, not recognizing that they are the contents *of perceptions*. So when "they have constantly found" the petals and scent "united together," their imaginations associate their ideas of the qualities but, given their ignorance of the perceptual mediation of their experience, they are unaware of the fact that the imagination is responsible for their belief in the necessary connection. Instead, they think that the qualities themselves are intrinsically linked; "they are apt to fancy . . . a separation to be in itself impossible and absurd" (T 1.4.3.9, SBN 223).

Philosophers, in contrast, who

abstract from the effects of custom, and compare the *ideas* of objects, immediately perceive the falshood of these vulgar sentiments, and discover that there is no known connexion among objects. Every different object appears to them entirely distinct and separate; and they perceive, that 'tis not from a view of the nature and qualities of objects we infer one from another, but only when in several instances we observe them to have been constantly conjoin'd.

(T 1.4.3.9, SBN 223; emphases added)

We saw in §4.3 that Hume, like Locke, takes philosophy to involve reflection on the mind (though, as I argued there, they understand reflection differently), so that we observe the primary perceptions involved in producing our vulgar opinion. And because we are no longer thinking of the rose's petals and scent, but are rather thinking of our *ideas* of them (by means of secondary ideas of those ideas), the associations between the primary ideas no longer have us in their sway. We are able to "abstract from the effects of custom"—the experience-engendered associations between primary ideas—when we reflect on the mind, and thus discover that the vulgar are mistaken in their beliefs about necessary connections: we do not have direct insight into an intrinsic connection between the scent and the petals.

Obviously this is an idiosyncratic interpretation of the philosophical project. Hume reads the tradition through his own method of anatomizing the mind in order to discover its fundamental principles. He also suggests that earlier philosophers implicitly understood his negative verdict on causal relations—his denial that we can have direct insight into necessary connections. They all recognized at some level that the ideas of the cause and of the effect were separable, and thus that the cause and effect were themselves distinct existences.[3] But Hume thinks that philosophers have tended to go wrong in their response to this discovery.

Some philosophers take their discovery about the associative source of our causal beliefs to mean that they should give up on them entirely. Hume does not address this option here, presumably because he already extensively analyzed the unsustainability of radical—"total" or "extravagant"—scepticism in SwR and SwS. Instead he

---

[3] The application of this point to theories of substance is more plausible. While the vulgar take themselves to have direct insight into the unity of an object, philosophers recognize the synchronic and diachronic diversity in our experience.

focuses on those philosophers who search for a non-mental foundation for our causal beliefs:

[I]nstead of drawing a just inference from this observation, and concluding, that we have no idea of power or agency, separate from the mind, and belonging to causes; I say, instead of drawing this conclusion, they frequently search for the qualities, in which this agency consists, and are displeas'd with every system, which their reason suggests to them, in order to explain it. They have sufficient force of genius to free them from the vulgar error, that there is a natural and perceivable connexion betwixt the several sensible qualities and actions of matter; but not sufficient to keep them from ever seeking for this connexion in matter, or causes.... At present they seem to be in a very lamentable condition, and such as the poets have given us but a faint notion of in their descriptions of the punishment of *Sisyphus* and *Tantalus*. For what can be imagin'd more tormenting, than to seek with eagerness, what for ever flies us; and seek for it in a place, where 'tis impossible it can ever exist?   (T 1.4.3.9, SBN 223)

Two points from the passage, each relating to what the philosophers described here seek, seem to be in tension with one another.

On the one hand, Hume has asserted elsewhere that "['t]is an establish'd maxim in metaphysics, That whatever the mind clearly conceives includes the idea of possible existence, or in other words, that nothing we imagine is absolutely impossible" (T 1.2.2.8, SBN 32; see §5.4 for a detailed consideration of this maxim). So his claim in the final sentence of the quoted passage that a mind-independent notion of causal power is impossible means that it is also inconceivable.

On the other hand, Hume also seems to allow that these philosophers do think of mind-independent causal powers: namely, as the goal for their fruitless search. His theory of motivation requires that with a few very primitive exceptions ("desire of punishment to our enemies, and of happiness to our friends; hunger, lust, and a few other bodily appetites," T 2.3.9.8, SBN 439; see also T 2.3.3.8, SBN 417), we have an idea of what we desire before we are moved by it. So, just as Sisyphus can conceive of successfully rolling the stone to the top of the hill and Tantalus can conceive of tasting the food and water that are out of his reach, these philosophers seem to be able to conceive of a kind of kind of necessary connection in things that goes beyond what we get from an internal feeling of necessity, even if Hume's argument in Part 3 of Book 1 of the *Treatise* shows that they will not be able to satisfy their desire to find such connections. Hume thus seems to want to have it both ways, with intrinsic necessary connections being both conceivable and inconceivable.

The ambivalence he demonstrates here reflects a subtlety in his view that has generated more than its fair share of discussion in the secondary literature over the last thirty years. Briefly, some interpreters—the so-called the "New Humeans," such as Galen Strawson, John Wright, and Peter Kail[4]—point to those places in Hume's

---

[4] John P. Wright, *The Sceptical Realism of David Hume* (Minneapolis, MN: University of Minnesota Press, 1983); Peter Kail, *Projection and Realism in Hume's Philosophy* (Oxford: Oxford University Press, 2007); Galen Strawson, *The Secret Connexion*, rev. edn. (Oxford: Oxford University Press, 2014). The label

corpus where he seems to hold that nature has a deep causal structure, even as he argues that we are unable to discover anything about it. They conclude that Hume is a metaphysical realist about causation, while remaining an epistemological sceptic: there are mind-transcendent necessities, even if we cannot know them. Kenneth Winkler, Peter Millican, and others defend the more traditional reading, where Hume's negative verdict about the idea of causation means that we cannot even *think* of mind-transcendent causal connections. The only impression of necessity arises from the association of ideas, and thus the only idea we can have of it is copied from this source. New Humeans try to escape this point by downplaying his theory of perceptions, so that we can have "notions" or "suppositions" of real causal connections, even if we have no ideas of them.[5] The problem is that Hume's sparse ontology of mind has no room for anything other than ideas and impressions, and indeed he uses 'notion' interchangeably with 'idea' in his investigation of causation (T 1.3.6.15, 1.3.14.20; SBN 93, 165).

In my view, Winkler and the traditionalists clearly have the upper hand in this debate, though the New Humeans are right to note those places where Hume seems to take seriously the possibility of mind-independent causal necessities. But I think that rather than endorsing causal realism in such passages,[6] his goal is to diagnose philosophers' tendency to seek for something more than what our minds make available to us.[7] Thus, in the climax to his discussion of causation in the *Treatise*, he considers an objection to his view: "What! the efficacy of causes lie in the determination of the mind! As if causes did not operate entirely independent of the mind, and wou'd not continue their operation, even tho' there was no mind existent to contemplate them, or reason concerning them" (T 1.3.14.26, SBN 167). He responds:

I can only reply to all these arguments, that the case is here much the same, as if a blind man shou'd pretend to find a great many absurdities in the supposition, that the colour of scarlet is not the same with the sound of a trumpet, nor light the same with solidity. If we have really no idea of a power or efficacy in any object, or of any real connexion betwixt causes and effects,

---

comes from a classic article by Kenneth Winkler, where he assesses the realist readings of Hume's analysis of causation, and finds them unsupported by the evidence ("The New Hume," *Philosophical Review* 100 [1991], 541–79); Peter Millican also offers an insightful refutation of the New Humeans in "Hume, Causal Realism, and Causal Science," *Mind* 118 (2009), 647–712. Many of the players in the debate responded, and there has been considerable back and forth. Representative papers on both sides, including Winkler's article, can be found in Rupert Read and Kenneth Richman (eds.), *The New Hume Debate* (London: Routledge, 2000).

[5] See, for example, Kail, *Projection*, 34, 84, 115.

[6] This point applies even to a semantic realism of the kind for which Kail argues (*Projection*, ch. 4).

[7] I do not mean to suggest that every passage on which the New Humeans rely should be interpreted in light of Hume's desire to diagnose false philosophical systems. Sometimes, as Winkler emphasizes, his point is that even though his account of causation is subjectivist—people's causal beliefs depends on their associative reaction to their particular experiences—he also allows for a kind of objectivity for causal claims—we aim to track the real constant conjunctions in nature, even if we do not yet observe the objects that are so conjoined ("New Hume," 548).

'twill be to little purpose to prove, that an efficacy is necessary in all operations. We do not understand our own meaning in talking so, but ignorantly confound ideas, which are entirely distinct from each other. I am, indeed, ready to allow, that there may be several qualities both in material and immaterial objects, with which we are utterly unacquainted; and if we please to call these *power* or *efficacy*, 'twill be of little consequence to the world. But when, instead of meaning these unknown qualities, we make the terms of power and efficacy signify something, of which we have a clear idea, and which is incompatible with those objects, to which we apply it, obscurity and error begin then to take place, and we are led astray by a false philosophy.

(T 1.3.14.27, SBN 168)

Here, Hume concedes that there might be features of objects "with which we are utterly unacquainted," but at the same time urges that using our ideas to characterize these features is pointless. Of course, in order to make the concession it is necessary for him to have an idea of such features, if only to deny our grasp of them. How is this possible?

Recall that in §3.3 we examined two different ways in which Hume allows for philosophers to think of objects. First, they can describe objects insofar as the vulgar encounter them by treating them as the same in kind as the content of perceptions but differing in "relations, connexions and durations" (T 1.2.6.9, SBN 68)—what I called *vulgar objects*. But it is also possible for philosophers to use relative ideas to think of objects "specifically different" (T 1.2.6.9, SBN 68) from perceptions and their contents—what I called *non-perceptual objects*. As I pointed out in §3.3.2, our grasp of such non-perceptual objects is very attenuated. It starts from the philosophers' introspective posture, where perceptions, considered as such, are the focus of our thoughts. We must then use our understanding of resemblance, developed through the experience of various vulgar objects, to think of those things that resemble perceptions, and finally we go on to negate this thought: non-perceptual objects are completely unlike anything we encounter.

This distinction allows Hume to explain the realist's objection to his account of causation and his own response to it. The account of non-perceptual objects shows that we can think of unknown qualities in objects, and thus acknowledge that there might be features in things that we entirely overlook. But as soon as we attempt to characterize those qualities, we must rely on our prior experiences, and thus are treating the objects vulgarly. So when philosophers try to say that there are intrinsic connections in things beyond what we are given in experience, Hume suggests that they have "ignorantly confound[ed] ideas, which are entirely distinct from each other": namely, those of non-perceptual objects and of necessary connections between vulgar objects.

With this analysis in mind, we can resolve the tension in the passage that compares false philosophers to Tantalus and Sisyphus. On the one hand, what the philosophers seek is inconceivable, in that we have no idea of necessary connection other than that arising from the experience-engendered association of ideas. On the other hand, by means of their idea of non-perceptual objects, they mistakenly think that they know what they are looking for, when they search for a deeper non-perceptual foundation for causal inferences. Recall that in §4.5.1 I showed how Hume makes a similar point in the penultimate paragraph of SwS. Philosophers who try to account for sensory access to the external world in terms of inner perceptions that are caused by resembling outer non-perceptual objects end up inadvertently relying on their grasp of vulgar objects *malgré eux*.

Hume continues his explanation of false philosophy by elaborating on the sense in which subscribers to it fail to realize that they have confounded incompatible ideas:

[A]s nature seems to have observ'd a kind of justice and compensation in every thing, she has not neglected philosophers more than the rest of the creation; but has reserv'd them a consolation amid all their disappointments and afflictions. This consolation principally con-sists in their invention of the words *faculty* and *occult quality*. For it being usual, after the frequent use of terms, which are really significant and intelligible, to omit the idea, which we wou'd express by them, and to preserve only the custom, by which we recal the idea at pleasure; so it naturally happens, that after the frequent use of terms, which are wholly insignificant and unintelligible, we fancy them to be on the same footing with the precedent, and to have a secret meaning, which we might discover by reflection. The resemblance of their appearance deceives the mind, as is usual, and makes us imagine a thorough resemblance and conformity. By this means these philosophers set themselves at ease, and arrive at last, by an illusion, at the same indifference, which the people attain by their stupidity, and true philosophers by their moderate scepticism. They need only say, that any phaenomenon, which puzzles them, arises from a faculty or an occult quality, and there is an end of all dispute and enquiry upon the matter.   (T 1.4.3.10, SBN 224)

Philosophers think that they are talking about real phenomena—non-perceptual faculties and occult qualities—when in fact the ideas at work in their reasoning are only those of the "wholly insignificant and unintelligible" *words*, 'faculty' and 'occult quality.' Thus they deceive themselves into thinking that they have found an extra-mental foundation for their causal beliefs, when in fact they are relying on the imagination's associations. Whereas the vulgar are ignorant of the role of perceptions and the imagination's associations in their thinking, and the false philosophers believe that they have provided it with a foundation, true philosophers, here identi-fied as "moderate sceptics," recognize that no such foundation can be offered. We must learn to live with the irremediable role of the imagination in our thinking about causes and substances. And this means that we can accept claims about the identity and simplicity of objects so long as we understand them "imperfect[ly]" (T 1.4.6.9, SBN 256). We are not tracking objects that are intrinsically unified at a time or across time. Rather, we have developed "grammatical" or "verbal" (T 1.4.6.21, SBN 262) rules to organize our common human reactions to changes in the environment, thus establishing thresholds for cases that will require us to recognize a new object, rather than a change in an old one (see §§3.2.3–3.2.5).

Hume's investigation of the idea of the vacuum provides a useful illustration of his point here. It ends with same dialectic whereby (false) philosophers object to his account for not penetrating into nature deeply enough, to which he responds by endorsing, in this case, a "modest scepticism" (T 1.2.5.26n12.2, SBN 639). Moreover, as we saw in §3.3.1, it is in the course of explaining the idea of the vacuum that he introduces the mechanism whereby philosophers mistake ideas of words for ideas of things on which he relies in the passage quoted earlier (and in fact I discussed part of that passage at that time).

Recall that Hume at first denies that we have an idea of the vacuum (T 1.2.3.16, SBN 39). Given his claim that the idea of space is an abstraction of the manner in which objects appear, it seems that thinking of space without thinking of objects arranged in it is impossible. How then can early-modern scientists debate the existence of a vacuum (T 1.2.5.2, SBN 54)? A "fiction" (T 1.2.3.11, SBN 37)[8] of the imagination enables us to think of empty space, and in this case the key to the fiction is the idea-substitution mechanism. Using the terminology I developed in §2.4, we can summarize Hume's argument as follows: though a vacuum cannot be experienced directly—it cannot be the proximate content of a perception—we can nonetheless have it as an intended object when we substitute the idea of two objects separated by an "invisible distance" for the idea of those objects where the distance between them is filled with perceptibles. Because of the relations between the content of the two substituted ideas, we overlook the differences between them, relying on the first idea when we need to think of the emptiness of the vacuum, and relying on the second idea when we need to think of its spatiality. The scientists, in their discussion of the vacuum, are thus in a position analogous to that of the vulgar with respect to causal connections. Just as the vulgar fail to recognize that their beliefs about causes arise from the imagination's experience-engendered association of ideas, so also the scientists fail to recognize that their thought of the vacuum depends on the imagination's mutual substitution of two ideas.

At the end of the discussion of the idea of the vacuum, Hume voices an objection to his view that foreshadows the objection to his account of causation that I quoted earlier (T 1.3.14.26, SBN 167): "'Twill probably be said...that I explain only the manner in which objects affect the senses, without endeavouring to account for their real nature and operations" (T 1.2.5.25, SBN 63). And his response is to "plead guilty"

by confessing that my intention never was to penetrate into the nature of bodies, or explain the secret causes of their operations. For besides that this belongs not to my present purpose, I am afraid, that such an enterprize is beyond the reach of human understanding, and that we can never pretend to know body otherwise than by those external properties, which discover themselves to the senses.   (T 1.2.5.26, SBN 64)

---

[8] The reference here is to Hume's account of the idea of the "unchangeable." He does not directly say that the idea of the vacuum results from a fiction, though given that he treats the idea of the unchangeable on the model of his account of the idea of the vacuum, I take it that the latter too qualifies as a fiction. See §§3.3.1 and 3.3.2.

If the scientists who debate the vacuum are, like the vulgar in their beliefs about causal connections, ignorant of the imagination's role in their thoughts, the objector here is like the false philosopher, who worries that once that role is acknowledged, some further foundation—something in the "real nature and operations" of objects— is needed to support her or his ideas. Hume's response is that it is hopeless to try to think beyond what can ultimately be traced back to sensation.

We saw in §3.2.1 that in the "Appendix" to the *Treatise* Hume elaborates on this point in an important footnote that he wanted to add to his guilty plea:

As long as we confine our speculations to *the appearances* of objects to our senses, without entering into disquisitions concerning their real nature and operations, we are safe from all difficulties, and can never be embarrass'd by any question.... If we carry our enquiry beyond the appearances of objects to the senses, I am afraid, that most of our conclusions will be full of scepticism and uncertainty. Thus if it be ask'd, whether or not the invisible and intangible distance be always full of *body*, or of something that by an improvement of our organs might become visible or tangible, I must acknowledge, that I find no very decisive arguments on either side; tho' I am inclin'd to the contrary opinion, as being more suitable to vulgar and popular notions. If *the Newtonian* philosophy be rightly understood, it will be found to mean no more. A vacuum is asserted: That is, bodies are said to be plac'd after such a manner, as to receive bodies betwixt them, without impulsion or penetration. The real nature of this position of bodies is unknown. We are only acquainted with its effects on the senses, and its power of receiving body. Nothing is more suitable to that philosophy, than a modest scepticism to a certain degree, and a fair confession of ignorance in subjects, that exceed all human capacity.
(T 1.2.5.26n12.1–2, SBN 638–9; emphases in original)

I take "modest scepticism" to be equivalent to the "moderate" scepticism of the true philosopher in AP. And Hume shows here that he is willing to accept theorizing about the vacuum once it is properly understood, just as the true philosopher will accept causal claims about objects and identity claims about substances, once they are properly understood. Thus, even though the idea of the vacuum results from a fiction of the imagination, and even though causal inferences and beliefs about substances depend on the imagination's associations, they can nonetheless be accepted by the true philosopher, who recognizes their human provenance.

In the footnote, Hume tells us that this kind of scepticism restricts its claims to the "appearances." He wanted this footnote to be appended so that it would appear three paragraphs prior to "Of the idea of existence, and external existence," with its discussion of the different conceptions of external objects that I investigated in §3.3, and I think Hume's point is best understood in its terms. For, as Donald Baxter emphasizes, once Hume has distinguished between what I have called vulgar and non-perceptual objects, he ends up with two different senses of 'reality' and 'appear-ance.'[9] On the one hand there are vulgar objects, which continue to exist with real

---

[9] "Hume's Theory of Space and Time," in D. F. Norton and J. Taylor (eds.), *Cambridge Companion to Hume*, 2nd edn. (Cambridge: Cambridge University Press, 2009), 116.

"relations, connexions and durations" (T 1.2.6.9, SBN 68) that will differ from their appearances in particular perceptions. On the other hand there are non-perceptual objects, the reality of which philosophers can barely conceive when they try to think of how things are absolutely independently of how they appear to us. The objection Hume raises to his discussion of the vacuum is put in terms of the latter reality/appearance distinction. He has accounted only for things in terms of the sensible qualities to which we have access, not in terms of a "real nature" that goes beyond our perceptual limitations. His guilty plea amounts to the admission that his positive claims are limited to vulgar objects. But he is unfazed by this objection because we have no significant access to the non-perceptual realm. Only "scepticism and uncertainty" can obtain when we try to say something about it because there is nothing we can appeal to to justify one position as opposed to another. An attempt to go beyond the "reach of human understanding" must fail.[10]

The comparison between Hume's treatments of the false philosophical conception of substance and the idea of the vacuum reveals what might seem like a problem for his view. False philosophers, he tells us, deceive themselves into thinking that they have found the wholly extra-mental foundation that they seek for their ideas, because the idea-substitution mechanism causes them to treat the ideas of words as if they had ideas of the things. In the case of the vacuum, however, true philosophers also rely on the idea-substitution mechanism in order to have empty space as an intended object. Why does Hume reject the outcome of the idea substitution in the first case but not in the second? One difference, of course, is that the true philosopher *acknowledges* the role of the idea substitution and thus has a conception of the vacuum in terms of the fiction, as "bodies . . . plac'd after such a manner, as to receive bodies betwixt them, without impulsion or penetration" (T 1.2.5.26n12.2, SBN 639). Is the only problem with the false philosophers' account of substance that they do not realize that they are engaging in a fiction? But why then does Hume treat 'faculty' and 'occult quality' as empty names, rather than as names the content of which is given by the mutual substitution of the idea of necessary connections between vulgar objects and the relative idea of non-perceptual objects?

I postpone my proposed resolution for this problem until I clarify further Hume's core metaphysical principles in §§5.3 and 5.4. It turns out that the false philosophers' fiction is merely verbal because they attempt to substitute *contradictory* ideas for one another.

5.2 Ancient Systems of the Internal World

I have suggested that Hume's analysis of true and false philosophy in "Of the antient philosophy" provides a template for his treatment of other systems of philosophy in

---

[10] See my "Adequate Ideas and Modest Scepticism in Hume's Metaphysics of Space," *Archiv für Geschichte der Philosophie* 92 (2010), 62–3.

Sections 4–6 of *Treatise* 1.4. Let us now turn to IS, where Hume addresses "the curious reasoners concerning the material or immaterial substances, in which they suppose our perceptions to inhere" (T 1.4.5.2, SBN 232). These philosophers respond to our inner experience with the same confusions as the ancients displayed with respect to experience of the world. In this section I use Descartes's version of the late-Scholastic theory of distinctions to consider Hume's argument that perceptions themselves qualify as substances, given the false philosophers' own definitions. There is no need to posit some further ground for perceptions—a soul in which they inhere.

It might seem a bit odd to treat Descartes as Hume's target when I have also identified his topic here as *ancient* systems of the internal world. But, as I suggested earlier, I take Hume to be using 'ancient' not as a merely temporal designator but as a substantive one, picking out those views that subscribe to substance ontology, whenever they were promulgated. Thus Descartes's substance dualism, just as Spinoza's substance monism (and even Locke's sceptical realism about substance), are aptly counted by Hume as ancient systems. They all fall prey to the same arguments. Note that my suggestion that Descartes, Locke, and Spinoza qualify as ancient philosophers, in Hume's sense, does not preclude their also being modern philosophers, in that each also subscribes to the primary–secondary quality distinction that he takes to define the modern system of the external world. Indeed, Hume must also not mean his philosophical taxonomy to be exhaustive: some philosophers will be neither ancient nor modern in various respects, as when Berkeley rejects both the primary-secondary quality distinction and substance metaphysics for the external world (though he remains an ancient with respect to the internal world given his commitment to the soul as a spiritual substance[11]).

Descartes presents his version of the theory of distinctions in *Principles* I 60–2 (AT VIIIA 28–30), in the course of giving the fundamentals of his ontology. The basic elements are substances—things "which exist in such a way as to depend on no other thing for [their] existence" (AT VIIIA 24). God is the only being to fully satisfy this definition, though Descartes also allows that created things count as substances in a secondary sense if they depend only on God. Two such substances are "really distinct" from one another, in that neither depends for its existence on the other. We recognize this real distinction when we "clearly and distinctly understand one apart from the other" (AT VIIIA 28). While substances are independent of other things, modes are dependent on substances for their existence. Two things are "modally

---

[11] At least according to the standard interpretations, though Berkeley's preferred specification of the concept of substance is controversial. See Talia Mae Bettcher, *Berkeley's Philosophy of Spirit: Consciousness, Ontology, and the Elusive Subject* (London: Continuum International Publishing, 2007); and Stephen H. Daniel, "Berkeley's Stoic Notion of Spiritual Substance," in Stephen H. Daniel (ed.), *New Interpretations of Berkeley's Thought* (Humanities Press, 2008), 203–30. Robert Muehlmann takes Berkeley's superficial commitment to a substance theory of mind to hide a deeper bundle account that prefigures Hume (*Berkeley's Ontology* [Indianapolis, IN: Hackett, 1992], ch. 6).

distinct" either when one is dependent on the other, but not *vice versa* (so that the second thing is a substance) or when each is dependent on another thing—a substance—though neither is dependent on the other. Finally, two things are "conceptually" or rationally "distinct" when it is unintelligible to think of the one without the other.

In the Sixth *Meditation*, Descartes famously argues that because we can clearly and distinctly perceive mind, characterized by thinking, apart from body, characterized by extension, and God could thus separate them in fact, the mind is a substance that is really distinct from body.[12] In contrast, two particular thoughts are modally distinct from one another, in that each depends on the mind that has them, though neither depends on the other. Finally, Descartes holds that there is merely a conceptual distinction between thought and the mind, so that thought counts as the "principal attribute" or nature of mind (AT VIIIA 25, 30-1). The mind is a *thinking* thing (*res cogitans*).

In IS, Hume seems to take delight in rejecting versions of all of these theses. Perceptions are not modes of the mind or soul, but rather themselves satisfy the definition of substance (T 1.4.5.5, SBN 233). Perceptions are not "actions" or "abstract modes" that are merely conceptually or rationally distinct from the mind, but have a separate existence from one another (T 1.4.5.26-28, SBN 244-6). His arguments take two forms. On the one hand, he relies on his previous treatments of substance to show that we do not have an idea of a mental substance as a subject of inherence. There is no impression source for an idea of internal substance in just the same way that there is not an impression source for an idea of external substance (T 1.4.5.2-4, SBN 232-3).

On the other hand, and more significantly for our purposes, he also uses two of his core metaphysical commitments—what are sometimes called the *conceivability maxim* and the *separability principles*—to show that perceptions do not need a subject of inherence:

Whatever is clearly conceiv'd may exist; and whatever is clearly conceiv'd, after any manner, may exist after the same manner. This is one principle, which has been already acknowledg'd. Again, every thing, which is different, is distinguishable, and every thing which is distinguishable, is separable by the imagination. This is another principle. My conclusion from both is, that since all our perceptions are different from each other, and from every thing else in the universe, they are also distinct and separable, and may be consider'd as separately existent, and may exist separately, and have no need of any thing else to support their existence. They are, therefore, substances, as far as this definition explains a substance. (T 1.4.5.5, SBN 233)

Hume's argument here starts from a premise that Descartes would accept: that perceptions are different from one another—though Descartes of course would say

---

[12] See Marleen Rozemond, *Descartes's Dualism* (Cambridge, MA: Harvard University Press, 1998) for a detailed exploration of Descartes's argument for the real distinction of mind and body.

that this is merely a modal distinction. But using principles that, as I show in §§5.3 and 5.4, have Cartesian roots, Hume argues that perceptions are in fact really distinct from one another, and thus qualify as substances under Descartes's definition.

Similarly, near the end of the Section he argues against the suggestion that perceptions are merely rationally distinct from the soul as follows:

> Our perceptions are all really different, and separable, and distinguishable from each other, and from every thing else, which we can imagine; and therefore 'tis impossible to conceive, how they can be the action or abstract mode of any substance.... As we conclude from the distinction and separability of their ideas, that external objects have a separate existence from each other; so when we make these ideas themselves our objects, we must draw the same conclusion concerning *them*, according to the precedent reasoning.   (T 1.4.5.27, SBN 245)

The argument here is perhaps disingenuous. Descartes does not argue that thoughts—the analogues in his system to Hume's perceptions—are each, taken singly, rationally distinct from the soul; rather, individual thoughts are modally distinct from one another and from the soul. Thought is rationally distinct from the soul when it is taken generally, as its principal attribute, so that "whatever we find in the mind is simply one of the various modes of thinking" (AT VIIIA 25). In the "Abstract," Hume acknowledges this feature of Descartes's account, but rejects it by appeal to his treatment of general ideas (T 1.1.7; see §2.4):

> *Des Cartes* maintained that thought was the essence of the mind; not this thought or that thought, but thought in general. This seems to be absolutely unintelligible, since every thing, that exists, is particular: And therefore it must be our several particular perceptions, that compose the mind. I say, *compose* the mind, not *belong* to it. The mind is not a substance, in which the perceptions inhere.   (T Abs.28, SBN 657–8)

But, given Hume's own view that minds are merely bundles of perceptions, he himself should admit that there is merely a distinction of reason between the mind and the perceptions that constitute it at any particular moment, even if he does not countenance a general attribute of perception. Ultimately, where Descartes wants to structure his view in terms of substance ontology, with thought as the essence of mind, Hume tries to do the opposite, with substances and modes being retained only as associatively generated intended objects (T 1.1.6), so that the mind is a collection of perceptions, each of which could exist without the others.

The problem with Hume's arguments against the Cartesian conception of mind as thinking substance is their reliance on his core metaphysical principles, neither of which receives a full defence and both of which are *prima facie* not easy to swallow. Indeed, by suggesting that our powers of conception give us guidance into the structure of things, they seem to reflect a Cartesian metaphysical confidence rather than a Humean sceptical modesty. In §§5.3 and 5.4 I address first the separability principles and then the conceivability maxim. I suggest that neither is as metaphysically ambitious as it appears at first glance, once the conception of reality at work in them is properly understood.

5.3 The Separability Principles

Hume introduces the separability principles rather abruptly in his discussion of general ideas:

[W]hatever objects are different are distinguishable, and that whatever objects are distinguishable are separable by the thought and imagination. And we may here add, that these propositions are equally true in the *inverse*, and that whatever objects are separable are also distinguishable, and that whatever objects are distinguishable are also different.

(T 1.1.7.3, SBN 18)

In that context, his goal is to show that the content of ideas, even general ideas, is fully determinate. Because the exact degree of a quality—say, the length of a line—is not different from the quality itself, and thus cannot be distinguished from it, nor thought of in a separate idea, the idea of a line-in-general cannot be generated by separating it out from the determinate features of the particular. Instead, as we saw in §2.4, the generality is created by the imagination's reactions to the particular.

But why believe the separability principles? They can be decomposed into six claims:

(OD) O_1 and O_2 are different objects → O_1 and O_2 can be distinguished by the mind;

(DO) O_1 and O_2 can be distinguished by the mind → O_1 and O_2 are different objects;

(OS) O_1 and O_2 are different objects → the idea of O_1 is separable from the idea of O_2;

(SO)   the idea of O_1 is separable from the idea of O_2 → O_1 and O_2 are different objects;

(DS) O_1 and O_2 can be distinguished by the mind → the idea of O_1 is separable from the idea of O_2;

(SD)   the idea of O_1 is separable from the idea of O_2 → O_1 and O_2 can be distinguished by the mind.

Whereas the first four principles assert an isomorphism between objects and our capacities of representation, the latter two concern the structure of those capacities themselves. I start with the latter two, which I take to be less problematic than the first four. I then turn to OD–SO and argue that Hume might have a defence of them available to him.

SD is the most trivial of the principles, in that it seems truistic that distinguishing between objects is a necessary condition for thinking of them in separate ideas. DS suggests that such distinctions are also sufficient for having the objects in separate ideas. The problem is that Hume himself allows for distinctions of reason, which "impl[y] neither a difference nor a separation" (T 1.1.7.17, SBN 25). The figure of a body and the colour that is so figured can be distinguished even if they are not separable in thought (or different in reality).[13] Hume accounts for this phenomenon in light of his parallel explanation of general ideas, where we can think of lines-in-general without thereby having a separate idea of the universal. In the case of distinctions of reason, we can think of the body's figure without thereby forming a separate idea of figure-apart-from-colour. Instead we form an idea of the object with its indistinguishable aspects (the proximate content), that then becomes the vehicle for a thought of the aspect in question (the intended object) because of our tendency to associate ideas of the object with ideas of others that also bear that aspect.[14] What is relevant for our purposes here is that Hume insists that two objects really count as distinguishable only if they can be thought by means of different ideas. That is, DS seems to be as much a definition of 'distinguishing' as it is a substantive claim about the relation between it and separation. What might look like a distinction between objects is not really one if their ideas cannot be separated.

While DS and SD clarify Hume's understanding of various mental acts, OD, OS, DO, and SO are more metaphysically robust, relating differences among objects to our capacities to register those differences in thought. Wherever there are differences in objects, we can in principle recognize them (OD) and conceive them separately (OS). And conversely, if we can separate out something in thought, then it exists in reality as a different object (DO, SO); there are no merely modal distinctions.

Hume applies these principles to both internal and external objects. Since one coloured or tangible point is different from another immediately adjacent to it, they can be distinguished (OD) and their ideas separated by the imagination (OS) (T 1.2.4.6, SBN 41). Since the length of a line is not different from the line itself, it cannot be distinguished from it (DO) (except through a distinction of reason) or thought of by means of a separate idea (SO) (T 1.1.7.3, SBN 18–19). Similarly, though with the O_i's now being played by perceptions, rather than external objects, "whatever we may imagine of the thing, the idea of a grain of sand is not distinguishable, nor separable into twenty, much less into a thousand, ten thousand, or an infinite number of different ideas" (T 1.2.1.3, SBN 27), and thus we have a minimal, partless idea (OS, OD). And the idea of time is not different from the idea of the succession of objects, and thus the idea of time is neither distinguishable nor separable from the idea of a succession (DO, SO) (T 1.2.3.10, SBN 36).

---

[13] Don Garrett offers a helpful discussion of this point in *Cognition and Commitment in Hume's Philosophy* (New York, NY: Oxford University Press, 1997), 74–5.

[14] The description I have given here is not quite right; it would yield, not the thought of say the redness of the red stop sign, but the thought of red things in general. It is not easy to pin down exactly the mental mechanics of Humean distinctions of reason, and Donald Baxter challenges their coherence in "Hume, Distinctions of Reason, and Differential Resemblance," *Philosophy and Phenomenological Research* 82 (2011), 156–82.

Some interpreters, such as Don Garrett, overlook the way in which Hume takes the principles to apply to both internal and external objects, reading OD–SO not in terms of how differences in *objects* are matched by our representational capacities, but instead in terms of how differences in *perceptions* match our capacities for distinguishing and separating ideas. On such a reading, the principles no longer appear to be metaphysically freighted, and Garrett thus takes them primarily to flow from the definitions of simple and complex perceptions.[15] But, while Hume himself does sometimes put the principles in terms that are congenial to Garrett's interpretation—"all *ideas*, which are different, are separable" (1.1.7.17, SBN 24; emphasis added)—he is elsewhere absolutely clear that the principles are to be taken to apply to the world as well as to the mind. We saw in IS, for example, that:

As we conclude from the distinction and separability of their ideas, that external objects have a separate existence from each other; so when we make these ideas themselves our objects, we must draw the same conclusion concerning *them*, according to the precedent reasoning.

(T 1.4.5.27, SBN 245)

And, as I noted above, he repeatedly uses the principles to move between claims about the mind and claims about the world. Garrett seems to have been misled by Hume's using 'perception' ambiguously—sometimes for that of which we are aware, and sometimes for the episode of awareness itself (see §§2.2 and §6.6).[16]

But once we recognize that the principles are meant metaphysically, it is hard to see why Hume thinks that they are true.[17] How can he be so sure that our minds are completely aligned with things in the world? Could there not be differences between objects that we simply are unable to register (*contra* OD and OS) or cases where our finding of such differences fails to accord with how things really are (*contra* DO and SO)?

Compare how Descartes—normally thought to be far more metaphysically confident than Hume—responds to similar principles. He openly rejects OD and OS, with their implication that all of nature's joints are open to us. In the Fourth *Meditation*, he argues that "it is the nature of a finite intellect to lack understanding of many things, and it is in the nature of a created intellect to be finite" (AT VII 60). Thus we have no reason to expect all differences between objects to be recognizable by us.

---

[15] Garrett, *Cognition*, ch. 3.

[16] Thus Garrett follows the standard interpretation where 'perception' is the Humean analogue for Locke's 'idea' (*Cognition*, 14)—a position I argue against in §6.6. In what I take to be a related mistake, Garrett also assumes that when ideas copy impressions they thereby become *about* impressions (*Cognition*, 66), thus overlooking the difference between Hume's secondary ideas, which are *about* primary perceptions (either ideas or impression), and more normal primary ideas, which acquire their content from the impressions they copy (see §4.3.2). Accordingly, for Garrett, the separability of ideas is a sign of differences in *impressions*, rather than in differences of objects (either external or internal).

[17] While some interpreters take Hume to eschew metaphysics entirely, Baxter argues convincingly that there remains a space for a Humean metaphysics when it is appropriately hedged with scepticism (*Hume's Difficulty* [London: Routledge, 2008], ch. 1).

Descartes does allow, however, that our registering differences between objects *in the right way* does have metaphysical significance. We have seen that he argues from our having clear and distinct perceptions of mind apart from body that they are different substances from one another—an inference that seems to rely on a version of DO (distinguishability of objects implies a difference between them). But his ultimate justification for this claim turns on his wholly un-Humean argument that a non-deceiving God exists who would not have created us with intellects that yielded error when they were being used correctly.

In the First *Objections* to the *Meditations*, Caterus worries that Descartes's real distinction argument is invalid: even if we can *distinguish* mind from body in this way, they might *in fact* be one thing, where we just happen to be able to focus on the different features (AT VII 100). Descartes replies by distinguishing cases where we "conceive [a thing] distinctly and separately from another by an abstraction of the intellect which conceives the thing *inadequately*" from cases where we have "such a distinct and separate conception of each thing that we can understand it as an entity in its own right" (AT VII 120; emphasis added). Only the latter case yields a real distinction. Thus Descartes suggests that he ultimately relies on SO (separability of ideas implies a difference in objects) rather than DO (distinguishability of objects implies a difference in objects), where the criterion for separability is the complete-ness of an idea's object. He goes on to say that we do in fact have conceptions of mind and body as "complete things," different from one another, and concludes that his argument escapes the objection.

In the Fourth *Objections*, Arnauld revisits the issue. He quite reasonably takes Descartes's reply to Caterus to suggest that we must have *adequate* ideas of mind and body in order to recognize the real distinction between these substances. He does not specify exactly what he means by 'adequate,' but presumably he has in mind the scholastic commonplace that *veritas est adaequatio rei et intellectus*.[18] Arnauld worries that "someone may...maintain that the conception you have of yourself when you conceive of yourself as a thinking, non-extended thing is an inadequate one; and the same may be true of your conception of yourself as an extended, non-thinking thing" (AT VII 200). Until we know that the idea captures the truth of the object, inferring properties of the object from facts about our ideas of it is invalid. The object might differ from our idea of it with respect to exactly those properties.

Descartes's response is to distinguish between complete and adequate conceptions of things, and to suggest that his argument needs only complete conceptions of mind and body—conceptions of them as complete—in order to secure their real distinction (AT VII 221). He denies that we need adequate conceptions. Indeed, he raises the stakes of Arnauld's objection by saying:

---

[18] See Jan A. Aertsen, *Medieval Reflections on Truth: Adaequatio rei et intellectus* (Amsterdam: Vrije Universiteit Boekhandel, 1984).

The difference between complete and adequate knowledge is that if a piece of knowledge is to be adequate it must contain absolutely all the properties which are in the thing which is the object of knowledge. Hence only God can know that he has adequate knowledge of all things. A created intellect, by contrast, though perhaps it may in fact possess adequate knowledge of many things, can never know it has such knowledge unless God grants it a special revelation of the fact.   (AT VII 220)

So, while Descartes can accept SO (separability of ideas implying difference in objects), so long as our ideas of the objects do capture their completeness, it cannot be generalized to a principle that would allow for more detailed derivations of other features of objects merely from our ideas of them. We cannot secure the adequacy of our ideas.[19]

Hume, however, does not follow Descartes in his reluctance to reason from facts about our perceptions to facts about the world. Not only does he accept DO and SO, he also argues in his exploration of spatiotemporal perceptions in Part 2 of Book 1 of the *Treatise* that we can ratify some of our ideas as adequate, and thus reach more substantive conclusions about their objects:

Wherever ideas are adequate representations of objects, the relations, contradictions and agreements of the ideas are all applicable to the objects; and this we may in general observe to be the foundation of all human knowledge. But our ideas are adequate representations of the most minute parts of extension.   (T 1.2.2.1, SBN 29)

And thus Hume concludes that extension itself must be as those ideas represent it— constituted out of finitely many indivisible parts.[20] Although in the concluding paragraph of the first *Enquiry* (EU 12.34, SBN 165) he calls for the burning of "any volume...of divinity or school metaphysics" that lacks quantitative or experimental reasoning, he offers in the *Treatise* what seems to be a robust metaphysics of space that rules out the existence of circles and isosceles right triangles, and the impossibility of dividing lines with an odd number of fundamental points into two equal portions.

Given the seeming metaphysical confidence embodied in the separability principles, why does Hume think that they are true? He prefaces their introduction in his discussion of general ideas with the statement that "we have already observ'd" that different objects are distinguishable, OD, and separable in thought, OS (T 1.1.7.3, SBN 18). I noted earlier that Garrett takes Hume to be referring us back to his definition of simple and complex ideas:[21]

---

[19] The previous three paragraphs borrow from my "Adequate Ideas and Modest Scepticism in Hume's Metaphysics of Space," *Archiv für Geschichte der Philosophie* 92 (2010), 42.

[20] Hume does not spend a great deal of time discussing the (in)adequacy of ideas, though he is presumably influenced by Locke's account at E II.xxxi. Nidditch notes that Locke's French translator, Pierre Coste, translates 'adequate' here as '*complete*,' with an appended marginal note indicating that "*en Latin adæquatæ*" (E II.xxxi.1n1). Thus Coste runs together Descartes's distinction between complete and adequate ideas. See my "Adequate Ideas" for a fuller discussion of these issues.

[21] *Cognition*, 68.

Simple perceptions or impressions and ideas are such as admit of no distinction nor separation. The complex are the contrary to these, and may be distinguished into parts. Tho' a particular colour, taste, and smell are qualities all united together in this apple, 'tis easy to perceive they are not the same, but are at least distinguishable from each other.

(T 1.1.1.2, SBN 2)

The fact that we cannot distinguish elements of a simple idea indicates that there is no other idea that could be separated out from it, SD. But we are not shown, as in OD and OS, that the object of the idea itself bears no parts. OD and OS are in play with the apple, where differences in its qualities can be distinguished, and presumably thought of in separate ideas, but Hume still does not rule out the possibility of there being further parts in the apple, beyond those we recognize. His point here, after all, is to define a simple idea in terms of our incapacity to make distinctions in its object (and separate our thoughts of the parts), rather than to make any claims about the relation of objects to ideas.

David and Mary Norton suggest that the "observation" Hume has in mind when introducing the separability principles comes at the end of his discussion of the "liberty of the imagination to transpose and change its ideas," where he says that "[w]herever the imagination perceives a difference among ideas, it can easily produce a separation" (T 1.1.3.4, SBN 10).[22] But this statement only supports DS's claim that the *perception* of a difference—I take this term to indicate a kind of 'distinguishing'—allows for the separation of an idea. It does not support the bolder claim that wherever there is a difference in objects we can recognize it and thus separate the objects in thought.

Moreover, immediately after asserting that he had "already observ'd" that different objects are distinguishable and separable in thought, OD and OS, Hume claims that their converses—that the separability of ideas of objects means that those objects are distinguishable, SD, and thus different, DO and SO—are "equally true" (T 1.1.7.3, SBN 18). While I have accepted SD as trivial, I have suggested that Hume is moving far too fast in his assertions of DO and SO.

Even though Hume's initial presentation of the separability principles does not explain why he endorses OD–SO, I think that a defence of them can be made on his behalf. The key is to understand what he means by 'object' in them. For, from our discussion of true and false philosophy in §5.1, as well as the discussion of external existence in §3.3, we know that 'object' can refer to either a vulgar or non-perceptual object. Which is in play in the separability principles? Clearly, Hume must have vulgar objects in mind, in that he allows for only the most attenuated conception of non-perceptual objects. And vulgar objects are, in part, defined by our (collective) tendencies to associate ideas so as to believe in the continued and distinct existence of their contents. But once the separability principles are read in terms of vulgar objects,

[22] "Editors' Annotations," in David F. Norton and Mary Norton (eds.), *Hume, A Treatise of Human Nature: A Critical Edition*, Vol. 2, *Editorial Material* (Oxford: Clarendon Press, 2007), 704.

they are no longer as metaphysically ambitious as they first seemed, and instead articulate an isomorphism between perceptions and what, in the footnote from the "Appendix" that we investigated in §5.1, he calls "appearances" (T 1.2.5.26n12.1, SBN 638).

So, whereas Descartes treats the objects in question as non-perceptual objects, and thus has to appeal to God's benevolence to secure his version of SO (ideas of objects as complete imply that the objects are different), Hume can argue that the separability of ideas of objects means that the objects in question are in fact different: since a vulgar object is nothing other than the possible intended object of a sensory impression, each of the separated ideas could serve in our awareness of such an object. Hume can similarly avoid the kinds of criticism that Arnauld and Caterus level at a Cartesian version of DO—the move from distinguishing between objects in thought to their being different in reality. Arnauld and Caterus worry that the distinction in the antecedent might be a mere distinction of reason, a result of our selective attention rather than a reflection of real differences between objects. Hume avoids this problem by his defining 'distinguish' for the purposes of the separability principles in terms of the possibility of having the distinguished objects in separate ideas, as in DS and SD. Distinction requires separability, and we have just seen that separability of ideas yields differences in vulgar objects.

If Hume means the separability principles to be restricted to vulgar objects, we can also see why he embraces the suggestion that *all* differences among objects are in principle recognizable by us—OD and OS—while even Descartes shies away from them. Descartes's worry is that God could establish features in things that are wholly beyond our cognitive reach. We saw in §5.1 that Hume concedes this point for *non-perceptual* objects. It is true that there might be qualities of some unknown kind in objects, and indeed those unknown qualities could in principle undermine the difference between the objects. But like the blind man making assertions about colours, we have no grasp of such differences, and thus their possibility "'twill be of little consequence to the world" (T 1.3.14.27, SBN 168). Since *vulgar* objects, in contrast, are defined in relation to our sensory capacities, Hume can treat their differences as available to us.

Finally, understanding Hume to be using 'object' to refer to vulgar objects in the separability principles also offers us a way to make sense of his claim that he has an adequate idea of the "most minute" part of extension and is thereby entitled to reach conclusions about extension itself on the basis of it. First, we rely on our introspective observations to form an idea with indivisible spatial image-content—the coloured or tangible pixel that we discussed in §§2.3 and 3.2.5. Such an idea might be used to provide the proximate content for all sorts of thoughts—of a grain of sand or one of its parts (T 1.2.1.3, SBN 27), or of an ink spot (T 1.2.2.4, SBN 27–8), or even of a planet. But we can conceive of an object that is itself minimal by putting this indivisible image-content into an associative context in which all associated ideas also have indivisible image-content. An ink spot or planet, in contrast, though they can be thought of by means of ideas with indivisible image-content when considered in terms of how they would look from the farthest visible distance, can also be thought of by means of associated ideas with divisible image-contents, when we consider them from a closer distance. To get the idea of an indivisible external object, we have to conceive of something while enmeshing it in associations that leave it as indivisible *as such*, no matter how close we approach it. Or perhaps more accurately, we need to conceive of something that is at the threshold of our discriminative capacities—something that only comes into view only when we have taken our observational powers to their utmost limits. In contemporary terms, we might be conceiving a quark or imagining what a fundamental particle at the final level of scientific discovery would be. Note that Hume does not say where exactly we will find the most minute parts of extension. As an example, he gives "the smallest atom of the animal spirits of an insect a thousand times less than a mite" (T 1.2.1.5, SBN 28). But he leaves open which particle will count as the most minute part of extension, presumably because it is a question best answered by natural philosophers. He only requires for his argument that we recognize that our observational powers have limits and that we can nonetheless imagine what the objects we would find there are like.

Arnauld's challenge, seconded by Descartes, asks why we should think that this idea of the most minute part of extension is an adequate representation of its object. But I have suggested that Hume understands this object as a vulgar object—one constituted by the imagination's associative reaction to our impressions and ideas. And the idea of the most minute object just is the idea of the minimal vulgar object. Thus any vulgar object must be at least as large as this minimal vulgar object. Hume's claim that extension conforms to our ideas of its most minute parts means only that the world, as it is conceived by us, must ultimately conform to our powers of conception. As we saw in §5.1, he has "confine[d] [his] speculations to the *appearances* of objects to our senses, without entering into disquisitions concerning their real nature and operations" (T 1.2.5.26n12.1, SBN 638).[23]

5.4 The Conceivability Maxim

In arguing that perceptions satisfy the Cartesian definition of substance, Hume appeals to not only the separability principles, but also the conceivability maxim, already quoted in connection with false philosophers' search for intrinsic necessary connections (§5.1):

'Tis an establish'd maxim in metaphysics, That whatever the mind clearly conceives includes the idea of possible existence, or in other words, that nothing we imagine is absolutely impossible. We can form the idea of a golden mountain, and from thence conclude that

---

[23] See Ainslie, "Adequate Ideas," 61–3.

such a mountain may actually exist. We can form no idea of a mountain without a valley, and therefore regard it as impossible. (T 1.2.2.8, SBN 32)

This maxim reappears throughout Book 1, as when he allows for the possibility that an event occur without a cause because it is conceivable that it occur spontaneously (T 1.3.3.3, BSN 79). There are three related issues that must be resolved in understanding Hume's commitment to the maxim. First, what is the idea of possibility on which he relies in it? Second, why does he take the maxim to be true? Finally, does he mean to endorse the *equivalence* of conceivability and possibility, or only the *sufficiency* of the former for the latter? That is to say, does he take inconceivability to entail impossibility, or just the converse? And if inconceivability does not entail impossibility, what grounds an impossibility claim, such as the one concerning the mountain and the valley, quoted previously?

Starting with the issue of the source of the idea of possibility, it is remarkable that while Hume spends many pages exploring the impression-source for the idea of necessity (T 1.3.2–14), he says almost nothing about whether and how we have an impression of possibility. One thought might be that Hume does not worry about this latter impression because he relies on an understanding of possibility based on the denial of the necessity of the negation of a claim. The extensive treatment of the impression of necessity would then suffice for an explanation of our having the idea of possibility. But it is somewhat unlikely that Hume thinks that the logical relation between possibility and necessity is all we need to get an idea of one on the basis of the idea of the other. As David Owen has emphasized, Hume follows the early modern tradition by focusing on the mind's interactions with its ideas rather than on the logical structure of propositions (see, for example, T 1.3.7.5n20, SBN 96–7n).[24] Moreover, given his lack of attention to an impression-source for the idea of negation, it is hard to see that his account of the impression of necessity can easily be adapted into an account of the impression of possibility by merely logical manoeuvres.[25]

Stephen Yablo has pointed out that the "establish'd maxim" quoted above is ambiguous between the suggestion that we *attribute* possible existence to any object we imagine and the claim that our imagining it *reveals* its possibility.[26] If the former reading is correct, then we need a robust idea of possibility that would be attached to that which we imagine, so that we could think of it *as possible*. I think, however, that it is unlikely that Hume means the maxim in this sense. Compare his account of the idea of existence, where he denies that we have a discrete idea of existence (T 1.2.6.1–6, SBN 66–7). If we did, the separability principles would apply and, in particular, SO would allow us to conclude from our separate idea of existence that

---

[24] *Hume's Reason* (Oxford: Oxford University Press, 1999).
[25] Lewis Powell has recently tried to construct an account of negation on Hume's behalf ("Hume's Treatment of Denial," *Philosophers' Imprint* 14, 26 [2014], 1–22).
[26] "Is Conceivability a Guide to Possibility?" *Philosophy and Phenomenological Research* 53 (1993), 4–5.

that existence was an object by itself. Instead, Hume argues that there is no distinction between thinking of an object and thinking of it as existing, and thus the ideas are not separable (SD): "Whatever we conceive, we conceive to be existent. Any idea we please to form is the idea of a being; and the idea of a being is any idea we please to form" (T 1.2.6.4, SBN 67). Of course, this is not yet to *believe* that something exists. Belief requires that the idea thus conceived is highly vivacious (see §6.6).

I think that Hume's treatment of possibility is best understood in a similar fashion to his treatment of existence. Given that conceiving of an object just is thinking of it as existing (though not, *ipso facto*, believing that it exists), conceiving of it just is thinking that it might exist—that it is possible. But now we face the second of the three issues noted previously. Why does our *thinking* that something might exist suffice for it to be a *real* possibility? In what sense do our powers of thought reflect the modal structure of things?

Hume says that he relies here on an "establish'd maxim in metaphysics" (T 1.2.2.8, SBN 32). David Norton and Mary Norton, in their compilation of Hume's sources, point to precedents only in Descartes and some of his followers.[27] Descartes endorses it as follows: "[P]ossible existence is contained in the concept or idea of everything that we clearly and distinctly understand" (AT VII 116).[28] I take it that Descartes holds that God's omnibenevolence guarantees that our best conceptions—the clear and distinct ones—map onto the realm of the possible.

Hume, of course, will not accept this Cartesian theocentric justification of the maxim. But, by now, we can see how he might argue for it: if the object the possibility of which is in question is a vulgar object, then we should not be surprised that our conception of it suffices for its possibility. Vulgar objects just are objects insofar as we can conceive them. So if we can conceive the object a certain way, and our ideas are ultimately dependent on prior impressions, then it is possible that those impressions will occur in exactly the order given by our conception. In conceiving a vulgar object, we are thereby showing that it is possible.

The third issue related to the conceivability maxim was whether Hume endorses its converse: does our being unable to conceive an object mean that it is impossible?

---

[27] In addition to Descartes, Norton and Norton cite Antoine Arnauld and Pierre Nicole's *Port Royal Logic* and Willem 's Gravesande's *Explanation of the Newtonian Philosophy*. Norton and Norton also note that Edmund Law rejected the maxim in his *Enquiry into the Ideas of Space* ("Editors' Annotations," 714).

Similarly, much of the current literature on necessity and possibility takes Descartes and Hume as its starting point. See Tamar Szabó Gendler and John Hawthorne, "Introduction: Conceivability and Possibility," in T. S. Gendler and J. Hawthorne (eds.), *Conceivability and Possibility* (Oxford: Oxford University Press, 2002), 1–70. For the pre-modern background to the maxim, see Lilli Alanen and Simo Knuuttila's "The Foundations of Modality and Conceivability in Descartes and his Predecessors," in S. Knuuttila (ed.), *Modern Modalities* (Dordrecht: Kluwer, 1988), 1–69.

[28] See also Axiom 10 in the "Geometrical Exposition" of the Second *Replies*: "Existence is contained in the idea or concept of every single thing, since we cannot conceive of anything except as existing. Possible or contingent existence is contained in the concept of a limited thing, whereas necessary and perfect existence is contained in the concept of a supremely perfect being" (AT VII 166).

I think not.[29] As Tycerium Lightner points out, what he calls the *inconceivability principle* does not appear in the text.[30] Moreover, we have already seen that Hume allows that objects might have qualities with which we are "utterly unacquainted" (T 1.3.14.27, SBN 168). So inconceivable qualities are openly admitted to be possible. For Hume, then, our powers of conception reflect the structure of the *vulgar* world, but because we can also think of *non-perceptual* objects, we can recognize the limits of our understanding.

If Hume rejects the inconceivability principle, how can he reach conclusions about impossibility? Following Lightner, I take Hume to hold the *contradiction principle*: "if an idea of a thing would be contradictory, then that thing is absolutely impossible."[31] Consider, for example, one of his arguments against the infinite divisibility of extension: "[I]f it be a *contradiction* to suppose, that a finite extension contains an infinite number of parts, no finite extension can be infinitely divisible" (T 1.2.2.2, SBN 29; emphasis added). Hume goes on to argue that this supposition does yield a contradiction. If a finite extension were infinitely divisible, then it would have an infinite number of parts, and these, he thinks, would yield an infinite expanse.[32] His conclusion that a finite extension cannot be infinitely divisible thus exemplifies the contradiction principle. Similarly with the point about impossibility of the mountain without a valley, quoted at the start of this section: because mountains are defined by their jutting up over their surroundings, they necessarily establish valleys beside them. Hume thus seems to accept Descartes's treatment of this issue (even while rejecting his treatment of existence and God): "It is just as much a contradiction to think of God (that is, a supremely perfect being) lacking existence (that is, lacking a perfection), as it is to think of a mountain without a valley" (AT VII 66). The contradiction of a mountain without a valley (or a non-existent perfect being) establishes its impossibility.

---

[29] R. F. Atkinson, in contrast, takes Hume to treat 'inconceivable' and 'contradictory' as equivalent ("Hume on Mathematics," *The Philosophical Quarterly* 10 [1960], 128). John Wright takes Hume initially to hold that inconceivability implies impossibility, but to later reject it in the case of absolute space (*Sceptical Realism*, 92, 103).

[30] D. Tycerium Lightner, "Hume on Conceivability and Inconceivability," *Hume Studies* 23 (1997), 113–32.

[31] Lightner, "Hume on Conceivability," 116.

[32] We saw in §5.3 that Hume holds that we have an idea of the "most minute part" of extension (T 1.2.2.1, SBN, 29). When I concatenate ideas of those parts, I find that the "compound idea of extension, arising from its repetition, always to augment, and become double, triple, quadruple, &c. till at last it swells up to a considerable bulk, greater or smaller, in proportion as I repeat more or less the same idea. When I stop in the addition of parts, the idea of extension ceases to augment; and were I to carry on the addition *in infinitum*, I clearly perceive, that the idea of extension must also become infinite. Upon the whole, I conclude, that the idea of an infinite number of parts is individually the same idea with that of an infinite extension; that no finite extension is capable of containing an infinite number of parts; and consequently that no finite extension is infinitely divisible" (T 1.2.2.2, SBN 29–30). For a more detailed consideration of Hume's argument here, especially its premise that an infinitely divisible extension must have an infinite number of parts, see Thomas Holden, *The Architecture of Matter: Galileo to Kant* (Oxford: Oxford University Press, 2004).

With these three issues relating to the conceivability maxim now resolved, we can return to the problem left outstanding in §5.1. I showed there that Hume thinks that philosophers use 'faculty' and 'occult quality' as if they referred to non-perceptual objects when in fact they are merely empty names. Without realizing it, they substitute the idea of the names for the relative idea of non-perceptual objects, thus creating the illusion of metaphysical insight.[33] The problem is why this use of the idea-substitution mechanism does not yield a new intended object, in the same way that Hume allows that scientists' fictional idea of the vacuum, when properly understood, suffices for scientific theorizing. The difference in these two cases, I suggest, is that the philosophers attempt to think of a *contradictory* object: a non-perceptual object that has vulgar features. But the non-perceptual object is only thinkable by denying any vulgar feature of it. The contradiction principle, however, states that contradictory objects are impossible, and this applies generally, to both vulgar and non-perceptual objects. As Hume states in the "Conclusion of this book," "when we desire to know the ultimate and operating principle, as something which resides in the external [non-perceptual] object, we either contradict ourselves or talk without a meaning" (T 1.4.7.5, SBN 267). In contrast, the two ideas that are mutually substituted for one another in the fiction of the idea of the vacuum are not contradictory, and thus our making that substitution can serve a constitutive role (see §3.4). So long as we understand the source of our ideas in experience, so long as we make "a fair confession of ignorance in subjects, that exceed all human capacity" and do not "carry our enquiry beyond the appearances of objects to the senses" (T 1.2.5.26n12.2, SBN 639), true philosophers can live with their natural tendency to substitute resembling (non-contradictory) ideas for one another. The problem arises when false philosophers use empty words to hide from themselves that they are trying to think a contradiction.

5.5 The Spinoza Argument

Now that we have clarified Hume's core metaphysical principles, let us return to the arguments in IS that rely on them. Hume uses OD and DS in his anti-Cartesian argument that perceptions satisfy the definition of substance. Because perceptions are different from one another, they are distinguishable (OD) and our secondary ideas of them are separable (DS). The conceivability maxim then can be applied to show that

---

[33] Or more likely, false philosophers switch between the idea of the name, the relative idea of the non-perceptual object, and an idea of qualities of vulgar objects (for example, the necessary connection between the flower's petals and its scent). They thus take themselves to discern a non-perceptual foundation—a faculty—in the flower responsible for its smelliness. See Lewis Powell, "How to Avoid Mis-Reiding Hume's Maxim of Conceivability" (*The Philosophical Quarterly* 63 [2013], 105–19) for a thoughtful account of how Hume can separate linguistic understanding from the kind of conceivability that the maxim concerns; thus we can understand something contradictory (such as a round square) without thereby conceiving it in the manner that triggers possibility.

they can exist by themselves. In the later argument against the suggestion that perceptions are "actions" or "abstract modes" of substances, he argues in the opposite direction, from the fact that, when we are reflecting on the mind, we can distinguish perceptions and thus (by DS) form separate (secondary) ideas of them, thus yielding (by SO) that they are different objects.

Note that my interpretation of the separability principles and the conceivability maxim (§§5.3 and 5.4) requires that the objects within their scopes be *vulgar* objects, whether those objects be external or, as in the arguments of IS, internal. Perceptions themselves are vulgar objects. I argued in Chapter 4 that Hume's account of introspection or reflection also yields this conclusion (§4.3.2): philosophers' introspective beliefs about the mind are structured similarly to the vulgar's beliefs about the world (and I took Hume's argument at T 1.4.5.27, SBN 245 as one piece of evidence in favour of this conclusion). I also argued that the double-existence theorists go wrong in their failure to understand this point (§§4.5.1 and 4.5.2). They posit a special unmediated, internal relation to perceptions that is superior to our mediated grasp of external objects. Hume's levelling of philosophical awareness of mind with vulgar awareness of things allows him to show that any philosophical attempt to discredit the vulgar point of view will simultaneously undermine the philosophical observations on which they would be based. We are left in the state of the true philosopher, recognizing that the world of appearances is immune both to philosophical vindication and philosophical repudiation.

Hume's rejection of substance accounts of the internal world moves swiftly, and its main argument is finished by the seventh of its thirty-five paragraphs. Although he then goes on to discuss the possibility of perceptions' having a "local conjunction" with the mind (see §5.6), he later returns to some "further reflections concerning" the "substance of the soul" (T 1.4.5.17, SBN 240). At this point Hume presents a rather peculiar analysis of Spinoza's philosophy—the only time that he offers a sustained investigation of another philosopher by name in the *Treatise*. But he does not seem all that interested in what Spinoza actually thought, nor in the details of his system. Instead, he analogizes Spinoza's account of the universe as a simple, intrinsically unified substance in which both thought and extension inhere to the account of the soul as a simple, intrinsically unified, immaterial substance in which perceptions inhere. Hume argues that Pierre Bayle's criticisms of Spinozism in the *Historical and Critical Dictionary* transfer over to criticisms of substance theories of the mind. And thus anyone who rejects Spinoza's "hideous hypothesis" (T 1.4.5.19, SBN 241) should also reject the doctrine of an immaterial soul.

The problem is that the "maxim" to which Hume appeals in effecting this transfer seem to conflict with the separability principles that were so crucial to his initial attack on substance theories of mind. But with Hume's account of true and false philosophy on the table (§5.1), I show in what follows that his use of the transfer maxim in the Spinoza argument is inoffensive. It makes sense only in the context of false philosophy, and thus does not threaten the true philosopher's use of the separability principles.

5.5.1 Using the Transfer Maxim

After offering a brief one-paragraph summary of Spinoza's monistic metaphysics, and recapitulating his claim from "Of the idea of existence, and of external existence" that "as every idea is deriv'd from a preceding perception, 'tis impossible our idea of a perception, and that of an object or external existence can ever represent what are specifically different from each other" (T 1.2.6.9, SBN 68), Hume says:

[S]ince we may suppose, but never can conceive a specific difference betwixt an object and impression; any conclusion we form concerning the connexion and repugnance of impressions, will not be known certainly to be applicable to objects; but that on the other hand, whatever conclusions of this kind we form concerning objects, will most certainly be applicable to impressions. The reason is not difficult. As an object is suppos'd to be different from an impression, we cannot be sure, that the circumstance, upon which we found our reasoning, is common to both, supposing we form the reasoning upon the impression. 'Tis still possible, that the object may differ from it in that particular. But when we first form our reasoning concerning the object, 'tis beyond doubt, that the same reasoning must extend to the impression: And that because the quality of the object, upon which the argument is founded, must at least be conceiv'd by the mind; and cou'd not be conceiv'd, unless it were common to an impression; since we have no idea but what is deriv'd from that origin. Thus we may establish it as a certain maxim, that we can never, by any principle, but by an irregular kind of reasoning from experience, discover a connexion or repugnance betwixt objects, which extends not to impressions; tho' the inverse proposition may not be equally true, that all the discoverable relations of impressions are common to objects.   (T 1.4.5.20, SBN 241–2)

This principle allows conclusions about objects to be applied to perceptions, but not *vice versa*. (I take the "irregular reasoning from experience" to concern connections between objects—their continued and distinct existence—that extend beyond the fragmentary impressions we have of them [see T 1.4.2.21, SBN 197]). We saw in §5.2, however, that the separability principles sanction conclusions about objects on the basis of our perceptions (DO and SO) (and, if we can ratify our ideas as adequate, we can draw even more conclusions about objects on the basis of our ideas, as in T 1.2.2's argument for the merely finite divisibility of space). Moreover, immediately following the Spinoza argument (T 1.4.5.17–25, SBN 240–4), Hume continues IS by arguing that perceptions are not "abstract modes" of the soul because the separability of our ideas of perceptions entails the perceptions' difference from one another (T 1.4.5.26–8, SBN 244–6)—again, an inference from facts about perceptions to facts about their objects.[34]

---

[34] Note that the Spinoza transfer maxim is put in terms of the relation between *impressions* and objects, while the separability principles are put in terms of the relation between *ideas* and objects. I do not think that much hinges on this difference, in that Hume insists that ideas and impressions differ only in their

Hume seems simply to ignore these tensions between the transfer maxim and the separability principles. Instead, after presenting the maxim, he says that "there are two different systems of beings presented, to which I suppose myself under a necessity of assigning some substance, or ground of inhesion" (T 1.4.5.21, SBN 242). On the one hand, there is "the universe of objects": "sun, moon and stars; the earth, seas, plants, animals, men, ships, houses, and other productions either of art or nature." On the other hand, there is the "universe of thought" (T 1.4.5.21, SBN 242): all of the impressions and ideas we have of the sun, moon, stars, plant, men, and so on (and in addition our reactions thereto). For Spinoza, members of the universe of objects are all modes of the attribute of extension, which modes inhere in the one simple substance, God or nature; and, though Hume does not dwell on it here, members of the universe of thought are all modes of the attribute of thought, which modes inhere in the same simple substance. But Hume is not interested in Spinoza's parallelism as such. Instead, he wants to use his transfer maxim to show that treating perceptions as inhering in a simple substance suffers from the same problems as those for which Spinoza was so often criticized.

Hume in particular focuses on Bayle's famous discussion of Spinoza in the *Historical and Critical Dictionary* (T 1.4.5.22n47, SBN 243n).[35] First, Bayle worries that Spinoza's making extension an attribute of God or nature means that God must himself be extended, and accordingly not simple (HCD, "Spinoza," 302). Hume adapts this point by suggesting that if extension is a mode of the one fundamental, indivisible substance, then either that substance must be itself extended or the extension must "contract itself, so as to answer to the indivisible substance" (T 1.4.5.23, SBN 243). Neither option, he intimates, is coherent. The transfer principle allows for this incompatibility in the universe of objects to apply to the universe of thought. Given that, for Hume, most visual and tactile perceptions of body are themselves extended (see §5.6), the transfer principle makes it clear that the mind itself must either expand itself to comprehend the extended perceptions, or those perceptions must contract themselves to fit into an indivisible, simple soul. If Spinoza's system is incoherent, then the doctrine of an immaterial soul as the subject in which perceptions inhere is similarly incoherent.

Second, Bayle elaborates on this first criticism by pointing out that any portion of matter counts as a distinct substance, and thus Spinoza's treating it as a mode is mistaken (HCD, "Spinoza," 305–6). Hume transfers this conclusion to the mind by suggesting that every perception could also count as a distinct substance, in that it

---

vivacity (T 1.1.7.5, SBN 19), and the vivacity of the perceptions in question is not at stake in either the maxim or the principles. Also, Hume uses the maxim to apply both to ideas and impressions, in that "all our ideas are deriv'd from our impressions" (T 1.4.5.21, SBN 243). Given that Hume's target in the Spinoza argument is the view that the mind is an indivisible immaterial substance in which *all* perceptions inhere, he needs the maxim to extend beyond impressions.

[35] For the influence of Bayle, especially the Spinoza article, see Jonathan Israel, *Radical Enlightenment* (Oxford: Oxford University Press, 2001), ch. 18.

ANCIENT PHILOSOPHY: SUBSTANCES AND SOULS   181

could exist by itself. In the "Appendix" to the *Treatise* for example, he points to the possibility of a creature's having a mind comprising only one perception—something "even below the life of an oyster" (T App.16, SBN 634). Just as Spinoza's claim that extension inheres in a simple substance is unsatisfactory, so also is the claim that perceptions inhere in a simple substance.

Third, Bayle objects that Spinoza's system of the external world leaves the one simple substance bearing inconsistent properties—a round table and a square table inhere in it at the same time, even though nothing can be both round and square simultaneously (HCD, "Spinoza," 306–7). The point transfers to the mind, Hume suggests. The perceptions of a round table and a square table cannot both inhere in the same mind simultaneously (T 1.4.5.25, SBN 244). Thus he concludes that anyone who condemns Spinozism as a form of atheism must give up the doctrine of the soul as an immaterial simple substance, for it too yields "a dangerous and irrecoverable atheism" (T 1.4.5.26, SBN 244).

5.5.2 False Philosophy of Mind

Of course, Bayle's criticisms of Spinoza are far from decisive; indeed, they result from a rather uncharitable reading of him. Hume's reconstruction of these criticisms is similarly weak, leading Norman Kemp Smith to say that, at the time Hume wrote the *Treatise*, he "had, it is evident, no knowledge of Spinoza's teaching, save what he derived from Bayle."[36] Thus one could easily conceive of possible retorts on the part

---

[36] *Philosophy of David Hume* (London: Macmillan, 1941), 325; see also Richard Popkin, "Hume and Spinoza," *Hume Studies* 5 (1979), 65–93. Paul Russell traces the claim that Hume is ignorant of Spinoza's *Ethics* back to the nineteenth century, though he notes that few who make it offer much in the way of argumentation. Russell also urges that whatever we conclude about Hume's familiarity with the *Ethics*, he probably knew the *Tractatus Theologico-Politicus* (*Riddle of Hume's 'Treatise'* [New York, NY: Oxford University Press, 2008], 72).

Wim Klever offers the most robust argument against the assumption that Hume had only indirect knowledge of Spinoza's metaphysics, going so far as to say that the *Treatise* reads as if Hume wrote it with a copy of the *Ethics* open beside him ("Hume Contra Spinoza?" *Hume Studies* 16 [1990], 92). I find the parallels between these two naturalists less obvious than Klever does; in particular, Spinoza's rationalistic commitment to the principle of sufficient reason is completely at odds with Hume's empiricist insouciance about the intelligibility of the world. When there are clear parallels between the two thinkers, I suspect that there might be a common cause for the similarity—typically Descartes, whose influence on Spinoza is obvious, and who reached Hume both directly and through his influence on Locke. Klever indicates six points of contact between Hume and Spinoza.

First, he reads Hume's lack of interest in exploring the physical causes of impressions as akin to Spinoza's metaphysical interdiction against the causal interaction of modes falling under different attributes. In fact, as Hume makes clear immediately after his discussion of Spinoza in "Of the immateriality of the soul," he puts no metaphysical barriers to any kind of causal interaction. In principle, anything can cause anything (T 1.3.15.1, SBN 173), and in fact we have evidence of the causal interaction of thought and matter, as when our hunger disturbs our concentration or when we willingly move our bodies (T 1.4.5.29–32, SBN 246–50). Moreover, it seems likely that Hume's methodological disinclination to investigating the physical causes of impressions stems not from Spinoza's metaphysical critique of Descartes, as Klever suggests, but from Locke's reconceptualization of the philosophical project away from the metaphysics of nature and towards what we would call the philosophy of mind. Similarly, where Klever sees Spinozistic roots for Hume's associationism, I take it that Locke is the more probable source.

of both Spinoza's defenders and of those partisans of the substantial soul. We face, then, the task of interpreting Hume's purposes in presenting the Spinoza argument, including its central transfer maxim.

Consider again the maxim. It allows conclusions about external objects to be transferred into conclusions about the mind, but not *vice versa*. As I have argued throughout this chapter, any time Hume discusses external objects we must clarify whether he means vulgar or non-perceptual objects. In this case, he must mean *non-perceptual* objects, for he emphasizes that the reason conclusions about perceptions cannot be transferred to objects is that we can "suppose, but never can conceive a *specific difference* between" the object and the perception. And that supposition means that the object might differ from the perception in such a way that the conclusion about the perception would be inapplicable to the object. (I suggested in §5.4 that Hume's rejection of the inconceivability principle sprang from a similar point.) The maxim allows that conclusions about non-perceptual objects, however, *if they could be reached*, must transfer to perceptions, since all of our thoughts ultimately are traced back to our encounters with objects. Reading the maxim in terms of non-perceptual objects means that the tension between it and the separability principles dissolves: the latter concern only vulgar objects, not non-perceptual objects.

Second, Klever notes that Spinoza puts forward a bundle theory of the mind: it is a complex idea of the body, constituted out of many more basic ideas of parts of the body. Here there is some resemblance to Hume's view, though the context for Hume's investigation of personal identity seems to have been set by the philosophical discussion of his contemporaries, "especially of late years in *England*"(T 1.4.6.15, SBN 259): namely, once more Locke and the responses he inspired by Butler, Collins, Clarke, and others. And of course, Hume shows no desire to establish the mind as a bundle of perceptions by creating a parallel between it and the body.

Third, Klever suggests that the "very sequence of chapters and topics in Book 1 of the *Treatise* and Book 2 of the *Ethics*" are parallel. One might just as easily point to Spinoza's need to preface Book 2 with Book 1 as a disanalogy here. And Russell argues that Hobbes' "Of Human Nature" is the likely source for Hume's organization of the *Treatise* (*Riddle*, ch. 6). I myself think that Hume need not be following any particular model in his composition, and that the topics he addresses were fairly standard in the early modern period.

Fourth, Klever sees similarities in Hume's and Spinoza's treatments of space and time, but he mischaracterizes the former as "conceiving of the universe as the infinite sum of all things and processes" ("Hume Contra Spinoza?" 95), even though Hume does not seem to commit himself to an infinite universe.

Fifth, Klever uses Hume's comments about the "intricacy" that can occur in mathematical reasoning (T 1.3.1.5, SBN 71) to attribute to him a view in which "systematicity as such is, as it were, the criterium, or even more fundamentally, the ground for all truth value" ("Hume Contra Spinoza?" 98). While Hume is happy to take systematicity where he finds it, I do not see him grounding truth in it. Moreover, while Klever sees Hume's method as in "full agreement" ("Hume Contra Spinoza?" 99) with that of Spinoza, I see no sign of a geometrical method in Hume. He is instead a "scientist of man" marshalling empirical evidence about the mind by means of introspection.

Sixth, Klever also sees a relation between Spinoza's treatment of ideas of sensation as being ideas of our bodies and Hume's sceptical treatment of our sensory beliefs in "Of scepticism with regard to the senses" (T 1.4.2). But Hume suggests that our sense impressions purport to disclose elements of the world to us, rather than facts about our bodies. Indeed, I suspect that Hume thinks it would be necessary to dissect someone before you could discover what is happening in his body. Perceptions, no matter how well we understand them, do not as such bear content about our bodies.

Of course, we saw in §5.1 that true philosophers deny that we can reach conclusions about non-perceptual objects. Only false philosophers think that they have insight into the world beyond how it appears to us. So the Spinoza transfer principle ends up being idle, except insofar as it can be used dialectically, to show false philosophers the consequences of their view, were it true. And this, I take it, is Hume's goal in the Spinoza argument. He is addressing opponents who claim to have insight into the deep structure of the internal and external worlds. The former, they say, is an indivisible, immaterial substance in which perceptions inhere, but they also claim that the latter does not conform to Spinoza's metaphysics. Hume uses the maxim to show the inconsistency of these positions.[37]

5.6 The Material Mind?

A final topic that Hume includes in IS is somewhat tangential to his consideration of ancient systems of the internal world with their embrace of substance metaphysics. He also wonders whether, if perceptions cannot belong to a mind by inhering in it, perhaps they could instead have a "local conjunction" (T 1.4.5.8, SBN 235) with it. He is a little unclear about exactly what he means by this phrase, but presumably his point is that if the mind is material, it is extended, and perceptions could thus be in the mind, not by inhering in it, but by being literally inside of it, in the same way that a chair can be in a house by being physically located inside of it.

Hume responds to this possibility by adapting an argument that he probably encountered in Ralph Cudworth's *True Intellectual System of the Universe*. In this sprawling work, Cudworth attempts to rebut all forms of atheism by appealing to a vast array of sources, ancient and modern. He relies primarily on Plotinus when arguing that the mind cannot be extended. Cudworth's main claim is that an extended mind would be divisible, and thus unable to account for the unity of thought. Each part of the mind would think different parts of an object without any part thinking of the whole (TISU I.v. 824).[38] But Hume's interest seems to have been captured by a related argument that Cudworth offers, again appealing to Plotinus as a source:

We cannot conceive a *Thought*, to be of such a certain *Length*, *Breadth*, and *Thickness*, *Mensurable* by *Inches* and *Feet*, and by *Solid Measures*. We cannot Conceive *Half*, or a *Third Part*, or a *Twentieth Part* of a *Thought*, much less of the *Thought* of an *Indivisible Thing*;

---

[37] Henry Allison reaches a similar conclusion: "The obvious problem here [in using the maxim] is that this [use] assumes the very un-Humean thesis that we can have knowledge of objects independently of our perceptions; but this may be excused on the grounds that Hume is mounting an *ad hominem* argument against the theologians, who presumably would assume that they have such knowledge" (*Custom and Reason*, 291).

[38] See the discussion in Ben Lazare Mijuskovic, *The Achilles of Rationalist Arguments* (The Hague: Martinus Nijhoff, 1974), ch. 3.

neither can we Conceive every *Thought* to be of some certain Determinate *Figure*, either *Round* or *Angular*; Spherical Cubical, or Cylindrical, or the like. Where if whatsoever is *Unextended*, be *Nothing, Thoughts* must either be meer *Non-entities*, or else *Extended* too, into *Length, Breadth*, and *Thickness*; *Divisible* into *Parts*; and *Mensurable*; and also (where Finite,) of a certain *Figure*. And consequently all *Verities* in us...must of necessity be *Long, Broad*, and *Thick*, and either *Spherically* or *Angularly Figurate*. And the same must be affirmed, of *Volitions likewise*, and *Appetites* or *Passions*, as *Fear* and *Hope*, *Love* and *Hatred, Grief* and *Joy*; and of all other things belong to *Cogitative Beings*, (*Souls* and *Minds*) as *Knowledge* and *Ignorance, Wisdom* and *Folly, Virtue* and *Vice, Justice* and *Injustice*, &c. that these are either all of them *Absolute Non-Entities*; or Else *Extended* into *Three Dimensions* of *Length, Breadth*, and *Profundity*; and *Mensurable* not only by *Inches* and *Feet*, but also by Solid *Measures*, as *Pints* and *Quarts*: and last of all (where they are Finite as in men) *Figurate*. But if this be *Absurd*, and these things belonging to *Soul* and *Mind*, (though doubtless as great Realities at least, as the things which belong to *Bodies*) be *Unextended*, then must the *Substances* of *Souls* and *Minds* themselves be *Unextended* also.   (TISU, I.v.828)

Here Cudworth tries to show that it is a mistake to hold that everything that exists must be extended. In particular, thoughts exist and are not extended; for if they were, then such things as volitions, appetites, and "verities" would have the kinds of properties that extended things have: determinate shapes, divisibility, length, breadth, and so on.[39] He concludes that unextended mental entities have no location, except insofar as they inhere in an immaterial soul that is united to a body.

Hume presents the argument as follows:

There is one argument commonly employ'd for the immateriality of the soul, which seems to me remarkable. Whatever is extended consists of parts; and whatever consists of parts is divisible, if not in reality, at least in the imagination. But 'tis impossible any thing divisible can be *conjoin'd* to a thought or perception, which is a being altogether inseparable and indivisible. For supposing such a conjunction, wou'd the indivisible thought exist on the left or on the right hand of this extended divisible body? On the surface or in the middle? On the back- or fore-side of it? If it be conjoin'd with the extension, it must exist somewhere within its dimensions. If it exist within its dimensions, it must either exist in one particular part; and then that particular part is indivisible, and the perception is conjoin'd only with it, not with the extension: Or if the thought exists in every part, it must also be extended, and separable, and divisible, as well as the body; which is utterly absurd and contradictory. For can any one conceive a passion of a yard in length, a foot in breadth, and an inch in thickness? Thought, therefore, and extension are qualities wholly incompatible, and never can incorporate together into one subject.   (T 1.4.5.7, SBN 234–5)

---

[39] Note that Cudworth also argues, following Descartes, that our capacity to conceive of thought without matter, and *vice versa*, means that thought and matter are really distinct. He openly endorses what in §5.4 I called the conceivability maxim: "[W]e having no other *Rule*, to Judge of the *Real Distinction* and *Separability* of things than from our *Conceptions*" (TISU I.v.828). Cudworth follows up this point with an endorsement of the inconceivability principle—that our incapacity to conceive of extended thoughts means that they are impossible.

He develops the argument by suggesting that it in fact cuts against both materialists and immaterialists. Because perceptions are heterogeneous—some are extended and some unextended—the incompatibility of an immaterial soul and extension means that extended perceptions could not be conjoined to such a soul, just as the unextended perceptions could not be conjoined to a material mind.

Hume spends most of his time here defending the suggestion that some perceptions are unextended and locationless ("no where" [T 1.4.5.10, SBN 235]), but I find his treatment of extended perceptions to be less than clear. We saw in §3.2.1 that Hume holds that we are not aware of space by having impressions of it. Instead, we are aware of objects disposed in a spatial manner, so that the idea of space is a general idea of such dispositions. But only visible and tangible objects can be disposed alongside one another, and thus Hume concludes that only spatial and tangible objects are extended. In IS, Hume argues that this account of extension means that complex visible and tangible perceptions are themselves extended, whereas the impressions that arise from the other sense modalities, as well as the various impressions of reflection—desires, passions, emotions—are unextended (as are the ideas that copy these impressions). Given that tangibility or visibility is a necessary condition of location, the non-tangible, invisible unextended perceptions are "no where" and, as Cudworth urges, cannot be conjoined to an extended mind.

But what does it mean to say that complex spatial and tangible perceptions are extended? Recall that in Chapters 2 and 3 I interpreted Hume's account of sensory experience to mean that in having, say, a visual impression as of a table, we have an impression with image-content that itself is constituted out of an array of indivisible coloured points (a tactile impression would have image-content made up of an array of indivisible tangible points). The impression in isolation does not count as an awareness of the table. Instead, the imagination's associative response to the impression, when there is constancy or coherence in the other impressions that occur along with it, leads us to think of a table that exists with a typical history for objects of that kind. In being aware of the image-content in this manner, we are thereby aware of the table as a public persisting object. Using the vocabulary I developed in Chapter 2, the table is the intended object of the impression, while the image-content is the proximate content. Insofar as the table is taken to be extended, the impression whereby we are aware of it must also count as extended. The table is a vulgar object after all, and thus is not different in kind from the image-content of the original impression; it is only different in "relations, connexions and durations" (T 1.2.6.9, SBN 69). The table is, say, two metres long. The visual impression which, in the right associative context, affords us an awareness of the table, includes an image-content containing, let us assume, a total of 572 visual minima. Recall that Hume is a finitist about both the content of impressions and the world (T 1.2.1–2). Thus the table itself might turn out, once science has improved its accuracy, to contain, say, 35,416,978,372 ultimate parts. The mind itself counts as extended insofar as some of its perceptions are extended.

Even though some perceptions are extended, Hume denies that they are spatially contiguous to one another. In the personal identity Section, where he discusses what he observes when he "enters most intimately into what [he] call[s] himself" (T 1.4.6.3, SBN 252), he notes that the introspected perceptions resemble and are causally connected to one another, and thus the secondary ideas of these perceptions are associated in such a way as to produce the belief that the observed perceptions are unified (see §6.5). But Hume says that contiguity "has little or no influence in the present case" (T 1.4.6.17, SBN 260). He does not explain himself, but I take it that his point is that although visual and tactile impressions are spatial, they do not have *locations*. Only when the impressions are sufficiently constant or coherent to be caught up in the associations that Hume describes in SwS will they yield the thought of an object in an ordered environment. My visual impression as of the table will thus have an extended image-content, but it will not, by itself, be located in my dining room. Rather, the table, as a vulgar object, is in the dining room. So my thought of the table might be associated with the thought of the carpet on which it sits, given the mind's tendency to associate contiguous objects (T 1.1.4.2, SBN 11). But the brown, trapezoidal image-content of the impression, when viewed via introspection as such, is not suitably *beside* anything in the way that would be necessary if contiguity were to play a role in generating the association of a (secondary) idea of the impression containing that image-content with other secondary ideas.

The problem Cudworth raises is how, if the mind is extended, something like virtue or knowledge could be located *in* it. Hume agrees that this is a problem. Non-sensory impressions (and the ideas that copy them) lack image-contents and thus cannot be located either inside or outside the extended visual and tangible perceptions that are responsible for our thoughts of objects: "A moral reflection cannot be plac'd on the right or on the left hand of a passion" (T 1.4.5.10, SBN 236). And even non-visual and non-tangible sense impressions, though they have image-content, do not have it in the right way for them to count as extended. Nonetheless, these impressions also contribute to our conception of the intended object. If we knock on the table, the sound impression is joined with the visual and tangible impressions so that we think of the table itself as sounding.

Hume takes there to be something of a paradox here. On the one hand, we take non-spatial qualities (sounds, tastes, and the like) to be located *in* their intended objects. On the other hand, the very notion of 'in' or 'out' cannot apply if a quality is non-spatial.

Here then we are influenc'd by two principles directly contrary to each other, *viz.* that *inclination* of our fancy by which we are determin'd to incorporate the [non-spatial quality such as] taste with the extended object, and our *reason*, which shows us the impossibility of such an union. Being divided betwixt these opposite principles, we renounce neither one nor the other, but involve the subject in such confusion and obscurity, that we no longer perceive the opposition. We suppose, that the taste exists within the circumference of the body, but in such a manner, that it fills the whole without extension, and exists entire in every part without

ANCIENT PHILOSOPHY: SUBSTANCES AND SOULS   187

separation. In short, we use in our most familiar way of thinking, that scholastic principle, which, when crudely propos'd, appears so shocking, of *totum in toto & totum in qualibet parte*: Which is much the same, as if we shou'd say, that a thing is in a certain place, and yet is not there.   (T 1.4.5.13, SBN 238)

Hume described a similar conflict between tendencies of the imagination and of reason in SwS, where the imagination causes us to believe in a world of persisting mind-independent objects while reason causes us to believe that perceptions are mind-dependent. I argued in Chapter 4 that he ultimately thought the verdict of reason in this case—that our access to the world is mediated by perceptions and the imaginations' associations—should be tempered by the recognition that this verdict is itself a product of the imagination's associative tendencies. But in the case of the vulgar tendency to spread non-spatial qualities throughout spatial entities, Hume holds that we should side with reason without qualification. As true philosophers, we can give up the supposition that non-spatial qualities have a location in any real sense, even if we can acknowledge their derivative, imagination-dependent location.

6

Modern Philosophy: Persons and Perceptions

In Chapter 5 we saw that Hume rejects substance metaphysics for both the external and internal worlds. His alternative view of the external world was presented in "Of scepticism with regard to the senses" (T 1.4.2, hereafter 'SwS'), but how does he understand the internal world? He answers this question in "Of personal identity" (T 1.4.6, hereafter 'PI'), where he argues that the mind is nothing but a "bundle or collection" of perceptions (T 1.4.6.4, SBN 252), lacking intrinsic unity both at a time and across time. We nonetheless believe it is unified because we associate our ideas of our perceptions when we reflect on them.

In §6.1 I start my exploration of Hume's arguments for this position through a consideration of Locke's revolutionary discussion of personal identity in the *Essay*, where he denies that persons should be understood in terms of substance metaphysics, and instead equates them with continuing consciousnesses, where 'consciousness' is defined as the ongoing internal grasp we have of ourselves as the subjects of our mental states (E II.xxvii.9). In §6.2 I suggest that the opening paragraphs in PI should be understood as Hume's argument against this conception of consciousness. Introspection shows that we are not aware of ourselves as the *subjects* of perceptions, and instead we discover simply the bundle of perception, without any 'I' that *has* them.

But is Hume entitled to this claim, especially when in the course of making it he seems to help himself to what a Lockian would say is the very notion of a conscious subject that he is trying to reject? In answering this question in §6.3 I emphasize that just as Hume addresses *ancient* systems of the external and internal worlds (in, respectively, "Of the antient philosophy" [T 1.4.3] and "Of the immateriality of the soul" [T 1.4.5, hereafter 'IS']), the opening argument of PI must be seen as his treatment of the *modern system of the internal world*, and thus must be read alongside "Of the modern philosophy" (T 1.4.4, hereafter 'MP'), his discussion of the modern system of the external world. In the latter, he defines modern systems by their endorsement of the primary–secondary quality distinction. I argue that the Lockian position on the self-conscious subject goes hand in hand with that distinction. I then show how the argument against the primary–secondary quality distinction in MP bolsters Hume's rejection of the Lockian account of persons in PI. In §6.4 I suggest that Hume holds that the modern philosophers fall into false philosophy when they argue for the primary–secondary quality distinction by supposing that their beliefs about the external world require an explanation, while their access to their inner representations comes for free.

I turn to Hume's positive theory of the unity of persons in §6.5. While the human mind, as a bundle of perceptions, is not intrinsically unified, the relations between those perceptions nonetheless cause us to believe it has unity when we reflect on them. (Notoriously, in the "Appendix" to the *Treatise*, published along with Book 3 in 1740, almost two years after the appearance of Books 1 and 2, Hume admits that he made one "very considerable" [T App.1, SBN 623] mistake in the earlier Books. There are "contradictions" in his account of personal identity that he is unable to "reconcile" [T App.21, SBN 636]. His account of the problem, however, is frustratingly unclear, and generations of Hume scholars have attempted to make sense of his concern. I postpone my treatment of this issue until Chapter 8.)

In §6.6 I note that Hume's endorsement of the bundle theory resolves a question that I left open in §2.2: how is it best to understand the structure of perceptions, the core element in his ontology of mind? I show that, for him, they ultimately must count as states of awareness—perceiv*ings*—rather than mental objects of some kind of inner sense.

6.1 Locke on Personal Identity

Locke's empiricism requires that every simple idea arise either from sensation or from "reflection," the introspective observation of our mental operations (E II.i.2–5).[1] His distinctive account of persons arises because neither source yields a full understanding of substances, mental or physical. We sense an object's shape, colour, heaviness, feel, and so on, but we do not similarly sense that in virtue of which these different qualities are united into one thing (E II.xxiii.4). Similarly, we reflectively observe the mind's perceiving ideas, compounding them into complex ideas, willing bodily or mental actions, and so on, but do not observe the substance in virtue of which these different mental features are united into one thing (E II.xxiii.5). Locke's scepticism about our insight into substances, both mental and material, sets the stage for his discussion of persons. Although we lack a clear grasp of material or immaterial substances, we are nonetheless able to recognize our own identity through time. Thus we must take persons to be something other than straightforward substances.

Locke discusses persons in a chapter, "Of identity and diversity" (E II.xxvii), that he added to the *Essay* for its second edition in 1694. He argues there that an inanimate, natural, material object is the same through time so long as it neither gains nor loses any of its constituent particles. Artifacts, in contrast, remain identical

---

[1] Note that most of this section is taken from one of my portions of the co-written essay (with Owen Ware) "Consciousness and Personal Identity," in Aaron Garrett (ed.), *Routledge Companion to Eighteenth Century Philosophy* (New York, NY: Routledge, 2014), 245–64.

through changes in their constitution so long as they preserve their function. Living things, similarly, can sustain changes—sometimes radical changes, as when an acorn grows into an oak—while remaining the same so long as they preserve their organization or "life" (E II.xxvii.5). Human beings, for example, remain the same even if they lose consciousness or undergo radical changes in personality, so long as they are the same living organisms (E II.xxvii.6). But Locke thinks that we can imagine, say, a prince and a cobbler switching bodies, so that the cobbler's memories and mental outlook would be located in the prince's body, and *vice versa*. No one would say that the prince *as a human being* is different because he is now possessed, as it were, by the cobbler. But neither would we say that, *as a person*, the prince remains in his original body; instead we would address the cobbler to discover what the prince thinks and desires (E II.xxvii.15). Persons are thus different from human animals.

Locke similarly distinguishes persons from spiritual substances or souls; for he points out that for all we know, given our fundamental ignorance of substances, someone might have the same *soul* as the one Socrates once had. But, lacking any memories of life in the *agora*, of teaching Plato, and so on, we would not thereby say that he was the same *person* as Socrates (E II.xxvii.14). Conversely, given our ignorance, it is possible that several substances have been sequentially supporting someone's mental life, with each substance passing on to the next all of its memories and consciousness. In that case, the person would be the same while her or his soul varied (E II.xxvii.13).

Thus Locke concludes that a person can be equated with neither a human animal nor with a soul. Instead a person is

a thinking intelligent Being, that has reason and reflection, and can consider it self as it self, the same thinking thing, in different times and places; which it does only by that consciousness, which is inseparable from thinking, and, as it seems to me essential to it: It being impossible for any one to perceive, without perceiving, that he does perceive. When we see, hear, smell, taste, feel, meditate, or will any thing, we know that we do so. . . . And as far as this consciousness can be extended backwards to any past Action or Thought, so far reaches the identity of that *Person*; it is the same *self* now it was then; and 'tis by the same *self* with this present one that now reflects on it, that that Action was done.   (E II.xxvii.9)

A person is a self-conscious rational subject of thought and action.

In interpreting this claim, recall our discussion of Locke's account of consciousness (§4.3.1), where we saw that he was adapting for his own uses the Cartesian view that in every mental state we are aware of ourselves in a special, intimate way, as the subjects of the state. If, as I suggested in §2.1, Locke thinks that the perception of an idea is akin to seeing an image in a mirror, the consciousness that accompanies perception is akin to my knowledge that *I* am the one looking in the mirror. This account of consciousness means that I end up with a pervasive sense of myself as I go about my business in the world: I know that I am the one who drinks the coffee, types the words, feels the hunger, or remembers having bought the cookies. This last, as a memory, is especially complex. I am conscious of myself, the one remembering, and, when shopping, I was conscious that I was the one finding the cookies, paying the money, bringing them home; in remembering, I know that I am the same 'I' as the one who found, paid, and brought.

The Cartesians use this notion of consciousness to ground the *cogito* argument, where the self we know through consciousness is a substance, a thinking thing (*res cogitans*). Locke also accepts a version of the *cogito*:

As for *our own Existence*, we perceive it so plainly, and so certainly, that it neither needs, nor is capable of any proof. For nothing can be more evident to us, than our own Existence. *I think, I reason, I feel Pleasure and Pain*; Can any of these be more evident than my own Existence? If I doubt of all other Things, that very doubt makes me perceive my own *Existence*, and will not suffer me to doubt of that. For if I know *I feel Pain*, it is evident, I have as certain a Perception of my own Existence, as of the Existence of the Pain I feel: Or if I know that *I doubt*, I have as certain a Perception of the Existence of the thing doubting, as of that Thought, which I call *doubt*. Experience then convinces us, that *we have an intuitive Knowledge of our own Existence*, and an internal infallible Perception that we are. In every Act of Sensation, Reasoning, or Thinking, we are conscious to our selves of our own Being; and, in this Matter, come not short of the highest degree of *Certainty*.   (E IV.ix.3)

But Locke rejects the claim that the self that we thereby come to know is a *substance*. Even if, for him, a substance underlies and supports the thoughts of which we are conscious, our ignorance of the nature of substances means we do not know it when our self-consciousness affords us knowledge of our own existence. Instead, we know ourselves as *persons*, where a person is that thing of which we are conscious when we grasp ourselves as the subjects of our mental lives.

Moreover, Locke thinks that this self-consciousness brings self-concern in its wake: "[A] concern for Happiness [is] the unavoidable concomitant of consciousness; that which is conscious of Pleasure and Pain, desiring that that *self*, that is conscious, should be happy." 'Person' is thus a "Forensick" term (E II.xxvii.26). In rewarding or punishing people for good or bad deeds we look not to the presence of an ongoing substance or a persisting human being, but rather to a connection between the consciousness of the one who did the deed and the one who is being held accountable. In human "Judicatures" we are often forced to rely on the identity of the human being as a proxy for the human person, but God in the afterlife ensures that we are properly rewarded or punished only for those deeds we did as conscious persons (E II.xxvii.22).

In defining 'person' in these terms, Locke is often thought to embrace a memory criterion for personal identity, whereby someone is the same as a person at an earlier time if and only if the later person remembers the earlier person's experiences. And indeed Locke does repeatedly appeal to a person's memory of her or his past throughout his discussion. But a memory criterion is open to serious objections both because it seems possible for someone to have forgotten (even irremediably so) previous experiences without thereby no longer having had them, and because it seems possible for someone to have false memories without thereby becoming the (non-existent?) person who did the deed that is supposedly remembered. Locke's critics argue that we need to return to the traditional notion of persons as immaterial substances.

Thomas Reid, for example, worries that Locke's view would violate the transitivity of identity. A brave officer might remember the experiences he had as a young boy, and a general "in advanced life" might remember the experiences of the brave officer, but the general might have forgotten his experiences as a boy. If Locke held a memory criterion, then the officer would be the same person as the boy, and the general would be the same person as the officer, but the general would not be the same as the boy.[2] Joseph Butler holds that Locke's appeal to memory makes the account circular. For a mental state counts as a memory if and only if represents a past state *of the person* whose state it is. A false memory counts as false because *the person* did not in fact have the experience in question. We thus need a notion of personal identity in order to secure the concept of memory.[3] Indeed, Locke himself seems to help himself to a memory-independent notion of personal identity in his account of the "Great Day," when God ensures that we are punished or rewarded only for the deeds that we in fact did; he reveals the "secrets of our hearts" in holding us responsible (E II.xxvii.26; see also II.xxvii.22). If our memories determined who we were in the past, there would be no secrets to be revealed; our not remembering them would mean we did not do them—someone else was their agent.

I will not address whether these criticisms of Locke are apt or, indeed, whether he does even hold a memory criterion for personal identity.[4] But, as Hume makes clear, this debate sets the background for his discussion in PI (T 1.4.6.15, SBN 258).

6.2 The Anti-*Cogito*

I think that the opening paragraphs of Hume's discussion in PI should be seen as his criticism of Locke's account of personal identity, though, unlike Butler or Reid, he is not interested in returning to an account based on the metaphysics of substance.[5] He tries there to reject Locke's model of self-consciousness in an argument that, in reference to the Cartesian roots of this model, I call the *anti-cogito*. However, as I show below, the problem is that with a proper understanding of the model, Hume's rejection of it can seem like a failure. In §6.3 I suggest that it can be rescued when it is

---

[2] *Essay on the Intellectual Powers of Man*, ed. D. R. Brookes (University Park, PA: Pennsylvania State University Press, 2002), 276.

[3] "Of Personal Identity," in *The Analogy of Religion*, 6th edn. (London: John Beecroft and Robert Horsfield, 1771), 439–50.

[4] See Shelley Weinberg, "The Metaphysical Fact of Locke's Theory of Personal Identity," *Journal of the History of Philosophy* 50 (2012), 387–415, for an interpretation of Locke where he is not a memory theorist of personal identity.

[5] The argument in this section and in §6.3 borrows from "Hume's Anti-*Cogito*," in Lorenzo Greco and Alessio Vaccari (eds.) *Hume Readings* (Rome: Edizioni di Storia e Letteratura), 91–120.

connected with his larger diagnosis of the flaws of modern philosophy in MP and of representationalist models of perception in general (what he calls "double-existence theories;" see §4.5) in SwS.

Hume introduces the target for his criticism in the first paragraph of PI:

There are some philosophers, who imagine [a] we are every moment intimately conscious of what we call our self; [b] that we feel its existence [c] and its continuance in existence; and [d] are certain, beyond the evidence of a demonstration, [e] both of its perfect identity and [f] simplicity. [g] The strongest sensation, the most violent passion, say they, instead of distracting us from the view, only fix it the more intensely, and make us consider their influence on *self* either by their pain or pleasure. [h] To attempt a farther proof of this were to weaken its evidence; since no proof can be deriv'd from any fact, of which we are so intimately conscious; [i] nor is there any thing, of which we can be certain, if we doubt of this.   (T 1.4.6.1, SBN 251)

This position includes three ontological claims: the self exists [b], it is perfectly simple at a time [f], and perfectly identical across time [c], [e]. Hume's target also involves a series of epistemological claims outlining how we know the existence of this unified self through a special, intimate, ever-present consciousness [a], [g], that carries the highest degree of certainty [d], [h], [i]. Four points about Hume's target are worth highlighting.

First, none of [a]–[i] invokes a notion of substance. Given my claim that substances are the crucial element of *ancient* systems of the internal world while PI concerns *modern* systems of the internal world, the absence of substance-talk in its opening paragraph should not come as a surprise. That said, there are many contributors to the secondary literature who see Hume as arguing against substantial theories of the self or mind in this Section of the *Treatise*, perhaps having been misled by Hume's later claim that the philosophers he criticizes rely on "the notion of a *soul*, and *self*, and *substance*" (T 1.4.6.6, SBN 254).[6] My suggestion is that those who see Hume as targeting substance views overlook that 'substance' is just one option here; the Lockian 'self' is another option. There is, as I suggested earlier, a similarity in [a]–[i] to various elements of Descartes's famous *cogito* argument for his own

---

[6] It is a common mistake in discussions of Hume to suppose that a substance view is his target in the personal identity section. See, for example, Roderick Chisholm, "On the Observability of the Self," *Philosophy and Phenomenological Research* 30 (1969), 12; P. Mercer, *Sympathy and Ethics* (Oxford: Clarendon Press, 1972), 29; J. L. Mackie, *Hume's Moral Theory* (London: Routledge, 1980), 160; John Bricke, *Hume's Philosophy of Mind* (Princeton, NJ: Princeton University Press, 1980), 59ff; Don Garrett, "Hume's Self-doubts about Personal Identity," *Philosophical Review* 90 (1981), 341, and *Cognition and Commitment in Hume's Philosophy* (New York, NY: Oxford University Press, 1997), 166, 168; Corliss Swain, "Being Sure of One's Self: Hume on Personal Identity," *Hume Studies* 17 (1991), 107–24; and Donald Livingston, *Philosophical Melancholy and Delirium: Hume's Pathology of Philosophy* (Chicago, IL: University of Chicago Press, 1998), 14.

That the self as substance is the target of Hume's anti-*cogito* also makes its appearance outside the Hume literature. See, for example, A. J. Ayer, *Language, Truth, and Logic* (Harmondsworth: Penguin, 1971), 167; P. F. Strawson, *Individuals* (London: Routledge, 1959), 103; Saul Kripke, *Naming and Necessity* (Cambridge, MA: Harvard University Press, 1980), 155n77, and *Wittgenstein: On Rules and Private Language* (Cambridge, MA: Harvard University Press, 1982), 121ff.

existence as a unified thinking substance, but Locke shows that one can endorse the *cogito* and the account of self-consciousness bound up with it without accepting Descartes's conclusion that the mind is a *substance*. Instead, for Locke, the self is a thinking *person*, conscious of itself as unified in its activities.

Second, although I have suggested that Locke is Hume's probable target in the argument that follows this paragraph, he does not endorse all of [a]–[i]. Most obviously, unlike Descartes, who uses the *cogito* as his fulcrum against sceptical doubt, Locke does not place the intuitive knowledge of self-existence at the centre of his epistemological project, [i]. Descartes, in his turn, would reject the target claims that equate our knowledge of self-*identity* with our knowledge of the existence of the self and its *unity at a time*. In particular, even when constrained by the hyperbolic doubt of an evil demon, we cannot be in error about our existence at a moment as a unified thinker, but we can be in error in our understanding of our sameness through time; it is possible that we were created only an instant prior with a false sense of identity. Descartes ultimately says in the "Synopsis" to the *Meditations* that it takes the "an account of the whole of physics" (AT VII, 13) to show that the soul continues identically, even after death. That is, he must establish that the mind is a thinking substance, really distinct from the body; that God exists and enables substances to persist by constantly recreating them; and that God is not a deceiver, thus guaranteeing that our sense of our continuity is not misleading. So, if Locke is not a perfect fit for the target view, Descartes is even less so. Overall, I have not been able to identify one philosopher who holds exactly [a]–[i];[7] nonetheless, Locke's endorsement of most of them makes it worthwhile for us to focus on him as Hume's target.

Third, whereas the philosophers in the target view emphasize not just the identity but also the simplicity—the unity at a time—of the self of which we are said to be conscious, [f], Locke does not thematize *simplicity* in his chapter of the *Essay* devoted to personal *identity* (and the identity of other things). Nonetheless, he does intimate that he accepts that the self of which we are conscious exemplifies a kind of unity at a time (even if it is possible that it is a product of or supported in a complex material system [E IV.iii.6; see §6.4]): we know that we are the *same* person who "sees, hears, tastes, feels, meditates, or wills" in the case of "*present* Sensations and Perceptions" (E II.xxvii.9; emphasis added). That is, although we can have diverse mental states at a time, we are conscious of ourselves as the one, unified subject of each. There is not a compound subject that is put together out of the different mental states, but one 'I' that stands over them all, aware of itself as the one having each of them.

Fourth, in clause [b] of the target, Hume identifies the intimate consciousness of self with a *feeling*. I noted in §4.3.1 that Locke equates consciousness both with the

---

[7] David and Mary Norton suggest that the target view is an amalgam of Descartes, Malebranche, Shaftesbury, Locke, Berkeley, and Butler ("Editors' Annotations," in David F. Norton and Mary Norton [eds.], *Hume, A Treatise of Human Nature: A Critical Edition*, Vol. 2, *Editorial Material* [Oxford: Clarendon Press, 2007], 807).

"perception of what passes in a Man's own mind" (E II.i.19) and with the perception that we are perceiving that accompanies every mental state (E II.xxvii.9, quoted in §6.1). But we have seen that the perception of perception that constitutes consciousness cannot be a garden-variety perception. If it were, Locke's thesis that all perceptions are conscious (E II.i.11) would entail an infinite hierarchy of perceptions, each accompanied by a further perception whereby we were conscious of it. Instead, for Locke, the perception involved in consciousness is a special kind of perception that makes us "sensible" (E II.i.10) that we are thinking even while we focus on whatever our ideas present to us. One might even say that we have a *feeling* of our continuous existence no matter what mental state we are in. Malebranche is particularly notable here, for he explicitly equates the consciousness (*conscience*) that accompanies all thought with an inner feeling (*sentiment intérieur*) that accompanies the perception of ideas.[8]

With this characterization of Hume's target now on board, let us turn to his attempt to defeat it. He asks his familiar question: do our experiences—impressions—lead us to think of the self as described in [a]–[i]? [a] says that our awareness of the self is ever-present, and [b] says that this awareness is a feeling. Since feelings are impressions in Hume's theory, there would have to be an ever-present impression if the target view were correct. But self-observation shows that there are no such impressions. Hume says:

> For my part, when I enter most intimately into what I call *myself*, I always stumble on some particular perception or other, of heat or cold, light or shade, love or hatred, pain or pleasure. I never can catch *myself* at any time without a perception, and never can observe any thing but the perception.   (T 1.4.6.3, SBN 252)

The mind is thus a "bundle or collection of different perceptions, which succeed each other with an inconceivable rapidity, and are in a perpetual flux and movement" (T 1.4.6.4, SBN 252). There is "no impression constant and invariable" (T 1.4.6.2, SBN 251). And so there is nothing that would allow us to conceive of the self as it is described in the target. Hume concludes that the target view is false (T 1.4.6.2–3, SBN 251–2).

The problem with this argument, however, is that Hume seems to help himself to the very thing he is at pains to deny: a grasp of himself as the subject of his inner observations. Thus his opponents could point to his admission that it is *he* who enters into himself, that it is *he* who stumbles onto his perceptions, and that it is *he* who observes himself as a bundle of perceptions. And he takes himself to be *the same*

---

[8] Malebranche repeatedly calls the awareness we have of ourselves "consciousness" [*conscience*], which he equates with "inner feeling" [*sentiment intérieur*]; this kind of awareness is contrasted with the idea-mediated knowledge we have of extension and the direct apprehension we have of God. But even though Malebranche hints that consciousness of self is "continually" present (ST III.i.1, 202), as in claim [a] of the target view, he is far from endorsing the view as a whole. For he thinks that because we only have consciousness of self, not an idea of it, we know extension much more perfectly than we do the self. And this means that he would reject [c]–[f] and [h]–[i] (see especially ST III.ii.7 and "Elucidation Eleven").

one who successively enters, stumbles, and observes. Hume has accounted only for the self-he-observes, omitting a consideration of the self-that-observes.[9] Locke would say that his notion of consciousness simply captures the self-awareness that is involved in knowing what we are doing. As we have seen, he denies that this self-awareness requires a *separable* piece of thought, an idea *in addition to* the other ideas we have at any given time. Rather, consciousness of ourselves is a component of every thought, an awareness that is *different in kind* from our regular awareness of our feelings, our reasonings, or the objects that surround us.

Hume seems to acknowledge this Lockian point when he says that on the target view, "self or person is not any one impression, but that to which our several ideas and impressions are supposed to have reference" (T 1.4.6.2, SBN 251). Nevertheless, it seems that he takes himself to be justified in searching for a *separate* impression that meets the target requirements because of one of the separability principles discussed in §5.3: perceptions with complex contents can be decomposed into perceptions that concern their constituents (T 1.1.7.3, SBN 18). Since the consciousness of self in a thought is meant to be different from the awareness of its object, he holds that the two awarenesses should be distinguishable, that we should be able to find their objects in separate experiences. His rejection of the target view follows.

Locke would still not be satisfied. He allows that the consciousness of self internal to a thought can be separated in the manner Hume describes so as for the self to become the object of a further thought. But that thought would have yet another consciousness of self internal to it; I would be conscious that *I* was thinking of my self. Consider Hume's own words: "[W]hen *I* enter most intimately into what *I* call *myself*, *I* always stumble...." (T 1.4.6.3, SBN 252; original emphasis on 'myself' only). That is to say that Locke and others who subscribe to the target view would not allow that applying the separability principle to self-consciousness is enough to defeat their view. For them, consciousness of self is an essential constituent of *every* thought; there is at best only a distinction of reason (T 1.1.7.17–18, SBN 24–5) between this self-consciousness and the awareness of an object that together make up a thought.

Does it follow that Hume's argument against the target view is a failure?[10] If PI is read in isolation, it is hard to see how it can count as a success. But of course

---

[9] Chisholm puts this point nicely: "[I]t looks very much as though the self that Hume professed to be unable to find is the one that he finds to be stumbling" (Chisholm attributes this observation to H. H. Price, referring the reader to *Hume's Theory of the External World* [Oxford: Clarendon Press, 1940], 5–6, but Price says there only that Hume's positive account of how the imagination produces our belief in the mind's identity seems to presuppose the real identity of the imagination; "On the Observability," 10).

[10] I think we see here the repetition of a phenomenon I noted in my discussion of Hume's rejection of Locke's theory of reflection (§4.4). Where Locke's observation of the mind leads him to believe that introspection is best understood on the model of inner sensation, Hume's observation of the mind leads him to believe that introspection is a form of thinking rather than sensation. When it comes to core features of their models of the mind, neither empiricist can secure their view simply by an appeal to introspective observation; for the model in question determines how that introspective observation is to be understood. In the opening paragraphs of PI, Hume relies on his model of the mind in observing merely a bundle of perceptions within himself, with no 'I' standing over and superintending it. But Locke's model

Hume did not intend for it to be read in isolation. The target view is the modern system of the internal world, and thus it should be read in conjunction with MP, where he rejects the modern system of the external world. In §6.3 I suggest that Hume's argument there shows why he is entitled to reject the Lockian model of consciousness in PI.

6.3 Modern Systems of the External World

Hume defines modern systems of philosophy in terms of a commitment to the primary–secondary quality distinction (T 1.4.4.3, SBN 226). And of course Locke subscribes to a version of this distinction (E II.viii), and thus his system qualifies as modern in this sense. Most contemporary interpreters of Locke take him to endorse it from a prior commitment to the mechanistic "new science" of the seventeenth century—the view that the physical world is ultimately composed of extended bodies characterized by a limited range of properties (the primary qualities such as size, shape, motion, and a few others), each of which could be adequately described by mathematics.[11] The world as it appears to us—exhibiting the secondary qualities of colour, smell, taste, and the like—is the outcome of our minds' reactions to the causal impact of arrangements of primary qualities on our sensory systems. The challenge for philosophers who endorse the primary–secondary quality distinction is in explaining how the mind works in such a way that the world appears to us to be drastically different from what it is in reality, while also showing that we can nevertheless come to recognize that reality. One such explanation makes use of the theses about self-consciousness that Hume targets in PI.

In the target view, each mental state, including those that purport to present the world, carries with it the subject's awareness that she is the one having that mental state. Recall Locke's claim that "In every Act of Sensation ... we are conscious to our selves of our own Being" (E.IV.ix.3). The question is thus repeatedly posed for each of us all the time: does this sensation accurately portray the world? Or is it *merely* how things look *to me*? Those aspects of a sensation that get at the truth of things in the right way are representations of primary qualities; the remainder of its representational content presents secondary qualities. The vulgar mistakenly treat the colours, smells, and tastes they sense as features of the world, while the scientist demotes these to secondary qualities, accepting only the geometrical (and other mathematical) properties presented in sensation as of a kind with the real properties of objects. Note, however, that if the primary–secondary quality distinction cannot be secured,

means that he observes himself as the one introspecting and also as the one who is subject to all the mental operations he observes. He thus inserts an element of self-awareness into every mental state. We seem to have reached an impasse.

[11] See Ed McCann, "Locke's Philosophy of the Body," in V. Chappell (ed.) *The Cambridge Companion to Locke* (Cambridge: Cambridge University Press, 1994), 56–88; and Lisa Downing, "The Status of Mechanism in Locke's *Essay*," *Philosophical Review* 107 (1998), 381–414.

we are left only with mere appearances and thus we have lost the suggestion that we are somehow able to escape our own personal take on the world. That is to say, because the target view models the mind in such a way that we are always aware of ourselves as standing over our mental processes, including sensation, we need the primary–secondary quality distinction to get outside of our minds and into the world.

Hume says that "many objections might be made" (T 1.4.4.6, SBN 227) to the primary–secondary quality distinction, and in MP he makes quick work of it by using Berkeleyan arguments to show that we can only conceive of objects' having primary qualities if we also take them to have secondary qualities (see P 1.9–15). And so, since perceptions of secondary qualities are acknowledged to be *mere* perceptions, lacking any "external model or archetype" (T 1.4.4.4, SBN 227), the intimate linking of primary and secondary qualities means that we lose our sense of an independent world altogether. "We utterly annihilate all these [external] objects, and reduce ourselves to the opinion of the most extravagant scepticism concerning them" (T 1.4.4.6, SBN 228). We are left only with our recognition of our perceptions, no longer believing that they reveal any of the world to us.

In my discussion of the final quarter of "Of scepticism with regard to the senses" in Chapter 4, I explored Hume's reaction to extravagant scepticism. I suggested that he used the empirical fact that philosophers could "maintain ... that opinion in words only, and were never able to bring themselves sincerely to believe it" (T 1.4.2.50, SBN 214) as a piece of evidence in favour of his preferred model of the mind (§4.4). A similar point applies here. Given that the primary–secondary quality distinction cannot be secured, the view of self-consciousness favoured by Locke means that we should be able to prescind from a commitment to the external world entirely. We should be able to maintain extravagant scepticism "sincerely" by remaining within the perspective that our consciousness of our mental states would afford. Since we cannot in fact adopt this kind of extravagant scepticism and the primary–secondary quality distinction is not viable, then we must reject the Lockian model of consciousness. Put more broadly, Hume makes the seemingly empirical claim that he does not find himself upon "intimate entry" into himself because he thinks that if he did find himself—if he did always recognize that his experience was marked as distinctively *his*—he would be unable thereafter to find anything other than himself. Modern systems of the internal world, like modern systems of the external world, are extravagantly sceptical.

So how, on this retelling of the anti-*cogito*, does Hume respond to the objection noted above, where he seems to help himself to a notion of himself as an *observer* of the mind, even if all he *observes* is the bundle of perceptions? Recall from the discussion in §4.3.2 that Hume thinks that the vehicles for mental observation are secondary ideas—ideas that are of primary perceptions, either impressions or ideas. And I suggested that, just as the vulgar are (normally) blind to how their encounters *with external objects* are mediated by perceptions as processed by the imagination, so also are philosophers (normally) blind to how their encounters *with perceptions* are mediated by secondary ideas as processed by the imagination. Philosophers are (normally) vulgar with respect to the mind, and the perceptions they observe are thus *vulgar objects*. If, as the objection to the anti-*cogito* has it, philosophers were self-conscious while observing their minds, they would have an awareness that their observations were being made from their own particular perspectives. And then, absent something like a primary–secondary quality distinction for the mind, they would fall into the "extravagant" sceptic's position of denying the existence not of an observer-independent world, but of an introspection-independent mind. Hume thinks that in each case it is by means of perceptions that the subjects in question are aware of the objects of their thought—but they remain (mostly) unaware of this fact.

This response to the objection might seem inadequate, in that it trades on finding our awareness of our mental states while introspecting to be limited in a manner analogous to our awareness of merely subjective secondary qualities while sensing. But it is by no means clear that these two classes of perception both are limited in the same way. As Roderick Chisholm points out, a sensory idea of, say, a tree is limited by being perspectival in that it presents the surface of the tree as it would appear to someone whose eyes were located at that particular position, or whose hands were sensitive to that particular degree. Given that sensation is mediated by the relevant organ, the perspectival quality of sensory perceptions is a reflection of the disposition of the organ in relation to the object perceived (compare T 1.4.2.45, SBN 210–11). And it is this perspectival, relational element that ultimately makes Hume argue that primary-quality perceptions are not different in kind from the admittedly subjective secondary-quality perceptions (T 1.4.4.3–4, SBN 226–7). But in the case of introspective awareness of our mental economies, there is no organ of perception. And so it might seem that there is no room for the perspectival dimension to our introspective awareness of our mental economies that Hume would need to yield the conclusion that self-consciousness in introspection leads to extravagant scepticism about the mind.[12]

But Hume would not, I think, be satisfied with this line of thought. Although there might not be organ-dependent perspective involved in our introspective investigation of our minds, he allows that there is another kind of limitation at work here. In particular, we have seen that Hume worries about what I have called *reflective interference* (§§1.4 and 4.7)—the possibility that in introspection, unlike sensation, the activity of observation might distort the object observed. He warns of this problem in the "Introduction" to the *Treatise*, where he notes that purposeful experiments have no place in the "science of man" because "reflection and premeditation would so disturb the operation of my natural principles, as must render it impossible to form any just conclusion from the phaenomenon" (T Intro.11, SBN

---

[12] Chisholm, "On the Observation," 12–13.

xix). But this point applies not just to active experimentation, but also to introspection more generally (T 1.4.7.8; SBN 268). Seeing a tree does not change the tree, but introspectively examining the mind while it is seeing might alter the relevant impression or the mental economy in which it participates. For the mind is the locus both of the agent of introspection and the object of introspection, which means that intimate entry into oneself changes the self entered into. And so, while sensation is limited because it presents its object to us only through the mediation of the relevant organ, introspective perception is limited because it gives us access only to the mind while it is being investigated, not the mind in its normal non-introspective posture. If Hume were self-conscious while introspecting, as the objection to the anti-*cogito* holds, he would be aware of the possibility of distortion created by his introspection. He would be left unable to make any conclusions about the mind when it is not being introspected, and his project of using introspection as a method for discovering the operations of the mind in everyday non-introspective life would be undermined.

I have shown that Hume's argument in the anti-*cogito* might seem like a failure, in that he seems to help himself to the kind of self-awareness that he is trying to deny. But when the argument is place into the larger context of the overall argument of Part 4 of Book 1, he is in fact vindicated. In order to avoid extravagant scepticism, self-consciousness of the kind that he is targeting in the anti-*cogito* presupposes un-self-consciousness, and thus the modern claim of a ubiquitous and fundamental self-awareness must fail.

6.4 Hume on the Primary–Secondary Quality Distinction

I have suggested that Hume addresses the primary–secondary quality distinction as part of his attack on modern systems of philosophy. But he also seems to allow that one of the arguments in favour of the distinction is "satisfactory" (T 1.4.4.3, SBN 226): namely, the causal argument based on the relativity of perceptions to conditions of the perceiver.[13] The problem is that he also seems to think that once this argument is accepted we are on the road to the annihilation of our conception of the world as perceiver independent. The final paragraph of MP thus notes a

direct and total opposition betwixt our reason and our senses; or more properly speaking, betwixt those conclusions we form from cause and effect, and those that persuade us of the continu'd and independent existence of body. When we reason from cause and effect, we conclude, that neither colour, sound, taste, nor smell have a continu'd and independent existence. When we exclude these sensible qualities there remains nothing in the universe, which has such an existence.   (T 1.4.4.15, SBN 231)

---

[13] See Annemarie Butler, "Hume's Causal Reconstruction of the Perceptual Relativity Argument in *Treatise* 1.4.4," *Dialogue* 48 (2009), 77–101.

Hume invokes the very same "contradiction" in the "Conclusion of this book" (T 1.4.7.4, SBN 266), where a footnote points us back to the discussion in MP. Janet Broughton thus takes him to be engaging in "completely unexceptionable" causal reasoning when he makes the relativity argument in favour of the primary-secondary quality distinction, even it if paves the way for extravagant scepticism. Accordingly, she suggests that Hume endorses the closing contradiction and uses that assumption as part of her case for what I call a sceptical reading of Hume's argument in the "Conclusion" (see §7.2).[14]

I think that there are three reasons for rejecting Broughton's reading, and for concluding instead that Hume does not endorse the closing contradiction in MP, but rather sees it as a manifestation of false philosophy.[15] First, that contradiction sits in tension with the argument that ends the following Section (T 1.4.5.29–33, SBN 246–51), where Hume uses causal reasoning between material bodies and percep-tions to reject the pervasive early-modern assumption of a fundamental incompati-bility of matter and mind; he no longer seems inclined to think that this kind of causal reasoning is tied up with the annihilation of our grasp of an independently existing universe. Second, the argument from perceptual relativity for the primary-secondary quality distinction has much in common with the Pyrrhonian experiments in SwS discussed in §4.1. I argued there that these experiments were meant ultimately to show that the bodies we take ourselves to encounter are *constituted by* the human imaginative response to sensory impressions (regularized by the social and normative effects of language), and that accordingly our impressions are not *caused by* external objects different in kind from what we experience. Moreover, a parallel story applies to the perceptions that philosophers introspectively encounter. But, third and most importantly, the modern philosophers make the error of taking their access to perceptions for granted, while assuming that access to external bodies requires an explanation. Let me elaborate on these three points.

Consider first the argument that closes IS. Hume has at that point rejected both the analysis of perceptions as belonging to a mind by inhering in it and the possibility that they instead have a "local conjunction" with it (see §5.6). He then considers a third option for the relation between perceptions and the mind: perhaps they are caused in it by bodily material processes. But many early moderns denied this possibility. They tended to assume that they could know *a priori* that the only changes a material system could undergo would be a rearrangement of its parts, and no such rearrangement would yield thought. Leibniz probably provides the clearest statement of this position:

[14] "The Inquiry in Hume's *Treatise*," *Philosophical Review* 113 (2004), 545.

[15] Louis Loeb describes Hume's reasoning here as "artificial" and "the one juncture where Hume's love of paradox determines the course of his argument" ("Stability and Justification in Hume's *Treatise*, Another Look—A Response to Erin Kelly, Frederick Schmitt, and Michael Williams," *Hume Studies* 30 [2004], 386). In *Stability and Justification in Hume's 'Treatise'* (Oxford: Oxford University Press, 2002), Loeb describes Hume's argument as "far from just and regular" and "contrived" (222).

Moreover, everyone must admit that *perception*, and everything that depends on it, is *inexplicable by mechanical principles*, by shapes and motions, that is. Imagine there were a machine which by its structure produced thought, feeling, and perception; we can imagine it as being enlarged while maintaining the same relative proportions, to the point where we could go inside it, as we would go into a mill. But if that were so when we went in we would find nothing but pieces which push one against another, and never anything to account for a perception. Therefore, we must look for it in the simple substance, and not in the composite, or in a machine....[16]

Similarly, Locke, despite allowing the possibility of a material mind through God's "superaddition" of thinking to body, nonetheless holds that God—the first cause of the universe—must be immaterial: "For it is as impossible to conceive, that ever bare incogitative Matter should produce a thinking intelligent Being, as that nothing should of itself produce Matter" (E IV.x.10). So, although God might "superadd" thought to matter to make human mentality, his own thinking must have an immaterial source. Whether Locke is consistent here has been a matter of intense debate in the secondary literature.[17]

Hume's response to these arguments is straightforward. His earlier treatment of causation shows that we do not have insight into intrinsic connections between causes and effects. Instead, we must rely on the observation of a constant conjunction between the two types of events when making causal inferences. So the fact that we do not have an *a priori* grasp on how a material system could cause a perception does not preclude their being causally linked. Causal connections turn out not to be the kind of thing that can be grasped *a priori*. Thus he prefaces his "rules by which to judge of causes and effects" with the statement that "there are no objects, which by the mere survey, without consulting experience, we can determine to be the causes of any other; and no objects, which we can certainly determine in the same manner not to be the causes. Any thing may produce any thing" (T 1.3.15.1, SBN 173). There is nothing that rules out the possibility of thought's being caused by the motion of matter:

For tho' there appear no manner of connexion betwixt motion or thought, the case is the same with all other causes and effects. Place one body of a pound weight on one end of a lever, and another body of the same weight on another end; you will never find in these bodies any principle of motion dependent on their distances from the center, more than of thought and perception. If you pretend, therefore, to prove *a priori*, that such a position of bodies can never cause thought; because turn it which way you will, 'tis nothing but a position of bodies; you

---

[16] "Monadology" (§17), in R. S. Woolhouse and Richard Francks (tr. and ed.), *G. W. Leibniz: Philosophical Texts* (Oxford: Oxford University Press, 1998), 270. For a valuable discussion of this argument, see Marleen Rozemond, "Mills Can't Think: Leibniz's Approach to the Mind–Body Problem," *Res Philosophica* 91 (2014), 1–28.

[17] In addition to Downing ("Status of Mechanism") and McCann ("Locke's Philosophy of Body"), see especially Margaret Wilson ("Supperadded Properties: The Limits of Mechanism in Locke," *American Philosophical Quarterly* 16 [1979], 143–50), and Michael Ayers ("Mechanism, Superaddition, and the Proof of God's Existence in Locke's *Essay*," *Philosophical Review* 90 [1981], 210–51).

must by the same course of reasoning conclude, that it can never produce motion; since there is no more apparent connexion in the one case than in the other. But as this latter conclusion is contrary to evident experience, and as 'tis possible we may have a like experience in the operations of the mind, and may perceive a constant conjunction of thought and motion; you reason too hastily, when from the mere consideration of the ideas, you conclude that 'tis impossible motion can ever produce thought, or a different position of parts give rise to a different passion or reflection.   (T 1.4.5.30, SBN 247–8)

He goes on to point out that not only is it possible for matter to cause perceptions, but there is evidence that it does. We can observe "that the different dispositions of [someone's] body change his thoughts and sentiments" (T 1.4.5.30, SBN 248)—just as the moderns did in noting that sensory perceptions depend "[u]pon the different situations of our health . . . [u]pon the different complexions and constitutions of men . . . [u]pon the difference of their external situation and position" (T 1.4.4.3, SBN 226). But where Hume seems to suggest in MP that this causal inference ultimately yields "extravagant" scepticism, he concludes in IS that we should recognize the causal impact of matter on mind.[18] How can he be so open to material causes for thought if he really took there to be an irremediable tension between causal reasoning and belief in body?

A second reason for rejecting Broughton's claim that the causal reasoning in MP is "completely unexceptionable" looks back to the Pyrrhonian experiments of SwS (T 1.4.2.45, SBN 210–11). In both places he appeals to the variability of our perceptions on the basis of our physical condition.[19] I argued in §4.1 that Hume's ultimate goal there is to use reflection to bring our sensory impressions into view in isolation, apart from the imaginations' reactions to them whereby they are the vehicles for our being aware of everyday objects ("what any common man means by a hat, or shoe, or stone" [T 1.4.2.31, SBN 202]). And, in fact, in everyday life, even when having anomalous perceptions as a result of unusual bodily situations, we normally continue to take ourselves to be in contact with the things around us. When we rub our eyes and temporarily see double or suffer from "sickness and distempers" (T 1.4.2.45, SBN 211) that interfere with our vision, we continue to take ourselves to be visually in touch with the world. I suggested in §§4.4 and 4.5 that the "extravagant" sceptics and double-existence theorists make the mistake of thinking that the fact that we can become reflectively aware of the perceptions that enable our awareness of

---

[18] This argument would not satisfy his opponents. They admit that the mind and body are joined in a union so that certain configurations of the body are linked to particular thoughts (see, for example, Descartes's discussion in the Sixth *Meditation*; for example, AT VII, 88). But these philosophers deny that the body alone is sufficient for the thought. Rather, God is ultimately responsible for ensuring that whenever our nervous system is affected in a certain manner, our mental states change accordingly. Hume's reply is that an intrinsic connection between God and the mental state is no more available than an intrinsic connection between the body and the mental state. The appeal to God is idle.

[19] As Loeb emphasizes, however, the argument in SwS is focused on the mind-dependency of perceptions, while the argument in MP is focused on the qualities that can be attributed to the external world (*Stability and Justification*, 218n5).

the external world means that we are always so aware, believing in the external world only on the basis of an inference from an inner perception (an inference that the extravagant sceptic rejects). It turns out, however, that a sensory impression can only count as an "image" as of the outer world on the basis of our retaining our grip on the vulgar objects of the outer world. Otherwise, our sensations are merely arrays of coloured and tangible points along with non-spatial tastes, smells, and so on.

Third, and crucially, we saw in §4.5.2 that Hume hints in SwS that his point about the parasitism of the extravagant sceptics' argument on their retention of the vulgar habits of the imagination that they are trying to undermine applies just as much to their conclusions about perceptions as it does to the double-existence theorists' conclusions about objects (T 1.4.2.46, 57; SBN 211, 218). As I emphasized in §4.3.2, philosophers' beliefs about perceptions depend on the similar principles of the imagination as those involved in the vulgar's beliefs about the world. Perceptions are themselves vulgar objects. But Broughton follows the modern philosophers Hume criticizes by missing out on this point about perceptions. They take our beliefs about the external world to require an *explanation*, while our beliefs about perceptions are *taken for granted*. Thus Hume presents the modern philosophers' argument as follows:

'Tis certain, that when different impressions of the same sense arise from any object, every one of these impressions has not a resembling quality existent in the object.... Many of the impressions of colour, sound, &c. are confest to be nothing but internal existences, and to arise from causes, which no way resemble them. These impressions are in appearance nothing different from the other impressions of colour, sound, &c. We conclude, therefore, that they are, all of them, deriv'd from a like origin.   (T 1.4.4.4, SBN 227)

Impressions are "confest to be nothing but internal existences," without any indication that our beliefs about them are also in need of explanation. The focus is resolutely on our belief about external bodies, and how we can come to understand them given the internal nature of our data. In §4.5.2, however, I suggested that Hume holds that philosophers' beliefs about perceptions ultimately arise from the principles of the imagination similar to those that yield the vulgar beliefs about external objects. The modern philosophers are not entitled to challenge the latter on the basis of an unexamined embrace of the former.

If the contradiction that closes MP is an artifact of the modern philosophers' unexamined assumptions, what is Hume's own attitude towards the kind of investigation that they undertake? As the argument that closes IS shows, we can reason causally between external objects and internal perceptions, but only when we retain the habits of imagination whereby both external and internal objects are vulgar objects.[20] Indeed, it is this kind of investigation that would allow us to spell out the

---

[20] Thus the causal connection between perceptions and their distal causes counts as a kind of what Eric Schliesser has dubbed "funky causation"—anything other than efficient, mechanical causation. Schliesser held a series of workshops on this topic at Ghent University in 2009–10.

rules of the imagination that determine sensory beliefs, as when we learn that objects partly submerged in water have visually distorted shapes and that what appear to be pools of water on flat highways during a hot, dry day are in fact merely optical illusions (T 3.3.3.2, SBN 603). What we cannot do is use a *causal* investigation of the relation between objects and perceptions to undermine their *constitutive* links.

6.5 The Belief in Mental Unity

Hume's introspective discovery that the mind is merely a bundle of perceptions means that it has no real unity (T 1.4.6.4; SBN 253).[21] So far as we can tell, there is nothing tying the perceptions together at a single time: The mind lacks *simplicity*. And, so far as we can tell, there is nothing tying the perceptions together across time: the mind lacks *identity*. It is important to note that these findings are primarily *philosophical*, rather than relevant to our everyday concerns. They depend on our taking up the reflective posture in which we observe our mental states, as opposed to the normal posture of everyday life where those states afford us an awareness of their content, without thereby making us aware of them.[22] Locke, in contrast, who takes every mental state to be accompanied by the subjects' awareness that they are in it, sees his exploration of personal identity as fundamentally practical; as we saw in §6.1, for him, 'person' is a "Forensick" term. In holding someone responsible we want to be sure that the one conscious of the pain or pleasure involved in the punishment or reward is the same as the one who was conscious of doing the deed. Hume, by rejecting Locke's model of consciousness, also rejects the practical dimension of his account of the unity of mind. If most people have never "entered most intimately" into what they call themselves, they will not observe themselves as a bundle of perceptions, nor need to form beliefs about its (dis)unity.[23] Hume does not, of course, deny that we are concerned about what happens to us, hold one another responsible for our good and bad behaviour, and care about the kinds of persons we are. But, unlike Locke, he thinks that this topic of "personal identity as it regards ... the concern we take in ourselves" is best treated by an investigation of the passions, not of mental

---

[21] The argument in this section borrows from my "Hume on Personal Identity," in E. Radcliffe (ed.), *A Companion to Hume* (Malden, MA: Blackwell, 2008), 144–7.

[22] Henry Allison agrees that Hume's account of the mind in T 1.4.6 is "not one that would occur to the vulgar" (*Custom and Reason in Hume* [Oxford: Clarendon Press, 2008], 244). Donald Livingston, in contrast, says that in this Section "the first-order question of what constitutes personal identity is in the foreground and the second-order question about the nature of philosophizing is in the background" (*Philosophical Melancholy and Delirium*, 14).

[23] Thus Hume uses 'mind' interchangeably with 'self,' 'person,' and 'soul' in PI. And his core endorsements of the bundle view tend to be couched in terms of the mind, rather than in the terms of personhood. Thus, "the mind is a kind of theatre ... [and] the successive perceptions only ... constitute the mind" (T 1.4.6.4, SBN 253); the "true idea of the human mind ..." (T 1.4.6.19, SBN 261). The tendency to focus on the unity of the *mind* is especially pronounced when Hume presents his positive view starting at T 1.4.6.15 (SBN 259).

unity (T 1.4.6.5; SBN 253).[24] The metaphysical issue of the unity of the bundle of perceptions, in contrast, Hume labels "personal identity as it regards our thought or imagination" (T 1.4.6.5; SBN 253). My discussion here is restricted to this latter issue.

Even if most of us rarely "enter most intimately" into ourselves in order to "observe" our perceptions, Humean philosophers rely on introspection in order to become clearer on the workings of the mind. For example, they notice that the repeated experience of conjoined objects causes the mind to associate the idea of one object with the idea of the other (T 1.3.8). These philosophers thus *believe* that the mind experiencing the conjunctions is the *same as* the one associating the ideas. Similarly, they observe that the co-presence of several impressions each of contiguous objects constitutes a "manner of appearance" responsible for the idea of space (T 1.2.3.5; SBN, 34); the philosophers thus *believe* that it is *one* mind undergoing the several simultaneous experiences. So even if introspecting philosophers can recognize that the bundle of perceptions they observe has no intrinsic unity at a time or across time, they nonetheless typically *believe* that it is unified. Accordingly, Hume's explanandum is not the *real* unity of the bundle of perceptions: there is none. Instead, his explanandum is our tendency to *believe* that the mind is unified when it is under observation.

His strategy is to explain this tendency in the same manner as he explains our everyday tendencies to find diverse and changing objects to be simple at a time and identical across time. Recall the account I presented in §3.2.5: such objects are just bundles of sensible qualities; they have no intrinsic unity in the same way that the mind as a bundle of perceptions has no intrinsic unity. But we nonetheless tend to believe that ordinary objects are simple at a time and identical across time because our ideas of their qualities are associated together, causing us to feel as though the qualities themselves belong together (T 1.4.2.31–6, 1.4.6.6–14; SBN 201–5, 253–8). For example, because the different parts of my dog are contiguous with one another, resemble one another, and are causally connected to one another, my ideas of these parts are associated together. Even as she sheds hair, gets covered in mud, and grows fat, her new conditions are related to those revealed by my previous perceptions of her. These relations cause the mind to associate together my various ideas of the dog, thus leading me to overlook the diversity of what I perceive at one time and the changes in it through time. It feels to me as if I have been observing the same, single, unchanging dog, even though in fact I have had many diverse perceptions. The dog, as the intended object of our thoughts and experiences, thus displays what Hume sometimes calls "imperfect" identity and, to extend his usage, imperfect simplicity (T 1.4.6.9; SBN 246; see §3.2.3). More generally, beliefs about the imperfect identity

---

[24] I discuss this facet of Hume's account of the self in "Scepticism about Persons in Book II of Hume's *Treatise*," *Journal of the History of Philosophy* 37 (1999), 469–92; see also Terence Penelhum, "Self-identity and Self-regard" and "The Self of Book I and the Selves of Book II," in *Themes in Hume: The Self, the Will, Religion* (Oxford: Clarendon Press, 2000), 61–98.

and simplicity of objects are the result of the mind's tendency to overlook its associating ideas of the parts or qualities of the object that resemble, are causally linked, or are contiguous with one another.

Hume appeals to the very same mental mechanism to explain why reflecting philosophers believe in the imperfect simplicity and identity of the bundle of perceptions when investigating the mind (T 1.4.6.15, SBN 259). Introspection affords them secondary ideas of their perceptions, and these are associated together because a sufficient number of those perceptions resemble one another and are causally connected with one another (he denies that contiguity can apply to perceptions themselves, as opposed to their objects [T 1.4.5.9–10, 1.4.6.17; SBN 235–6, 260; see §5.6]). Just as the association of my *ideas* of my dog makes me believe that the *dog* is unified, so also the association of the philosophers' *ideas* of their perceptions make them believe that the *bundle of perceptions* is unified:

[I]n pronouncing concerning the identity of a person, we [do not] observe some real bond among his perceptions ... [but] only feel one among the [secondary] ideas we form of them.
(T 1.4.6.16; SBN 259)

[I]dentity is nothing really belonging to these different perceptions, and uniting them together; but is merely a quality, which we attribute to them, because of the union of their ideas [that is, the secondary ideas of the perceptions] in the imagination, when we reflect upon them [that is, the different perceptions].   (T 1.4.6.16; SBN 260)

Thus the difference between our ordinary beliefs in the imperfect unity of everyday objects and the philosophers' beliefs in the imperfect unity of the mind is a difference in level, not in kind. The ideas that are associated in the everyday cases are ideas *of external objects*—of dogs, apples, tables, and the like. The ideas that are associated in the philosophers' case are (secondary) ideas *of perceptions* (where the perceptions in question might be of dogs, apples, tables, and the like).

It might seem, however, as if Hume is mistaken in thinking that there are sufficient relations between the perceptions in the mind-bundle to support the associations needed to produce the belief in mental unity.[25] The dog, for example, does not cause the apple or the table; and although these objects might have "philosophical" relations of resemblance (as, say, having mass), they do not seem to resemble in the way necessary for the imagination to associate their ideas (T 1.1.5.1, SBN 13–14). But Hume does not need relations between the dog, the apple, or the table in his explanation of the belief in mental unity. I do not believe that these disparate items are *themselves* unified; I believe that my *perceptions* of them are.[26] And there are many

---

[25] S. C. Patten makes this objection in "Hume's Bundles, Self-consciousness, and Kant," *Hume Studies* 2 (1976), 59–75. My response is in line with that of Barry Stroud in *Hume* (London: Routledge and Kegan Paul, 1977), 125–7. Garrett also offers a similar response ("Hume's Self-Doubts," 347–50, and *Cognition*, 172–3).

[26] Abraham Roth worries that Hume's explanation of personal identity is in conflict with his explanation of our belief in the unity of ordinary objects. But he overlooks the difference in level that I have

relations between the perceptions in our bundles. The impression of the dog causes and resembles the idea of it; the impression of the apple resembles the impression of the dog, in that each is especially vivacious. An impression of willing might have been the cause of my moving my attention from the dog to the table, thus serving as a contributing cause to the impression and idea of it. And so on. Hume need only think that the mind-bundle is a network of ideas and impressions that has lines of causal influence and resemblance running throughout it in order for his explanation of the belief in mental unity to succeed. As he puts it:

> [T]he true idea of the human mind, is to consider it as a system of different perceptions or different existences, which are link'd together by the relation of cause and effect, and mutually produce, destroy, influence, and modify each other. Our impressions give rise to their correspondent ideas; and these ideas in their turn produce other impressions. One thought chaces another, and draws after it a third, by which it is expell'd in its turn. In this respect, I cannot compare the soul more properly to any thing than to a republic or commonwealth, in which the several members are united by the reciprocal ties of government and subordination, and give rise to other persons, who propagate the same republic in the incessant changes of its parts. And as the same individual republic may not only change its members, but also its laws and constitutions; in like manner the same person may vary his character and disposition, as well as his impressions and ideas, without losing his identity. Whatever changes he endures, his several parts are still connected by the relation of causation.   (T 1.4.6.19, SBN 261)

It does not seem unreasonable for him to think that there will be sufficient relations among the perceptions to support associations between our secondary ideas of them, thus generating the belief in imperfect mental unity.

Just as Locke appeals to memory in his explanation of personal identity, Hume also appeals to memory as part of his explanation of this network of relations in the bundle. Introspecting philosophers observe an impression followed by a vivacious idea that copies and thus resembles it (T 1.1.1.3, SBN 2–3). Because ideas of resembling perceptions tend to be associated together and thus contribute to the belief that the bundle of perceptions is unified, Hume says that when we remember we do not simply *recognize* an identity that is secured independently of memory; rather, memory's role in supporting the resemblance-based associations between ideas of perceptions "contributes to [the] production" of the belief in the identity of the mind (T 1.4.6.18; SBN 261). Moreover, memory is also involved in the causation-based associations between ideas of perceptions (T 1.4.6.20; SBN 262).

emphasized here, between the association of ideas of an ordinary object to produce a belief in its unity and the association of ideas *of perceptions* to produce a belief in their unity ("What was Hume's Problem with Personal Identity?" *Philosophy and Phenomenological Research* 61 [2000], 91–114). Vijay Mascarenhas makes a similar mistake in "Hume's Recantation Revisited," *Hume Studies* 27 (2001), 288–9. Anik Waldow also overlooks the difference between the association of ideas as a result of constant or coherent impressions, where we end up believing that an external object exists, and the association of (secondary) ideas of introspectively observed perceptions, where we end up believing that a unified mind exists ("Identity of Persons and Objects: Why Hume Considered both as Two Sides of the Same Coin," *Journal of Scottish Philosophy* 8 [2010], 147–67).

Introspecting philosophers discover many causal connections between perceptions: impressions cause ideas (T 1.1.1), the idea of a future pleasure causes desire (T 2.3.9), the passion of love causes the passion of benevolence (T 2.2.6), and so on. But in order for philosophers to *believe* that these causal connections obtain, they must observe the constant conjunction of the relevant perceptions in such a way that they come to associate their ideas of the perceptions. Even if they do not need *explicit* memories of, say, *this* episode of love followed by *that* episode of benevolence, they need to retain the impact of their observation of the conjunction. It is this retentive memory that stands behind the developing tendency to associate their ideas of love and benevolence—their disposition to believe that the passion of love causes the passion of benevolence. Because memory is involved in the production of both the resemble-based and causation-based association of ideas of perceptions, Hume sees himself here as aligned with Locke against his critics in making memory productive of the belief in personal identity.

But Hume also acknowledges the critics' point that a person can forget an experience—even irremediably forget it—and it can nonetheless be counted as one of her experiences, albeit an unremembered one. Once philosophers learn that the causal connections and resemblances between the perceptions that are observed in the bundle are responsible for their beliefs that their minds are unified, they can then acknowledge that if there are causal connections between the observed perceptions and other earlier ones, those earlier ones can also be believed to be part of the same bundle. An unremembered experience, then, can be recognized as part of a person's mind if it can be causally connected to the perceptions that are observed to constitute her bundle (T 1.4.6.20; SBN 262).

Hume concludes his analysis of our belief in the identity of mind by a consideration of how it would treat "all the nice and subtle questions concerning personal identity" (T 1.4.6.21, SBN 262), presumably thinking of Lockian puzzle cases such as the prince and the cobbler. In §3.2.5 I emphasized that Hume's account of identity depends on our understanding of what is "natural and essential" to things of a certain kind (T 1.4.6.14, SBN 258), where our grasp of this nature and essence invokes his earlier account of general ideas. And we have seen (§2.4) that this account has an important linguistic element that brings with it a normative and social dimension. Hume's response to the Lockian puzzle cases makes the linguistic element in his account of the imperfect unity of the mind explicit. These puzzles

can never possibly be decided, and are to be regarded rather as grammatical than as philosophical difficulties. Identity depends on the relations of ideas; and these relations produce identity, by means of that easy transition they occasion. But as the relations, and the easiness of the transition may diminish by insensible degrees, we have no just standard, by which we can decide any dispute concerning the time, when they acquire or lose a title to the name of identity. All the disputes concerning the identity of connected objects are merely verbal, except so far as the relation of parts gives rise to some fiction or imaginary principle of union, as we have already observ'd.   (T 1.4.6.21, SBN 262)

Given that there is no intrinsic unity to persons, there is no fact of the matter waiting for us to discover when we consider, say, the prince and the cobbler. Instead, there are only our associative reactions to our experiences. When we encounter cases that are deviant with respect to our expectations for things of a certain kind—minds in this case—then there might be no "just" answer to the "dispute." Our associations need not converge in the same direction, and, given the deviance of the case, the grammatical rules that have developed around the term 'mind' do not yield a verdict on which associations are right.[27] The problem is when "false" philosophers hypostatize their imaginative tendencies through the fictions "of a *soul*, and *self*, and *substance*" (T 1.4.6.6, SBN 254) that outstrip what we find by our self-observation. They then assume that appeal to such fictions will allow us to answer whether it is the "self" or "soul" of the prince that now resides in the cobbler's body. The true philosopher, in contrast, will accept our inability to answer the question of identity in such an unusual case. There is no determinate answer when we confront the prince or the cobbler.

In concluding my discussion of Hume's positive explanation for the belief in mental unity—and to prepare us for his second thoughts on the topic in the "Appendix" to the *Treatise* (see Chapter 8)—consider the introspective posture that stands behind his account. In §2.2 I noted that Hume appeals to three different levels of introspection. Sometimes, as in most of Parts 1 and 3 of Book 1, he takes the vulgar world of objects for granted and looks within himself to see how the mind operates in forming perceptions or in reasoning. But in much of Parts 2 and especially 4, he examines the mind in its coming to believe in the vulgar world of objects itself. When it comes to PI, however, I have argued that Hume's positive account is primarily meant to address the beliefs of *introspecting philosophers*. Why do they think that the mind that they introspectively observe is one mind? Thus Hume must enter into a third level of introspection by examining his mind *as it introspects*. He, as it were, watches himself as he "enters most intimately" into himself. Thus he can 'see' that secondary ideas are being associated together in producing his thoughts about the mind. Normally, when he philosophizes, secondary ideas are *at work* in producing beliefs about various mental items without thereby calling attention to themselves.

I have emphasized that for Hume, philosophers are normally vulgar with respect to the mind, so that they normally take themselves to be immersed in the perceptions that they observe in the same manner as the vulgar take themselves to be immersed in the world that they sense (§4.3.2). So when he explains the belief in mental unity, his explanandum is the belief in the unity of the perceptions *that the philosophers observe*, and the secondary ideas that are the vehicles for this observation are not

---

[27] David Pears, in contrast, thinks that Hume's incapacity to account for distinction between a single mind, with its train of perceptions, and the case where the train is transferred telepathically to another mind, reveals a shortcoming in his view ("Hume's Recantation of his Theory of Personal Identity," *Hume Studies* 30 [2004], 260).

within the scope of the belief. In the third level of introspection, the role of secondary ideas comes into focus. Hume thinks about them by forming what we might call *tertiary ideas*. The hyper-introspecting philosopher nonetheless remains unaware *of* these tertiary ideas even as they afford him an awareness *of secondary ideas*. In §8.2 I suggest that Hume's second thoughts about the explanation of the belief in mental unity arise from a problem generated when philosophers *recognize* that their beliefs about mental unity depend on the presence of unobserved secondary ideas that are being associated within them. For then they recognize their mind to contain both observed primary perceptions and unobserved secondary ideas, and a new question about the belief in mental unity arises: why do they think that it is the same mind containing both kinds of ideas? Why do they believe that the reflecting mind and the mind reflected upon are one mind?

6.6 Perceptions

If Hume finds a bundle of perceptions when he "enters most intimately" into himself, what does he find? What exactly is a perception? Even though perceptions are at the centre of Hume's project of investigating the mind, he makes it surprisingly difficult to answer this question. In §2.2 I noted that he uses 'perception' ambiguously—most frequently to mean the imagistic mental object of which we are aware when having a thought or sensation, and sometimes to mean the episode of sensing or thinking itself. We are now in a position to resolve this ambiguity. Although most interpreters assume that Hume treats perceptions as inner objects of some kind of special awareness,[28] I think that Hume's identification of the mind with a bundle of perceptions means that he must reject this invocation of 'awareness.' If perceptions were objects of some kind of inner awareness, then the mind would be a bundle of perceptions and in addition a set of awarenesses. Instead, despite his frequent description of perceptions as mental objects, I take Hume's considered view to be that perceptions are mental episodes, states of awareness, or perceiv*ings*; we can reinterpret his invocations of perceptions as mental objects as shorthand for 'that of which we are aware of in an episode of perceiving.' In what follows, I bring together elements of the story I have told in previous chapters to flesh out this view. I then show how it resolves some problems that have traditionally been thought to plague his account of the mind.

In §2.3 I noted that Humean sensory perceptions have what I called *image-content*—most primitively unextended coloured or tangible points, or non-spatial

[28] See, for example, Jonathan Bennett, *Locke, Berkeley, Hume: Central Themes* (Oxford: Clarendon Press, 1971), 222; Stroud, *Hume*, ch. 2; Robert Fogelin, *Hume's Skepticism in 'A Treatise of Human Nature'* (London: Routledge and Kegan Paul, 1985), ch. 6; Wayne Waxman, *Hume's Theory of Consciousness* (Cambridge: Cambridge University Press, 1994), 10, 18; Garrett, *Cognition*, 14; David Norton, "Editor's Introduction," in *David Hume: A Treatise of Human Nature*, ed. David F. Norton and Mary J. Norton (Oxford: Oxford University Press, 2000), 116–17.

smells, tastes, and the like. A person is aware of image-content when a sensory perception is in her mind-bundle—either an impression or an idea depending on the nature of the awareness. She has no further awareness or consciousness *of* the perception; rather, the perception *is* the awareness-of-image-content package. Thus, for Hume, sensory perceptions have two inseparable aspects: the image-content, and what he calls the "action of the mind" (T 1.3.8.16, 3.3.1.2; SBN 106, 456) whereby we are aware of that content. There is no image-content in the mind without some kind of awareness of it (though it might be very weak),[29] and there is no sensory awareness without its being the awareness of image-content. (I will suggest in what follows that there are *non-sensory* episodes of awareness, such as impressions of reflection like desire or pride, that do not have image-content.)

We have already seen two other places where Hume relies on sensory perceptions' including awareness as an aspect. First, in §4.3.2, I noted that Hume allows that ideas can copy perceptions in two different ways. Normally we acquire an idea by copying the image-content of a prior impression. The idea in this case would have the same image-content as the impression, but as a case of thinking rather than sensing, our *awareness* of the image-content would be different. Nonetheless, both the impression and the idea that copies it have the same awareness-of-image-content structure. But Hume also allows a second way in which ideas can copy perceptions, when they present not simply the image-content of the prior perception, but also the manner in which we were aware of the image-content—what Hume calls "the action of the mind in the meditation, that certain *je-ne-scai-quoi*, of which 'tis impossible to give any definition or description" (T 1.3.8.16, SBN 106). In these cases we end up thinking not of something of which we were previously aware, but rather of our *having been aware* of it. The resulting copy is a secondary idea of a prior perception.

The second place where we have seen Hume relying on the two aspects of sensory perceptions occurs in his explanation of what I called in §3.2.1 the *idea-substitution mechanism*. When two objects are related by resemblance, contiguity, or causation, the mind often substitutes the idea of one for the idea of the other without our realizing it. Hume notes that this substitution occurs most easily in the case of resembling objects. For in that case, not only do the objects resemble one another, but also "the *actions of the mind*, which we employ in considering them, are so little different that we are not able to distinguish them" (T 1.2.5.21, SBN 61; emphasis added).[30] This possibility of a double resemblance between ideas—on the one hand between their content and on the other between the mental actions by means of

---

[29] The being of the image-content is its being an object of awareness. Thus Hume endorses the claims about mental transparency about image-contents that I explored in §2.3.

[30] Note that the quoted passage starts: "Resembling *ideas* are not only related together, but the actions of the mind, which we employ in considering them...." (T 1.2.5.21, SBN 61; emphasis added). I noted that Hume uses perception language ambiguously. Here Hume makes it seem as if the "actions of the mind" are *considerings* by which we are aware of the idea. That is, he is using 'idea' in an object sense rather than the

which we are aware of the content—reappears in SwS when Hume explains the vulgar belief in the continued existence of that of which they have interrupted and yet "constant" experience (see §3.2.3). Such experience feels like the uninterrupted experience of an unchanging object, and thus we mistake one for the other. Hume adds a footnote stating that there are two different resemblances operative here: the resemblance between those things of which we are aware (the unchanging object or the constant content), and the resemblance that "the act of the mind in surveying a succession of resembling objects bears to that in surveying an identical object" (T 1.4.2.35n39, SBN 205n).

Once we interpret perceptions as having two aspects, it becomes easier to understand Hume's account of the vivacity, force, or liveliness of perceptions (he uses these terms synonymously [T 1.3.7.7, SBN 629]). He says on a number of occasions that impressions and the ideas that copy their image-content differ only in vivacity (T 1.1.7.5, SBN 19; see also 1.1.1.5, 1.1.1.8, 1.1.3.1, SBN 2, 5, 8). It follows that vivacity is best understood not as a feature of the image-content, but rather as a characterization of the manner in which we are aware of perceptions' content. In the case of impressions we cannot help but be aware of the image-content. In the case of ideas we can reject the image-content, say, by conceiving of something else. Nonetheless, some ideas—notably memories (T 1.3.5) and beliefs (T 1.3.7)—count as having high vivacity because they are resistant to this kind of rejection; their content forces itself on us so that we are constrained to think of things as the idea presents them, even if we remain able, with effort, to think otherwise (if we could not, they would be impressions). We can, for example, imagine that our team won the championship, thus overriding our memory of the loss. We can conceive that the bright summer sun will not cause its normal rash, even though we also believe, sadly, that the rash will occur. But we cannot stop seeing the table in front of us without turning our head or shutting our eyes.

In the "Appendix" to the *Treatise*, he clarifies his view slightly: where he had earlier said that "two ideas of the same object can only be different by their different degrees of force and vivacity," he now holds that "two ideas of the same object can only be different by their different *feeling*" (T App.22, SBN 636). But even in the revised view, Hume still holds that ideas have two elements: their content, and their vivacity or feeling—the manner in which we are aware of their content. Hume's use of the analogy to feeling here is, I think, suggestive; for in Book 2 of the *Treatise*, he makes it clear that while it is impossible to have a perception with an image-content that does not have some vivacity, there are some perceptions without image-contents: namely, emotions and passions (T 2.3.3.5, SBN 415). If the manner by which we are aware of image-contents can be called a feeling, then perhaps feelings proper are nothing but different 'flavours' of vivacity. They would not be *objects* of some special kind of inner awareness; rather, they would be the different ways of being oriented towards

episode-of-thinking sense that I think he ultimately favours when he explains that the mind does not include considerings (or other mental actions) over and above the bundle of perceptions.

things—colourings of our outlooks on the world. Just as the vivacity of our sensory perceptions makes a difference to how we treat their particular contents (for example, whether we take them to exist), our passions and emotions, lacking image-contents, would make a difference to how we treat some or all of the objects we happen to sense and to think of while in their grip. For example, an angry person views everything around her to be conspiring against her to some degree, while someone in love sees the whole world as revolving around his beloved.[31]

I will not pause to develop this suggestion here. Instead, let us consider the challenges that Hume's account of vivacity poses for the standard interpretations of the theory of perceptions, where they are taken to be objects of some kind of inner awareness. Given that, in this interpretation, a perception just is the mental object, its vivacity must be a feature of that object: namely, the intensity or brightness of that of which we are aware.[32] But this interpretation of vivacity leaves Hume without the resources to respond to two notable objections.[33]

The first arises when the suggestion that impressions and ideas differ because of their vivacity is combined with the equations of ideas with thoughts and of impressions with sensations and feelings. Consider sensations that are dim—the buzz of the lights in my office that I cannot help but hear—or thoughts that are gripping—the intellectual project of understanding Hume's philosophy. If the vivacity of the perceptions is meant to capture the intensity of the mental content, it seems like the gripping thoughts have far more intensity than the barely heard buzz. And yet the latter, as sensations, are impressions, while the former, as thoughts, are ideas. But impressions are supposed to have more vivacity than ideas.

Once perceptions are understood as mental episodes, with vivacity characterizing not the content, but the manner in which we are aware of the content, this problem evaporates. The dim buzz of the lights and all other sensings, no matter how faint, count as impressions because we are passive with respect to them, even if their objects do not demand our attention. We cannot help but have them when our sense organs have been stimulated properly. Thus Hume equates involuntariness with the "superior force and violence" that characterize impressions (T 1.4.2.16, SBN 194).[34]

[31] My discussion has focused on sensory perceptions and their role in our everyday awareness of objects in the world around us. But Hume also allows that we have ideas of relations, and these too are amenable to being interpreted as mental episodes. A two-place relation involves the joint awareness of two objects in a certain manner. Hume specifies seven different kinds of relations in Treatise 1.1.5. I take him there to be indicating the seven general 'flavours' of vivacity available to us in our comparisons of objects.

[32] Waxman introduces consciousness as over and above perceptions in an attempt to address this problem (Hume's Theory of Consciousness).

[33] Janet Broughton offers an overview of the standard problems with interpretations of Hume's theory of perceptions and a solution that I take to be congenial to what I offer here in "What Does the Scientist of Man Observe?" Hume Studies 18 (1992), 155–68.

[34] Hume himself seems to have been somewhat confused about this matter. Sometimes he does seem to want to use 'vivacity' to capture not just the involuntariness of a perception, but also a characteristic whereby the object of the perception is the focus of our thinking: "[E]verything that strikes upon us with vivacity, and appears in a full and strong light, forces itself, in a manner, into our consideration, and ...

The second problem for the standard interpretation of perceptions as mental objects also relates to the issue of vivacity. When he first distinguishes impressions from ideas by their amount of vivacity, he makes it seem as if he wants them to differ only in degree. But he also clearly wants them to differ in kind, for he notes that it is possible for them "to approach" to one another in their vivacity so as for us not to be able to tell whether we are dealing with an impression or idea. When we dream or when we are ill with fever, our ideas are "receiv'd on the same footing" as our impressions (T 1.1.1.1, 1.3.10.9; SBN 2, 123); and Hume claims in his account of motivation that we all commonly "confound" those impressions that are calm passions with those ideas that qualify as Humean reason (T 2.3.3.8, SBN 417). But if impressions just are more vivacious perceptions than ideas, a low-vivacity impression should not be "confounded" with an idea; it should *be* an idea. Similarly, if an idea has enough vivacity to be "receiv'd" as an impression, it should *be* an impression.[35]

The problem arises here because, with the assumption that perceptions are the objects of a special inner awareness, their vivacity becomes one feature of that of

when it is once present, it engages the attention, and keeps it from wandering to other objects" (T 2.2.2.15, SBN 339).

But in the "Appendix" to the *Treatise*, Hume admits that his earlier discussion of vivacity had been oversimplified, especially in its suggestion that this feature of our perceptions is one-dimensional, so as to increase or decrease uniformly (T App.2–9, SBN 623–7). In one of the additions he wanted to make to the body of the *Treatise*, he allows that:

The force of our mental actions ... is not to be measur'd by the apparent agitation of the mind. A poetical description may have a more sensible effect on the fancy, than an historical narration. It may collect more of those circumstances, that form a compleat image or picture. It may seem to set the object before us in more lively colours. But still the ideas it presents are different to the *feeling* from those, which arise from the memory and the judgment.   (T 1.3.10.10, SBN 631)

Since Hume notes here that the "poetical descriptions" engage our attention more than "historical narrations" without thereby having the kind of feeling constitutive of belief, I think that his final view is that vivacity is best understood two-dimensionally, where one dimension measures involuntariness (say, any positive number on the x-axis indicates involuntariness, and so impressions always fall on the right side of the y-axis), and the other dimension measures the extent to which the object presented engages our attention.

In fact, the proposed two dimensions of vivacity can be mapped onto the mental-episode theory's two aspects of perceptions. The dimension of vivacity that tracks involuntariness describes a feature of the *awareness* in a perception *qua* awareness-of-an-image; the dimension of vivacity that tracks the engagement of our attention describes a feature of the *image* of which we are aware in a perception *qua* awareness-of-an-image. So the "poetical description" is voluntary while nonetheless being the focus of our thoughts, and so has a vivacity of, say, (−7, 7); the "historical narration" is believed, but it does not capture our attention, and so belongs at (−1, −3), its x-coordinate remaining negative to indicate that this belief is not an impression, but high enough for it to be beyond the threshold that qualifies a perception as a belief (say a perception is a belief if its x-coordinate is greater than or equal to −1). Similarly, the vivacity of my hearing of the background buzz of the lights in my office would be plotted at (1, −4) to indicate involuntariness but low intensity, while my current beliefs about Hume's concept of vivacity might be located at (−0.5, 5) that is belief combined with mental engagement.

[35] This is in fact what Hume himself claims in his explanation of sympathy: the process of emotional contagion whereby someone comes to feel the same thing as another person simply by witnessing it. Hume suggests that the observer's idea of the other person's sentiment acquires so much vivacity that it is converted from an idea into an impression, leading the observer herself to start feeling the sentiment (T 2.1.11.3–4, SBN 317).

which we are aware. Stroud, for example, says that Hume "wants to distinguish impressions from ideas on the basis of some features the two kinds of perceptions can be found to possess by a straightforward inspection of the contents of the mind.... He restricts the range of evidence to the contents of the mind alone."[36] But if this were true, then a perception's vivacity would be manifest to us, and it would not be possible to mistake an impression for an idea. His transparency thesis about image-contents (§2.3) means that we should not make any mistakes about vivacity, construed here as a feature of a mental image.

By interpreting sensory perceptions as episodes of awareness—as awareness-of-image-content packages—this problem disappears. The vivacity of the perception determines whether it is an idea or an impression, but if vivacity is understood as involuntariness then we cannot expect the one having it to be able to tell immediately whether she can control her entertaining its image-content. The dreamer usually does not realize he can avoid the dream, while we all fall prey to thinking that our decisions about what to do happen independently of our passion-influenced views of the situation.

It is important to note, then, how Hume's talk of someone's "confounding" an idea for an impression (or *vice versa*) must be understood. Interpreting perceptions as mental episodes means that the one having them does not usually have any awareness *of* her perceptions; rather, she has an awareness of the perception's image-content (unless, that is, she simultaneously has a secondary idea of the perception, as a result of spontaneous or philosophically induced introspection). And so her mistaking her impression for an idea cannot be assimilated to what, in §3.4, we called an *epistemic* error, as when she sees her friend Lisa and mistakes her for Reva; for in such cases, the object misrecognized (Lisa) *is* the object of awareness, and thus the perceiver could come to see her mistake and so to correct herself. But by treating perceptions as mental episodes, the object of awareness is, say, proximately the tiger-image and ultimately the *tiger* itself that is being dreamt of, not the *idea* of the tiger by means of which the dreamer thinks of it. Her mistake, then, in supposing herself to have an impression of a tiger cannot be an epistemic error, in that she does not have any opinions about the status of the perception in question—she has no secondary idea by means of which she would be thinking *about* her tiger-*idea* (unless she is introspecting while dreaming). Hume instead characterizes her mistake *psychologically*: the perception in question is caught up in the associations that normally would occur only in connection with the perception with which the present one is being "confounded" (T 1.2.5.20–1, SBN 60–2). The tiger-idea in the dream triggers the reactions that normally accompany a tiger-impression, such as fear and the desire to flee. Since the 'error' here is only recognizable to someone observing the perceiver's mind, it is not one that she could *correct*; her mind is just operating naturally.

---

[36] Stroud, *Hume*, 30.

Who, then, can make the correct identification of the kind of perception she is experiencing? In the normal case, where the perceiver is not dreaming, her own introspective access to her mind would allow her to "enter most intimately" into herself in order to "observe" her perceptions (T 1.4.6.3, SBN 252). She could then, for example, try to resist the image-content of the tiger by thinking of other things. But Hume does not insist that the perceiver, while introspecting, has the last word on what goes on in the mind. His methodological commitment to "gleaning up" his "experiments...from a cautious observation of human life" (T Intro.10, SBN xix) means that sometimes other people might have better insight into the perceiver's mental life than she has for herself.[37] They can insist that there is no tiger in the vicinity even if she cannot help but seem to be aware of one—consider a pharmacologically induced tiger hallucination that she cannot wake up from, as opposed to the dream of a tiger. If there is no tiger around, then she cannot be sensing one, no matter how it seems to her.

The account of perceptions I have presented here shows again how Hume relies on the vulgar perspective even when he engages in philosophy. The scientists of man conclude that there is no tiger in the vicinity by retaining their own vulgar grasp of the everyday world of objects. They also determine whether a perception is an idea or an impression by testing for its voluntariness—trying to conceive otherwise—and thus rely on their retention of imagination-generated causal associations. Hume, of course, does not forefront this retention of the vulgar perspective in his initial presentation of his theory of perceptions. But in Part 4 of Book 1, where "systems of philosophy" are themselves the focus of investigation, the irremediable vulgarity of the mind, even for philosophers, is a recurring theme.

---

[37] Broughton, "What does the Scientist of Man Observe?"

7

True Scepticism

Book 1 of the *Treatise* ends with what must be the most literary stretch of writing in the English-language philosophical canon.[1] Though the Section in question has a prosaic title[2]—"Conclusion of this book" (T 1.4.7, hereafter 'CtB')—Hume presents there a dramatic first-person narration of his responses while looking back at his discoveries about the nature of human reason and about how we come to believe that our senses reveal to us a world of public objects. He describes his increasing dismay at what he has accomplished, doubting both its truth and whether we should believe in the verdicts of reason or the senses if his account of them is true. The climax is what amounts to a nervous breakdown:

> The *intense* view of these manifold contradictions and imperfections in human reason has so wrought upon me, and heated my brain, that I am ready to reject all belief and reasoning, and can look upon no opinion even as more probable or likely than another. Where am I, or what? From what causes do I derive my existence, and to what condition shall I return? Whose favour shall I court, and whose anger must I dread? What beings surround me? and on whom have I any influence, or who have any influence on me? I am confounded with all these questions, and begin to fancy myself in the most deplorable condition imaginable, inviron'd with the deepest darkness, and utterly depriv'd of the use of every member and faculty.
>
> (T 1.4.7.8, SBN 268–9)

Dinner, conversation, and a few games of backgammon with friends allow Hume to escape from the paralysis he so vividly presents here. He goes on to say that, though his recovery leaves him at first unwilling to return to philosophy, his curiosity gets the better of him, and the "Conclusion" finishes with Hume's declaration that he will continue with his investigations of human nature—though with a newly chastened attitude. As a "true sceptic," he "will be diffident of his philosophical doubts, as well as of his philosophical conviction; and will never refuse any innocent satisfaction, which offers itself, upon account of either of them" (T 1.4.7.14, SBN 273). And so in Books 2 and 3 of the *Treatise*, Hume investigates the passions and the moral sentiments free from the angst that dominates CtB.

---

[1] Michael Williams calls it "one of the most dramatic expositions of skeptical doubt ever set down" ("The Unity of Hume's Philosophical Project," *Hume Studies* 30 [2004], 267).

[2] Indeed, Hume uses the same title for the concluding Section of Book 3 (T 3.3.6).

As I noted in my Introduction, Hume's 1734 letter to a physician makes it hard to avoid thinking that CtB is a retelling of his personal experiences with philosophy, though the letter ends with the turn away from philosophy and the immersion in public activities (in this case, as a merchant in Bristol), rather than with the return to philosophy that we know that Hume eventually made. Perhaps because of its evidently autobiographical elements, its notable difference of tone from the rest of the *Treatise*, and its recapitulation of topics that seemed to have already been fully discussed elsewhere, earlier scholars tended to ignore CtB, treating it as an expression of what Hume later called his "ruling passion," the "love of literary fame" (MOL, xl).[3] But Annette Baier, in her seminal book *A Progress of Sentiments*,[4] inaugurated a new era of Hume scholarship, in part by putting CtB at the centre of her interpretation (I discuss her reading in §7.4).

In what follows, I offer my take on this fascinating text. I build on the interpretations I offered in Chapters 1 and 4 of what I take to be the crucial sceptical Sections, "Of scepticism with regard to reason" (T 1.4.1, hereafter 'SwR') and "Of scepticism with regard to the senses" (T 1.4.2, hereafter 'SwS'). There, I argued that Hume uses our reactions to sceptical challenges—our incapacity to believe their conclusions despite finding no error in their reasoning—as evidence in favour of his model of the mind. We are fully engaged by our mental processes, naturally believing the conclusions of our reasoning and the verdicts of our senses rather than standing over and superintending them. We *can* reflect on these processes to consider whether we *should* accept what we naturally believe, and normally this means we continue to be engaged in our reasoning and sensing in having second thoughts about, say, possible errors in our calculations or the likelihood that we are in non-standard conditions for sensation. Philosophy, however, wants something more—a vindication of our cognitive capacities as enabling us to get things right. It turns out that philosophy is impotent when it takes on this task. Reflection interferes with our mental processes, undermining both our tendencies to believe and our capacities to reflect. But, I suggested, this was a problem only *for philosophy*, and leaves us, in common life, continuing to believe our reasonings and sensings without trouble.

My suggestion, detailed in §7.5, is that in CtB Hume's chief concern is to understand the place of philosophy in his model of the mind. Against those who think that we *require* a philosophical defence of our basic cognitive capacities, I argue that for Hume, philosophy is *optional*, appropriate only for those who are so inclined. When we do pursue it, it turns out that we are unable to answer some of its core questions because of reflective interference. And, in many ways, we would be better off were we not tempted by philosophy. The pathologies of "false philosophy" that I detailed in

---

[3] See, for example, John Passmore, *Hume's Intentions*, 3rd edn. (London: Duckworth, 1980), 133.
[4] Annette Baier, *A Progress of Sentiments* (Cambridge, MA: Harvard University Press, 1991).

Chapters 5 and 6 mean that this activity is risky, even if not as dangerous as the path of religious superstition. I make this argument by first addressing what I take to be the three main interpretive options for CtB: sceptical readings (§7.2), naturalist readings (§7.3), and dialectical readings (§7.4).[5]

---

[5] Williams also sees three main options for interpreters of Hume's scepticism. While he and I agree in our identification of two of the options (the sceptical and naturalist readings), his third option differs from mine. He identifies a "critical" interpretation, where the goal is the proto-positivist debunking of metaphysical conceits such as substance ontology, intrinsic necessary connections, and the like ("Unity," 267–71). I think that all interpretations of Hume's scepticism must make room for his anti-metaphysical stance, so I do not see the "critical" option as amounting to a fully-fledged interpretive alternative.

A fourth option for understanding Hume's scepticism has emerged more recently: the moralized interpretation, which takes his references to utility and agreeableness in the latter parts of CtB (e.g. T 1.4.7.12–13, SBN 271–2) to mean that he wants to appeal to his moral theory in some fashion as a solution to the challenges of the earlier parts of the Section. (In Book 3, Hume identifies the virtues with traits that are useful or agreeable to their possessors or to those who interact with them.) The relative novelty of moralized interpretations has meant that there is not yet a dominant version, and thus I have not devoted a section to them in my later discussion.

David Owen has offered one version, though he also can be grouped with the naturalist interpreters insofar as he takes Hume to solve the sceptical challenge to reason articulated in SwR by taking our nature to restrict reason's application (*Hume's Reason* [Oxford: Oxford University Press, 1999], 195). But he also thinks that in CtB Hume worries about why we should follow reason when there are other sources for belief available (such as education or superstition). Owen concludes that Hume opts for reason because it is more useful and agreeable (*Hume's Reason*, 212). Michael Ridge offers a similar argument in "Epistemology Moralized: David Hume's Practical Epistemology," *Hume Studies* 29 (2003), 165–204.

Karl Schafer argues that the Owen/Ridge approach loses out on a distinctively epistemic mode of assessment, which he sees as emerging from Hume's emphasis on curiosity and ambition in the latter parts of CtB. Schafer suggests that these two passions ground a "special form of Humean virtue... that comes into view" when they determine our evaluations of character traits ("Curious Virtues in Hume's Epistemology," *Philosophers' Imprint* 14, 1 [2014], 14).

Hsueh Qu argues against what I have been calling the moralized interpretations for failing to pay due heed to Hume's clear desire in Book 3 of the *Treatise* to separate moral evaluation from epistemic evaluation: "Laudable or blameable... are not the same with reasonable or unreasonable" (T 3.1.1.10, SBN 458; "Hume's Practically Epistemic Conclusions?" *Philosophical Studies* 170 [2014], 501–24).

More generally, I think that despite the presence of the language of utility and agreeableness in CtB, none of the moralized interpreters has yet explained how exactly Hume's defence of true scepticism in CtB relates to his use of these concepts in his moral theory. In particular, he thinks that virtues are contrastive in nature, and are thus by definition rare (Es. 83, "Of the dignity or meanness of human nature"; the point is also present in the *Treatise*, where Hume equates the virtues with those qualities that elicit pride [T 3.3.1.3, SBN 575] and requires that causes of pride must be rare [T 2.1.6.4, SBN 291]). How can our approval of reasoning over superstition (as in Owen and Ridge) or of good forms of reasoning over bad (as in Schafer) be limited to the rare cases of those who do so exceedingly well?

A related problem is that the moralized interpreters have tended to run together Hume's preference for *philosophy* with his defence of *reason* (Owen, *Hume's Reason*, 212; Ridge, "Epistemology Moralized," 186; Schafer, "Curious Virtues," 10–11). As I detail in §7.5, Hume's concern in the latter part of CtB is whether and how to *philosophize*, where he eventually endorses it for the pleasure it gives him and its superiority to superstition. He is clear that he does not expect everyone to become philosophers and is instead expressing his own particular taste for this activity. Insofar as this preference for philosophy can be integrated into Hume's moral philosophy it would be that the tendency towards philosophy counts as what I have called a "trait of taste" ("Character Traits and the Humean Approach to Ethics," in Sergio Tenenbaum [ed.], *Moral Psychology* [Amsterdam: Rodopi, 2007], 102), akin to the tastes for hunting and the pursuit of women (Henry I), or expensive amusements (Anne of Denmark) that Hume includes in the character sketches of royalty in his *History of England* (Indianapolis, IN: Liberty Classics, 1983; ch. 6, 277; vol. 5, ch. 49, 122). Such traits count as virtues when the spectator assessing them shares the interest in the pastime, but they do not demand approval from everyone in the manner of most Humean virtues.

The most venerable interpretive option, dating back to Hume's initial readers,[6] takes him to be strongly sceptical, holding that we *should not* believe the verdicts of reason or the senses even if we cannot help but do so. The only alternative, then, is to ignore the sceptical arguments and continue with our lives and our philosophy regardless of the fundamental contradictions to which we cannot help but be committed. I call interpretations that fall into this general pattern *sceptical* interpretations, and in §7.2 I focus on the sceptical interpretations of CtB offered by Janet Broughton and Phillip Cummins. I suggest that these kinds of interpretations ultimately cannot make sense of Hume's continued commitment to philosophy as he goes on, in Books 2 and 3 of the *Treatise*, to investigate the mind's operations—our passions and moral responses—in great detail. Following Cummins, I call this the *integration* problem.

The *naturalist* interpretation of the "Conclusion," in contrast, sees Hume not as showing us to have self-defeating cognitive natures, but as revealing a ground for our beliefs in a source that is different from reason: namely, our natural tendencies to accept what reason and the senses urge. So even though reason speaks against the verdicts of reason and the senses, the fact that *nature* leaves us unable to disbelieve them means that they are justified nonetheless. Reason's authority over us is trumped by the authority of nature. Norman Kemp Smith inaugurated this interpretive school in the early twentieth century,[7] and in §7.3 I focus both on him and on Don Garrett, who has offered a subtle and sophisticated interpretation of CtB as an argument for the embrace of our natural propensities as norms for belief.[8] I argue, however, that by attributing a normativity to nature, both Kemp Smith and Garrett undermine the normativity of reason, leaving Hume in an untenable position that he would not embrace. I call this the *normativity* problem.

Baier's innovation is to make sense of Hume's project in the *Treatise* by seeing it as a fundamentally dialectical work.[9] In her reading of CtB he develops a series of

Thus, even though Hume only hints at traits of taste in the *Treatise* (for example, T 3.3.3.9, SBN 606), I take the most promising line of moralized interpretation to be Peter Kail's in "Hume's Ethical Conclusion," in M. Frasca-Spada and P. J. E. Kail (eds.), *Impressions of Hume* (Oxford: Clarendon Press, 2005), 125–39 (though Kail offers a version of the naturalist interpretation in *Projection and Realism in Hume's Philosophy* [Oxford: Oxford University Press, 2007], 67–9). He argues that Hume's goal in CtB is to reject the Malebranchian obligation to philosophize, with its Augustinian emphasis that such a search after truth brings us close to God.

[6] Hume's response to the sceptical interpretation of his earliest readers is found in "A Letter from a Gentleman to his Friend in *Edinburgh*."

[7] "The Naturalism of David Hume" (I) and (II), *Mind* (1905), 149–73 and 335–47; *The Philosophy of David Hume* (London: Macmillan, 1941).

[8] *Cognition and Commitment in Hume's Philosophy* (New York, NY: Oxford University Press, 1997), and "Hume's Conclusions in 'Conclusion of this book'," in S. Traiger (ed.), *Blackwell Guide to Hume's 'Treatise'* (Malden, MA: Blackwell, 2006), 151–75.

[9] *Progress*, 2, 13, 15, 18, 20, 27. See also W. E. Morris, "Hume's Conclusion," *Philosophical Studies* 99 (2000), 89–110; Amelie Rorty, "From Passions to Sentiments: The Structure of Hume's *Treatise*," *History of Philosophy Quarterly* 10 (1993), 165–79; and Donald Livingston, "Hume on the Natural History of Philosophical Consciousness," in P. Jones (ed.), *The 'Science of Man' in the Scottish Enlightenment:*

conceptions of our cognitive situation, each of which ultimately shows its limitations, thus yielding a revision of that conception that, until the final embrace of "true" scepticism (T 1.4.7.14, SBN 273), will then face its own limitations. Hume thus effects a transition from a "rationalist" analysis of the human thinker to one that is "social and passionate."[10] Baier differs from the sceptical and naturalist interpreters by rejecting the assumption that *Hume* finds the challenges to reason and the senses compelling. CtB's *narrator* is clearly moved by them, but it would be a mistake to equate Hume with the narrator. I discuss what I call the *dialectical* interpretation in §7.4. The problem I find with Baier's approach is that it leaves Hume too distanced from the sceptical challenges to reason and the senses. Why would he call himself a "true" sceptic in its closing paragraphs if the sceptical problems afflict only those with overly intellectualist conceptions of human nature? I call this the *scepticism* problem.

Thus I find none of the sceptical, naturalist, or dialectical interpretations of CtB satisfactory, though I suggest in what follows that each contains a germ of truth. In §7.5 I present my alternative interpretation—what I call the *philosophical* interpretation. I compare it to the sceptical, naturalist, and dialectical interpretations in §7.6, showing that it avoids the integration, normativity, and scepticism problems. I conclude in §7.7 with some reflections on the sources of Hume's true scepticism. But first it will be helpful to have a more detailed overview of CtB in hand.

7.1 Overview of the "Conclusion"

CtB has fifteen paragraphs, falling into five main divisions: first, the "desponding reflections" (T 1.4.7.1–7, SBN 263–8), in which Hume reviews various of the arguments that he presented elsewhere in Book 1 and draws sceptical conclusions from them; second, the climactic nervous breakdown (T 1.4.7.8, SBN 268–9), which I quoted at the start of the chapter; third, the "splenetic sentiments" (T 1.4.7.9–10, SBN 269–70) expressed by Hume when nature not only allows him to escape from the breakdown, but also tempts him to reject philosophy altogether; fourth, the slow return of an inclination to philosophize (T 1.4.7.11–13, SBN 270–2); and fifth, the embrace of "true" scepticism as Hume's preferred "system of philosophy" (T 1.4.7.14–15, 272–4). Let us briefly consider each in turn.

7.1.1 Desponding Reflections (T 1.4.7.1–7)

Hume starts CtB by raising a version of the Pyrrhonian doubts that he explored earlier in SwR. There he worried that the "natural fallibility of [his] judgment"

Hume, Reid and their Contemporaries (Edinburgh: Edinburgh University Press, 1989), 68–84. In *Philosophical Melancholy and Delirium: Hume's Pathology of Philosophy* (Chicago, IL: University of Chicago Press, 1998), Livingston expands his dialectical interpretation beyond the *Treatise* to encompass Hume's philosophical project as a whole, including his treatment of morality, politics, and history.

[10] *Progress*, 278.

(T 1.4.1.6, SBN 183) meant that any given stretch of reasoning must be checked before it could be trusted; but that check is itself another stretch of reasoning and thus it in turn must be checked; and so on, leaving him with no stopping point where he could achieve rational satisfaction in the outcome of his reasoning. In CtB, Hume wonders whether the long stretch of reasoning about the mind that he has undertaken in Book 1 is in fact successful. His conclusions have certainly been unorthodox, and he cannot expect to find very many others who will accept what he has had to say. Why should he himself believe it?

Hume then radicalizes this first Pyrrhonian doubt by raising the question of whether, even if his account of the mind is accurate, his reasoning should be trusted. For in Part 3 of Book 1 he has shown that causal reasoning depends on the imagination's tendency to associate the idea of the cause and the idea of the effect whenever we have had previous conjoint experiences of similar objects. Why accept what the imagination induces us to believe? It seems "so trivial, and so little founded on reason" (T 1.4.7.3, SBN 265). And this concern ramifies, in that Hume showed in SwS that our beliefs about the objectivity of what our senses reveal to us are also rooted in the imagination's "trivial" (T 1.4.2.56, SBN 217) propensities. Similarly, in the Section "Of personal identity" (T 1.4.6) he showed that our belief in the unity of the perceptions that are the vehicles for our sensing, feeling, and thinking is itself a product of the imagination's propensities. Indeed, even the belief that there are perceptions other than those which are "immediately present to consciousness" (T 1.4.7.3, SBN 265) depends on the imagination's tendency to present memories more vivaciously than it does other ideas (T 1.1.3). Hume thus acknowledges that in his account of the mind, "the memory, senses, and understanding are . . . all of them are founded on the imagination" (T 1.4.7.3, SBN 265). So why should he believe in their verdicts?

Hume draws out related sceptical implications of two of the other topics discussed in Book 1. He says that, in "Of the modern philosophy" (T 1.4.4), he showed that the causal reasoning involved in the primary–secondary quality distinction reveals to us that we should not believe in the existence of mind-independent objects, even though the imagination normally generates such a belief in us. So, not only are the imagination's propensities responsible for both our causal reasoning and our beliefs about the world, but these propensities turn out to lead us into a "manifest contradiction" (T 1.4.7.4, SBN 266). He goes on to express even deeper dissatisfaction when he reflects on the fact that our causal reasoning leaves us unable to discover "that energy in the cause, by which it operates on the effect," instead yielding only "that determination of the mind, which is acquir'd by custom, and causes us to make a transition from an object to its usual attendant" (T 1.4.7.5, SBN 266).

Hume ultimately poses for himself a "very dangerous dilemma" in trying to decide which of the imagination's propensities are worthy of assent. On the one hand, if he chooses to follow the "trivial suggestions" of the imagination, he would end up embracing contradictions, errors, absurdities, and obscurities. On the other hand, if he rejects those trivial suggestions, assenting only to the suggestions of the "general and more establish'd properties of the imagination" that constitute the understanding, he would end up succumbing to the constant deferral of belief described in SwR. Moreover, he cannot even make it a policy to commit himself to those aspects of the imagination that allowed him to escape that regress—the difficulty of entering into "remote views of things" (T 1.4.7.7, SBN 268). For such remote views are essential to science and philosophy; and if following these aspects of the imagination is elevated into a policy, then it is not clear why other propensities of the imagination should not also be endorsed, in which case he would find himself back on the first horn of the dilemma. Finally, a policy of avoiding remote views contradicts itself, for it gets its plausibility only on the basis of an abstruse argument. Hume thus summarizes the dilemma at the core of his desponding reflections as a choice between "a false reason"—one that promiscuously accepts the trivial propensities of the imagination—and "none at all"—the reason that cannot settle on any conclusions, instead destroying all belief entirely.

7.1.2 Confounding Paralysis (T 1.4.7.8)

Hume notes "what is commonly done" with these difficulties: they are "seldom or never thought of," and when they are considered they are "quickly forgot" (T 1.4.7.7, SBN 268). But that makes things even worse, for his "present feeling and experience" make it manifest to him that "reflections very refin'd and metaphysical" do matter to him (T 1.4.7.8, SBN 268). In particular, they leave him ready to give up all his beliefs, both those generated by reason and by the senses. The climactic paragraph I quoted at the start of this chapter expresses his dismay at where he has found himself, what he now sees as the "most deplorable condition imaginable." He even starts to lose control of his body; he is "utterly depriv'd of the use of every member and faculty" (T 1.4.7.8, SBN 269). He is lost in "philosophical melancholy and delirium" (T 1.4.7.9, SBN 269).

7.1.3 Splenetic Sentiments (T 1.4.7.9–10)

Nature, Hume says, comes to the rescue by "relaxing this bent of mind" spontaneously, or when social life (dinner, a game of backgammon, merriment with friends) intervenes to "obliterate all these chimeras." And once he has re-engaged with the world, his speculations seem "cold," "strain'd," "ridiculous" (T 1.4.7.9, SBN 169). Indeed, he is tempted to "throw all [his] books and papers into the fire" and to "resolve never more" to sacrifice normal life for the "sake of reasoning and philosophy." His "blind submission" to the understanding and the senses "shew[s] most perfectly" his "sceptical dispositions and principles." And he is under no "obligation" to return to philosophy; that would be "torturing [his] brain with subtilities and sophistries" (T 1.4.7.10, SBN 269–70).

7.1.4 An Inclination to Philosophize (T 1.4.7.11–13)

Philosophy is unable to oppose these anti-philosophical moods. The "force of reason and conviction" does not require us to investigate "principles of moral good and evil, the nature and foundation of government, and the cause of . . . passions and inclinations." Nonetheless:

I am *uneasy* to think I approve of one object, and disapprove of another; call one thing beautiful, and another deform'd; decide concerning truth and falshood, reason and folly, without knowing upon what principles I proceed. I am concern'd for the condition of the learned world, which lies under such a deplorable ignorance in all these particulars.   (T 1.4.7.12, SBN 271)

The return to philosophy is driven primarily by his feelings:

[I]f we are philosophers, it ought only to be upon sceptical principles, and from an inclination, which we feel to the employing ourselves after that manner. Where reason is lively, and mixes itself with some propensity, it ought to be assented to. Where it does not, it never can have any title to operate upon us. . . . I feel an ambition to arise in me of contributing to the instruction of mankind, and of acquiring a name by my inventions and discoveries. These sentiments spring up naturally in my present disposition; and shou'd I endeavour to banish them, by attaching myself to any other business or diversion, I *feel* I shou'd be a loser in point of pleasure; and this is the origin of my philosophy.   (T 1.4.7.11–12, SBN 270–1)

But Hume also notes a second reason to return to philosophy: the need to combat "superstition" and "religion." The problem is that human weakness causes many people, in searching for the causes of the events surrounding them, to be tempted to project their minds into a strange world, filled with "scenes, and beings, and objects, which are altogether new"—and completely unlike what we find in "the visible" world, the "sphere of common life," or "that narrow circle of objects, which are the subject of daily conversation and action." Because superstition is so prevalent and influential on the "popular opinions of mankind," the question becomes whether we should prefer it or philosophy when it comes to speculation. Hume opts for philosophy: "if just, [it] can present us only with mild and moderate sentiments; and if false and extravagant, its opinions are merely the objects of a cold and general speculation, and seldom go so far as to interrupt the course of our natural propensities." Where "religion" is "dangerous" and likely to inspire "great extravagancies of conduct," philosophy is, at worst, "ridiculous," barring some truly anomalous cases of philosophers, like the Cynics, who actually try to implement their philosophical principles as a way of life (T 1.4.7.13, SBN 271–2).

7.1.5 True Scepticism (T 1.4.7.14–15)

How then to pursue philosophy? Hume first re-emphasizes that there is no obligation to philosophize, that it depends on its practitioners' "easy disposition," "good humour," and "application." He does not want to make philosophers out of those "many honest gentlemen,[11] who being always employ'd in their domestic affairs, or amusing themselves in common recreations, have carried their thoughts very little beyond those objects, which are every day expos'd to their senses." Indeed, it would be better if philosophers were to be more like these gentlemen, "shar[ing] . . . in this

---

[11] Hume emphasizes that they are to be found "in *England* in particular" (T 1.4.7.14, SBN 272).

gross earthy mixture, as an ingredient, which they commonly stand much in need of, and which wou'd serve to temper those fiery particles, of which they are compos'd." With the moderation of their "warm imagination[s]," philosophers

might hope to establish a system or set of opinions, which if not true (for that, perhaps, is too much to be hop'd for) might at least be satisfactory to the human mind, and might stand the test of the most critical examination.... For my part, my only hope is, that I may contribute a little to the advancement of knowledge, by giving in some particulars a different turn to the speculations of philosophers, and pointing out to them more distinctly those subjects, where alone they can expect assurance and conviction.   (T 1.4.7.14, SBN 273)

Hume thus urges those who are so inclined to join him in his project.

The conduct of a man, who studies philosophy in this careless manner, is more truly sceptical than that of one, who feeling in himself an inclination to it, is yet so over-whelm'd with doubts and scruples, as totally to reject it. A true sceptic will be diffident of his philosophical doubts, as well as of his philosophical conviction; and will never refuse any innocent satisfaction, which offers itself, upon account of either of them.   (T 1.4.7.15, SBN 273)

Hume closes CtB by noting that his sceptical principles do not preclude him from making "positive" and "certain" assertions when his investigations so move him. He notes that he had earlier been willing to "make use of such terms as these, *'tis evident, 'tis certain, 'tis undeniable.*" His excuse is that "such expressions were extorted from me by the present view of the object, and imply no dogmatical spirit, nor conceited idea of my own judgment, which are sentiments that I am sensible can become no body, and a sceptic still less than any other" (T 1.4.7.15, SBN 274).

7.2 Sceptical Interpretations

An interpretation of CtB counts as sceptical to the extent that it sees Hume as endorsing the "desponding reflections." They are not merely *prima facie* justified, awaiting further ratification or rebuttal (say by nature), but speak to our true cognitive condition. As such, these interpretations have tended to emphasize the first seven paragraphs of CtB (§7.1.1) and the climactic crisis of paragraph eight (§7.1.2). Robert Fogelin, for example, says that Hume "*ends up* in a morass of skeptical doubt. He *ends up* there ... because he comes to see that the mechanisms that ultimately fix our beliefs are mere makeshifts not worthy of our epistemic approval from the very perspective he has come to occupy."[12] Wayne Waxman says that "Hume's survey of human understanding in *A Treatise of Human Nature ends* with a vertiginous descent into despair;" and "*Treatise* I *concludes* with reason locked in self-destructive yet inescapable combat with itself."[13]

---

[12] "Garrett on the Consistency of Hume's Thought," *Hume Studies* 24 (1998), 167; emphases added.
[13] *Hume's Theory of Consciousness* (Cambridge: Cambridge University Press, 1994), 1, 278; emphases added. Louis Loeb also endorses a version of the sceptical interpretation, taking Hume to hold that we

This is not to say that either interpreter entirely ignores what happens *after* the climactic moment in CtB, where Hume returns to philosophy, but both suggest that we are given a merely psychological description of our failure to accept the negative verdict on our capacities. Fogelin suggests that Hume thinks we overcome this verdict not by responding to the challenges in the desponding reflections, "but by bringing our reflections to an end."[14] Waxman argues that, for Hume, we are unable to sustain the mental posture where reason's contradictions are manifest to us: "[N]o attitudes or modes of awareness are less suitable to be so combined than those of immediate consciousness [used for philosophical investigation] and [of] imagination [used in common life]."[15] Even though we recognize the contradictions inherent in our reason, we are nonetheless "moderate" in our reaction to them. We mostly ignore them as we go on with both life and philosophy.

Fogelin admits that Hume's response so characterized seems inadequate: "It is ... unclear how human faculties can be disciplined to stay within the modest bounds that Hume, in his calmer moments, prescribes."[16] Notably, in Book 2, Hume resumes his investigation of the causal structure of the human mind with detailed analyses of the passions, but does not pause once to worry about (what sceptical interpreters see as) his negative epistemic verdict on the very activity of causal reasoning. Cummins calls this the *integration problem*: "Hume appears paradoxically to endorse the triumph of skepticism and, yet, continue his pursuit of just the kind of knowledge the triumph of skepticism would entirely preclude."[17] Cummins and Broughton[18] are the two sceptical interpreters of CtB who have come closest to offering Hume a response to this problem, though I suggest neither ultimately succeeds.

Broughton emphasizes Hume's conception of his project as an *inquiry* that will have transformative effects upon the inquirer (her approach thus has some commonalities with the dialectical interpreters discussed in §7.4). The narrator who

should "reject all belief as unjustified, at least for the reflective person, even though some beliefs are irresistible" (*Stability and Justification in Hume's 'Treatise'* [Oxford: Oxford University Press, 2002], 14). I think, however, that Loeb's interpretive commitments—where he takes the justification of a belief for Hume to reflect its stability—mandate a different interpretation of CtB. Surely Hume's point there is the *instability* of the sceptical conclusions, and thus Loeb should take them to be *unjustified*. If Loeb accepted this criticism, his reading of CtB would look more like my preferred 'philosophical' interpretation (see §7.5). Loeb himself revises his view extensively in "Stability and Justification in Hume's *Treatise*, Another Look—A Response to Erin Kelly, Frederick Schmitt, and Michael Williams," *Hume Studies* 30 (2004), 339–404.

[14] *Hume's Skepticism in the 'Treatise of Human Nature'* (London: Routledge and Kegan Paul, 1985), 92. His position ultimately resembles Richard Popkin, "David Hume: His Pyrrhonism and his Critique of Pyrrhonism," *The Philosophical Quarterly* 1 (1951), 385–407. James O'Shea aptly describes this kind of interpretation as attributing to Hume a "mood pluralism" ("Hume's Reflective Return to the Vulgar," *British Journal for the History of Philosophy* 4 [1996], 310). The problem then becomes one of reconciling the verdicts we reach when in different moods.

[15] *Hume's Theory*, 278.

[16] *Hume's Skeptical Crisis: A Textual Study* (New York, NY: Oxford University Press, 2009), 137.

[17] "Hume's Diffident Skepticism," *Hume Studies* 25 (1999), 43.

[18] "The Inquiry in Hume's *Treatise*," *Philosophical Review* 113 (2004), 537–56.

voices seemingly complete confidence in the causal investigation of human nature in the early portions of the *Treatise* must ultimately "absorb...the conclusion that virtually all of our beliefs about the world around us are entirely unwarranted."[19] The result is a new ironical self-understanding. The inquirer in Book 2 can continue with his[20] causal investigation of the mind, not because the sceptical challenges are "quickly forgot" (T 1.4.7.7, SBN 268), but because he treats his new results "in a detached way."[21]

My concern is that Broughton's claim that Hume is committed to the negative verdicts about his beliefs means that no amount of irony or detachment will avoid the integration problem. Compare a sceptic about Roman Catholicism who comes to see that belief in the Christian God, Jesus as the son of God, and the resurrection is entirely unwarranted. She might, however, continue to attend mass, partake in the Eucharist, confess her sins, and so on, because she enjoys the pageantry or the social ritual. This is fine for her, of course, but it gives no reason to anyone who is not similarly inclined to participate in the Church's activities. Broughton might say that, in the philosophical analogue, this is exactly Hume's point. The return to philosophy is driven by feelings and inclinations (§7.1.4). Hume urges that there is no "obligation" to philosophize.

But this reading of CtB is too nihilistic. For when Hume returns to philosophy, he continues to aim at the truth even if he is willing to settle for opinions that "might at least be satisfactory to the human mind, and might stand the test of the most critical examination" (T 1.4.7.14, SBN 272). For Broughton, Hume's negative conclusion means that he can only ask those who are pleased by his results to accept them. Instead, he wants those who are pleased by *philosophy* to join him as he attempts to *find out more* about human nature. A solution to the integration problem needs to explain why someone who follows Hume for the remainder of the *Treatise* should accept the *reasoning* he displays there.

Broughton might be able to avoid this problem with her interpretation if she allowed that Hume moderated his negative conclusion, perhaps by adopting irony not just towards the ongoing project of philosophy in Books 2 and 3, but also to the conclusions he has reached in the "desponding reflections" of CtB. Hume does say that "the true sceptic will be diffident of his philosophical doubts, as well as of his philosophical conviction" (T 1.4.7.14, SBN 273). If she accepted this amendment to

---

[19] "The Inquiry," 539.

[20] I take Hume's narrator throughout the *Treatise* to be gendered as male (see especially the discussion in T 3.3.5.2 [SBN 614–15] of "good women's men"). Broughton also makes this assumption.

[21] "The Inquiry," 550. Broughton takes Hume's emphasizing that his return to philosophy is rooted in non-rational parts of his nature (§7.1.4) to mean that he remains fully committed to the negative verdicts on his cognitive capacities, and in this she differs from Cummins, who sees Hume as doubting his doubts. I think Broughton should similarly conclude that the inquirer would end up with ironic detachment towards both his "philosophical doubts, as well as...his philosophical conviction" (T 1.4.7.14, SBN 273).

her view, it would end up as quite similar to Cummins' interpretation.[22] For him, Hume's point in CtB is to show that, even if the sceptical challenges cannot be met on their own terms, our curiosity overcomes our indolence (§7.1.4) and we develop a cautious attitude towards them—"an unwillingness to take them as conclusive even though they seem unanswerable."[23] In this reading, our doubts about our abstruse philosophical doubts allow us to continue philosophizing, though now as "diffident" sceptics.

Ultimately I do not think that Cummins and Broughton are successful in their attempts to free Hume from the integration problem. Because both interpreters think that Hume is genuine in his "desponding reflections," doubts about or ironic distancing from the sceptical challenges can be maintained only if we leave our reflections behind us. Otherwise, despite our doubts or irony, we would still *believe* the negative verdicts, albeit in a complicated manner. Thus if Hume were endorsing Cummins' or Broughton's strategy, we would expect, when he continues his inquiry in Books 2 and 3, to find him averting his eyes,[24] as it were, from the arguments summarized in CtB. But this is not what we find. For he repeatedly harks back to his account of the understanding in Book 1 in order to provide what he considers to be *rational* support for his conclusions about the passions and morals. Most notably, he reminds himself, at one point, that "[t]he essence and composition of external bodies are so obscure, that we must necessarily, in our reasonings, or rather conjectures concerning them, involve ourselves in contradictions and absurdities" (T 2.2.6.2, SBN 366). He seems here to go out of his way to remind himself of CtB and SwS. Elsewhere, he uses his account of causation as evidence in favour of his associationist explanations of both the person-oriented indirect passions (T 2.1.5.11, SBN 290) and sympathy (T 2.1.11.8, SBN 318–20), which he later declares to be the "chief source of moral distinctions" (T 3.3.6.1, SBN 618); similarly, he spends several Sections of the *Treatise* showing how the workings of the

---

[22] Both Cummins and Broughton take Hume to show his hand in the "Introduction" to the *Treatise*, and both invoke the following passage, where he considers the "common prejudice against metaphysical reasonings of all kinds" and against

[…] every kind of argument, which is any way abstruse, and requires some attention to be comprehended. We have so often lost our labour in such researches, that we commonly reject them without hesitation, and resolve, if we must for ever be a prey to errors and delusions, that they shall at least be natural and entertaining. And indeed nothing but the most determined scepticism, along with a great degree of indolence, can justify this aversion to metaphysics.

(T Intro.3, SBN xiv; see Cummins, "Diffident Skepticism,"
44, 60, and Broughton, "The Inquiry," 552–3)

Hume seems to reject this prejudice by saying that one should expect philosophical discussions of the type that he is introducing to be abstruse, though, as the author of CtB, he is well aware that he too will fall prey to a determined scepticism and a great degree of indolence. But he also knows that he then continues to investigate philosophical questions in Books 2 and 3, though doubting his earlier doubts (Cummins) or having a new detached attitude towards his inquiry (Broughton).

[23] "Diffident Skepticism," 59.

[24] Note the interesting repetition of visual metaphors in CtB: angels covering their eyes (T 1.4.7.6, SBN 267) and blind submission (1.4.7.10, SBN 269).

imagination described in Book 1 are interwoven with the passions described in Book 2 to bring about the particular motivations that we experience, such as hope and fear (T 1.3.10, 2.3.6–8). Thus he says in the introductory passages of Book 3: "I am not … without hopes that the present system of philosophy will acquire new force as it advances; and that our reasonings concerning *morals* will corroborate whatever has been said concerning the *understanding* and the *passions*" (T 3.1.1.1, SBN 455). Hume does not seem to have *turned away* from his achievements in Book 1 when he continues with his philosophical investigations in Books 2 and 3; rather, he seems to *embrace* them, despite the qualms of CtB.

Cummins' meta-doubts or Broughton's detachment might explain how it is psychologically possible to engage in *other* intellectual endeavours—natural philosophy or mathematics, say—where the mind's mechanisms are not at the centre of our attention. But even then, once we have learned that our cognitive capacities are fundamentally unsound, there no longer is any *reason* for our continued attraction to these topics. Recall that Hume's account of practical reason holds that when we discover the impossibility of success in an endeavour, our desire to engage in it no longer keeps us in its sway (T Intro.9, 2.3.3.7; SBN xviii, 416). If we really believed that we are as cognitively disordered as the sceptical interpretation of Hume suggests, it is hard to see how we would ever continue to philosophize.

7.3 Naturalist Interpretations

Where the sceptical interpreters take the initial "desponding reflections" of CtB (§7.1.1) to give Hume's considered assessment of our cognitive condition, the naturalist interpreters emphasize the significance of our not believing the sceptical challenges (§7.1.3) and the eventual return of our confidence in reason and the senses (§7.1.4) that follows on the climactic nervous breakdown and the splenetic anti-philosophical sentiments. They take Hume's point in the latter parts of the CtB to be not merely psychological, but also philosophical. We are to learn that, despite the sceptical arguments against the verdicts of reason and the senses, our natural faith in them shows them to be justified. Kemp Smith labels beliefs that are so justified *natural beliefs*, and takes Hume to hold that they have "*de facto* prescriptive rights which Nature, in thus predetermining us to them, has conferred upon them."[25] For Garrett, our natural propensities have a "title" over us that neutralizes any philosophical challenges they might face. I argue in what follows, however, that they end up leaving Hume unable to manage the conflicts that can arise between our propensities and our reflective verdicts.

---

[25] *Philosophy of David Hume*, 125. David Owen's statement of the naturalist view is especially clear: "Reason's hold on us is limited, and a good thing too. If its influence were unlimited, it would entirely destroy itself. It is only because its influence is limited by other aspects of our nature that it can have any influence at all. We can be rational only if we are only partly rational" (*Hume's Reason*, 195).

Although Kemp Smith does not investigate CtB in detail, he does discuss Hume's original presentations of the various topics recapitulated in the "desponding reflections." And like the sceptical interpreters I criticized in §7.2, he holds that Hume believes the sceptical attacks on reason and senses are sound. Reason *does* reveal that we ought not to believe any stretch of reasoning; reason *does* show that the senses reveal only our subjective states, not a world of independently existing objects. But Kemp Smith thinks that Hume wants us to learn that "Nature" trumps these rational arguments by means of our incapacity to accept them.[26] And so we should be thankful to nature for providing us with beliefs that are fundamental to our wellbeing where reason lets us down.

It is somewhat unclear what Kemp Smith means by 'natural beliefs.' His examples usually have to do with the belief in body as existing independently of us and the belief that these bodies have causal interactions with one another;[27] sometimes he also includes the causal principle (that every event has a cause) as a natural belief.[28] But Kemp Smith cannot mean that the vulgar have conscious commitment to these beliefs. Indeed, as he openly admits, particular instantiations of them can be wrong, as when we hallucinate or make causal errors.[29] Rather, Kemp Smith seems to be drawing attention to Hume's account of certain principles of the imagination that operate such as to reliably produce the particular, though fallible, beliefs in the existence of body and in casual connections. Natural beliefs are thus better thought of as natural *tendencies* to believe.

These tendencies are not open to rational justification. In fact, Kemp Smith takes Hume's sceptical arguments to mean that they generate only beliefs that are false, strictly speaking. He thinks that Hume appeals to "immediate consciousness"—what Kemp Smith takes to be an infallible immediate awareness of our mental states—to show that causal beliefs depend not on a grasp of an intrinsic connection between the objects under investigation, but rather on an inner impression of reflection, generated only once suitable experience has brought us to associate the ideas of the cause and the effect; and beliefs about body are really only beliefs about perceptions, not independently existing objects.[30] For Kemp Smith, our continuing to follow the natural beliefs despite reason's verdict against them reveals that reason's place in our mental economy is less exalted than is traditionally believed. The role of the sceptical arguments, he suggests, is to help us keep our tendencies to believe in check;

---

[26] *Philosophy of David Hume*, 129–32.   [27] *Philosophy of David Hume*, 124, 455.
[28] *Philosophy of David Hume*, 127.   [29] *Philosophy of David Hume*, 455.
[30] *Philosophy of David Hume*, 454–8. Kemp Smith differs from Waxman (*Hume's Theory*), however, in that where Waxman wants the beliefs generated by immediate consciousness to be akin to all other beliefs in being based on vivacity (though he takes vivacity to characterize consciousness, not perceptions), Kemp Smith thinks that immediate consciousness is a source for beliefs that, being infallible, are different in kind from vivacity-dependent beliefs generated by the imagination. In §4.3.2 I argued that Humean consciousness is best understood in terms of secondary ideas of primary perceptions, where we believe that the primary perceptions exist because of mechanisms of the imagination akin to those that generate the belief in the existence of sensory objects.

for example, to stop us from becoming carried away with our desire for causal explanations before we attempt to discover a cause of the universe. As Kemp Smith says, "nothing short of the dispassionate questionings of a sceptical philosophy can avail to keep [us] in wholesome conformity with Nature's ends."[31]

Kemp Smith's naturalist interpretation has the benefit of avoiding the integration problem plaguing the sceptical interpretations. Because we are to embrace our natural tendency to believe our reasoning, there is nothing surprising about Hume's continuing to reason about human nature throughout Books 2 and 3 of the *Treatise*. But Kemp Smith is susceptible to a different objection—one that is especially evident when his interpretation is applied to CtB.

The problem is that it is hard to see how the natural beliefs are meant to work in concert with the "desponding reflections" (§7.1.1). Kemp Smith's view that the sceptical arguments are sound means that he thinks Hume is *right* when he refuses to assent to the various "trivial" mechanisms of the imagination discussed in the "desponding reflections." So at what point do we abandon our commitment to the truth of the arguments for the sake of the natural beliefs? Only after the nervous breakdown at the climax of CtB (§7.1.2)? Does this mean that the sceptical arguments are justified when we attend to them, but not afterwards? Or is Kemp Smith simply offering us a variant of Fogelin's interpretation, where we forget reason's verdicts shortly after recognizing them, in which case the integration problem returns to haunt us?

More generally, Kemp Smith tries to have Hume rely on two normative principles: reason and the natural beliefs. When they clash, "Nature" is supposed to have the greater authority. But what about the reasoning that led us into the clash with Nature, such as the "desponding reflections"? Are we to continue believing in our rational conclusions until we suddenly find that we cannot any longer do so? That would be a case not of our finding out what we *should* believe, but of our finding out what we *do* believe. And what of other cases where we do not want to go where reason takes us. Usually this is a case of irrationality, not of recognizing an authority different from reason. Let us call this the *normativity* problem: how is Nature's normativity to be integrated with the normativity of reason?[32]

Garrett offers the most sustained naturalist interpretation of CtB, though he differs from Kemp Smith by rejecting the suggestion that Hume *endorses* the "desponding reflections" (§7.1.1). Instead, Garrett takes Hume only to be *describing* his reactions to various challenges to his fundamental beliefs, without being fully persuaded by any of them: "In no case does he claim that an entire class of *fundamental* human beliefs is false or unworthy of belief, nor that such a class of beliefs should be rejected or

---

[31] *Philosophy of David Hume*, 130.

[32] Williams makes a similar point when he says that the "naturalistic reading is incomplete unless it explains how Hume's psychology of belief acquires a normative edge" ("Unity," 269). See also Ruth Weintraub, "The Naturalistic Response to Scepticism," *Philosophy* 78 (2003), 369–86.

suspended."[33] This suggestion allows Garrett to make some headway on avoiding the normativity problem that plagued Kemp Smith. For if Hume does not see the sceptical argument in the desponding reflections as sound, then integrating the demands of reason and of nature might be an easier task.

Garrett thinks that Hume does exactly this in the eleventh paragraph of the "Conclusion," which ends with what Garrett calls the *title principle*: "Where reason is lively, and mixes itself with some propensity, it ought to be assented to. Where it does not, it never can have any title to operate over us" (T 1.4.7.11, SBN 270). Although the sceptical arguments that start CtB are supported by reason, Hume's reactions to them show that they ought not to be assented to—not because other reasons are elicited that undermine the sceptical arguments' initial plausibility, but because the arguments do not mix themselves with our propensities.

I have two problems with Garrett's invocation of the title principle. First, it too yields an unsatisfactory reading of the "desponding reflections" in the first portion of the CtB. It is true that, as Garrett emphasizes, Hume describes there his reactions to the sceptical challenges to his beliefs rather than saying that we should accept their conclusions. But it is important to see that his reactions—despair, melancholy, dread, and so on—take the form they do because of what the sceptical challenges are urging on him. He feels negative emotional assessments *because* he discovers that his reasoning is probably flawed, or that it is merely the expression of trivial propensities in the imagination. It is not that the feelings show that the reasoning does not have a title over him; rather, it is because of the title that reasoning has over him that he experiences negative emotional reactions to the sceptical arguments.

The second problem with Garrett's reading is that it is not clear how his invocation of the title principle solves the normativity problem. For it seems to suggest that once we have reasoned to a conclusion, we are to wait to see if it mixes itself with our propensities so as to produce a belief. If it does yield a belief, we should believe it; if it does not yield a belief, we should not believe it. Moreover, as Hume's narrator himself demonstrates in CtB, individuals will be dominated by different propensities at different times, and different people will have different propensities from one another. Are they thereby justified only at the moment that their propensities "mix" with their beliefs? Even if "superstition...seizes strongly on the mind" (T 1.4.7.12, SBN 271)?[34] As in Kemp Smith's naturalist interpretation, Garrett's title principle gives us only what we *do* believe, not what we *should* believe.[35]

---

[33] *Cognition*, 208. Ridge argues persuasively that Garrett's attempt to read the "desponding reflections" in CtB non-normatively is unsatisfactory ("Epistemology Moralized," 196–8n8).

[34] For a similar criticism of the title principle, see Schafer, "Curious Virtues," 14.

[35] Henry Allison accepts Garrett's positioning of the title principle as the key for understanding Hume's argument in CtB, but offers a different account of it. He takes it to be "second-order normative principle, the applicability of which is limited to reasoning that passes the first-order normative test" (embodied in the "logic" Hume articulates in T 1.3.15). Allison suggests that the title principle gives Hume a "license to suspend the rules in this case [that is, the desponding reflections] and perhaps in other cases as well," thus allowing his "diffidence regarding his philosophical doubts to trump his diffidence regarding his

7.4 Dialectical Interpretations

The third school of interpreters of CtB tries to avoid the problems facing the sceptical and naturalist interpretations by questioning whether Hume is speaking *in propria persona* in its more negative moments. After all, as we saw in Chapter 1, in SwR—the core argument of which plays a key role in the "desponding reflections," especially its "dangerous dilemma" (see §7.1.1)—Hume presents a sceptical argument with what seems to be a straight face only to say immediately thereafter that his "intention...in displaying so carefully the arguments of that fantastic sect, is only to make the reader sensible of the truth of [his] hypothesis" that causal reasoning is a product of the imagination's associations rather than the "cogitative part of our nature" (T 1.4.1.8, SBN 183). So Baier suggests that CtB's sceptical arguments are similarly designed to effect a final transition in the reader away from intellectualist conceptions of human nature—where the cogitative part of the mind is different in kind from and transcendent with respect to the rest of our mental capacities—and towards a conception of human nature in which our passions are fully integrated with our reason.

Perhaps the best evidence in favour of a dialectical interpretation is found in the Section "Of the antient philosophy" (T 1.4.3), where Hume describes three different ways in which our thinking can be organized: the vulgar outlook, false philosophy, and true philosophy (T.1.4.3.9, SBN 222–3). Recall the discussion in §5.1. We saw there that Hume illustrates this distinction using his account of causation: the vulgar think that the necessary connection between causally related objects is a feature in them that ties them together, while the philosophers, both true and false, recognize that it is only the mind's associating together its *ideas* of the causally related objects on the basis of prior experience that leads to the belief in the necessary connection. But false philosophers worry that their discovery has drastic epistemological consequences, wholly discrediting causal reasoning, and so, in an attempt to save it, they self-deceptively invent new "unintelligible" words, such as "*faculty* and *occult quality*," that they take to refer to something unperceivable in the objects that connects them together causally (T.1.4.3.10, SBN 224). True philosophers, in contrast, take the mind-involving character of causal connections not to undermine the integrity of causal reasoning. The fact that the causal relations are *constituted* by the mind's associative reactions to naturally conjoined kinds of objects does not mean that causal beliefs are false simply as such (of course, a particular causal belief will still be false if it turns out to be the result of a *merely experienced* conjunction of two types of objects, rather than an *actual* conjunction of them). Hume comments that the true philosophers thus "return back to the situation of the vulgar, and...regard all these

philosophical conviction" ("Hume's Philosophical Insouciance: A Reading of Treatise 1.4.7," *Hume Studies* 31 [2005], 335). The result is a "dogmatism of the present moment" ("Hume's Philosophical Insouciance," 337). My objection to Allison's version of this argument is that it, like Garrett's, leaves Hume without adequate normative resources to object when, say, an enthusiast or a false philosopher embraces her or his own particular such dogmatism.

disquisitions [about the nature of the causal connection] with indolence and indifference" (T 1.4.3.9, SBN 223), in that their philosophical understanding of the principles of human nature responsible for causal reasoning does not lead them to reject it, even if does lead them to a different understanding of what causal connections are from that of the vulgar.

Now consider again Hume's presentation of the "desponding reflection" concerning his prior treatment of causation (T 1.4.7.5, SBN 266–7; see §7.1.1). He expresses severe *disappointment* in his failure to discover the "energy" or "tie" connecting a cause and its effect. Henry Allison notes that, "[g]iven his deflationary analysis of causality, Hume's worry at this point is more than a little surprising."[36] Ted Morris suggests rather that we should see in the disappointment expressed here the presence of the *false* philosophical mindset, not that of the true philosopher, where the discovery of the mind-involving character of our causal thinking is accepted with equanimity.[37]

Similarly, Hume's discussion in CtB's fourth paragraph of the "contradiction" between the causal reasoning that leads to the primary–secondary quality distinction and the imaginative principles responsible for our belief in body harks back to the Section "Of the modern philosophy" (T 1.4.4). Recall from Chapter 6 that Hume thinks that the "modern system" of the "external world" (T 1.4.2.57, SBN 218) has the primary–secondary quality distinction as its "fundamental principle" (T 1.4.4.3, SBN 226). But it too is a form of false philosophy, for he tells us that the principle is open to "many objections" (T 1.4.4.6, SBN 227). I suggested in §6.4 that the reasoning of the modern philosophy, by taking our introspective access to perceptions for granted, confuses constitutive and causal relations. The "contradiction" that Hume recapitulates in CtB is similar. Philosophers can engage in causal reasoning between vulgar objects and perceptions, but to do so they must continue to rely on the tendencies of the imagination whereby we come to believe in both the internal and external worlds. They can, for example, note that sometimes an object yields impressions that present it as yellow (when the observer has jaundice, assuming—falsely—that this disorder distorts the colours he or she would see) and sometimes impressions that present it as white (when the observer is well and the object is properly lit). In fact, when the impressions are suitable ordered, the person having them will, through the imagination's reactions, take her- or himself to be encountering one continuing object. But philosophers cannot use this relativity of perceptions to discredit our beliefs about the world. For, as Hume shows in SwS (see §4.7), an attempt to use reasoning of this sort to discredit beliefs about the world discredits itself by undermining the introspective observation of perceptions that drives the reasoning. The modern philosophers

---

[36] "Hume's Philosophical Insouciance," 326. Loeb says similarly: "Hume's exposition of his theories of causation and belief in part 3 hardly prepares the reader for the tone of these passages" ("Another Look,"386).

[37] "Hume's Conclusion," 96, 107.

succumb to the contradiction in CtB only because they believe that they have insight into the internal world of perceptions independently of the workings of the imagination. But it is not a contradiction that Hume himself must face. He does not buy into its enabling assumptions.

The dialectical interpreters take these overt indications that the narrator of CtB is being tempted by false philosophy to mean that *all* of the "desponding reflections" are to be treated similarly—not as concerns that Hume himself takes seriously, but as concerns that would only animate someone who held an incorrect conception of philosophy. But *why* would Hume do such a thing? Why would he write the "Conclusion" starting from the position of false philosophy? The answer is given in the same passage where Hume first introduces the distinction between the different kinds of philosophical outlooks. For he says there that these outlooks "rise above each other, according as the persons, who form them, acquire new degrees of reason and knowledge" (T 1.4.3.9, SBN 222). So Hume seems to hold that reaching true philosophy requires a progression *through* false philosophy. Indeed, we can see from the example of causation how this makes some sense. The discovery that necessary connections are not in objects in any straightforward manner should lead us to search for such connections in objects in some more complex manner (such as occult qualities); and it is only when we have demonstrated the inadequacy of these alternative explanations that we should move on to the true philosophical position of seeing causal connections as being mind involving. The dialectical interpreters hold that the "Conclusion" is meant as a narration of this movement through false philosophy to true philosophy, as it pertains not just to causation but also to the mind's hold on an objective world. We have to "acquire new degrees of reason and knowledge" to recognize that Hume's discoveries about the mind-involving character of our fundamental beliefs do not mean that we are forced to give up on those beliefs by embracing the version of false philosophy that he calls "extravagant" scepticism (T 1.4.2.50, 1.4.4.6; SBN 214, 228).

Baier suggests that Hume's version of true philosophy involves seeing the mind as "social and passionate,"[38] rather than primarily intellectual. So the ongoing descriptions of feelings that Garrett noted in his discussion of the "Conclusion" are, for Baier, the signs of Hume's narrating the slow recognition that true philosophy requires that those feelings be recognized as *part* of reason, rather than as impediments that lie *outside* of reason.

One problem with Baier's version of the dialectical interpretation is that it requires her to see Hume as using 'reason' equivocally, sometimes as the narrow intellectualist conception of reason, as when it yields the sceptical regress explored in SwR, and sometimes as his own preferred conception of reason, where the passions are acknowledged to play an essential role. But, as Garrett argues, it is hard to find this

---

[38] *Progress*, 278.

equivocation in the text.[39] Hume seems to use 'reason' fairly consistently throughout the *Treatise* to describe the faculty responsible for discovering relations, whether they admit of knowledge or of probability (T 1.3.2.2, SBN 73). Moreover, it is this sense of 'reason' that is at the centre of the sceptical challenge in SwR. So it is not as easy as Baier suggests for Hume to escape from that challenge by rejecting the conception of reason at work in it. For the challenge seems to run using Hume's preferred (univocal) sense of reason.

The problem Baier has with the sceptical challenge to reason is related to a second problem with the dialectical interpretation—one that will afflict other versions of it as well. If the "desponding reflections" that open CtB are enunciated from the outlook of a false philosopher, why does Hume's move to true philosophy not involve a *solution* to them? Baier, for example, sees an expansion of reason as meaning that the challenges to reason and to our belief in an objective world no longer have any power. Why then does Hume continue to call himself a "true" sceptic? It seems that Hume should see himself as an *anti*-sceptic if his move to true philosophy means that the "desponding reflections" are left behind. I will call this interpretive problem the *scepticism* problem: in what sense does Hume remain a sceptic at the end of CtB?

7.5 The Philosophical Interpretation

I have suggested that each of the three interpretive approaches to the "Conclusion" suffers from a problem: sceptical interpretations face the integration problem; naturalist interpretations face the normativity problem; and dialectical interpretations face the scepticism problem. I also think that each approach has its advantages: sceptical interpretations help us to see why Hume thinks of himself as a "true sceptic;" naturalist interpretations correctly emphasize the special place of Kemp Smith's natural beliefs; and dialectical interpretations' reading of the "desponding reflections" as the product of false philosophy helps to explain the anomalous character of this stretch of text, where Hume both dramatically changes the tone of his exposition and seems to abandon earlier positions. The challenge is to synthesize the positive features of each interpretive approach without falling prey to the problems of any of them. I suggest that meeting this challenge first requires a better understanding of the false philosophy that drives the "desponding reflection," and then recognizing that Hume's real concern in CtB is to understand how philosophy fits into everyday life. Thus I call my interpretation of Hume's scepticism the *philosophical* interpretation.

I start by finding a different conception of false philosophy from the rationalist version suggested by Baier in her version of the dialectical interpretation. Consider a point shared by the sceptical interpreters and Kemp Smith's naturalist interpretation.

---

[39] *Cognition*, 84–5.

They take for granted our awareness of the mental processes that drives the "desponding reflections:" namely, our observation of "those perceptions, which are immediately present to our consciousness" (T 1.4.7.3, SBN 265). Recall that it is our becoming self-conscious about our reasoning and our sensing of the world that triggers our doubts about their credentials. But by taking our awareness of our mental processes (and what seem to be their "trivial propensities") for granted, Kemp Smith ends up assuming that the Humean mind involves our *standing over* our perceptions, witnessing the associations of our ideas that constitute our mental processes. Fogelin takes what he calls the phenomenal perspective, where we are aware of the "realm of perceptions (impressions and ideas) and nothing more" to be "the privileged perspective, the perspective that reveals how things really are when all artificial impositions are suppressed."[40] Waxman develops for Hume a *theory* of consciousness, where every perception is the object of a non-perceptual consciousness that stands over them.[41] Cummins and Broughton, in more subtle ways, also share the assumption that our awareness *of* our perceptions comes for free.[42] The "desponding reflections" work by asking whether we have any good reason to accept the outcomes of the processes of which we are aware from this perspective.

In keeping with the insight of the dialectical interpreters, I want to suggest that we should see the model of the mind that takes our awareness *of* our perceptions (rather than their contents) for granted, not as Hume's considered view, but as how false philosophers understand themselves when they enter into the "desponding reflections." That is, I think that both the naturalist and sceptical interpretations, in failing to recognize that CtB narrates the transition from false to true philosophy, end up attributing to Hume a view of the mind that he in fact wants to reject.

In Chapters 1, 4, and 6 we saw considerable evidence against taking Hume to think that we are normally aware *of* our perceptions (as such) when we reason and believe (see, in particular, my discussion of our "consciousness" of our perceptions in §§2.3 and 4.3.2). Perceptions afford us awareness of their *contents*, but we remain mostly blind (a term I borrow from T 1.4.7.10, SBN 269) to the perceptions and the imagination's operations on them that produce our vulgar sense of immersion in the world. Of course, we *can* reflect both as part and parcel of everyday life and, in a more disciplined fashion, when we are philosophizing. *Then* we observe the mind as a bundle of perceptions, and we can note how our fundamental beliefs depend on the ebb and flow of vivacity within its members. And this is how the narrator describes

---

[40] *Skeptical Crisis*, 91.   [41] *Hume's Theory*.

[42] Broughton is less clear than Waxman on how she understands Hume to model our awareness of our perceptions. But we saw in §6.4 that she takes the modern philosophers to offer a "completely unexceptionable causal inference that leads us to distinguish between primary and secondary qualities" ("The Inquiry," 545), as if the awareness of the variable internal impressions needed to make this inference does not itself require explanation. Cummins overlooks how Hume, in SwS, notes that philosophers' double-existence theories of perception involve their reliance on the imagination's associations to generate not just the belief in an external, represented object, but also in the internal, representing perception (T 1.4.2.46, SBN 211; see §4.5.2) ("Diffident Skepticism," 51–2).

his situation at the opening of CtB, when he thinks that his only criterion for belief is the vivacity of his *ideas*. But normally, we do not inspect our ideas to decide whether to believe. If I have doubts about my reasoning I appeal to such things as my prior experience of conjoined objects (in the case of causal beliefs), and if I have doubts about my sensing I appeal to such things as my being in standard observational circumstances. The narrator of CtB, in contrast, has assumed the reflective posture where he observes his mind, leaving the normal checks on our beliefs unavailable to him.

If the reflective awareness that drives the "desponding reflections" were our fundamental or basic or default mental posture, then the incapacity to resolve the "dangerous dilemma" of T 1.4.7.6–7 (SBN 267–8) *should* be paralyzing. I argued in Chapters 1 and 4 that Hume rejects the Cartesian model of reasoning and the Lockian model of sensation—models in which "consciousness" of our mental processes is taken to be a fundamental feature of the mind—by appealing to the fact that we are not fully able to prescind from the verdicts of reason and the senses. We do not *need* to decide whether to believe. We are not fundamentally self-conscious. In the "splenetic sentiments" of CtB (§7.1.3), Hume shows that even if we cannot solve the dangerous dilemma, we can still play backgammon, dine, converse, reason, and sense: "I may, nay I must yield to the current of nature, in submitting to my senses and understanding; and in this blind submission I shew most perfectly my sceptical disposition and principles" (T 1.4.7.10, SBN 269).

Hume recognizes that it is philosophical curiosity that drives the narrator into the abyss; we are not forced into it.[43] And thus he needs to understand how this kind of philosophical curiosity fits into his own system of philosophy. The final two subsections of CtB (§§7.1.4 and 7.1.5), by exploring that question, give us the moral of the whole Section. Four points emerge.

First, Hume notes that philosophy is entirely optional, dependent on the propensities of the individual and her or his inclinations at the time. Because we are fundamentally carried along by reason and the senses, no one *must* take up the reflective posture whereby we observe their operations. Some people, like the "honest gentlemen" in England, are never inclined to turn inward and to question the soundness of their cognitive natures, though no doubt they continue, when appropriate, to check their reasoning (by further reasoning) or correct their sensations (by further sensings). Hume emphasizes that "they do well to keep themselves in their present situation" and disavows any need to "refin[e] them into philosophers" (T 1.4.7.14, SBN 272). The unexamined life can be well worth living.[44] But Hume notes that some people do want to examine their lives; this is the "origin of...

---

[43] Thus, in the conclusion of Book 2, "Of curiosity, or the love of truth" (T 2.3.10), Hume emphasizes that philosophy, like hunting, is driven by the pleasure its practitioners take in it, buttressed by the possibility that its findings might be useful (T 2.3.10.8, SBN 451).

[44] See my "Hume, a Scottish Socrates?" *Canadian Journal of Philosophy* 33 (2003), 133–54.

philosophy." When "tir'd with amusement and company" and feeling their "mind[s] all collected within" themselves, they find themselves "*inclin'd* to carry [their] view into all those subjects, about which [they] have met with so many disputes in the course of [their] reading and conversation" (T 1.4.7.12, SBN 271).

Second, philosophy does have its benefits. It is helpful to understand our cognitive situation better so that we can avoid succumbing to ungrounded superstition. Even if many people might lack the special curiosity that is typical of philosophy, where we explore the principles of human nature and the merits of our tendencies to believe, they nonetheless are often animated by their ignorance and their fear to try to explain the workings of the world around them. In his *Natural History of Religion*, Hume explores the natural human tendency to posit supernatural entities to explain our condition, even if proper causal reasoning would not sanction them. And in his *Essays* and the *History of England*, he repeatedly emphasizes how political life becomes distorted by religious beliefs. So a better understanding of the dangers of superstitious belief will serve the public.

Third, although philosophy has its benefits, it also has its limits. The "desponding reflections" arise because Hume's narrator asks a series of legitimate (though not mandatory) philosophical questions. Once we understand how reason and sensory belief are instantiated in human nature—through tendencies of the imagination—what are the ultimate merits of their verdicts? I argued in Chapters 1 and 4 that we learned in SwR and SwS that even though these questions are legitimate, philosophy turns out to be unable to answer them. Our reflections interfere with the capacities we are exploring and we end up causing confusion in ourselves. I take the climactic paralysis of T 1.4.7.8 (SBN 268–9; see §7.1.2) to show how repeated probing of our fundamental tendencies ends up undermining their operations so that we lose our grip on the world around us and our capacity to believe. We *cannot* answer the "dangerous dilemma" (T 1.4.7.7, SBN 268) because we lose our ability even to ask the questions embodied in its two horns. It turns out, then, that philosophy does not have the means to provide a fundamental verdict on our cognitive condition. Because we need to retain our vulgar propensities in order to reason about our reason and to engage in introspective observation of the mind, philosophers' repeated distancing of themselves from those propensities means that they have pulled the rug out from under themselves. And this is a problem for philosophy and its aspirations, not for our everyday reasoning and sensing. The "splenetic sentiments" (§7.1.3) show that we can get on just fine without a philosophical grounding for our beliefs. The lesson, then, is that there is no reason to think that philosophy can succeed in every task it sets for itself. As Hume says, his "only hope is, that I may contribute a little to the advancement of knowledge, by giving in some particulars a different turn to the speculations of philosophers, and pointing out to them more distinctly those subjects, where alone they can expect assurance and conviction" (T 1.4.7.14, SBN 273). It turns out that the justification of our fundamental cognitive tendencies is not one of those subjects where philosophy can succeed.

Fourth, Hume has learned from his "splenetic sentiments" and his "blind submission" to the "current of nature" in "submitting to his senses and understanding" (T 1.4.7.10, SBN 269) that we are almost inescapably in the grip of our fundamental imaginative tendencies. As I argued in Chapter 4, there is a sense that, for Hume, we are inevitably vulgar, carried into the beliefs that our reasoning and sensing yield. Even when we are reflecting, we remain under the sway of the imagination when we accept our second-level rational beliefs or our introspective observations. Nonetheless, the "liberty of the imagination" leaves us able to temporarily suspend the imagination's associations and induce the total loss of conviction described in the climactic paragraph (T 1.4.7.8, SBN 268–9). But nature soon returns and the imagination resumes its work in producing our grip on things.

The question then becomes how to make sense of our irremediable vulgarity. The "total" and "extravagant" sceptics of SwR and SwS pretend that they can maintain the posture of disbelief. CtB shows convincingly that the best that they can hope for is a moment of stunned paralysis. False philosophers typically invent words that hide from themselves their lack of what they take to be an urgent need: a foundation for their beliefs. As Hume says, this response is mostly "ridiculous" and "its opinions are merely the objects of a cold and general speculation, and seldom go so far as to interrupt the course of our natural propensities" (T 1.4.7.13, SBN 272). He does allow, however, that some philosophers end up with what he elsewhere calls "artificial lives," where they fight persistently against their natures, and end up embracing "extravagancies of conduct" that set them apart from the rest of humanity.[45] But "true" philosophers accept our common human nature. They accept that our core beliefs about the world—that it exists independently from us and that it has a causal structure—reflect the human point of view. They accept that they are unable to show that the human point of view is privileged, that it is guaranteed to get things right in some absolute sense. They are thus "diffident" in their "philosophical doubts" and their "philosophical conviction" (T 1.4.7.14, SBN 273). Hume describes "moderate" scepticism (I take this to be equivalent to "true" scepticism) as a return "back to the situation of the vulgar," where they regard "all these disquisitions with indolence and indifference." But they differ from the vulgar, in that they have "acquire[d] new degrees of reason and knowledge" (T 1.4.3.9, SBN 222–3). They now *understand* the mind's operations and the limits of philosophy's capacity to understand the deep structure of things, inner and outer, and are thus able to continue their research into human nature.

Hume signals this rapprochement with our irremediable vulgarity, even in our philosophical moments, in the last paragraph of CtB. He notes that true sceptics will continue to be carried along by their imaginative propensities that "incline us to be

---

[45] See the discussion of the "artificial lives" of Pascal and Diogenes in the "Dialogue" that Hume appended to the second *Enquiry* (Tom L. Beauchamp [ed.], *An Enquiry concerning the Principles of Morals: A Critical Edition* [Oxford: Clarendon Press, 1998], 122).

positive and certain in *particular points*, according to the light, in which we survey them in any *particular instant*" (T 1.4.7.15, SBN 273). And this is fine, so long as we understand that it does not signal a deep insight into a world beyond human experience, a world of "real nature[s] and operations;" that would be a subject that "exceed[ed] all human capacity" (T 1.2.5.26n12.1–2, SBN 638–9).

7.6 Problems Solved

To clarify the philosophical interpretation of Hume's true scepticism, it will be helpful to compare it to the three other interpretive strategies, showing that it retains their virtues while avoiding their vices.

Like the dialectical interpreters, the philosophical interpretation sees Hume in CtB as narrating the transition from false philosophy to true philosophy. Baier suggests that the conception of false philosophy with which Hume starts CtB stems from an intellectualist conception of mind; it is replaced by one in which reason is made social and passionate. I suggested earlier that this left her facing the scepticism problem. Why does Hume call himself a "true" sceptic once he has cleansed himself of false philosophy? In fact, it is not obvious why, on Baier's reading, Hume thinks that philosophers would be tempted into the intellectualism that she finds to be so dangerous in the first place.

On the philosophical reading, however, the false philosophy that starts CtB has an obvious source: it stems from philosophers' remaining vulgar about the mind. Philosophy, both true and false, starts when we reflect on the mind, when we "abstract from the effects of custom, and compare the ideas of objects" (T 1.4.3.9, SBN 223). From this introspective posture we can look for a justification of our tendencies to believe—something that would shore up our reliance on the "trivial propensities" of the imagination. In the case of the associations involved in causal reasoning, we can look for something that would ground our beliefs: namely, "that energy in the cause, by which it operates on its effect; that tie, which connects them together; and that efficacious quality, on which the tie depends" (T 1.4.7.5, SBN 266). The narrator of CtB expresses dissatisfaction that this "ultimate and operating" principle is not forthcoming and that we are left only with our associative tendencies. I take this to mean that he has yet to make the transition to true philosophy, where he understands that he does not in fact have privileged access to the mind. It too is mediated by the imagination and its associative principles.

Baier faced the scepticism problem because she sees Hume as offering a revised conception of mind that no longer faces the sceptical challenges. In my philosophical interpretation, however, Hume allows for the legitimacy of the philosophical question of whether and how to trust our tendencies to believe. It turns out that his question cannot be answered using the only method for philosophy he countenances. Thus he ends up as a sceptic about what philosophy can accomplish, and also a sceptic who embraces his fundamental tendencies to believe blindly. Philosophy can neither justify nor undermine them. We move from false to true philosophy when we "return to the situation of vulgar" (T 1.4.3.10, SBN 224) by relying on our reasoning, sensing, and introspecting, though now with an understanding of our situation.

Note how the philosophical interpretation also differs from the sceptical interpretation. Because the sceptical interpreters do not acknowledge how the "desponding reflections" are parasitic on our introspective beliefs, they take Hume to conclude that we ought not to believe our reasoning or sensing. That we do continue to believe is a sign of irrationality, mitigated at best by doubting our philosophical doubts or adopting an ironical stance. The integration problem then looms, as Hume shows no qualms about his endeavours as he continues to philosophize in Books 2 and 3.

In the philosophical interpretation the narrator learns that the philosophical challenge to reason and the senses is itself unstable. So we do not reach a negative verdict on our cognitive condition, and thus it is not surprising that Hume can continue to philosophize with such equanimity in the rest of the *Treatise*. We cannot offer a *fundamental* justification of our causal reasoning or our introspective observations, but this does not stop us from justifying particular causal claims about perceptions, using the same norms for causal belief that apply to common life (namely the "logic" of T 1.3.15).

Finally, the philosophical interpretation, like the naturalist interpretation, gives a special place to Kemp Smith's natural beliefs, understood not as discrete beliefs but as fundamental imaginative tendencies by which, when reasoning, we believe the conclusions we reach, and when sensing or reflecting, we believe in the independent existence of the objects we observe. But the naturalist interpreters faced the normativity problem because they introduced Nature (or the propensities that have a "title" over us) as a justification for beliefs that is different from reason. On the philosophical interpretation, reason *is* the natural source of normativity, with the mechanism yielding sensory and introspective beliefs as a secondary such source. Reasoning and sensing are implemented in human nature to yield vivacious beliefs, and while their "authority" is not "entire" (T 1.4.1.5, SBN 182) it is authority nonetheless. Nothing foreign to them must support them in order for them to be embraced. Of course, we can still second-guess ourselves if there are appropriate motivations in place that require due care. But such reflective correction will involve the same fundamental capacity as the one being corrected. We check our reasoning with reasoning and our sensing with sensing, though in the latter case, we also reason about which sensing is more likely to be accurate, where the norms for accuracy are those determined by the core structures of the imagination involved in sensing.

In fact, when we look at the paragraph where Garrett finds his title principle, it is apparent that Hume does not introduce it to serve a separate normative role in our deciding what to believe. Rather, as the philosophical interpretation emphasizes, it speaks to whether we should philosophize. Hume urges us to do so only if we feel like it:

Nay if we are philosophers, it ought only to be upon sceptical principles, and from an inclination, which we feel to the employing ourselves after that manner. Where reason is lively, and mixes itself with some propensity, it ought to be assented to. Where it does not, it never can have any title to operate upon us. (T 1.4.7.11, SBN 270)

That is to say that *philosophy* does not have an exalted place in human life so that we all must undertake it. We do not need to philosophize in order to reason and sense as successfully as we can.

7.7 Sources of Scepticism

Hume's true scepticism, as I have interpreted it, arises from his embrace of two theses. First, philosophers try to get at the roots of our vulgar beliefs by considering objects that are *different from* the objects of everyday life. Thus philosophers focus on the perceptions in the mind that afford us an awareness of vulgar objects, rather than the hats, shoes, and stones themselves (or even the "most minute" [T 1.2.2.1, SBN 29] particles of the natural philosophers).

Second, however, the structure and methods of our dealings with everyday objects are *the same as* the structure and methods of philosophers' dealings with perceptions. In both cases, if we want to discover how things are in the vicinity, then we need to "observe" (T 1.4.6.3, SBN 252) our surroundings, either by sensation in the case of hats, shoes, and stones, or by introspection in the case of perceptions. Hume's empiricism denies the possibility of some deeper, non-sensory source of insight. Furthermore, belief in the continued and distinct existence of what we encounter (via sensation in the case of the vulgar and via introspection in the case of the philosophers) depends on the operations of the imagination. Hence I argued, in §§4.3.2 and 4.5.2, that Hume treats both perceptions and everyday objects as what in §3.3.1 I called *vulgar objects*. Finally, the reasoning we undertake about those objects depends primarily on the experience of prior constant conjunctions of similar sorts of objects, either external objects in the normal case, or internal objects in the case of philosophers.

As a consequence of the second thesis, philosophers investigating the mind encounter the reflective interference that I have suggested drives Hume into true scepticism. In investigating the mental structures that yield our everyday life, philosophers must rely on those very structures. And because of this, any attempt to discredit our vulgar beliefs serves similarly to discredit itself. The attempt is "destroy'd by [its] subtility" (T 1.4.1.12, SBN 186).

Nonetheless, as a consequence of the first thesis, Hume can keep his everyday beliefs insulated from his philosophical conclusions. Although philosophy cannot "justify" these beliefs in a "manner" (T 1.4.7.57, SBN 218) that would guarantee their truth, its failure results from the limitation in its method that the second thesis encodes. Thus the true sceptic can continue to instinctively embrace the verdicts of reason and the senses (and introspection) while recognizing that they are the contingent products of human nature. Moreover, he or she can continue to undertake the corrective moves that are internal to the process of reasoning or sensing—asking someone else for reassurance, taking another look, checking an inference—even without the external guarantee that such corrections get at some absolute truth, independent of the human perspective.

Other philosophers would approach these issues differently from Hume. Some would be willing to accept that philosophers are concerned with different objects from those of everyday life, and that the methods and structures for our dealing with those objects are the same in both cases. But rather than learning that philosophy cannot answer the questions it poses about its objects, these philosophers believe that they can ratify our ways of thinking. Consider, for example, some ordinary language philosophers. They study the *language* we use in, say, our sensory beliefs, rather than the *objects* we sense, but they think that the credentials of that use are in order, and can be shown to be in order.

Hume differs from philosophers of this stripe because of his conviction that there is a kind of arbitrariness to our cognitive capacities. They are mere instincts, akin to the nesting instincts of birds (T 1.3.16.9, SBN 179), or as he emphasizes in the "desponding reflections" outlined in §7.1.1, they are rooted in "trivial" (T 1.4.7.3, SBN 265) propensities of the imagination. After Darwin, we now think of instincts as embodying a kind of rationality by expressing how the species in question has come to inhabit its particular niche, and perhaps this recognition offers a route for avoiding a contemporary version of Hume's true scepticism.[46]

Still other philosophers would differ from Hume in other ways, either by taking the objects of study in philosophy to be the same as the objects of everyday life, or by distinguishing the methods of philosophy from those of everyday life. There are thus three other possibilities to consider, each of which might yield a different kind of sceptical reaction.

First, a philosopher, such as perhaps Aristotle, could hold that the objects of philosophical scrutiny are the objects of everyday life, and the methods of philosophical scrutiny are the same as those in everyday life. Should those methods turn out to be defective—consider the ancient Pyrrhonian suggestion that an argument for any thesis could be balanced with another argument against it (§1.2)—then the sceptical outcome would threaten our everyday beliefs, perhaps yielding a kind of tranquility as we freed ourselves from worry about their justification, or—more likely—creating an extreme cognitive crisis.

Second, someone could hold that philosophers study the objects of everyday life but with a fundamentally different approach. Descartes, for example, takes philosophers to rely on reason in their understanding of body—extension—while the vulgar use their senses. This kind of approach creates an opening for scepticism if the philosophical perspective serves to discredit vulgar beliefs, without being able to craft a suitable replacement using its own resources. A different kind of philosopher who agrees that

---

[46] See, for example, Ronald de Sousa, *Why Think? Evolution and the Rational Mind* (Oxford: Oxford University Press, 2007).

philosophy and everyday life share the same objects but use different methods could hold, unlike Descartes, that the verdicts of everyday life are superior to those of philosophy. Some kinds of common-sense philosophy might exemplify this tendency, whereby no philosophical verdict could dislodge the justifications of our everyday beliefs.

The third option would be to hold that philosophy studies different objects from those that occupy us in everyday life and that it uses different methods from everyday life. Plato, for example, or Leibniz might be thought to endorse this option, while combining it with a commitment that the philosophical objects—Forms or monads—are more truly real than the mere phenomena that engross the vulgar. The sceptical reaction here might lead to a kind of solipsism, where the unreality of the vulgar world seems to leave the philosopher alone with their privileged objects, disconnected from everyday life entirely.

Hume argues for the first thesis only in the "Introduction" to the Treatise, where he emphasizes that the study of any feature of *the world* requires an understanding of the structures of *the mind* that make the study possible. He is less direct about his support of the second thesis (and much of the argument in this book has been my attempt to bring it to light). His official statements in support of it often take the form of mere assertion: an introspective look within shows that introspection relies on the same principles of the imagination as those involved in vulgar sensory belief (T 1.4.6.5, SBN 253); by "running over" many of his perceptions, he reaches the "observation" that (almost) all simple ideas acquire their content from prior simple impressions (T 1.1.1.5, SBN 4); and so on.

But I have suggested that Hume ultimately uses our experiences with sceptical arguments to support his core commitments. He has offered us a way to understand both their power and their impotence. They cannot be "radically cur'd" (T 1.4.2.57, SBN 218), but we need not embrace their conclusions (on pain of irrationality) in part because any attempt to do so simultaneously undermines the arguments. Instead, we learn that philosophy's incapacity to address some of the questions it poses means that the vulgar can continue to form rational and sensory beliefs without need of a philosophical dispensation. And, for those who are curious in the right way, there are still many areas of concern worthy for philosophers to pursue. As we saw in §7.1.4, Hume explains that he is interested in

the principles of moral good and evil, the nature and foundation of government, and the cause of those several passions and inclinations, which actuate and govern me. I am uneasy to think I approve of one object, and disapprove of another; call one thing beautiful, and another deform'd; decide concerning truth and falshood, reason and folly, without knowing upon what principles I proceed.   (T 1.4.7.12, SBN 271)

He here sets the agenda that he goes on to pursue in Books 2 and 3 of the *Treatise*, no longer perturbed by his incapacity to offer a special vindication of his fundamental tendencies to believe, but accepting of the fact that he inhabits what he now recognizes to be the human perspective.

8

Second Thoughts

Books 1 and 2 of the *Treatise* were published together in January 1739. Book 3 came out in November of the following year, and included an "Appendix" where Hume confesses that he had made one "considerable mistake" in the earlier two Books. (He also takes the opportunity to clarify there what he meant by the 'vivacity' of a perception—see §6.6—and to include several passages that were to be inserted into the main body of any revised edition of the *Treatise*.) The mistake concerns his analysis of personal identity. He says: "I find myself involv'd in such a labyrinth, that, I must confess, I neither know how to correct my former opinions, nor how to render them consistent" (T App.10, SBN 633). After reviewing his argument from his original treatment of that topic in "Of personal identity" (T 1.4.6, hereafter 'PI'), Hume asserts that he faces an inconsistency when he tries to "explain the principles, that unite our successive perceptions in our thought or consciousness" (T App.20, SBN 636). The problem for interpreters is that the commitments that he says lead to the inconsistency are not in fact inconsistent, nor do they concern issues specific to personal identity. The challenge, then, is to find on Hume's behalf a problem in his original treatment of personal identity that is linked to the commitments in the "Appendix" that are supposed to yield the inconsistency. Given the paucity of text, there have probably been as many interpretations of Hume's second thoughts in the "Appendix" as there are Hume scholars.

I offer my explanation of the inconsistency in what follows. In Chapter 6 I argued that in PI, Hume shows that when we reflectively observe our minds as bundles of perceptions, we believe it is unified when our secondary ideas of the perceptions under observation are associated together so that we overlook the diversity of the perceptions at a time and through time. But what of the secondary ideas? Normally they are not themselves observed, and so their presence in the mind while producing the belief in mental unity is not in tension with the belief. When, however, philosophers come to *believe* that their belief in mental unity is the result of the association of unobserved secondary ideas, then a tension does emerge. They believe that the secondary ideas are part of their unified minds, but Hume's explanation for that belief does not encompass the secondary ideas. The problem that Hume recognizes in the "Appendix," I suggest, is how philosophers can believe that the reflecting mind is the same as the mind reflected upon.

I support this suggested reading by first, in §8.1, reviewing the relevant portions of the "Appendix," and introducing seven criteria that a successful interpretation should meet.[1] In §8.2 I develop and defend my claim that Hume comes to recognize a problem with his view relating to reflective thought. In §8.3 I address some of the other main options for interpreting the "Appendix" and show how they fail to satisfy one or more of the criteria. I conclude with some reflections on the impact of Hume's problem on the overall success of his project.

8.1 Interpreting the "Appendix"

Hume addresses the issue of personal identity in thirteen paragraphs of the "Appendix" (T App.10–22, SBN 633–6). After the introductory comment about finding himself in a "labyrinth" on this issue, Hume reviews the reasoning of PI and endorses almost all of it. He starts by noting that, lacking any impressions of "self or substance" as having "strict and proper identity" (what Hume calls "perfect" identity in PI [T 1.4.6.1, SBN 251]), we also have no ideas of a self that is unified in this way. Instead, just as everyday objects, such as a chimney or a table, exist independently of one another, so also do our perceptions. Thus, when we reflect on ourselves, we observe only perceptions and "['t]is the composition of these ... which forms the self" (T App.15, SBN 634). In fact, we can conceive of a mind—one "reduc'd even below the life of an oyster" (T App.16, SBN 635)—consisting of only one perception, without needing to posit, in addition, a self or substance that *has* the perception. Hume concludes that such a posit will not be needed when more perceptions are added into a mind.

Thus far, Hume has simply recapitulated what I called his anti-*cogito* argument (§6.2), where he claimed that the mind is a bundle of perceptions without a self or substance that unites them through a special kind of reflective self-awareness. In the twentieth paragraph he turns to his explanation of why, despite its plurality, we believe the mind to be unified. It is here that he says the problem emerges:

> [H]aving thus loosen'd all our particular perceptions, when I proceed to explain the principle of connexion, which binds them together, and makes us attribute to them a real simplicity and identity; I am sensible, that my account is very defective, and that nothing but the seeming evidence of the precedent reasonings cou'd have induc'd me to receive it.
>
> (T App.20, SBN 635)

Nonetheless, he continues in a primarily recapitulative fashion. "If perceptions are distinct existences, they form a whole only by being connected together" (T App.20,

---

[1] In "Hume's Self-doubts about Personal Identity" (*Philosophical Review* 90 [1981], 337–58), Don Garrett noted three "conditions" that, of the many then extant interpretive options for the "Appendix," he suggested his alone met. In "Hume's Reflections on the Identity and Simplicity of Mind" (*Philosophy and Phenomenological Research* 62 [2001], 557–78) I built on these conditions by listing seven criteria for success in interpretations of the "Appendix" problem, the first three of which were similar to Garrett's. In a more recent contribution ("Rethinking Hume's Second Thoughts about Personal Identity," in Jason Bridges, Niko Kolodny, and Wai-hung Wong [eds.], *The Possibility of Philosophical Understanding: Essays for Barry Stroud* [New York, NY: Oxford University Press, 2011], 15–40), Garrett offers five criteria that include his three original conditions, and two new ones that overlap considerably with my seven criteria.

SBN 635). But the understanding cannot discern connections between distinct existences. Instead, we

feel a connexion or determination of the thought to pass from one object to another.... [T]he thought alone finds personal identity, when *reflecting* on the train of past perceptions, that compose a mind, the *ideas of them* are felt to be connected together, and naturally introduce each other.   (T App.20, SBN 635; original emphasis only on 'feel')

Note that Hume does not deny that perceptions are connected, even if those connections are not rationally discernible (that is, discernible by the understanding). Rather, our *feeling* them to be connected means that they have a kind of unity ("imperfect" unity; see §§3.2.3 and 6.5) because of our imaginations' reactions to them. Thus we see here what seems to be the same position as the one I explicated in §6.5, where the belief in mental unity is produced when, reflecting on our minds, our (secondary) ideas of our perceptions ("the ideas of them") are associated together. The difference from the earlier account is that here he introduces a restriction to "*past* perceptions" that was not included in PI. Hume then compares his view to that of "most philosophers," though presumably he primarily has John Locke in mind: they "seem inclin'd to think, that personal identity *arises* from consciousness; and consciousness is nothing but a reflected thought or perception." He notes that "[t]he present philosophy so far has a promising aspect" (T App.20, SBN 635).

Hume then announces his concern: "[A]ll my hopes vanish, when I come to explain the principles, that unite our successive perceptions in our thought or consciousness" (T App.20, SBN 635–6). Thus the first criterion for a successful interpretation of the "Appendix" is the identification of the relevant *principles*.[2] He elaborates: "In short there are two principles, which I cannot render consistent; nor is it in my power to renounce either of them, viz. *that all our distinct perceptions are distinct existences*, and *that the mind never perceives any real connexion among distinct existences*" (T App.21, SBN 636). These principles, however, are not inconsistent and not particularly linked to the issue of personal identity. The second criterion thus requires a specification of the *inconsistency*; other Humean claims must be shown to be in play in the discussion and inconsistent with the two he provides.[3] Hume goes on to note that were he able to show that "our perceptions inhere in something simple and individual, or did the mind perceive some real connexion among them," the problem would evaporate. So a third criterion is that whatever problem is identified, these two options would allow for a

---

[2] Garrett notes that an interpretation should show that Hume's problem concerns the "'connecting principles' he has provided (causation and resemblance)" ("Hume's Self-doubts," 355). He later calls this the "origin" criterion ("Rethinking," 23).
[3] This is Garrett's first condition in "Hume's Self-doubts" (355). It is incorporated into his "crisis" criterion in the later article: "[I]t should concern a problem that, had he noticed it, would have appeared to him to be a very serious one, definitively threatening contradiction and absurdity that would involve him in a 'labyrinth' and be sufficient to inspire skepticism" ("Rethinking," 23).

plausible *escape*.[4] Instead, he "pleads the privilege of sceptic": "[T]his difficulty is too hard for my understanding. I pretend not, however, to pronounce it absolutely insuperable. Others, perhaps, or myself, upon more mature reflection, may discover some hypothesis, that will reconcile those contradictions" (T App.21, SBN 636). An interpreter must thus also explain how this plea fits into an overall understanding of Hume's self-confessed scepticism (I call this the *sceptic's plea* criterion[5]).

The three other criteria for interpretations of the "Appendix" speak to how this stretch of text relates to the project of the *Treatise* overall. First, Hume takes the problem with his account of personal identity to be the single substantive mistake in all of Books 1 and 2 (T App.1, SBN 623). Thus an interpretation should not suggest that Hume identifies a problem that he would also have recognized to have ramifications beyond the issue of personal identity (the *singularity* criterion).

Second, the view of the self as a bundle of perceptions that Hume presents in PI first made its appearance in "Of scepticism with regard to the senses" (T 1.4.2, hereafter 'SwS'), where he relies on it to makes sense of the possibility of perceptions' continued existence when "absent from the mind" (T 1.4.2.38, SBN 207). (In §3.3 I discussed this passage and its many idiosyncrasies.)[6] Furthermore, Hume seems to maintain the bundle view throughout his career, writing in the posthumous *Dialogues Concerning Natural Religion* that "the soul of man ... [is] a composition of various faculties, passions, sentiments, ideas; united, indeed, into one self or person, but still distinct from each other."[7] Thus whatever problem Hume has in his treatment of personal identity in the "Appendix," he must plausibly be able to treat it as having *insulation* from his other uses of the bundle theory, especially in the *Treatise*.[8]

A final challenge for any interpreter of the "Appendix" is finding a problem that Hume could have noticed shortly after having finished the first two Books of the

---

[4] This is Garrett's third condition in "Hume's Self-doubts" (355). He calls it the "solution criterion" in "Rethinking" (23). Galen Strawson seems to view this criterion as the only requirement for successful interpretations of the "Appendix" problem (*The Evident Connexion: Hume on Personal Identity* [Oxford: Oxford University Press, 2011], part 3).

[5] Garrett does not include this criterion in either "Hume's Self-doubts" or "Rethinking."

[6] In addition, the self is the "object" of the indirect passions, where pride and humility make us think of "that succession of related ideas and impressions, of which we have an intimate memory and consciousness" (T 2.1.2.2, SBN 277). Many interpreters take Hume here to be suggesting that the object of the indirect passions is the idea of self as explicated in PI. I have argued against this assumption in "Scepticism about Persons in Book II of Hume's *Treatise*," *Journal of the History of Philosophy* 37 (1999), 481–2. Briefly, it is hard to see why Hume would think that pride or humility would make us think of our *minds*, with each perception treated equally as a constituent of the bundle; rather, they make us think of ourselves as characterized by the feature of which we are proud or ashamed (see, for example, T 2.1.5.6, 2.1.8.8; SBN 287, 303). If, however, an interpreter rejects my separation of PI's idea of mind from Book 2's idea of self as it occurs in the indirect passions, then she or he must insulate the problem of the "Appendix" from Book 2. Hume does not seem to think the problem requires a revision of the treatment of pride and humility.

[7] The character in the *Dialogues* making this statement is Demea, but the other characters accept it without comment (*Dialogues concerning Natural Religion*, ed. N. Kemp Smith [Indianapolis, IN: Bobbs-Merrill, 1947], 159).

[8] Garrett combines my insulation and singularity criteria into what he calls the "scope criterion" ("Rethinking," 23).

Treatise, but not one so obvious that he should have recognized it when he first wrote PI. I call this the *charity* criterion.[9]

8.2 Unity in Reflection

In order to motivate my interpretation of the "Appendix," consider that Hume stays in recapitulative mode up to and including the claim that, for him, as for "most philosophers," personal identity arises from "consciousness or reflected thought," where he takes the identity to depend on the imagination's associative reactions to our perceptions when we reflect on them. The problem he then points to concerns how our perceptions are united "in our *thought* or *consciousness*" (T App.20, SBN 635–6; emphases added). Of course, for Hume, thought is the realm of ideas (T 1.1.1.1, SBN 1), and I have argued in §4.3.2 that he understands reflection in terms of the formation of secondary ideas of primary perceptions.[10] We have seen, however, that 'consciousness' is a tricky term in early modern philosophy (§§2.3 and 4.3). Locke, for example, should be understood as distinguishing consciousness from reflection. For him, reflection is an optional process of turning within ourselves to observe our mental operations, and it yields ideas of reflection with these operations as their objects. But he thinks that *all* ideas—ideas of sensation and ideas of reflection—are conscious (§4.3.1). I argued in §4.3.2 that Hume sometimes uses 'consciousness' in the way that Locke uses 'reflection.' And this seems to be the case in this portion of the "Appendix,"[11] where he has already noted that "thought alone finds personal identity, when *reflecting*" and associating ideas of the mind's (past) perceptions (T App.20, SBN 635, emphasis added; see also T App.15, SBN 634). Thus when Hume describes his problem as concerning the explanation of the unification of "successive perceptions" in our "thought or consciousness," he must mean that the problem concerns the secondary ideas—the successive ideas, associations of which he takes to constitute personal identity.

---

[9] Garrett's "difficulty criterion" ("Rethinking," 23) is similar, though he focuses on the need to account for Hume's having difficulty in expressing the problem that he takes himself to have discovered.

[10] An alternative reading would take "thought or consciousness" here to be echoing the phrase at T 1.1.1.1 (SBN 1), where he says that "[a]ll the perceptions of the human mind [both impressions and ideas] . . . strike upon the mind, and make their way into our *thought or consciousness*" (emphasis added). In this usage, 'thought and consciousness' captures the way in which all perceptions are states of awareness. I take Hume's use of the phrase in the "Appendix" to involve his more precise meanings of 'thought' (as ideas) and 'consciousness' (as the secondary ideas generated by reflection) because of his prior invocation in the paragraph of how "thought . . . finds personal identity, when reflecting on the train of past perceptions . . . the ideas of them are felt to be connected together" (T App.20, SBN 635).

[11] In T App.4, SBN 625, he rejects the suggestion that belief involves a separable impression by saying that it "is directly contrary to experience, and our immediate consciousness." He seems to be using 'consciousness' here to mean the awareness we have of a perception's content (see §6.6). That is, he introspectively examines what happens when he hears the voice of a friend as if from an adjacent room, and then comes to believe that the friend is in that room. He notes that the belief is not achieved by a separate impression but rather is internal to the thought of the friend.

Four problems might be identified here. First, the problem might concern the *associations*. Thus Galen Strawson suggests that Hume realizes that he needs to find "a ground" for the principles of association to which he appeals in the explanation of belief in personal identity (though Strawson does not acknowledge Hume's appeal to secondary ideas in the explanation of this belief).[12] But this suggestion clearly fails the singularity criterion. Were Hume concerned about the need for a ground for the principles of association, he would not think that his only mistake arose in PI. The principles of association are ubiquitous in Books 1 and 2, and indeed, in the "Abstract" to the *Treatise*, Hume declares that his use of them is what entitles him to "so glorious a name as that of an *inventor*" (T Abs.35, SBN 661).

Second, the problem might concern the *secondary ideas*. Thus John Bricke thinks that Hume realizes that although he has an account of the difference between a primary idea and the impression it copies (namely, they have different vivacity), he is unable to distinguish the secondary idea that is *of* a primary idea from the primary idea itself.[13] I addressed this issue in §4.3.2, where I argued that Hume has two different notions of copying available to him: the duplication of *image-content* on the one hand, and the portrayal of *the way in which we are aware* of that content on the other hand. Bricke overlooks the latter. And of course, were Hume's problem with secondary ideas in general, the problem would not be specific to his account of personal identity. As the vehicles for thoughts about the mind, he relies on them throughout Books 1 and 2. Thus Bricke's suggestion also fails the singularity criterion.

Third, the problem might concern the *succession* of secondary ideas in our "thought or consciousness" as their associations produce the belief in mental unity. Thus Wayne Waxman thinks that Hume's problem in the "Appendix" arises when he realizes that his explanation of the belief in personal identity presupposes the successiveness of perceptions to one another *prior* to their being associated by the imagination. (Waxman does not see this problem as concerning secondary ideas, but rather perceptions in general.)[14] But, Waxman thinks, a Humean succession is constituted out of the association of its elements. I find this suggestion doubtful. First, Hume allows that objects exist in succession "independent of our thought and reasoning" (T 1.3.14.28, SBN 168). Second, Waxman supposes that perceptions must be retained in memory before the imagination can associate them. And thus he supposes that we must have "consciousness" of the succession of perceptions before

---

[12] *Evident Connexion*, 105. Strawson's overlooking the role of secondary ideas means that when he identifies Hume's problem as having its root in the association of *ideas*, he must ignore Hume's concern with how *impressions* fit into the bundle (141n54): sensory impressions, after all, are not themselves associated; rather the primary ideas that copy them or the secondary ideas that are *of* them are. But Hume clearly is worried about the how the observation of the "perceptual flux and movement" (T 1.4.6.4, SBN 252) of impressions due to the turning of our eyes in their sockets can be combined with a belief in the unity of mind.

[13] *Hume's Philosophy of Mind* (Princeton, NJ: Princeton University Press, 1980), 74–99.

[14] "Hume's Quandary Concerning Personal Identity," *Hume Studies* 18 (1992), 233–53.

we can associate its elements (it is exactly this "consciousness" that creates the problem he takes Hume to recognize in the "Appendix"). But Hume does not think that association is something *done to* perceptions of which we are already aware; rather, the association of ideas is what explains why we think of one object after having experienced (or thought of) another. And third, Waxman treats "consciousness" as if it were presupposed in all association, whereas Hume is concerned about the kind of consciousness that occurs when we reflectively examine our minds. Finally, as Waxman admits, his problem would go to the heart of Hume's treatment of association, and thus it is hard to reconcile with the singularity and insulation criteria (§8.1).[15]

A fourth possibility for Hume's problem in explaining the principles that "unite our successive perceptions in our thought or consciousness"—the possibility I prefer—focuses on how the successive secondary ideas that, when we reflect on the mind, make up our "thought or consciousness" are themselves taken to be unified with the rest of the mind. Why do scientists of man believe that the secondary ideas, the vehicles for their introspective reflection, are unified with those perceptions that they observe within themselves (by means of the secondary ideas)? The secondary ideas are distinct existences, and accordingly there are no real connections linking them with the rest of the mind. Nor are there further ideas of them (tertiary ideas?), associations of which would bring the scientists of man to believe that the secondary ideas are unified with the other observed perceptions. My suggestion is that Hume realizes in the "Appendix" that he believes that secondary ideas are part of the mind and yet is unable to explain this belief.[16]

This interpretation of the "Appendix" meets the charity criterion because it can explain why Hume did not see the problem in his original treatment of personal identity. Recall that his explanandum there was philosophers' belief in the simplicity and identity of the minds *that they observe*. Because secondary ideas are not themselves under observation—they are instead the vehicles for observation—Hume did not need to explain a belief that included them in its scope. Just as the vulgar take themselves to be immersed in the world, overlooking the role of perceptions in affording them their sense of immersion, so also introspecting scientists of man normally take themselves to be immersed *in the mind*, overlooking the role of secondary ideas in affording them their sense of immersion. They are vulgar with respect to the mind (§4.3.2). As I emphasized in §§5.1 and 7.5, Hume thinks that it is only when philosophers make the transition to "true" scepticism that they *recognize* this ineliminable vulgarity.

In Hume's original treatment of personal identity, philosophers' taking their access to the mind for granted shows up in at least two places. Consider his analogy between

---

[15] See my "Hume's Reflections," 568n22.

[16] I first offered this suggestion in "Hume's Reflections." Most of this paragraph, and the four following, are borrowed from "Hume on Personal Identity," in E. Radcliffe (ed.), *A Companion to Hume* (Malden, MA: Blackwell, 2008), 151–3.

the mind and the performance of a play, with the perceptions being compared to the actors:

The mind is a kind of theatre, where several perceptions successively make their appearance; pass, re-pass, glide away, and mingle in an infinite variety of postures and situations. There is properly no *simplicity* in it at one time, nor *identity* in different; whatever natural propension we may have to imagine that simplicity and identity. The comparison of the theatre must not mislead us. They are the successive perceptions only, that constitute the mind; nor have we the most distant notion of the place, where these scenes are represented, or of the materials, of which it is compos'd.   (T 1.4.6.5; SBN 253)

When Hume goes on to explain that the association of ideas of the actors/perceptions is responsible for the belief in the unity of the play/mind, he helps himself to a seat in the audience of his mind, as it were. The spectator is the one believing that the play is unified because of the association of ideas within him, just as the spectator of the mind is the one believing that the mind is unified because of the association of secondary ideas within him. Hume does not worry that the secondary ideas are themselves part of the mind that is believed to be unified, because he has restricted the scope of the belief to be explained to those perceptions in the mind that are *observed*. The fact that unobserved perceptions (the secondary ideas) are involved in his explanation does not matter so long as the explanandum remains restricted.

Similarly, Hume analogizes the scientists of man's views of their minds to the view we would have if "we cou'd see clearly into the breast of another, and observe that succession of perceptions, which constitutes his mind or thinking principle" (T 1.4.6.18; SBN 260).[17] The relations among the observed perceptions would cause our secondary ideas of the perceptions to be associated together, yielding the belief that the other person's mind is unified. Hume ends the thought experiment by saying: "The case is the same whether we consider ourselves or others" (T 1.4.6.18; SBN 261). Of course, the case is not the same. When investigating someone else's mind, the secondary ideas, associations of which produce the belief in mental unity, are not in the same mind as the perceptions that are believed to be unified. When investigating our own minds, the secondary ideas are in the same mind as those perceptions believed to be unified. But so long as the role of secondary ideas in producing the belief remains unthematized—so long as the introspecting philosophers remain oblivious to the perceptual mediation of their awareness of their minds—then Hume's explanation counts as a success.

In the "Appendix," when reviewing the portion of his original explanation of personal identity that he takes to be "promising" (T App.20; SBN 635), Hume makes a similar separation of the observing philosophers from the bundles of perceptions that they observe, this time by considering only their *retrospective* beliefs about their minds: "[T]he thought alone finds personal identity, when reflecting on the train of

---

[17] I called this the first level of introspection in §2.2.

past perceptions, that compose a mind, the [secondary] ideas of them are felt to be connected together, and naturally introduce each other" (T App.20; SBN 635; emphasis added). Here the scope of the belief about the mind does not extend to the secondary ideas: they are in the present, but the belief concerns only the mind *in the past*.

I think that Hume enters the "labyrinth" of difficulties about personal identity when he acknowledges that by appealing to the association of secondary ideas in his explanation of the belief in mental unity, he is no longer ignorant of their occurrence in the mind. He is in a position where he *knows* that his belief in the unity of the observed perceptions is produced by the association of unobserved secondary ideas; thus he knows that his mind includes both observed and unobserved perceptions, both of which he takes to be present in the *same mind*. How can he explain this new belief in mental unity—not the belief that the observed perceptions are unified, but the belief that the secondary ideas are unified along with the observed perceptions? Bringing the secondary ideas themselves under observation, by means of tertiary ideas, would allow for a process of association that would explain the belief in the unity of the secondary ideas with the observed perceptions. But these tertiary ideas remain unobserved, and any belief about their unity with the rest of the mind remains unexplained. Hume's problem in the "Appendix," then, occurs when he comes to *believe* his original explanation of the belief in personal identity. He is left believing that unobserved secondary ideas are in his mind, being so associated as to produce the belief in mental unity. The scope of that belief, however, has changed, for he now believes that there are unobserved perceptions in his mind in addition to the observed ones that his reflection reveals to him. His original explanation of the belief no longer works.

The principles criterion from §8.1 requires that an interpreter specify why Hume's problem arises when he tries to "explain the principles" that unite perceptions "in thought or consciousness." My interpretation takes the principles to be the association of secondary ideas, and Hume's problem with explaining them to be a problem with explaining how we believe secondary ideas to be in the same mind as the perceptions that are observed within us when we reflect on them. The contradiction criterion can then be met as follows:

(a) When we reflect on the mind, we observe a bundle of perceptions.
(b) We believe the observed perceptions in (a) to be unified with one another at a time (simple) and across time (identical).
(c) Beliefs in an object's unity can be explained only by (1) appeal to its intrinsic features ("something that really binds...[it] together" such as "real connexions" between its constituents or a substantial ground), or (2) the association of ideas of its constituents (T 1.4.6.16, SBN 259).
(d) Distinct perceptions are distinct existences (T App.21, SBN 636).
(e) The mind does not perceive "real" connections between distinct existences (T App.21, SBN 636).

(f) The observed perceptions in (a) are distinct existences (from [d]).

(g) We do not perceive real connections between the observed perceptions in (a) (from [e] and [f]).

(h) Perceptions do not inhere in the mind, nor do we conceive of them as doing so (T 1.4.5.2–6, SBN 232–4).

(i) There are no intrinsic features of the observed bundle in (a) that explain our belief in its unity (b) (from [g] and [h]).

(j) The mind's believed unity (in [b]) "is nothing really belonging to these different perceptions [observed in (a)], and uniting them together; but is merely a quality, which we attribute to them, because of the union of their [secondary] ideas in the imagination, when we reflect upon" the perceptions (T 1.4.6.16, SBN 259) (from [c] and [i]).

(k) We believe that the unobserved secondary ideas in (j) are in the *same unified* mind as the observed perceptions in (a).

(l) The secondary ideas in (j) are distinct existences (from [d]).

(m) Nothing real connects the secondary ideas (in [j]) to one another or to the observed (primary) perceptions in (a) (from [l] and [e]).

(n) There is no association of (tertiary) ideas of the secondary ideas in (j) with one another or with the (secondary) ideas of the observed perceptions in (a) (with [h], [k], and [m], contradicting [c]).

(a)–(j) encapsulate Hume's argument in PI. But when we get to (k)—accepting the explanation for our belief in personal identity and thus believing that the mind-bundle contains unobserved secondary ideas in addition to observed primary perceptions—the problem emerges. There is a belief in the unity of the mind, (k), that cannot be explained in the ways he countenances for beliefs in unity, (c)—either substantial unities (denied in [h]), real connections (denied in [m]), or associations of ideas of its elements (denied in [n]).

This reconstruction also meets the escape criterion, for it makes it clear why Hume would count real connections (between the secondary ideas and the other perceptions in the bundle) or a unified substance in which all the perceptions, primary and secondary, inhered, as a solution to the problem. It would allow him to explain the belief in (k) in one of the two ways that (c) allows, *viz.* the options in (1).

Were Hume to take one of these two possible escapes he would be introducing radical changes into his philosophy, and could not keep the problem he has identified here as an isolated, "single" mistake. Instead, he "pleads the privilege of the sceptic." In Chapters 1, 4, and 7 I have argued that Hume's "true" scepticism involves recognition of the limits of philosophical inquiry. It turns out that certain tasks—notably the vindication of our tendencies to believe the verdicts of our reason and our senses—cannot be completed, in part because our reflections interfere with the mental capacities we are investigating. In the "Appendix," Hume seems to be adding the belief in mental unity to the topics that philosophy cannot fully address. Again, the problem can be seen as stemming from reflective interference. In this case, reflection adds new (secondary) ideas to the mind-bundle, thus changing the object we are investigating. As we become true sceptics and accept that our beliefs depend on the imagination's processes, we also recognize that our minds contain ideas, the association of which are responsible for our fundamental thoughts and beliefs, even while we are not aware *of* them (though we are, of course, aware of their contents).

Finally, the interpretation of the "Appendix" that I have offered here also meets the remaining two criteria set out in §8.1. First, it identifies a *single* problem in Hume's account. I take him to recognize that because the vehicles for mental observation are secondary ideas which themselves remain unobserved, it will always be impossible to have all of the mind in view all at once. But the only time he needs to have this panoramic perspective on the mind is in his explanation of our belief in its unity. In other cases, if he needs to consider the role of secondary ideas, he can always step back and bring them into view by formulating tertiary ideas of them. It follows that the "Appendix," which on my view depends on Hume's recognition of this problem with mental observation, is a withdrawal only from the account of the belief in mental simplicity and identity.

Second, my interpretation also locates a problem for Hume that is quite narrow, thus making it plausible that he would regard it as *insulated* from the rest of Books 1 and 2. As I see it, he rejects only his associationist account of the belief in mental unity, not the bundle theory of the mind. Therefore, he can in the "Appendix" legitimately leave the bundle theory's appearance elsewhere in the *Treatise* unaddressed, and we should not be surprised to find that he later recapitulates it in the *Dialogues*. Moreover, the problem that the interpretation finds in the explanation of the belief in mental unity depends crucially on the fact that the mechanism invoked to account for it itself involves perceptions that fall within the scope of the belief. Hume can continue to rely on the very same mechanism to explain beliefs that are not self-referential in this way, and thus he need not revisit those parts of the *Treatise* outside of the personal identity section that attempt to explain our beliefs in the unity of external objects (T 1.4.2, 1.4.3).[18]

Jonathan Ellis and Terence Penelhum have each raised objections to the position I attribute to Hume. Ellis worries that it is unclear whether

Hume believes that people (even philosophers) really *have* such beliefs, that is, beliefs about *occurrent* secondary perceptions to the effect that these (still occurrent) secondary perceptions are 'themselves' part of a simple mind—or that Hume believes that such a beliefs are even possible.[19]

---

[18] I have borrowed this paragraph from "Hume on Personal Identity," 155.

[19] "The Contents of Hume's Appendix and the Source of His Despair," *Hume Studies* 32 (2006), 212–13. Ellis takes the footnote in the first sentence of T App.20 (SBN 635) to be a crucial piece of evidence for understanding the "Appendix" (202). This sentence reads: "[W]hen [fn] I proceed to explain the principle of connexion, which binds them [the perceptions in the bundle] together, and makes us attribute to them a

Ellis's objection has two elements. First, he could be suggesting that Hume does not have the resources to account for a non-observational belief that a secondary idea is in the mind (in contrast to the situation where we reflect on ourselves reflecting and thus form a tertiary idea of the secondary idea). But if Hume could not avail himself of beliefs about perceptions being in his mind even while we were not reflecting on them, then his project of using reflection for the science of man would be undermined. The whole point is to understand the mind's workings as we go about our everyday business of sensing objects around us, trying to understand the world, and so on. In §4.3.2 I suggested that Humean philosophers rely on beliefs about perceptions that are akin to the vulgar's beliefs about everyday objects: perceptions continue to exist even when not being introspectively observed and are independent of the introspective observation. And though he does not thematize these beliefs, I suggested that insofar as he accepts the analogy between vulgar sensory awareness and philosophical introspective awareness, he could adapt the four-step mechanism he developed in SwS to explain the former (§3.2) in order to explain the latter. We would think of an unobserved perception, and then the relevant associations would qualify this secondary idea so that it served as a belief in the perception's current existence. Of course, the secondary idea of the perception in this case is a higher-level idea, and it in turn is unobserved. In applying this to the case of the truly sceptical philosopher who recognizes that his beliefs about the mind are the result of associations of unobserved secondary ideas, this belief in the current existence of unobserved secondary ideas would be supplemented by the general idea of an associative mechanism. All of these would involve the introduction of yet more unobserved ideas into the mind, continuing to populate the mind-bundle with perceptions, the belief in the unity of which with the rest of the mind remains unexplained.

The second element of Ellis's concern focuses on my suggestion in (k) that the unobserved perceptions are taken to be part of the *same, unified* mind as the observed perceptions. Ellis puts this in terms that are stronger than I would, in terms of a belief that the secondary ideas belong to a mind that is "simple" *tout court*. I take Hume to have accepted that the mind is a bundle and thus not "perfectly" simple, but is rather "imperfectly" unified at a time and across time. The introspecting philosopher believes that his secondary ideas—the same ones affording him awareness of the perceptions he does observe—are being associated to produce his belief in the unity of the observed mind. And that means that he takes those secondary ideas to be

---

real simplicity and identity; I am sensible, that my account is very defective." In the original edition, the footnote referred us to a page containing the final sentence of T 1.4.6.16 (and a bit of the penultimate one), all of T 1.4.6.17, and the first sentence of T 1.4.6.18 (SBN 260). These passages describe the need to find how our (observed) perceptions trigger the principles of association in the manner needed to produce the belief in their unity. In my interpretation, Hume is starting to explain there how the association of secondary ideas occurs when we observe the mind-bundle, and thus his problem in the "Appendix" does arise in the portion of PI to which the footnote refers: he is now aware of the unobserved secondary ideas that are producing his belief in mental unity.

operative in *his own* mind. "[W]hat [he] calls" *himself* when he "enters most intimately" into it now includes the perceptions that constitute the entering, not merely the perceptions that he "stumbles" upon (T 1.4.6.3, SBN 252).

Terence Penelhum makes a different objection to my account. He thinks that Hume could respond to the problem I see him as facing in the "Appendix" by explaining the unity of the secondary ideas with the rest of the mind in the same way as he explains that the bundle includes unremembered past experiences.[20] Secondary ideas are *caused* by the perceptions that they have as their objects (T 1.1.1.11; SBN 6).[21] Perhaps then the causal relations between secondary ideas and the rest of the bundle can serve the same role as the causal relations between observed perceptions and the unremembered past experiences that bring those experiences within the boundaries of the bundle.[22] The problem is that in order to explain the *belief* that secondary ideas are in the mind by means of their causal relations with other perceptions, there would need to be further ideas as vehicles of this belief. Hume requires that a causal belief take the form of vivacious idea resulting from the association of the idea of the cause and the idea of the effect.[23] So the belief that a secondary idea is caused by the perception that is its object requires an association between a tertiary idea of the original secondary idea and a secondary idea that takes the perception that is the object of the original secondary idea as its object. Believing that secondary ideas are causally connected with the bundle thus involves the presence of further higher-order ideas, and the belief in the unity of these further ideas with the rest of the mind will remain unexplained.

In fact, the same problem will reoccur for any associative mechanism that might be offered to explain the belief in the unity of the mind. The association of ideas can explain beliefs about only the *objects* of those ideas, as happens when the association of the *idea* of fire and the *idea* of smoke causes the belief that *fire causes smoke*. In this case, someone can know that her belief about fire's causal powers is a result of the association of ideas in her mind without that knowledge undermining the belief, though, as we saw in our discussion of the "Conclusion" to Book 1 of the *Treatise* (T 1.4.7) in Chapter 7, self-awareness about one's psychological propensities can induce a kind of vertigo. But the situation is different when it is a belief about the unity of the mind that is to be explained. Since an associative mechanism can explain a belief about only the *objects* of the ideas being associated, not about the *ideas*

---

[20] "Hume, Identity and Selfhood," in *Themes in Hume: The Self, the Will, Religion* (Oxford: Clarendon Press, 2000), 117–19.

[21] My discussion of Hume's analysis of introspection as being partly analogous to sensation (§4.3.2), in addition to his ambivalent attitude about making causal inferences from sensory impressions to their object causes (§6.4), should give us pause in assuming that the relation between perceptions and the secondary ideas that are of them is straightforwardly causal.

[22] Ellis makes this suggestion as well (213).

[23] Normally, a causal belief requires an impression of the cause or of the effect. But Hume allows that in the case of secondary ideas, where we focus on the perceptions rather than their objects, an idea "supplies the place of an impression" (T 1.3.8.15, SBN 106) in our causal reasoning (see §4.3.2).

themselves (in this case the higher-level ideas of other perceptions), there will be ideas in the mind different from those believed to be unified. This would not be a problem if the person in question were ignorant of the presence of those ideas, for Hume is not trying to explain the *actual* unity of the mind, just our *beliefs* about it, even if those beliefs fail to match the real contents of our bundle of perceptions. What Hume cannot allow is for someone to believe that her mind is unified at the same time as she *believes* this belief to be the result of ideas being associated in her; for she is then admitting that there are ideas that she takes to be part of her mind even though the associative mechanism posited to explain her beliefs about mental unity does not encompass them. Hume's problem in the "Appendix" arises when he takes seriously what it would be like to believe that the mind is as he describes it.[24]

8.3 Other Interpretations

I noted earlier that Hume's second thoughts in the "Appendix" have generated a surfeit of interpretive response. Clearly the text underdetermines the possibilities.[25] I consider three of the more popular 'families' of interpretations here.

8.3.1 Explanatory Failure Interpretations

The interpretation I offered in §8.2 sees Hume as discovering a flaw only in his earlier explanation for the *belief* in mental unity. It takes the insulation criterion—Hume's seeming not to feel the need to revisit other uses of the bundle theory, notably in SwS (T 1.4.2.38, SBN 207)—to mean that he never doubts his finding that the mind is "nothing but a bundle or collection of different perceptions . . . in a perpetual flux and movement" (T 1.4.6.4, SBN 252). As I emphasized in my exposition of the relevant portion of the "Appendix" in §8.1, most of it consists of recapitulation of his arguments from PI, with the problem emerging only when he addresses the issue of what "makes us attribute to them [the perceptions that we observe] a real simplicity and identity" (T App.20, SBN 635).

Other interpreters share my strategy of taking Hume to be identifying a problem in his explanation of how the attribution of personal identity takes place. John Passmore[26] and Wade Robison,[27] for example, both suggest that there is an inconsistency between equating the mind with a bundle of perceptions and also allowing for various mental activities, such as *associating* ideas of resembling, contiguous, or causally related objects; *mistaking* a series of related objects for a unified object; or

---

[24] This paragraph is mostly borrowed from my "Hume, a Scottish Socrates?" *Canadian Journal of Philosophy* 33 (2003), 151.

[25] There is also a tendency for interpreters to find a problem in the "Appendix" that gets at what they take to be a core problem for empiricism, though such interpretations find it hard to meet most of the criteria I outlined in §8.1 (notably singularity, insulation, and charity).

[26] *Hume's Intentions*, 3rd edn. (London: Duckworth, 1980), 82–3.

[27] "Hume on Personal Identity," *Journal of the History of Philosophy* 12 (1974), 181–93.

spreading an impression of necessity onto objects believed to be causally connected. There seems to be something over and above the perceptions that *does* things to them. But as Garrett[28] and Barry Stroud[29] have emphasized, Hume can explain away any mental-action talk simply by redescribing the action in terms of changes in the bundle of perceptions constituting the mind; mental powers can be redescribed as conditionals true of these changes. Moreover, given the centrality of these mental activities to Hume's project throughout Books 1 and 2, it seems hard to see how he would think he has identified only one, seemingly quite limited, error is his prior reasoning. Passmore's and Robison's suggestion thus fails the singularity criterion from §8.1.

Donald Baxter points to a different problem that he takes Hume to have recognized. How can we represent the bundle of perceptions as both many and one simultaneously?[30] More specifically, the problem is that the secondary ideas, the associations of which Hume appeals to in PI, are *many*, and yet they must represent the bundle as *one*. Baxter thinks that Hume comes to realize that his theory of representation, which Baxter takes to require resemblance between a perception and that which it represents, precludes this representational feat.

I disagree because, as I argued in §§2.4 and 3.2, Hume distinguishes between the representational content of a perception when it is taken in isolation, and the representational content it acquires when the dynamics of the imagination are solidified as a fiction. Thus an idea might in isolation represent a particular, but represent a universal when the imagination responds appropriately. Similarly, while a single secondary idea in isolation represents the primary perception it copies, in the dynamic context where it is associated with other secondary ideas, it (and the others) represents the bundle as a unified (albeit imperfectly) vulgar object.[31]

Moreover, like Passmore and Robison, Baxter's interpretation sees Hume as finding a problem that would go to the root of many of the core doctrines in (especially) Book 1 of the *Treatise*. It is thus difficult to see how it can satisfy the singularity criterion.[32]

8.3.2 The Dissolvers

Whereas the first group of interpreters focuses, as I do, on Hume's statement that his problem arises when, having "loosen'd all our particular perceptions" (T App.20,

---

[28] "Hume's Self-doubts," 344; *Cognition*, 170.

[29] *Hume* (London: Routledge and Kegan Paul, 1977), 130–1.

[30] "Hume's Labyrinth Concerning the Idea of Personal Identity," *Hume Studies* 24 (1998), 203–33. See also *Hume's Difficulty: Time and Identity in the 'Treatise'* (London: Routledge, 2008), ch. 5.

[31] Martha Brandt Bolton makes what I take to be a similar point in her "Fiction in Hume's Account of the Idea of Identity: Comments on Don Baxter, *Hume's Difficulty: Time and Identity in the 'Treatise'*," Eastern Division Meeting of the American Philosophical Association (Philadelphia, December 2008).

[32] Baxter suggests that Hume could find a problem with his account of personal identity without realizing its more general applicability, especially to SwS, because he focuses there on how we believe that the object of constant impressions is unified; the resemblance between the different perceptions obscures their multiplicity ("Hume's Labyrinth," 223–6).

SBN 635), he tries to explain our attribution of unity to them, the next two groups note that he also describes his problem as concerning the "principle of connexion, which binds them together" or the "principles, that unite our successive perceptions in our thought or consciousness" (T App.20, SBN 635). These phrases can make it seem as if Hume's concern in the "Appendix" is not merely our *belief* in mental unity, but in some kind of *metaphysical* unity exemplified by the bundle itself.

But it should come as a surprise that Hume would turn to the issue of a deeper kind of unity to the mind than that arising from the association of ideas of its members. In the prior paragraph, for example, he notes that philosophers have become "reconcil'd to the principle" that the idea of an external object is nothing more than a set of ideas of its qualities, and he seems ready to accept a "like principle with regard to the mind" (T App.19, SBN 635). Thus Tom Beauchamp argues that Hume is mistaken in his claim that he has made an error in his treatment of personal identity. He should have had the courage of his empiricist convictions in accepting that there is no metaphysical foundation for our belief in mental unity.[33] Corliss Swain is similarly taken aback by Hume's search for a real unity in the mind, and concludes that he means in the "Appendix" only to reaffirm that substance metaphysicians will be unable to find such unity. He does not, on her reading, mean to present a problem for his own preferred account of the personal identity.[34]

Jane McIntyre agrees with Beauchamp that Hume was mistaken in thinking that his original discussion PI was flawed, but she offers him what she takes to be a solution to the problem of accounting for a deeper unity than that arising from the association of ideas. In particular, she suggests that because Hume allows temporally 'thick' simple impressions and ideas (most clearly in Book 2; see §3.2.2), bundles will have overlapping constituents through time, and thus will exemplify a kind of unity that does not require either real connections or substantial inherence.[35]

The problem for Beauchamp, Swain, and McIntyre is how they can meet the singularity and charity criteria. Why would Hume suggest, in the opening paragraph of the "Appendix," that he will be correcting one (and only one) "considerable *mistake*" (T App.1, SBN 623; emphasis added) in his earlier discussion? He does seem to think that there is a problem that he finds to be "insuperable" (T App.21, SBN 636).

8.3.3 *The Bundling Interpretations*

The most popular option for interpreting the "Appendix" shares the dissolvers' assumption that Hume's concern is accounting for a unity to the mind that is

---

[33] "Self Inconsistency or Mere Self Perplexity?" *Hume Studies* 5 (1979), 37–44.

[34] "Being Sure of One's Self: Hume on Personal Identity," *Hume Studies* 17 (1991), 107–24.

[35] "Is Hume's Self Consistent?" in D. Fate Norton, N. Capaldi, and W. L. Robison (eds.), *McGill Hume Studies* (San Diego, CA: Austin Hill, 1979), 79–88; "Further Remarks on the Consistency of Hume's Account of the Self," *Hume Studies* 5 (1979), 55–61.

more metaphysically robust than that arising from the association of ideas.[36] John Haugeland initiated this interpretive approach by focusing on the issue of how perceptions end up in bundles in the first place.[37] Consider my coming to recognize a causal link between, say, fire and smoke. Only if the fire-impression-tokens are in *the same bundle* as the smoke-impression-tokens will I come to believe that fire causes smoke. But Hume also appeals to causal links between perceptions to explain the belief that the bundle is unified. It seems as if perceptions must come pre-bundled for the causal habits to develop. Stroud also offers a version of this problem, focusing on how Hume can explain the discreteness of one person's bundle from that of another person.[38] David Pears worries that Hume cannot account for how a perception that is in one mind must be in that mind and cannot be in a different mind when there are only contingent relations between the elements of a bundle.[39]

Don Garrett offers what I take to be the most sophisticated version of a bundling interpretation.[40] He points out that Hume thinks that most perceptions (all non-visual and non-tangible ones) are not spatial and are thus "no where" (T 1.4.5.10, SBN 235–6; see §5.6). Consider, then, two qualitatively identical non-spatial impressions—say two simultaneous smellings of a rose. What makes one of them belong in one person's bundle of perceptions and the other in another's? Any perceptions that resemble one of the smellings will just as much resemble the other. And, lacking any spatial qualities, any perception (perhaps an impression of pleasure) that is conjoined with one of them will just as much be conjoined with the other. As Hume admits in his treatment of causation, the requirement of constant *spatial* conjunction of objects similar to the cause and to the effect is restricted to those situations where the cause and effect are spatial; otherwise, merely temporal succession is required (T 1.3.2.6; SBN 75). So there are no causal or resemblance relations by which the two smellings differ. How, then, can they be in two minds? Thus Garrett suggests that, in the "Appendix," Hume recognizes that he cannot

[36] Peter Kail thinks that the "new Hume" shows himself in the "Appendix" by taking causal connections to require more than the constant conjunction of the relevant kinds of objects, the observation of some of which leads us to associate our ideas of the objects. Even if we can only know of such conjunctions, the "new Hume" is committed to intrinsic necessary connections between causes and effects. The bundle, as involving a system of causally linked perceptions, is thus unified by real connections. The problem Kail takes Hume to recognize in the "Appendix" is how he can also hold that perceptions are distinct and separable from one another (*Projection and Realism in Hume's Philosophy* [Oxford: Oxford University Press, 2007], ch. 6). As I argue in §5.1, I find the "new Humeanism" underlying Kail's interpretation of the "Appendix" to be implausible.

[37] "Hume on Personal Identity," in *Having Thought: Essays in the Metaphysics of Mind* (Cambridge, MA: Harvard University Press, 1998), 63–71. For many years prior to publication, this essay circulated in manuscript, where it was also credited to Paul Grice. Haugeland clarifies his sole authorship in the published version, noting that the view is his alone, though it was developed in conversation with Grice (364).

[38] *Hume*, 134–40.

[39] *Hume's System* (Oxford: Oxford University Press, 1990), 135–51; "Hume's Recantation of his Theory of Personal Identity," *Hume Studies* 30 (2004), 257–64.

[40] "Hume's Self-doubts;" *Cognition*, ch. 8; "Rethinking."

simply rely on resemblance and causation to explain how perceptions are linked together in a mind-bundle.

I do not disagree with Garrett and the other bundling interpreters that Hume presupposes that perceptions come pre-bundled. When I introspectively enter into myself I do not observe all the perceptions in the world; I observe only 'my' perceptions. If "we cou'd see clearly into the breast of another," we "observe that succession of perceptions, which constitutes *his* mind or thinking principle" (T 1.4.6.18, SBN 260; emphasis added), but not the perceptions someone (or every-one) else has. If an omniscient God looked into the breasts of all sentient creatures simultaneously, he would see 'islands' of perception-bundles, not an undifferentiated mass of all the perceptions in the universe—what Haugeland suggests would be a "perception salad."[41] Instead, Hume seems to treat it as a brute fact that when we reflect, we observe a limited set of perceptions. And, of course, he does not shy from brute facts (T Intro.9, 1.1.4.6; SBN xviii, 13). But there is a problem still to be addressed. We see this bundle of perceptions as *one unified mind*, despite the evident multiplicity of its constituents. This is Hume's explanandum in PI.[42]

I suggested in §4.3.2 that Hume sees the structure of introspection as being similar to the structure of sensation (see T 1.4.6.5, SBN 253 for an explicit application of this similarity in his discussion of PI). It is a brute fact that we have the sense modalities that we do, each with their particular acuity. I can see only those objects surrounding me, not all the objects in the world. Similarly, when I watch a play I observe the actors on the stage in the theatre, not the people on the streets outside. Our observations are limited. But there is still a question as to why we treat those divisible, complex objects that we sense as making up a unified desk, computer, wall, carpet, and the like; there is a question of why we take the play to be a continuous event, rather than a series of discrete speeches. So also in the case of introspection: when I look within, I am thereby aware of only a particular set of perceptions—'mine' not 'yours.'

I see no evidence in the text of either the *Treatise* proper or the "Appendix" itself that Hume ever worries about why or how to divide up a universe of perceptions into bundles. In his discussion of substance theories of the mind in "Of the immateriality of the soul," Hume does allow that any perception could exist on its own; there are no dependence relations between the different perceptions in a bundle, nor between

---

[41] "Hume on Personal Identity," 69. I owe thanks to Alison Simmons for challenging me to consider what an omniscient observer of minds would see.

[42] Note that where Garrett worries that the lack of spatial characteristics makes it impossible for Hume to account for how, say, the smelling of the rose causes one person's pleasure rather than another person's simultaneous pleasure, I take it that Hume's second definition of 'cause' at T 1.3.14.31 (SBN 170) rules this out, given its requirement that "the mind" associate the ideas of causally connected objects. The first person will be (brutely) unable to observe the other person's pleasure and thus will not develop the associative reaction whereby her idea of the smelling is associated with the idea of the other person's pleasure. The suggestion that the first person can form secondary ideas only of 'her' smelling and pleasure is simply another reflection of Hume's having taken the bundling of perceptions into minds as a brute fact. The bundling interpreters who think Hume owes us an account of this fact will remain dissatisfied.

them and some kind of substantial ground (T 1.4.5.5, SBN 233; see §5.2). Presumably, if a perception were to exist separately from the others in the bundle, it would be something like the sub-oyster mind Hume describes in the "Appendix" (T App.16, SBN 635).

The closest Hume comes to what might suggest a concern about bundling is in the portion of SwS where the bundle view is first introduced. Recall from §3.3.1 that he there digresses to consider the Berkeleyan question of how the vulgar believe that what Hume now identifies as a perception (or its image-content) could be absent from the mind. His answer is that because the mind is nothing but a "heap" of perceptions, "every perception is distinguishable from another, and may be consider'd as separately existent." Thus "there is no absurdity in separating any particular perception from the mind; that is, in breaking off all its relations, with that connected mass of perceptions, which constitute a thinking being" (T 1.4.2.39, SBN 207). But note that this statement occurs during the short stretch of SwS where Hume uses 'perception' and 'object' interchangeably (T 1.4.2.31, 40; SBN 202, 207); we cannot treat it as enunciating a fundamental point about how he conceives of the mind. In §3.3.1 I suggested that Hume here is rather ham-handedly pointing out that philosophers must conceive of vulgar objects as akin to the image-content of our sensations, even if they are different in "relations, connexions and durations" (T 1.2.6.9, SBN 68). But I see no sign that Hume thereby must worry about how a given perception of smell, say, should be bundled into one mind or another. Insofar as the person in the vicinity of the rose smells it, she has that impression. When she reflects, she observes that perception; a secondary idea of the impression occurs in the mind. When she becomes a true sceptic, she starts to believe that unobserved perceptions are in her imperfectly unified mind. These are simply the parameters of human cognition. The problem for Hume, I have suggested, is in explaining the belief in the unity, once we come to see things his way.

My final concern with bundling interpretations is that they do not meet the insulation criterion. If Hume were worried that conceiving of the mind as a bundle of perceptions created a problem for his system, he would have had to revisit its first appearance in SwS. And, presumably, the problem would ramify beyond the issue of personal identity, making it difficult for bundling interpretations to meet the singularity criterion.

8.4 Consequences

In §8.2 I sketched out how I understand Hume's sceptical plea in the "Appendix." The belief in the unity of the mind proves to be too difficult a problem for him to solve, given that it involves a kind of self-referentiality akin to the reflective interference that I suggested yielded the true sceptic's recognition of philosophy's limitations in the cases of justifications for our tendencies to accept the verdicts of reason and the senses (§§1.5, 4.7, and 7.5). Thus, Hume concludes that he can continue to investigate the mind in the manner he has presented in the *Treatise*. Most of the core doctrines of Book 1 are recapitulated in the *Enquiry concerning Human Understanding*, though notably the issue of personal identity does not reappear. But in a letter of 1751 he reaffirms that the "philosophical principles are the same" in both the *Treatise* and the first *Enquiry* (L 1, 158). And in "My Own Life," written at the end of his life, he declares that once he had finished the *Treatise* his philosophical views changed only in their "manner" of presentation, not in their "matter" (MOL, xxxv).

A different kind of philosopher would have a different response to the difficulty Hume has uncovered in the "Appendix." Recall my suggestion in §7.7 that the sources of his scepticism are his taking philosophy and everyday life to concern themselves with different kinds of objects (internal perceptions as opposed to external hats, stones, and the like), while also holding that similarly structured processes are used for accessing both kinds of objects; I have argued that introspective reflection and sensation depend, for Hume, on similar fictions of the imagination. But consider a non-Humean philosopher who notices the non-observational belief in mental unity that I have suggested is at the root of the "labyrinth" of personal identity. This philosopher might conclude that Hume is mistaken in thinking that philosophers must rely on processes analogous to sensation in forming beliefs; some of our commitments might have a non-sensory source, say as a precondition for our everyday thinking and sensing.

Immanuel Kant, most obviously, takes this approach. He shares Hume's view that introspection reveals only a bundle of mental representations: "Consciousness of self according to the determinations of our state in inner perception is merely empirical, and always changing. No fixed and abiding self can present itself in this flux of inner appearances." But our capacities to represent this flux and the objects of everyday life both presuppose a kind of mental unity—a "pure original unchangeable consciousness"—that he calls "transcendental apperception."[43] Throughout the first *Critique*, Kant appeals to this special commitment to mental unity to ground our sensory and rational faculties. Thus the very "difficulty" that Hume found to be "too hard for [his] understanding" (T App.21, SBN 635) is, for Kant, the key to his philosophical project.

I do not mean to suggest that Hume himself should have prefigured Kant by making an exit from the labyrinth through a reconceptualization of what philosophy is and how to pursue it. There are costs to taking that route—notably, the heavy machinery of transcendental idealism. Despite Kant's seeming capacity to address some of the issues where Hume takes philosophy to be impotent, we should remain wary:

Whatever has the air of a paradox, and is contrary to the first and most unprejudic'd notions of mankind is often greedily embrac'd by philosophers, as shewing the superiority of their science, which cou'd discover opinions so remote from vulgar conception. On the other

---

[43] *Critique of Pure Reason*, tr. Norman Kemp Smith (New York, NY: St Martin's Press, 1965), A107.

hand, any thing propos'd to us, which causes surprize and admiration, gives such a satisfaction to the mind, that it indulges itself in those agreeable emotions, and will never be perswaded that its pleasure is entirely without foundation. From these dispositions in philosophers and their disciples arises that mutual complaisance betwixt them; while the former furnish such plenty of strange and unaccountable opinions, and the latter so readily believe them.

(T 1.2.1.1, SBN 26)

Bibliography

Historical Sources

Where appropriate, I have listed the date of the work's first publication, along with the contemporary version I have used.

Aristotle. *The Complete Works of Aristotle*, ed. Jonathan Barnes, Vol. 2 (Princeton, NJ: Princeton University Press, 1984).

Arnauld, Antoine. *Of True and False Ideas* (1683), tr. and intr. Stephen Gaukroger (Manchester: Manchester University Press, 1990).

Augustine. "Against the Academicians" (386), in Peter King (tr. and intr.), *Augustine: Against the Academicians and The Teacher* (Indianapolis, IN: Hackett, 1995).

Barnes, Jonathan (ed.). *The Presocratic Philosophers* (London: Routledge and Kegan Paul, 1982).

Bayle, Pierre. *Historical and Critical Dictionary: Selections* (1697/1740), tr. and ed. Richard H. Popkin (Indianapolis, IN: Hackett, 1991).

Berkeley, George. *A Treatise Concerning the Principles of Human Knowledge* (1710) and *Three Dialogues between Hylas and Philonous* (1713), in A. A. Luce and T. E. Jessop (eds.), *Works of George Berkeley, Bishop of Cloyne*, Vol. 2 (London: Thomas Nelson and Sons, 1949).

Burton, Robert. *Anatomy of Melancholy*, 6th edn. (1651), ed. F. Dell and P. Jordan-Smith (London: George Routledge and Sons, 1931).

Butler, Joseph. "Of Personal Identity," in *The Analogy of Religion* (1736), 6th edn. (London: John Beecroft and Robert Horsfield, 1771), 439–50.

Cheyne, George. *The English Malady: Or, A Treatise of Nervous Diseases of all Kinds; as Spleen, Vapours, Lowness of Spirits, Hypochondriacal and Hysterical Distempers, &c.*, 2nd edn. (London: George Strahan and J. Leake, 1734).

Cicero. "Academica" (45 BC), in H. Rackham (tr.) *'De Natura Deorum' and 'Academica'* (Cambridge, MA: Harvard University Press, 1933).

Clarke, Samuel. *A Letter to Mr. Dodwell; Wherein All Arguments in his Epistolary Discourse Against the Immortality of the Soul Are Particularly Answered, &c.*, 6th edn. (London: James and John Knapton, 1731).

Cudworth, Ralph. *The True Intellectual System of the Universe* (1678). Facsimile reprint of the 1678 Richard Royston edition (Stuttgart: Friedrich Frommann, 1964).

Descartes, René. *The Philosophical Writings of Descartes*, Vols. I–II, tr. J. Cottingham, R. Stoothoff, and D. Murdoch (Cambridge: Cambridge University Press, 1984); Vol. III, tr. J. Cottingham, R. Stoothoff, D. Murdoch, and A. Kenny (Cambridge: Cambridge University Press, 1991).

Diogenes Laertius. *Lives of Eminent Philosophers*, Vol. 2, rev. edn., ed. and tr. R. D. Hicks (Cambridge, MA: Harvard University Press, 1972).

Fieser, James (ed.). *Early Responses to Hume's Metaphysical and Epistemological Writings*, II, 2nd edn. (Bristol: Thoemmes Press, 2005).

Hume, David. *A Treatise of Human Nature* (1739–40), ed. L. A. Selby-Bigge; 2nd edn., ed. P. H. Nidditch (Oxford: Clarendon Press, 1978).

Hume, David. *A Treatise of Human Nature: A Critical Edition* (1739–40), Vol. 1, ed. David F. Norton and Mary Norton (Oxford: Clarendon Press, 2007).

Hume, David. "Letter from a Gentleman to his Friend in *Edinburgh*" (1745), in David Fate Norton and Mary Norton (eds.), *David Hume, A Treatise of Human Nature: A Critical Edition*, Vol. 1 (Oxford: Clarendon Press, 2007), 419–31.

Hume, David. *Essays: Moral, Political, and Literary* (rev. edn.) (1741/1777), ed. Eugene F. Miller (Indianapolis, IN: Liberty Fund, 1987).

Hume, David. *Enquiries concerning Human Understanding and Concerning the Principles of Morals* (1748/1751), ed. L. A. Selby-Bigge; 3rd edn., ed. P. H. Nidditch (Oxford: Clarendon Press, 1975).

Hume, David. *An Enquiry concerning Human Understanding: A Critical Edition* (1748), ed. Tom L. Beauchamp (Oxford: Clarendon Press, 2000).

Hume, David. *An Enquiry concerning the Principles of Morals: A Critical Edition* (1751), ed. Tom L. Beauchamp (Oxford: Clarendon Press, 1998).

Hume, David. "A Dialogue" (1751), in Tom L. Beauchamp (ed.), *David Hume: An Enquiry concerning the Principles of Morals: A Critical Edition* (Oxford: Clarendon Press, 1998), 110–23.

Hume, David. *History of England* (1754–61) (Indianapolis, IN: Liberty Classics, 1983).

Hume, David. *Dialogues concerning Natural Religion* (1779), ed. N. Kemp Smith (Indianapolis, IN: Bobbs-Merrill, 1947).

Hume, David. *Letters of David Hume*, ed. J. Y. T. Grieg (Oxford: Clarendon Press, 1932).

Husserl, Edmund. *Ideas: General Introduction to Pure Phenomenology* (1913), tr. W. R. Boyce-Gibson (London: George Allen and Unwin, 1931).

James, William. *The Principles of Psychology* (1890) (Cambridge, MA: Harvard University Press, 1981).

Johnson, Samuel. *A Dictionary of the English Language: The First and Fourth Editions* (1755, 1773), ed. A. McDermott (Cambridge: Cambridge University Press, 1996).

Kant, Immanuel. *Critique of Pure Reason* (1781/1787), tr. N. Kemp Smith (New York, NY: St Martin's Press, 1965).

Leibniz, G. W. "Monadology" (1714), in R. S. Woolhouse and Richard Francks (tr. and ed.), *G. W. Leibniz: Philosophical Texts* (Oxford: Oxford University Press, 1998), 267–81.

Leibniz, G. W. *New Essays concerning Human Understanding* (1765), tr. and ed. P. Remnant and J. Bennett (Cambridge: Cambridge University Press, 1996).

Locke, John. *An Essay concerning Human Understanding*, 4th edn. (1700), ed. P. H. Nidditch (Oxford: Clarendon Press, 1975).

Locke, John. *Essai philosophique concernant l'entendement humain* (1700), tr. P. Coste, ed. G. J. D. Moyal (Paris: Vrin, 2004).

Locke, John. *Works*, Vol. 4 (Correspondence with Stillingfleet, 1697, 1699) (London: T. Tegg et al., 1823).

Long, A. A., and D. N. Sedley, *The Hellenistic Philosophers*, Vols. 1–2 (Cambridge: Cambridge University Press, 1987).

Malebranche, Nicolas. *Search after Truth* (1712), tr. and ed. T. M. Lennon and P. J. Olscamp (Cambridge: Cambridge University Press).

Mandeville, Bernard. *A Treatise on the Hypochondriack and Hysterick Diseases* (1730), intr. Stephen H. Good (Delmar, NY: Scholars' Facsimiles & Reprints, 1976).

Ramazzini, Bernardino. *Diseases of Workers* (1700), tr. Wilmer Cave Wright, intr. George Rosen (New York, NY: Hafner Publishing Company, 1964).

Reid, Thomas. *Essays on the Intellectual Powers of Man* (1785), ed. D. R. Brookes (University Park, PA: Pennsylvania State University Press, 2002).

Sextus Empiricus. *Outlines of Pyrrhonism*, tr. R. G. Bury (Cambridge, MA: Harvard University Press, 1976).

Spinoza, Benedict. *Collected Works of Spinoza*, Vol. 1, ed. and tr. E. Curley (Princeton, NJ: Princeton University Press, 1985).

Secondary Sources

Aertsen, Jan A. *Medieval Reflections on Truth: Adaequatio rei et intellectus* (Amsterdam: Vrije Universiteit Boekhandel, 1984).

Ainslie, Donald C. "Scepticism about Persons in Book II of Hume's *Treatise*," *Journal of the History of Philosophy* 37 (1999), 469–92.

Ainslie, Donald C. "Hume's Reflections on the Identity and Simplicity of Mind," *Philosophy and Phenomenological Research* 62 (2001), 557–78.

Ainslie, Donald C. "Hume, a Scottish Socrates? Critical Notice of Terence Penelhum's *Themes in Hume*," *Canadian Journal of Philosophy* 33 (2003), 133–54.

Ainslie, Donald C. "Hume's Scepticism and Ancient Scepticisms," in Jon Miller and Brad Inwood (eds.), *Hellenistic and Early Modern Philosophy* (New York, NY: Cambridge University Press, 2003), 251–73.

Ainslie, Donald C. "Character Traits and the Humean Approach to Ethics," in Sergio Tenenbaum (ed.), *Moral Psychology* (Amsterdam: Rodopi, 2007), 79–110.

Ainslie, Donald C. "Hume on Personal Identity," in E. Radcliffe (ed.), *A Companion to Hume* (Malden, MA: Blackwell, 2008), 140–57.

Ainslie, Donald C. "Adequate Ideas and Modest Scepticism in Hume's Metaphysics of Space," *Archiv für Geschichte der Philosophie* 92 (2010), 39–67.

Ainslie, Donald C. "Hume's Anti-*Cogito*," in Lorenzo Greco and Alessio Vaccari (eds.), *Hume Readings* (Rome: Edizioni di Storia e Letteratura, 2013), 91–120.

Ainslie, Donald C., and Owen Ware. "Consciousness and Personal Identity," in Aaron Garrett (ed.), *Routledge Companion to Eighteenth Century Philosophy* (New York, NY: Routledge, 2014), 245–64.

Alanen, Lilli, and Simo Knuuttila, "The Foundations of Modality and Conceivability in Descartes and his Predecessors," in S. Knuuttila (ed.), *Modern Modalities* (Dordrecht: Kluwer, 1988), 1–69.

Allison, Henry. "Hume's Philosophical Insouciance: A Reading of Treatise 1.4.7," *Hume Studies* 31 (2005), 317–46.

Allison, Henry. *Custom and Reason in Hume: A Kantian Reading of the First Book of the 'Treatise'* (Oxford: Clarendon Press, 2008).

Annas, Julia. "Hume and Ancient Scepticism," in Juha Sihvola (ed.), *Ancient Scepticism and the Sceptical Tradition, Acta Philosophica Fennica* 66 (Helsinki: Societas Philosophica Fennica, 2000), 271–85.

Annas, Julia, and Jonathan Barnes. *The Modes of Scepticism: Ancient Texts and Modern Interpretations* (Cambridge: Cambridge University Press, 1985).

Árdal, Páll. "Convention and Value," in G. Morice (ed.), *David Hume: Bicentenary Papers* (Austin, TX: University of Texas Press, 1977), 51–68.

Ashley, L., and M. Stack. "Hume's Theory of the Self and its Identity," *Dialogue* 13 (1974), 239–54.

Atkinson, R. F. "Hume on Mathematics," *The Philosophical Quarterly* 10 (1960), 127–37.

Ayer, A. J. *Language, Truth, and Logic* (Harmondsworth: Penguin, 1971).

Ayers, Michael. "Mechanism, Superaddition, and the Proof of God's Existence in Locke's *Essay*," *Philosophical Review* 90 (1981), 210–51.

Ayers, Michael. *Locke: Epistemology* (London: Routledge, 1991).

Baier, Annette. "Master Passions," in A. O. Rorty (ed.), *Explaining Emotions* (Berkeley, CA: University of California Press, 1980), 403–23.

Baier, Annette. *A Progress of Sentiments: Reflections on Hume's 'Treatise'* (Cambridge, MA: Harvard University Press, 1991).

Baier, Annette. "A Voice, as from the Next Room," in *Death and Character: Further Reflections on Hume* (Cambridge, MA: Harvard University Press, 2008), 205–23.

Barnes, Jonathan. "The Beliefs of a Pyrrhonist," *Proceedings of the Cambridge Philological Society* 208, NS 28 (1982), 1–29.

Baxter, Donald. "Hume's Labyrinth Concerning the Idea of Personal Identity," *Hume Studies* 24 (1998), 203–33.

Baxter, Donald. *Hume's Difficulty: Time and Identity in the 'Treatise'* (London: Routledge, 2008).

Baxter, Donald. "Hume's Theory of Space and Time," in D. F. Norton and J. Taylor (eds.), *Cambridge Companion to Hume*, 2nd edn. (Cambridge: Cambridge University Press, 2009), 105–46.

Baxter, Donald. "Hume, Distinctions of Reason, and Differential Resemblance," *Philosophy and Phenomenological Research* 82 (2011), 156–82.

Beauchamp, Tom. "Self Inconsistency or Mere Self Perplexity?" *Hume Studies* 5 (1979), 37–44.

Bennett, Jonathan. *Locke, Berkeley, Hume: Central Themes* (Oxford: Clarendon Press, 1971).

Bettcher, Talia Mae. *Berkeley's Philosophy of Spirit: Consciousness, Ontology, and the Elusive Subject* (London: Continuum International Publishing, 2007).

Bolton, Martha Brandt. "Locke on the Semantic and Epistemic Roles of Simple Ideas of Sensation," *Pacific Philosophical Quarterly* 85 (2004), 301–21.

Bolton, Martha Brandt. "The Taxonomy of Ideas in Locke's *Essay*," in L. Newman (ed.), *Cambridge Companion to Locke's 'Essay concerning Human Understanding'* (New York, NY: Cambridge University Press, 2007), 67–100.

Bolton, Martha Brandt. "Fiction in Hume's Account of the Idea of Identity: Comments on Don Baxter, *Hume's Difficulty: Time and Identity in the 'Treatise'*," presented at the Eastern Division Meeting of the American Philosophical Association (Philadelphia, PA, December 2008).

Bricke, John. *Hume's Philosophy of Mind* (Princeton, NJ: Princeton University Press, 1980).

Broughton, Janet. "What Does the Scientist of Man Observe?" *Hume Studies* 18 (1992), 155–68.

Broughton, Janet. "The Inquiry in Hume's *Treatise*," *Philosophical Review* 113 (2004), 537–56.

Broughton, Janet. "Hume's Explanation of Causal Inference," in Paul Hoffman, David Owen, and Gideon Yaffe (eds.), *Contemporary Perspectives on Early Modern Philosophy* (Peterborough, ON: Broadview Press, 2008), 289–305.

Buckle, Stephen. *Hume's Enlightenment Tract: The Unity and Purpose of an Enquiry Concerning Human Understanding* (Oxford: Oxford University Press, 2001).

Burnyeat, Myles. "Can the Sceptic Live his Scepticism?" in M. Schofield, M. Burnyeat, and J. Barnes (eds.), *Doubt and Dogmatism* (Oxford: Clarendon Press, 1980), 20–53.

Burnyeat, Myles. "Idealism and Greek Philosophy: What Descartes Saw and Berkeley Missed," *Philosophical Review* 91 (1982), 3–40.

Burnyeat, Myles. "The Sceptic in his Place and Time," in R. Rorty, J. B. Schneewind, and Q. Skinner (eds.), *Philosophy in History* (New York, NY: Cambridge University Press, 1984), 225–54.

Burton, John Hill. *Life and Correspondence of David Hume* (New York, NY: Burt Franklin, n.d.).

Butler, Annemarie. "Hume's Causal Reconstruction of the Perceptual Relativity Argument in *Treatise* 1.4.4," *Dialogue* 48 (2009), 77–101.

Butler, Annemarie. "Vulgar Habits and Hume's Double Vision Argument," *Journal of Scottish Philosophy* 8 (2010), 169–87.

Chappell, Vere. "Locke's Theory of Ideas," in V. Chappell (ed.), *Cambridge Companion to Locke* (Cambridge: Cambridge University Press, 1994), 26–55.

Chisholm, Roderick. "Notes on the Awareness of the Self," *The Monist* 49 (1965), 28–35.

Chisholm, Roderick. "On the Observability of the Self," *Philosophy and Phenomenological Research* 30 (1969), 7–21.

Costa, Michael. "Hume on the Very Idea of a Relation," *Hume Studies* 24 (1998), 71–94.

Coventry, Angela, and Uriah Kriegel. "Locke on Consciousness," *History of Philosophy Quarterly* 25 (2008), 221–42.

Cummins, Philip. "Hume's Diffident Skepticism," *Hume Studies* 25 (1999), 43–65.

Daniel, Stephen H. "Berkeley's Stoic Notion of Spiritual Substance," in Stephen H. Daniel (ed.), *New Interpretations of Berkeley's Thought* (Humanity Books, 2008), 203–30.

de Sousa, Ronald. *Why Think? Evolution and the Rational Mind* (Oxford: Oxford University Press, 2007).

Dicker, Georges. "Three Questions about *Treatise* 1.4.2," *Hume Studies* 33 (2007), 115–53.

Downing, Lisa. "The Status of Mechanism in Locke's *Essay*," *Philosophical Review* 107 (1998), 381–414.

Ellis, Jonathan. "The Contents of Hume's Appendix and the Source of His Despair," *Hume Studies* 32 (2006), 195–231.

Falkenstein, Lorne. "Hume and Reid on the Simplicity of the Soul," *Hume Studies* 21 (1995), 47–56.

Falkenstein, Lorne. "Hume on Manners of Disposition and the Ideas of Space and Time," *Archiv für Geschichte der Philosophie* 79 (1997), 179–201.

Flage, Daniel. "Relative Ideas Re-viewed," in R. Read and K. Richman (eds.), *The New Hume Debate* (London: Routledge, 2000), 138–55.

Fodor, Jerry A. *Hume Variations* (Oxford: Clarendon Press, 2003).

Fogelin, Robert. *Hume's Skepticism in the 'Treatise of Human Nature'* (London: Routledge and Kegan Paul, 1985).

Fogelin, Robert. "Garett on the Consistency of Hume's Thought," *Hume Studies* 24 (1998), 161–70.

Fogelin, Robert. *Hume's Skeptical Crisis: A Textual Study* (New York, NY: Oxford University Press, 2009).

Fosl, Peter. "The Bibliographic Bases of Hume's Understanding of Sextus Empiricus and Pyrrhonism," *Journal of the History of Philosophy* 16 (1998), 93–109.

Frede, Michael. "Stoics and Skeptics on Clear and Distinct Impressions," in *Essays on Ancient Philosophy* (Minneapolis, MN: University of Minnesota Press, 1987), 151–76.

Frede, Michael. "The Skeptic's Beliefs," in *Essays on Ancient Philosophy* (Minneapolis, MN: University of Minnesota Press, 1987), 179–200.

Frede, Michael. "The Skeptic's Two Kinds of Assent and the Question of the Possibility of Knowledge," in *Essays on Ancient Philosophy* (Minneapolis, MN: University of Minnesota Press, 1987), 201–22.

Garrett, Don. "Hume's Self-doubts about Personal Identity," *Philosophical Review* 90 (1981), 337–58.

Garrett, Don. *Cognition and Commitment in Hume's Philosophy* (New York, NY: Oxford University Press, 1997).

Garrett, Don. "Hume's Naturalistic Theory of Representation," *Synthese* 152 (2006), 301–19.

Garrett, Don. "Hume's Conclusions in 'Conclusion of this book'," in S. Traiger (ed.), *Blackwell Guide to Hume's 'Treatise'* (Malden, MA: Blackwell, 2006), 151–75.

Garrett, Don. "Once More into the Labyrinth: Kail's Realist Explanation of Hume's Second Thoughts about Personal Identity," *Hume Studies* 36 (2010), 77–87.

Garrett, Don. "Rethinking Hume's Second Thoughts about Personal Identity," in Jason Bridges, Niko Kolodny, and Wai-hung Wong (eds.), *The Possibility of Philosophical Understanding: Essays for Barry Stroud* (New York, NY: Oxford University Press, 2011), 15–40.

Gendler, Tamar Szabó, and John Hawthorne, "Introduction: Conceivability and Possibility," in T. S. Gendler and J. Hawthorne (eds.), *Conceivability and Possibility* (Oxford: Oxford University Press, 2002), 1–70.

Grant, Edward. *Much Ado about Nothing: Theories of Space and Vacuum from the Middle Ages to the Scientific Revolution* (Cambridge: Cambridge University Press, 1981).

Grene, Marjorie. "The Objects of Hume's *Treatise*," *Hume Studies* 20 (1994), 163–77.

Haugeland, John. "Hume on Personal Identity," in *Having Thought: Essays in the Metaphysics of Mind* (Cambridge, MA: Harvard University Press, 1998), 63–71.

Holden, Thomas. *The Architecture of Matter: Galileo to Kant* (Oxford: Oxford University Press, 2004).

Israel, Jonathan. *Radical Enlightenment* (Oxford: Oxford University Press, 2001).

Jackson, Stanley W. *Melancholia and Depression: From Hippocratic Times to Modern Times* (New Haven, CT: Yale University Press, 1990).

Kail, Peter J. E. "Hume's Ethical Conclusion," in M. Frasca-Spada and P. J. E. Kail (eds.), *Impressions of Hume* (Oxford: Clarendon Press, 2005), 125–39.

Kail, Peter J. E. *Projection and Realism in Hume's Philosophy* (Oxford: Oxford University Press, 2007).

Kemp, Catherine. "Two Meanings of the Term 'Idea': Acts and Contents in Hume's *Treatise*," *Journal of the History of Ideas* 61 (2000), 675–90.

Kemp Smith, Norman. "The Naturalism of David Hume" (I) and (II), *Mind* 14 (1905), 149–73 and 335–47.

Kemp Smith, Norman. *The Philosophy of David Hume* (London: Macmillan, 1941).

Klever, Wim. "Hume Contra Spinoza?" *Hume Studies* 16 (1990), 89–106.

Klever, Wim. "More about Hume's Debt to Spinoza," *Hume Studies* 19 (1993), 55–74.

Kripke, Saul. *Naming and Necessity* (Cambridge, MA: Harvard University Press, 1980).

Kripke, Saul. *Wittgenstein: On Rules and Private Language* (Cambridge, MA: Harvard University Press, 1982).

Kulstad, Mark. *Leibniz on Apperception, Consciousness, and Reflection* (Munich: Philosophia, 1991).

Lähteenmäki, Vili. "The Sphere of Experience in Locke: The Relations between Reflection, Consciousness, and Ideas," *Locke Studies* 8 (2008), 59–100.

Lennon, Thomas, and Robert Stainton (eds.). *The Achilles of Rationalist Psychology* (Dordrecht: Springer, 2008).

Lightner, D. Tycerium. "Hume on Conceivability and Inconceivability," *Hume Studies* 23 (1997), 113–32.

Loeb, Louis. *Stability and Justification in Hume's 'Treatise'* (Oxford: Oxford University Press, 2002).

Loeb, Louis. "Stability and Justification in Hume's *Treatise*, Another Look—A Response to Erin Kelly, Frederick Schmitt, and Michael Williams," *Hume Studies* 30 (2004), 339–404.

Livingston, Donald. *Hume's Philosophy of Common Life* (Chicago, IL: University of Chicago Press, 1984).

Livingston, Donald. "Hume on the Natural History of Philosophical Consciousness," in P. Jones (ed.), *The 'Science of Man' in the Scottish Enlightenment: Hume, Reid and their Contemporaries* (Edinburgh: Edinburgh University Press, 1989), 68–84.

Livingston, Donald. *Philosophical Melancholy and Delirium: Hume's Pathology of Philosophy* (Chicago, IL: University of Chicago Press, 1998).

Mackie, J. L. *Hume's Moral Theory* (London: Routledge, 1980).

Mascarenhas, Vijay. "Hume's Recantation Revisited," *Hume Studies* 27 (2001), 279–300.

McCann, Edwin. "Locke's Philosophy of Body," in V. Chappell (ed.), *Cambridge Companion to Locke* (Cambridge: Cambridge University Press, 1994), 56–88.

McIntyre, Jane. "Is Hume's Self Consistent?" in D. Fate Norton, N. Capaldi, and W. L. Robison (eds.), *McGill Hume Studies* (San Diego, CA: Austin Hill, 1979), 79–88.

McIntyre, Jane. "Further Remarks on the Consistency of Hume's Account of the Self," *Hume Studies* 5 (1979), 55–61.

Meeker, Kevin. "Hume's Iterative Probability Argument: A Pernicious Reductio," *Journal of the History of Philosophy* 38 (2001), 221–38.

Mercer, Philip. *Sympathy and Ethics: A Study of the Relationship between Sympathy and Morality with Special Reference to Hume's 'Treatise'* (Oxford: Clarendon Press, 1972).

Mijuskovic, Ben Lazare. *The Achilles of Rationalist Arguments: The Simplicity, Unity and the Identity of Thought and Soul from the Cambridge Platonists to Kant: A Study in the History of Argument* (The Hague: Martinus Nijhoff, 1974).

Millican, Peter. "Hume, Causal Realism, and Causal Science," *Mind* 118 (2009), 647–712.

Millican, Peter (ed.). *Reading Hume on Human Understanding: Essays on the First 'Enquiry'* (Oxford: Clarendon Press, 2002).

Morris, W. E. "Hume's Scepticism about Reason," *Hume Studies* 15 (1989), 39–60.

Morris, W. E. "Hume's Conclusion," *Philosophical Studies* 99 (2000), 89–110.

Mossner, Ernest. "Hume's Epistle to Dr. Arbuthnot, 1734: The Biographical Significance," *Huntington Library Quarterly* 7 (1944), 135–52.

Muehlmann, Robert. *Berkeley's Ontology* (Indianapolis, IN: Hackett, 1992).

Newman, Lex. "Locke on Sensitive Knowledge and the Veil of Perception—Four Misconceptions," *Pacific Philosophical Quarterly* 85 (2004), 273–300.

Newman, Lex. "Locke on Knowledge," in L. Newman (ed.) *The Cambridge Companion to Locke's 'Essay concerning Human Understanding'* (New York, NY: Cambridge University Press, 2007), 313–51.

Norton, David Fate. "Editor's Introduction," in David Fate Norton and Mary Norton (eds.), *David Hume: A Treatise of Human Nature* (Oxford: Oxford University Press, 2000).

Norton, David Fate. "Historical Account of *A Treatise of Human Nature* from its Beginnings to the Time of Hume's Death," in David Fate Norton and Mary Norton (eds.), *David Hume, A Treatise of Human Nature: A Critical Edition*, Vol. 2, *Editorial Material* (Oxford: Clarendon Press, 2007), 433–588.

Norton, David Fate, and Mary Norton (eds.). *David Hume, A Treatise of Human Nature: A Critical Edition*, Vol. 2, *Editorial Material* (Oxford: Clarendon Press, 2007).

Norton, David Fate, and Mary Norton. "Editors' Annotations," in David Fate Norton and Mary Norton (eds.), *David Hume, A Treatise of Human Nature: A Critical Edition*, Vol. 2, *Editorial Material* (Oxford: Clarendon Press, 2007), 685–979.

Olshewsky, Thomas. "The Classical Roots of Hume's Skepticism," *Journal of the History of Ideas* 52 (1991), 269–87.

O'Shea, James. "Hume's Reflective Return to the Vulgar," *British Journal for the History of Philosophy* 4 (1996), 285–315.

Owen, David. *Hume's Reason* (Oxford: Oxford University Press, 1999).

Passmore, John. *Hume's Intentions*, 3rd edn. (London: Duckworth, 1980).

Pears, David. *Hume's System* (Oxford: Oxford University Press, 1990).

Pears, David. "Hume's Recantation of his Theory of Personal Identity," *Hume Studies* 30 (2004), 257–64.

Penelhum, Terence. *Hume* (London: Macmillan, 1975).

Penelhum, Terence. "Self-identity and Self-regard," in *Themes in Hume: The Self, the Will, Religion* (Oxford: Clarendon Press, 2000), 61–87.

Penelhum, Terence. "The Self of Book I and the Selves of Book II," in *Themes in Hume: The Self, the Will, Religion* (Oxford: Clarendon Press, 2000), 88–98.

Penelhum, Terence. "Hume, Identity and Selfhood," in *Themes in Hume: The Self, the Will, Religion* (Oxford: Clarendon Press, 2000), 99–126.

Popkin, Richard. "David Hume: His Pyrrhonism and his Critique of Pyrrhonism," *The Philosophical Quarterly* 1 (1951), 385–407.

Popkin, Richard. "So, Hume did Read Berkeley," *Journal of Philosophy* 61 (1964), 773–8.

Popkin, Richard. "Hume and Spinoza," *Hume Studies* 5 (1979), 65–93.

Popkin, Richard. *The History of Scepticism from Erasmus to Spinoza* (Berkeley, CA: University of California Press, 1979).

Popkin, Richard. "Sources of Knowledge of Sextus Empiricus in Hume's Time," *Journal of the History of Ideas* 54 (1993), 137–41.

Powell, Lewis. "How to Avoid Mis-Reiding Hume's Maxim of Conceivability," *The Philosophical Quarterly* 63 (2013), 105–19.

Powell, Lewis. "Hume's Treatment of Denial," *Philosophers' Imprint* 14 (2014), 1–22.

Price, H. H. *Hume's Theory of the External World* (Oxford: Clarendon Press, 1940).

Qu, Hsueh. "Hume's Practically Epistemic Conclusions?" *Philosophical Studies* 170 (2014), 501–24.

Radner, Daisie. "Thought and Consciousness in Descartes," *Journal of the History of Philosophy* 26 (1988), 439–52.

Read, Rupert, and Kenneth Richman (eds.). *The New Hume Debate* (London: Routledge, 2000).

Rickless, Samuel. "Is Locke's Theory of Knowledge Inconsistent?" *Philosophy and Phenomenological Research* 77 (2008), 83–104.

Ridge, Michael. "Epistemology Moralized: David Hume's Practical Epistemology," *Hume Studies* 29 (2003), 165–204.

Robison, Wade. "Hume on Personal Identity," *Journal of the History of Philosophy* 12 (1974), 181–93.

Rocknak, Stefanie. "The Vulgar Conception of Objects in 'Of Skepticism with regard to the Senses,'" *Hume Studies* 33 (2007), 67–90.

Rorty, Amelie O. "From Passions to Sentiments: The Structure of Hume's *Treatise*," *History of Philosophy Quarterly* 10 (1993), 165–79.

Rosenberg, Alexander. "Hume and the Philosophy of Science," in D. F. Norton (ed.), *Cambridge Companion to Hume* (Cambridge: Cambridge University Press, 1993), 64–89.

Roth, Abraham S. "What was Hume's Problem with Personal Identity?" *Philosophy and Phenomenological Research* 61 (2000), 91–114.

Roth, Abraham S. "The Psychology and 'Language' of Identity in the *Treatise*: Unity, Number, or Something In Between?" presented at the 41st International Hume Conference (Portland, OR, July 2014).

Rozemond, Marleen. *Descartes's Dualism* (Cambridge, MA: Harvard University Press, 1998).

Rozemond, Marleen. "Mills Can't Think: Leibniz's Approach to the Mind–Body Problem," *Res Philosophica* 91 (2014), 1–28.

Russell, Paul. *The Riddle of Hume's 'Treatise': Skepticism, Naturalism, and Irreligion* (New York, NY: Oxford University Press, 2008).

Schafer, Karl. "Curious Virtues in Hume's Epistemology," *Philosophers' Imprint* 14, 1 (2014), 1–20.

Schliesser, Eric. "Hume's Missing Shade of Blue Reconsidered from a Newtonian Perspective," *Journal of Scottish Philosophy* 2 (2004), 164–75.

Schmidt, Claudia. *David Hume: Reason in History* (University Park, PA: Pennsylvania State University Press, 2003).

Stewart, M. A. "Hume's Intellectual Development, 1711–1752," in M. Frasca-Spada and P. J. E. Kail (eds.), *Impressions of Hume* (Oxford: Clarendon Press, 2005), 11–58.

Stove, D. C. *Probability and Hume's Inductive Scepticism* (Oxford: Clarendon Press, 1973).

Strawson, Galen. *The Evident Connexion: Hume on Personal Identity* (Oxford: Oxford University Press, 2011).

Strawson, Galen. *The Secret Connexion: Causation, Realism, and David Hume*, rev. edn. (Oxford: Oxford University Press, 2014).

Strawson, Peter F. *Individuals* (London: Routledge, 1959).

Strawson, Peter F. *Skepticism and Naturalism: Some Varieties* (New York, NY: Columbia University Press, 1985).

Stroud, Barry. *Hume* (London: Routledge and Kegan Paul, 1977).

Swain, Corliss. "Being Sure of One's Self: Hume on Personal Identity," *Hume Studies* 17 (1991), 107–24.

Thiel, Udo. "Hume's Notions of Consciousness and Reflection in Context," *British Journal for the History of Philosophy* 2 (1994), 75–115.

Traiger, Saul. "Impressions, Ideas, and Fictions," *Hume Studies* 13 (1987), 381–99.

Waldow, Anik. "Identity of Persons and Objects: Why Hume Considered both as Two Sides of the Same Coin," *Journal of Scottish Philosophy* 8 (2010), 147–67.

Waxman, Wayne. "Hume's Quandary Concerning Personal Identity," *Hume Studies* 18 (1992), 233–53.

Waxman, Wayne. *Hume's Theory of Consciousness* (Cambridge: Cambridge University Press, 1994).

Weinberg, Shelley. "The Coherence of Consciousness in Locke's *Essay*," *History of Philosophy Quarterly* 25 (2008), 21–40.

Weinberg, Shelley. "The Metaphysical Fact of Locke's Theory of Personal Identity," *Journal of the History of Philosophy* 50 (2012), 387–415.

Weintraub, Ruth. "The Naturalistic Response to Scepticism," *Philosophy* 78 (2003), 369–86.

Williams, Christopher. *A Cultivated Reason: An Essay on Hume and Humeanism* (University Park, PA: Pennsylvania State University Press, 1999).

Williams, Michael. "The Unity of Hume's Philosophical Project," *Hume Studies* 30 (2004), 265–96.

Wilson, Fred. "Is Hume a Sceptic with Regard to the Senses?" *Journal of the History of Philosophy* 27 (1989), 49–73.

Wilson, Fred. *Hume's Defense of Causal Inference* (Toronto, ON: University of Toronto Press, 1997).

Wilson, Fred. *The External World and our Knowledge of It: Hume's Critical Realism, an Exposition and a Defence* (Toronto, ON: University of Toronto Press, 2008).

Wilson, Margaret. "Supperadded Properties: The Limits of Mechanism in Locke," *American Philosophical Quarterly* 16 (1979), 143–50.

Winkler, Kenneth. "The New Hume," *Philosophical Review* 100 (1991), 541–79.

Winkler, Kenneth. "Hume on Scepticism and the Senses," in D. C. Ainslie and A. Butler (eds.), *Cambridge Companion to Hume's 'Treatise'* (New York, NY: Cambridge University Press, 2015), 135–64.

Wright, John P. *The Sceptical Realism of David Hume* (Minneapolis, MN: University of Minnesota Press, 1983).

Wright, John P. "Dr. George Cheyne, Chevalier Ramsay, and Hume's Letter to a Physician," *Hume Studies* 29 (2003), 125–41.

Yablo, Steven. "Is Conceivability a Guide to Possibility?" *Philosophy and Phenomenological Research* 53 (1993), 1–42.

Yolton, John. *Thinking Matter: Materialism in Eighteenth-Century Britain* (Minneapolis, MN: University of Minnesota Press, 1983).

Yolton, John. *Perceptual Acquaintance from Descartes to Reid* (Minneapolis, MN: University of Minnesota Press, 1984).

Index